Forgiving Others and Trusting God…
A Handbook for Survivors of Child Abuse

Experience Healing for Deep Wounds that Hinder Your Relationship with the Father

J. E. Norris-Bernal

XULON
PRESS

Dedication

*T*o Jesus Christ (ישו עהמשיח), *my Lord and Savior. I would never have survived my own abuse, been able to forgive those who abused me, and learned to trust my Abba Father without His life, death, and resurrection. To my wonderful husband, Manuel, without whose support and sacrifice I could not have written this book or fulfilled the Lord's call on my life. Finally, to my brother, Jimmy, who has been gone many years but is still very much alive in my heart.*

Acknowledgments

How can I possibly express my gratitude to Father God, my Abba? One of His attributes that I have repeatedly experienced over my lifetime is His mercy. I was supposed to write this book seven years ago, but I let myself become distracted. I am so thankful that the Lord once again created the time and space in my life so I could complete this particular assignment.

I am so grateful to my Mom. You drove me back and forth to our church all those years, enabling me to gain a solid foundation for my faith and life as a believer. Equal to that is my gratitude to the Lord for how you nurture, encourage, and set a godly example for me to this day. You are the mentor/friend everyone dreams of having, and I absolutely love to spend time with you! In addition to all this, you are my proofreader par excellence.

I am especially thankful for my brother, John, who has a pure heart and a fresh outlook on how to follow the Lord. Our background of abuse and the subsequent healing process have actually strengthened our relationship. When either of us refers to past emotional trauma, the other "gets it" before we can even complete sentences. Your unwavering love and support mean everything to me.

I also want to acknowledge my godly grandparents, Albert and Helen Schilt, for a priceless spiritual heritage, and my great aunt, Ada Schrey, who quietly lived a life of profound faith that left a deep impression on me. I am also thankful for my Grandpa Glen, who systematically undid a great deal of the abuse by my father without even realizing it.

Words cannot adequately express my thanks to the clients with whom I have had the privilege of working during the past 22 years as a therapist, then life coach. We have labored together with the Lord in working toward healing and restoration in the midst of much pain. For reasons of confidentiality, I cannot mention names, but please know that your lives have taught and inspired me. We have shared private moments of "agony and ecstasy" that I will never forget. Your courage and determination in working on these tough issues have truly amazed and inspired me.

I am thankful for Ed Lixey, who was obedient in communicating what he heard the Lord say and confirming that I was supposed to write books. Your words gave me the vision and encouragement necessary to fulfill this aspect of the Lord's call on my life.

I wish to express my deep gratitude to the Lord for the believers who have been obedient in sharing with me what the Lord was showing them. You have lifted and edified me more than you will ever know this side of eternity: Mavis Lewis, Anna Grove, Rick Wright, Marion Lundy, Ruth Corneal, Stan Johnson, Ken Peters, Ed Lixey, and Stephen Hanson. I know the Lord is pleased with your committed and submitted lives, your compassion, and your deep desire that the Body of Christ be fully trained and equipped to come into the measure of the stature of the fullness of Christ.

Leaders in various churches I have attended over the years who have had a profound impact on my walk with the Lord include Walter Gerber, Doug Essick, Herb Ezell, Archa Glass, and Jack Hayford. Dr. Hayford and Herb Ezell were spiritual fathers to me whom the Lord used to heal my heart.

I would be remiss if I didn't mention authors whose works deeply touched me and influenced my life: Frances Roberts, David Wilkerson, Dumitru Duduman, Michael Boldea, Corrie Ten Boom, Dietrich Bonhoeffer, Bob Sorge, Rick Renner, Graham Cooke, Marsha Burns, Steve Wohlberg, Vern Kuenzi, Andrew Strom, and Joy Dawson. Some of you have gone home to be with the Lord, and I never had the privilege of speaking with you personally; nevertheless, I wanted to honor you for the rich heritage of faith you have imparted to me.

I want to acknowledge my wonderful brothers and sisters in the Lord. Each of you has been a precious gift to me, and I don't know where I would have been without your friendship, love, support, and prayers. My thanks go to Helen Warn, Barbara Arellano, Steve Finn, Terri Helms, Bill Dresser, Debbie Correa, Mike Wourms, Dr. John Ellis, Betty Jones, Steve Orcutt, Mike and Debbie Nelson, Cathy Wilson, Israel Cohen, and Renee Morales.

I am thankful for my Hebrew class buddies Bob Thornburg and Susan Hinton. You are blessings in my life!

I want to thank Jerry Jensen, Editor of *Voice* magazine, who prodded me to have confidence in my writing, as well as editing, skills.

Finally, I am indebted to the wonderful believers at Xulon Press for assisting me in publishing this vital message for the walking wounded in the Body of Christ.

Table of Contents

Introduction

She was probably 14, maybe 15, years old and known to her classmates as somewhat shy and quiet... someone who would never call attention to herself. Later in life, she would resonate with the term "invisible" – for that's what she wanted to be. One night, she was home alone. Her father wasn't home from work, her mother was at choir rehearsal, and her two brothers were out doing whatever they did when given the freedom.

It was, perhaps, 9:00 p.m. She heard a car roll into the driveway and its engine silenced. She heard slow steps on the front porch, the door opening, and then his footsteps echoing off the slate tile entryway. Although he was nearly always drunk, he didn't stumble or weave his way around... his tolerance had kept up with the increasing amounts of alcohol he drank.

Oh no, she cried to herself. *He's home too early, and I'm all alone with him.* She next heard him making his way to the kitchen to see whether her mother had left a dinner plate for him in the oven. Extremely rare, now, were the times they ate together as a family. He got home from work later and later, it seemed.

She instinctively reached for the little knobs on the closet. As she slipped in and made a place to sit down with the clothes covering her and the shoes next to her, she gave an audible sigh of relief. *I hope he thinks I'm gone, too. No way do I want to be alone with him. He might hurt me, and there's no one here to defend me.*

Although in some part of her awareness, she knew she was being ridiculous – that he could find her if he wanted and she wasn't a little girl to be hiding in a closet – she sat there in the darkness until she heard another car pull up and a second family member enter the house. Only then did she feel as though she could leave her small fortress and be safe.

You must be thinking this girl feared a physical beating or some sort of overt sexual abuse. No... what she feared the most was her father's tongue. Ever since her mother had told her father, in no uncertain terms, that he was not to physically discipline their three children in any way, he had intentionally come up with an alternative. If he couldn't beat his kids, then he would devastate them with his words – belittling, shaming, and threatening words. Every kind of verbal and emotional abuse he could mete out was his way of coping with his own rage and unresolved emotional conflicts.

You have probably already guessed that the teenager hiding in the closet was me, and you would be right. I would do anything to avoid my father whenever he had been drinking. Even when he hadn't had his nightly dose of alcohol, I had to test the waters carefully to see what kind of mood he was in before I'd interact with him. The things he could say would just be too hurtful or revolting.

Revolting? You ask. I suffered from what is called "covert sexual abuse" at the hands of my father. This entailed his (1) detailed probing of my nonexistent sex life, (2) continuing evaluation of my developing body, and (3) none-too-welcome, comprehensive accounts of his and my mother's sexual relationship. His coarse and vulgar language, meant to shock, never failed to "gross me out" (the term we used back then for being repulsed by someone or something). His crude labels for women and their body parts would invariably make me cringe and feel queasy.

I actually received the least of the overt verbal abuse (enough, though), but all the covert sexual abuse. I always felt sorry for my two brothers, as I was the only female child, and the middle one at that. One brother was two years older, the other three years younger. They received the full brunt of my father's conscious, intentional verbal and emotional abuse. He very nearly succeeded in destroying all of us – had it not been for the Lord in our hearts and our nurturing mother, we believe, no, we **know**, we would be dead now.

Actually, one of us didn't make it – he died in 1988 of AIDS. No one will ever convince me that my father's treatment of him (which was the worst, because he looked so much like and reminded my father of himself) had no connection to his entering a promiscuous and destructive lifestyle that eventually killed him. In addition, an "older friend"/male adviser molested him as an early adolescent. My younger brother and I narrowly escaped the same fate, because we participated in many of the same addictive, self-destructive behaviors in our older brother's repertoire as a way of coping with the abuse.

As far as overt sexual abuse, I experienced that as well. An adolescent friend of the family molested me when I was about eight years old; then the youth pastor of my church sexually abused me when I was 13 and 14. I subsequently learned that because a pastor is such an important authority and so utterly trusted, this type of abuse is considered incest. Through "counseling" me, he capitalized on my vulnerability – I always felt so ugly and inferior. My father hadn't missed any opportunities to let me know how unattractive I was and that he just "prayed" that somehow, some way, I would be transformed into a beauty one day. As the saying goes, it doesn't take a rocket scientist to conclude that my relationships with men would be troubled from the get-go because of Dad's abusive treatment.

The scars of child abuse stay with people their entire lives, unless there is deliberate intervention on someone's part to get them help. I was blessed to receive that help and to grieve the losses of childhood abuse. However, that didn't help me in forgiving my abusers or trusting the Lord. A well-documented theory is that our concepts of Father God are based primarily on who our fathers are and what our relationships with them were like. Throw in the youth pastor, and I had a completely distorted view of the Lord. Trust Him? I didn't have any idea how to begin to do that.

Sadly enough, I even once looked up the word "trust" in the dictionary to begin to find some direction as to how to have a personal relationship with the Lord. There is a saying in recovery circles that in alcoholic families there are three unspoken rules everyone abides by: "Don't talk," "Don't trust," and "Don't feel." These three rules characterized my family-of-origin. So to try to trust God with any, much less every, part of my life **felt impossible**. I like the *Amplified Bible* for the translation of one very applicable Bible verse concerning matters of abuse. It clearly delineates the direct cause-and-effect link between how a parent (particularly the father) treats his children and their subsequent development throughout childhood and adolescence. Here is the connection between the two:

> *Fathers, do not provoke or irritate or fret your children – do not be hard on them or harass them; <u>lest they become</u> discouraged and sullen and morose and feel inferior and frustrated; do not break their spirit (emphasis added) (Colossians 3:21, Amplified Bible).*

I have worked for the last 22 years in the field of mental health in different capacities and used this verse countless times to help clients see something important. I tell them that as they relate abusive aspects of their childhood to me, they are not "parent-bashing," "gossiping," "making excuses for their own behavior," being disobedient to the instruction in Philippians 3:13 – "... forgetting what lies behind..." or ignoring the commandment to honor their parents. The One Who created us tells us in His Word that when children are treated in certain ways, they will become troubled and dysfunctional. Studies have shown that children undergo developmental arrest at the time of their abuse. In other words, the child continues to grow physically, but emotional maturation is seriously stunted or stops altogether at that point.

Therefore, just because their bodies mature doesn't mean abused children grow up emotionally and spiritually – or that they don't carry around all the feelings described in Colossians 3:21. I also show this verse to clients because it accurately reflects the issues that lead them to seek professional help. They indeed are **discouraged** and **sullen** (angry) and **morose** (depressed) and **feel inferior, frustrated, broken**, and that some part of their soul died during whatever abuse they suffered.

Colossians 3:21 and Philippians 3:13 ("forgetting what lies behind") don't mention anxiety specifically, which almost inevitably follows the trauma of abuse (although when children feel inferior, it would follow that they would be anxious). There are differing opinions on how many times we are told not to be afraid in the Bible, but the best estimate I've found is around 100 – a staggering amount of times for us to be given this exhortation. **In my opinion, child abuse is the primary antecedent of fear and anxiety.**

In the *Amplified Bible*, the verb "trust" is described as "to lean on (leaning of the whole human personality on), rely on and be confident in." We see it in Psalm 37:3: "Trust (lean on, rely on and be confident) in the Lord, and do good; so shall you dwell in the land and feed surely on His faithfulness, and truly you shall be fed."

That's great… except individuals who have been abused haven't the slightest idea how to do this. Whenever we've been betrayed by someone close to us, we automatically shut down and become unable to trust that person and many, if not all others. **I don't want to give the impression that this book refers solely to parental or primary caregiver abuse; rather it pertains to abuse suffered at the hands of anyone. Of course, abuse can take place when we're very young all the way through our adult lives. Domestic violence and emotional abuse are rampant in our society today.** The incidence of elder and dependent adult abuse is rising. *For every person, no matter their age and stage in life, forgiving our abusers and learning to trust the Lord are absolutely vital if we are ever to mature in Christ.* <u>**I will be concentrating solely on child abuse to narrow the scope of this book. The survivor stories throughout the text and Appendix B all pertain to children.**</u>

As noted in the Acknowledgments, I will be using many stories from clients I have treated. Any identifying information has been disguised. I have repeatedly observed that the extent to which my clients forgave their abusers is directly correlated with their emotional and spiritual well-being today. Many times, their overall physical health is positively affected as well. (See Chapters Two and Three for more on that subject.)

I will refer to many sources and use numerous quotations in this book. There has been an incredible amount written on forgiveness and trust, so why re-invent the wheel? You only need to give a cursory glance at the Bibliography, which is by no means comprehensive, to see the abundance of literature on these subjects. Far more gifted authors than I have expounded upon forgiving others and trusting God. I have endeavored to give all authors quoted credit for their work and recommendations to read their books, when applicable

My main motivation in writing this book and working directly with people on these issues is to see the Church become all that our Father means her to be. Most Christians I have spoken with initially believe they have forgiven *all* and discover that they haven't really forgiven *at all*. This condition of the heart is seriously crippling many in the Body of Christ, and they aren't even aware that there's a problem!

The other important factor as to why I could write another book on these subjects is that believers still, in this age of abundance of help for emotional problems, paint on their smiles and greet their brothers and sisters in Christ at church services as though they are full of peace and joy. They project an image of walking intimately with the Lord and trusting Him for everything in their lives. What a sham! What a shame!

I initially set out to write a book on the End Times. I got a fraction of it done but just kept dragging my feet, being overwhelmed with the massive amounts of information already out there and troubled with my lack of passion in writing about Bible prophecy (which I *am* passionate about…).

I had to get really quiet to hear the Lord and when I did, He basically impressed upon me that this subject… working with troubled people toward healing and learning to trust God (a process spanning one's entire life)…was what my whole life has been about. They represent the *calling* and *passion* of my life.

⸻ ∞ ⸻

Therefore, if forgiving others and trusting God is difficult, if not impossible, for you, I invite you to place your hand in mine and we'll walk through the rough places together… and allow the ultimate Comforter and Counselor to bring forgiveness and trust into your lives that we might be whole and worship the Lord together!

⸻ ∞ ⸻

[If you have any doubt at all as to whether you are saved – a born-again believer in Jesus – please go straight from here to Appendix A to receive that assurance or to recommit your life to the Lord. The great amount of space devoted herein to trusting God will be meaningless to you unless you know beyond a shadow of a doubt that you are saved and continually making Jesus Lord of your life.]

Fathers, do not irritate and provoke your children to anger [do not exasperate them to resentment], but rear them [tenderly] in the training and discipline and the counsel and admonition of the Lord. – Ephesians 6:4 (Amplified Bible). Fathers, do not provoke or irritate or fret your children [do not be hard on them or harass them], lest they become discouraged and sullen and morose and feel inferior and frustrated. [Do not break their spirit.] – Colossians 3:21 (Amplified Bible)

An average of nearly four children dies every day as a result of child abuse or neglect. Sixty-one percent of the children were victims of neglect, meaning a parent or guardian failed to provide for the child's basic needs. Forms of neglect include educational neglect, physical neglect, and emotional neglect. Another 44 percent were victims of abuse, including physical abuse, sexual abuse, and emotional abuse. – Jennifer Collins

A review of 500 studies of child sexual abuse found that about half of long-term abuse victims will suffer long-term mental health problems. Depression, suicide, substance and behavioral addictions, and failed marriages are among the outcomes for those who attempt to bury their suffering inside, as so many people even among their own families have advised them. – David Briggs

The consequences of your denial will be with you for a lifetime and will be passed down to the next generations. Break your silence on abuse! – Patty Hopson

Child abuse casts a shadow the length of a lifetime. – Herbert Ward

Abuse creates toxic shame - the feeling of being flawed and diminished and never measuring up. Toxic shame feels much worse than guilt. With guilt, you've done something wrong, but you can repair that - you can do something about it; but with shame, you are inadequate and defective. Toxic shame is the core of the wounded child. – John Bradshaw

Someday, maybe, there will exist a well informed, well considered and yet fervent public conviction that the most deadly of all possible sins is the mutilation of a child's spirit. – Dr. Erik Erikson

A child's tear rends the heavens. – Yiddish proverb

Those children who are beaten will in turn give beatings, those who are intimidated will be intimidating, those who are humiliated will impose humiliation, and those whose souls are murdered will murder. – Alice Miller

Abuse is the gift that keeps on giving. – Author unknown

Alcoholism programs identify emotional neglect by parents as a major theme of life for children in alcoholic homes…. Alcohol is almost always a factor in family violence. Up to 80% of all cases involve drinking, whether before, during, or after the critical incident – Suzanne Somers

Chapter One

The Many Faces of Abuse: Why Dredge Up the Past?

To deal comprehensively with child abuse, we begin by examining the term "abuse" itself. The word is defined in the *Complete and Unabridged Collins English Dictionary* as follows:

abuse vb [əˈbjuːz] (tr): 1. to use incorrectly or improperly; misuse; 2. to maltreat, esp. physically or sexually; 3. to speak insultingly or cruelly to; revile. n [əˈbjuːs]: 1. improper, incorrect, or excessive use; misuse; 2. (Sociology) maltreatment of a person; injury; 3. insulting, contemptuous, or coarse speech; 4. an evil, unjust, or corrupt practice… [C14 (vb): via Old French from Latin abūsus, past participle of abūtī to misuse from AB-¹ + ūtī to USE]

Child abuse can take many forms. Dr. Steven Tracy, in his authoritative work, *Mending the Soul: Understanding and Healing Abuse*, identified and defined the following five types of child abuse:

Sexual abuse is the exploitation of a minor for the sexual gratification of another person through sexual contact or sexual interaction. Abusive sexual contact can be described on a descending continuum and includes intercourse, attempted intercourse, oral sex, genital contact, breast contact, intentional sexual touching of buttocks or thighs, simulated intercourse, touching of clothed breasts, and sexual kissing. Abusive sexual interaction includes deliberate exposure of a minor to pornography or sexual activity and exhibitions. This graphic description in necessary because many mistakenly believe sexual abuse must involve sexual intercourse, or at least genital contact, with a minor. Furthermore, even when people accept that sexual abuse encompasses a broad range *of behaviors, they often assume that only abuse involving intercourse creates severe damage. On the contrary, <u>all sexual abuse is extremely damaging</u> (emphasis added).*

<u>Physical abuse</u> is legally defined as any nonaccidental injury to a minor by an adult or caregiver. This could include blows, shakings, burnings, or other physical assaults that cause injury to the child… This can include threats, shovings, slaps, hair-pulling, punches, kicks, injuring or killing of pets, destruction of personal possessions, assaults with inanimate objects, and assaults with lethal weapons.

<u>Neglect</u> is closely connected with physical abuse. Overtly it is the opposite of physical abuse but produces similar results. Instead of a failure of actions (physical abuse), it is a failure to act. Neglect is the failure of a parent or guardian to provide a minor with adequate food, clothing, medical care, protection, supervision, and emotional support.

<u>Spiritual abuse</u> is the inappropriate use of spiritual authority (the Bible, ecclesiastical tradition, or church authority) to force a person to do that which is unhealthy. Often it will involve a forceful or manipulative denial of that person's feelings and convictions.

<u>Verbal abuse</u> is a form of emotional maltreatment in which words are systematically used to belittle, undermine, scapegoat, or maliciously manipulate another person. <u>Verbal abuse can be every bit as damaging as physical or sexual abuse, and in some cases it's even more damaging</u> (emphasis added). Those who haven't experienced abuse often can't understand this. The somewhat subjective nature of verbal abuse can make it more insidious and difficult to confront (which can also make it more damaging).[1]

Every type of abuse mentioned here has been experienced by clients I have seen over the years and myself. At the outset, it is important to set a parameter that applies to every part of this book. *We should never "compare" our abuse with anyone else's.* Abuse such as I identified in the Introduction (emotional and verbal abuse) can leave just as many scars as more violent or physical abuse. *NO abuse should ever be considered mild, marginal, or unimportant.*

John and Paula Sandford and Norm Bowman, in their comprehensive work, *Choosing Forgiveness*, describe what happens to a person when they are victimized by child abuse. They refer to the abuse as a "crippling injury," define what makes up this category, and enumerate the resulting "deep wounds of the spirit" as follows:

A crippling injury is comprised of the following events: traumatic experiences in early childhood, repeated over a long period; unresolved grief; deprivation of love and nurture; emotional, physical or sexual abuse; traumatic loss; terror, being out of control; offender unrepentant and often not specifically identifiable. The deep wounds of the spirit include: absence of basic trust; feeling of abandonment; deep-seated anger; feeling of rejection; mistrust and hostility; powerlessness; lingering anxiety; pervasive fear; victimization; bitter attitude toward life; and isolation/withdrawal.[2]

Over the years, I have played nearly every part possible involving child abuse: victim, survivor, mental health professional reporting cases and treating victims, advocate in court cases, helpless observer when nothing could be done from the outside to stop it, etc. The toxicity and lingering effects of abuse have necessitated my being actively engaged in the spiritual warfare I have waged for over two decades. On a positive note, as much grief as I initially feel for victims of abuse, I feel that much more satisfaction as they heal and grow up "safe" this time.

Many believers are of the opinion that what happened to them as children should have no bearing on their lives as adults, and they claim to have "forgiven and forgotten." I would submit to you that this is an entirely false and unbiblical premise. Let us return to a verse referred to in the Introduction again and see what Paul is actually referring to:

I do not consider, brethren, that I have captured and made it my own [yet]; but one thing I do – it is my one aspiration: forgetting what lies behind and straining forward to what lies ahead, I press on toward the goal to win the [supreme and heavenly] prize to which God in Christ Jesus is calling us upward (Philippians 3: 13-14, Amplified Bible).

What is Paul speaking of when he refers to "forgetting what lies behind"? Certainly not the wounds of child abuse, or any kind of abuse, for that matter. What he was speaking of here was his own identity without Jesus, his own accomplishments, what the Jewish people considered impressive in those days, etc. In other words, Paul is speaking about himself – his flesh – with his impeccable qualifications and clear authority before he was knocked off his horse on the road to Damascus. The enumeration of these is as follows:

For we [Christians] are the true circumcision, who worship God in spirit and by the Spirit of God, and exult and glory and pride ourselves in Jesus Christ, and put no confidence or dependence [on what we are] in the flesh and on outward privileges and physical advantages and external appearances. Though for myself I have [at least grounds] to rely on the flesh. If any other man considers that he has or seems to have reason to rely on the flesh and his physical and outward advantages, still more have I! Circumcised when I was eight days old, of the race of Israel, of the tribe of Benjamin, a Hebrew [and the son] of Hebrews; as to the observance of the Law I was of [the party of] the Pharisees. As to my zeal I was a persecutor of the church, and by the Law's standard of righteousness – supposed] justice, uprightness and right standing with God – I was proven to be blameless and no fault was found with me (Philippians. 3:3-6, Amplified Bible).

In the book of Acts, Paul gives us one further qualification, a clear advantage of his early in life. He is addressing the commander of the regular Roman garrison, as well as his Jewish brethren and fathers:

I am a Jew, born in Tarsus of Cilicia, but reared in this city. At the feet of Gamaliel I was educated according to the strictest care in the Law of our fathers, being ardent – even a zealot – for God, as all you are today. [Yes,] I harassed (troubled, molested and persecuted] this Way [of the Lord] to the death, putting in chains and committing to prison both men and women (Acts 22:2-3, Amplified Bible).

Therefore, if anyone had cause to be ever so confident about his earthly education, accomplishments, position, and authority, it was Saul of Tarsus. Now we'll see his overall evaluation of these advantages:

But whatever former things I had that might have been gain to me, I have come to consider as (one combined) loss for Christ's sake. Yes, furthermore I count everything as loss compared to the possession of the priceless privilege – the overwhelming preciousness, the surpassing worth and supreme advantage – of knowing Christ Jesus my Lord, and of progressively becoming more deeply and intimately acquainted with Him, of perceiving and recognizing and understanding Him more fully and clearly. For His sake I have lost everything and consider it all to be mere rubbish (refuse, dregs), in order that I may win (gain) Christ, the Anointed One (Philippians. 3:7-8, Amplified Bible).

One other interpretation that I found as I did research on the subject of "forgetting what lies behind" is quite literal in context. This individual wrote that what Paul means about that is "forgetting," in a metaphorical way, refers to not dwelling on sins we have confessed and repented of. The only One who can truly forget is God (which I can't fathom). We see evidence of this in the book of Jeremiah. God tells us that when He forgives us, He "remembers our sins no more" (Jeremiah 31:34). This does not mean that the all-knowing God forgets because He forgives us. Rather, He chooses not to bring up our sin to Himself or others.[3]

A full understanding of the verse where Paul, by example, exhorts us to forget what lies behind is foundational to understanding God's view of child abuse. He **does not** expect us to "forgive and forget." He wants us to forgive, yes, forget, only in the literary sense of the word. We will cover this subject more thoroughly in Chapter Five. In the meantime, I will leave the reader with a real-life example of why we **must** "dredge up the past" or it will remain – buried alive.

—❦—

She was one of my first clients. We'll call her Sarah. She was 68 years old when she first came to see me. Sarah was widow who lived with and took care of her mother, and had two adult children and a grandchild. I was a 35-year-old intern at the time and figured, *Whoa there, how could this woman possibly trust me or think I might possess any knowledge or wisdom that could set her free?* Fortunately for both of us, this turned out to be a non-issue, helping me to apply the principle that Paul once spoke of to Timothy, "Let no one despise your youth... " (I Timothy 4:12).

Sarah had strong faith and served the Lord with all her might, but she was moderately depressed and anxious, and her familial relationships were troubled. She definitely was not through grieving the death of her husband, resented her mother in a huge way, and felt that her children kept their distance from her. As I gently began to probe her background, I asked Sarah whether she had ever been sexually abused when she was a little girl. She answered with a resounding "No!" and changed the subject. I am nothing if not persistent, so I listed the various forms sexual abuse could take and that forced intercourse was not the only definition of molestation/sexual abuse (as Dr. Tracy explained in his definition of sexual abuse). She began to sob and admitted that when she was a little girl growing up on a farm, her older brothers took turns making her take off her clothes and fondling her. She had never told anyone, including her husband, of this horrible abuse and the theft of her innocence.

Therefore, we began to explore the ramifications of the abuse. Sarah claimed to have had a fulfilling sex life with her husband, but the sexual identity of one of her adult children was in question and there was extended intra-familial sexual abuse that she began to identify. She had troubling dreams that sometimes turned into nightmares, which left her with vague sense of **anxiety** all the time. Many times, Sarah would attempt to minimize the impact that her brothers' abuse had on her, and I would remind her of the growing list of its continuing effects on her life. Finally, she became convinced that there was validity to the idea that the sexual abuse had altered her life and continued to affect her children and grandchild. We worked through her pain, she forgave her brothers, and the Lord performed a deep healing in her soul.

When Sarah was ready to "graduate" from counseling, there was a marked difference in her countenance. She actually radiated the Lord's grace and mercy and was able to love others in a Christ-like way. She continued to grow spiritually and eventually realized the dream of living on her own in another state (which she couldn't begin to trust the Lord for before counseling). She thanked me repeatedly for being stubborn in confronting her denial and working through the healing process. I redirected her to the Lord and His boundless love and care for her – that even at this late date in her life, she could become whole.

I felt the incredible fulfillment that a counselor does when one of her clients goes all the way through the healing process and comes out on the other side a transformed person. I praise the Lord for this early "success," for it was He that did the healing, not I. The Holy Spirit is our Comforter and Counselor, and I am simply honored to be included in the process of seeing lives changed and thrilled to see true intimacy with the Lord come about in a fellow believer's life.

⸺⊗⊗⊗⸺

One final objection to "dredging up the past" that clients have often verbalized is "What about the Fifth Commandment to 'Honor thy father and mother'? Isn't this (dealing with the abuse at the hands of a parent) just the opposite of what God tells us to do?" For quite a while, I had no quick or easy answer for this question, other than redirecting them to Ephesians 6:4 and Colossians 3:21. If a parent is unrepentant and continues to be abusive, how can their adult child honor them in all honesty?

Somewhere in the midst of my years as a therapist, I heard an answer that made complete sense to me. **Survivors of abuse can live their lives in such honorable ways that the parent is respected (honored) by virtue of being the parent of such an admirable child!**

The singer famous for his performance of "Raindrops Keep Falling on My Head," B. J. Thomas, was abused as a child in an alcoholic family and by a paternal uncle. His meteoric rise to fame coincided with years of horrendous drug abuse that except for the grace of God could have easily resulted in his death. He wrestled with multiple addictions **before and after being born again, which illustrates the principle that abuse just never "goes away" by itself).** His wife, Gloria, and Nashville writers J. D. Martin and Gary Harrison composed the song "Broken Toys," which Thomas then recorded. This song has been adopted by child abuse agencies throughout the country:

Broken Toys

Such a pretty little face,
with a heart that's been torn.
Living in a borrowed space,
from the moment she was born.
How many times she's cried,
but never tears of joy.
Someone's taken a little girl
and made a broken toy.

Two sad little eyes,
painted heartbreak blue...
The simplest of his dreams,
never will come true.
Someone else's pain
fell on this little boy.

Someone's taken a soldier,
and made a broken toy.

Broken toys,
who will mend these broken toys?
For every one we break,
a broken life takes its place.
That one day will break toys of its own.
Oh Lord, we've got to mend these broken toys.
And let them be children again,
give back the innocence stolen from them.

Broken toys,
who will mend these broken toys?
For everyone we break,
a broken life takes its place.
That one day will break toys of its own.
Oh Lord, we've got to mend these broken toys.

You might be asking, **"Can't I go through the healing process and be close to the Lord without forgiving the awful things done to me that have left me so messed up and scarred? Why does the Lord ask me to forgive _____? What he/she/they did is unforgiveable! I just can't, and furthermore, I don't want to!"** Let's go on in our journey to learn the answer to these very valid questions.

In a way, forgiving is only for the brave. It is for those people who are willing to confront their pain, accept themselves as permanently changed, and make difficult choices. Countless individuals are satisfied to go on resenting and hating people who wrong them. They stew in their own inner poisons and even contaminate those around them. Forgivers, on the other hand, are not content to be stuck in a quagmire. They reject the possibility that the rest of their lives will be determined by the unjust and injurious acts of another person. – Beverly Flanigan

The Risen Christ proclaimed not that we "have to forgive," but rather, that at last we CAN forgive – thereby freeing ourselves from consuming bitterness and the offender from our binding condemnation. This process requires genuine human anger and grief, plus – and here is the awful cost of such freedom – a humble willingness to see the offender as God sees that person, in all his or her terrible brokenness and need for God's saving power. I would never tell another, 'You have to forgive.' But my uncomfortable duty as a Christian is to confess the truth, so lethal to our self-centered human nature: 'Jesus, who suffered your sin unto His own death, calls you likewise to forgive, so that God's purposes may be accomplished in both you and your offender. – Gordon Dalbey

Forgiving is something that you do for yourself. It is one way of becoming the person you were created to be – and fulfilling God's dream of you is the only way to true wholeness and happiness. You NEED to forgive so that you can move forward with life. An unforgiven injury binds you to a time and place someone else has chosen; it holds you trapped in a past moment and in old feelings. – Carol Luebering

Forgiveness is not always easy. At times, it feels more painful than the wound we suffered to forgive the one that inflicted it. And yet, there is no peace without forgiveness. – Marianne Williamson

Forgiving does not erase the bitter past. A healed memory is not a deleted memory. Instead, forgiving what we cannot forget creates a new way to remember. We change the memory of our past into a hope for our future. – Lewis B. Smedes

Early in my pastoral ministry, I noticed an interesting fact: nearly all the personal problems that drive people to seek pastoral counsel are related in some way to the issue of forgiveness. The typical counselee's most troublesome problems would be significantly diminished (and in some cases solved completely) by a right understanding of what Scripture says about forgiveness. People who come for counseling generally fit into one or both of two categories. There are some who need to understand how God's forgiveness is extended to sinners, and there are others who need to learn to be forgiving. – John MacArthur

When you forgive, you in no way change the past – but you sure do change the future. – Bernard Meltzer

Chapter Two

Why Forgive, Anyway?

Although everyone understands the term "forgiveness," it never hurts to begin with the dictionary definition (from the *Merriam Webster Online Dictionary*):

for·give: verb*fər-'giv; fòr-*\for·gave\-'gāv; \for·giv·en\-'gi·vən; \for·giv·ing. Definition of *FORGIVE:* Transitive verb: 1. *a*: to give up resentment of or claim to requital for <*forgive* an insult> *b*: to grant relief from payment of <*forgive* a debt>. 2. to cease to feel resentment against (an offender): PARDON <*forgive* one's enemies>. Intransitive verb: to grant forgiveness; for·giv·able\-'gi·və-bəl*adjective* for·giv·ably\-blē*adverb* for·giv·er. *Noun:* Examples of *FORGIVE: 1.* Can you ever *forgive* me for being so selfish? 2. I've never *forgiven* myself for the way I treated her; 3. We must ask God to *forgive* us for our sins; 4. When he feels he's been insulted, he finds it hard to forgive; 5. He finds it hard to *forgive* an insult; 6. We must ask God to *forgive* our sins; 7. The government has agreed to *forgive* some of the debt. Origin of *FORGIVE:* Middle English, from Old English *forgifan,* from *for-* + *gifan* to give. First Known Use: before 12th century Related to *FORGIVE:* Synonyms: PARDON; Antonyms: RESENT; Related Words: ABSOLVE, ACQUIT, CLEAR, EXCULPATE, EXONERATE, VINDICATE; REMIT, SHRIVE; CONDONE, DISREGARD, EXCUSE, IGNORE, PASS OVER, SHRUG OFF; DISCHARGE, LIBERATE, REDEEM, RELEASE, UNBURDEN.

There are many reasons for us to forgive others – the primary being because the Lord instructs us to. Many believers know and give intellectual assent to this exhortation, but to walk it out is a whole other story. One way to get a sincere believer's attention is to have them recite and carefully attend to the following portion of the Lord's Prayer, "Forgive us our debts [trespasses] as we forgive our debtors [those who trespass against us]." People can pray, more or less by rote, and include this phrase hundreds of time in their lives and never realize its true meaning. When they recognize what they are saying, they sometimes "freak out"! Jesus spells it out quite clearly:

If you forgive those who sin against you, your heavenly Father will forgive you. But if you refuse to forgive others, your Father will not forgive your sins (Matthew 6:14-15).

Attention: It is extremely important to qualify these statements. They are in no way intended to heap further guilt, shame, and/or fear on survivors who have not yet forgiven their abusers. I am utterly convinced that the Lord does not give us what seem to be impossible tasks, without also giving us the grace and empowerment with which to implement them.
So no freaking out, okay? Please read on.

In *The Handbook of Bible Application*, Neil Wilson, Editor, asks this very question: Why should we forgive one another? He lists the following reasons:

1. Forgiveness is a mark of the Christian life.
2. Forgiveness is contrary to the pattern of the world.
3. Forgiveness is an act of the will.
4. If we expect to be forgiven, we need to practice forgiveness.[1]

Ultimately, there are two very important reasons to consider forgiving our abuser(s): (1) Because in so many ways it frees us survivors to become everything the Lord created us to be; and (2) To make us 100 percent whole, thus completing the healing process. It's like some other difficult things the Lord asks of us. Why does He not want His children to engage in any form of sexual activity other than with their spouses? This command is completely for their protection and future blessing… it certainly isn't because God is some kind of a heavenly killjoy. As I often rather bluntly inform my clients, "If all the Lord intended sex for was procreation, He wouldn't have created an orgasm." The same principle applies to forgiveness. Whenever the Lord insists on our doing things His way, it is for our blessing and protection.
Another crucial point to be made early on is the fact that as the Lord invites you to forgive and heal, He will give you many different opportunities to do so over your lifetime. Since He knows your end from your beginning, it only makes sense that He knows if or when you will. So in no way is this book intended to be used as a hammer with which to hit you on your head. It is meant to encourage you, the abuse survivor, to start the process of healing and forgiveness that you may live a free, unfettered life!
In the recent past, a new development in the field of psychotherapy caught my attention and spurred me on in writing this book. Where once it was thought that certain offenses against people were unforgiveable and a person was absolutely justified in not forgiving, now based on scientific research done over many years' time, therapists, **Christian or not**, largely agree that forgiveness is the right (healthy) thing to do. I began to receive brochures from secular organizations offering continuing education seminars on granting forgiveness as a means to achieve better mental health.

Nearly all mental health practitioners, no matter what their worldviews, currently agree that forgiveness is necessary for a survivor of abuse to really heal and get on with life.

I had to laugh when, in the early part of 2010, I received a brochure advertising a seminar entitled *The Forgiveness Solution: A Powerful Clinical Approach to Lasting Change*. The organization offering the seminar is PESI, which is known for their outstanding therapeutic seminars. They are definitely **not** coming from a Christian perspective; instead, the only acceptable worldviews for PESI are secular humanism or some New Age type of spirituality. They do not employ any speakers who could even vaguely be termed Christian. What I found so amusing was the description of the contents being presented:

1. <u>Radical new approach</u> that gets to the core of emotional, relational and behavioral issues; 2. <u>Forgiveness techniques</u> to shift perceptions, choose differently, change attitudes, redirect energy and make constructive decisions in behavior and relationships; 3. Transform anger, hurt, guilt, resentment, bitterness, disappointment, shame and dysfunctional relationships; 4. Learn <u>tools for assessing unforgiveness</u> and life satisfaction along with a <u>variety</u> of <u>healing techniques</u> all established through <u>extensive clinical experience and empirical research</u>; and 5. Learn from one of the most experienced clinicians and clinical researchers in the area of forgiveness, healing and change (emphasis added).[2]

Radical new approach? Hardly! The first example of one person forgiving another is found in the biblical account of Joseph and his brothers, who abused and betrayed him in approximately 1894 B.C. That hardly seems "new" to me. Forgiveness techniques? Not so much a technique… more like obedience to the Word of God. Tools for assessing unforgiveness? We really don't need to look further than Acts 8:23, Romans 3:14, Ephesians 4:13 and Hebrews 12:15, which all address bitterness. Variety of healing techniques? There is a lot of hubris contained in this advertisement, because anyone who has progressed in their Christian walk knows that God is the only true Healer – we are just conduits through which He flows. Extensive clinical experience and empirical research? They really didn't have to go to all that trouble, now did they? All the experience and research in the world will simply point back to the veracity and wisdom of the Bible. Actually, it's a sad state of affairs when people take as long as between two and four thousand years to discover a truth that sets them free when it has been right in front of their noses all that time!

Mayo Clinic has earned the reputation as a place where people with terminal diagnoses and no hope can be treated and returned to health. In their article on *Forgiveness: Letting Go of Grudges and Bitterness* (which refers to no foundational spiritual approach to healing), the same conclusion is reached:

Nearly everyone has been hurt by the actions or words of another…. These wounds can leave you with lasting feelings of anger, bitterness and even vengeance – but if you don't practice forgiveness, you may be the one who pays most dearly. By embracing forgiveness, you embrace peace, hope, gratitude and joy…. Letting go of grudges and bitterness makes way for compassion, kindness and peace. Forgiveness can lead to: healthier relationships, greater spiritual and psychological well-being, less stress and hostility, lower blood pressure, fewer symptoms of depression, anxiety and chronic pain, and lower risk of alcohol and substance abuse.[3]

Another continuing education course coming from a strictly secular perspective is entitled *The Science of a Meaningful Life: Forgiveness and Gratitude.* Once again, scientists have merely validated millennia-old biblical injunctions and principles of living. Here is a brief description of this seminar:

Dr. Luskin will teach participants the 'Nine Steps to Forgiveness' training he has validated through successful studies, including his famed Stanford Forgiveness Project. This research, as well as others' research, has consistently shown that forgiveness increases physical vitality, optimism, hope, compassion, and self-confidence while reducing anger, blood pressure, hurt, depression, and stress. Dr. Luskin's presentation will combine lecture with a hands-on approach to forgiveness. Participants will explore forgiveness with the goal of reducing hurt and helplessness, letting go of anger and grudges, and increasing their feelings of confidence and hope. They will also learn how to facilitate forgiveness in others through a combination of cognitive therapy and narrative approaches, intermixed with mindfulness and guided imagery practices [Note: mindfulness and guided imagery are New Age concepts and therapeutic techniques.][4]

Apparently, England was a bit ahead of the United States as far as forgiveness being recognized as healing by those who are secular in their approach. R. T. Kendall informs us of the following in his book, *Total Forgiveness*:

The June 4, 2000 issue of London's <u>Daily Express</u> carried an article with this headline: 'Can You Learn to Forgive?' It began with the following declaration 'Bearing a grudge can hold you back and even damage your health.' The writer of the article, Susan Pape, had interviewed Dr. Ken Hart, a lecturer at Leeds University, who had been running the 'world's first forgiveness course' – a seminar designed to help people forgive their enemies and let go of grudges. Participants ranged from a jilted husband to victims of burglary and bullying. All had one thing in common: they were angry and bitter, and they wanted revenge. <u>This was not, as far as I know, a Christian course. Evidently, it was a case of people doing something biblical without even realizing it. It is one indication that the world is starting to recognize the merits of a lifestyle of forgiveness</u> (emphasis added).[5]

In the Journal of Mental Health Counseling, an article by Steven J. Sandage and Everett L. Worthington, Jr., written in January 2010, *Comparison of Two Group Interventions to Promote Forgiveness: Empathy as a Mediator of Change,* contained similar findings, with one exception:

Undergraduate student volunteers (N = 97) were randomly assigned to one of two six-hour forgiveness psychoeducational seminars or to a wait-list control group... forgiveness was conceptualized in relation to the care-giving behavioral system. Both the Empathy Forgiveness Seminar and the Self-Enhancement Forgiveness Seminar facilitated forgiveness to a greater degree than the wait-list control group at post-test and six-week follow-up. Empathy mediated changes in participants' forgiveness scores regardless of seminar condition…. Clinical models have tended to focus on forgiveness as one way individuals, couples, and families attempt to cope with hurt and resentment after a relational conflict or betrayal. Surveys of mental health professionals have generally found that most clinicians view forgiveness as (a) an issue that arises often in therapy, and (b) potentially therapeutic for some clients. Reducing unforgiveness has been shown to have benefits for physical health, mental health, and relationships…. However, some therapists question whether forgiveness is a worthy goal for clients who either suffer from severe trauma, such as abuse. or hold cultural and moral values that diverge from forgiveness [emphasis added].[6]

Oops! What happened? Now therapists are deciding who should and shouldn't forgive? We also know that if people hold "cultural and moral values that diverge from forgiveness," they probably aren't too interested in pursuing a relationship with the God of the Bible.

One final quote, from a non-Christian viewpoint regarding the benefits of forgiveness, is found in the Harvard Health Publications article, "2010 Health Resolution – Walk in Forgiveness":

It has been said that harboring resentment and holding back forgiveness is like drinking poison and hoping the other person dies. Physics dictates that what goes on in the mind will have an effect on the physical body. It is also interesting to note that forgiveness is something nearly all Americans want – 94% surveyed in a nationwide Gallup poll indicated it was important to forgive – but only 48% said they usually tried to forgive others. Besides making you miserable and zapping your enjoyment from life, unforgiveness comes with a laundry list of negative health effects. Psychologist Loren Toussaint of Luther University in Iowa was among the first to demonstrate a long-term link between people's health and their ability to forgive. In what many call the new science of forgiveness, numbers of overwhelming case studies have shown the benefits of extending forgiveness: reduced stress and hostility; fewer symptoms of depression, anxiety and chronic pain; lower risk of alcohol and substance abuse; improved heart function/lower

blood pressure; improved relationships; greater spiritual and psychological well-being; and improved sleep (emphasis added).[7]

The world is finally catching up to the benefits of obeying the Lord's instruction to forgive one another**. It only took four millennia**… Now let's examine what happens **when we won't forgive**.

Bitterness is the only chemical that will destroy its own container – YOU! – James Earls

Unforgiveness is the act of drinking poison and hoping someone else dies – Unknown

If we say that monsters [people who do terrible evil] are beyond forgiving, we give them a power they should never have… they are given the power to keep their evil alive in the hearts of those who suffered most. We give them power to condemn their victims to live forever with the hurting memory of their painful pasts. We give the monsters the last word. – Lewis B. Swedes

Vengeance is having a videotape planted in your soul that cannot be turned off. It plays the painful scene over and over again inside your mind…. And each time it plays, you feel the clap of pain again…. Forgiving turns off the videotape of pained memory. Forgiving sets you free. – Lewis B. Smedes

Not to forgive is to be imprisoned by the past, by old grievances that do not permit life to proceed with new business. Not to forgive is to yield oneself to another's control… to be locked into a sequence of act and response, of outrage and revenge, tit for tat, escalating always. The present is endlessly overwhelmed and devoured by the past. Forgiveness frees the forgiver. It extracts the forgiver from someone else's nightmare. – George Herbert

Hurt leads to bitterness, bitterness to anger, travel too far that road and the way is lost. – Terry Brooks

It is a simple but sometimes forgotten truth that the greatest enemy to present joy and high hopes is the cultivation of retrospective bitterness. — Robert G. Menzies

The one who pursues revenge should dig two graves. – Old Chinese Proverb

Many are quite comfortable saying they will not forgive. In a 1988 Gallup poll on forgiveness, 94 respondents indicated that it was important to forgive. But only 48 percent said they make it a practice to forgive. – Christ Brauns

Forgiveness is the key that unlocks the door of resentment and the handcuffs of hate. It is a power that breaks the chains of bitterness and the shackles of selfishness. – William Arthur Ward

When we are bitter, we delude ourselves into thinking that those who hurt us are more likely to be punished as long as we are set on revenge. We are afraid to let go of those feelings. After all, if we don't make plans to see that justice is done, how will justice be done? We make ourselves believe that it is up to us to keep the offense alive. – R. T. Kendall

Chapter Three

What Happens When We Won't Forgive

After citing all the reasons why we need to enter the process of forgiveness, we will now examine the costs and consequences of not forgiving. All of us know people who are filled with bitterness and resentment. These people are neither pleasant nor appealing – if we are being honest, we don't really want to be around them for any length of time. The trouble is…. it is so **easy** to become bitter when we have been deeply wounded, because that's the natural human reaction. It sneaks up on us before we even realize it, and most of the time we're not even aware of our own condition.

For the purpose of this book, the words "bitterness" and "unforgiveness" are used interchangeably. It is always good to have a full definition of a word one is examining. Here is the definition of the word "bitterness" in the *Merriam-Webster's Online Dictionary*:

> *Bitterness: Main Entry: ¹bit·ter Pronunciation: \'bi-tər\ Function: adjective. Etymology: Middle English, from Old English biter; akin to Old High German bittar bitter, Old English bītan to bite — more at* BITE. *Date: before 12th century. 1a: being or inducing the one of the four basic taste sensations that is peculiarly acrid, astringent, or disagreeable and suggestive of an infusion of hops — compare* SALT, SOUR, SWEET; *b: distasteful or distressing to the mind:* GALLING *<a bitter sense of shame>; 2: marked by intensity or severity: a: accompanied by severe pain or suffering <a bitter death>; b: being relentlessly determined:* VEHEMENT *<a bitter partisan>; c: exhibiting intense animosity <bitter enemies>; d: (1): harshly reproachful <bitter complaints>; (2): marked by cynicism and rancor <bitter contempt>; e: intensely unpleasant especially in coldness or rawness <a bitter wind>; 3: expressive of severe pain, grief, or regret <bitter tears>; bit·ter·ish \'bi-tə-rish\ adjective; bit·ter·ly adverb; bit·ter·ness noun.¹*

Let us examine the applicable Bible verses concerning bitterness. We will find out what bitterness looks like in a variety of situations.

You saw their abominations and their idols which were among them – wood and stone and silver and gold; so that there may not be among you man or woman or family or tribe, whose heart turns away today from the LORD our God, to go and serve the gods of these nations, and that there may not be among you <u>a root bearing bitterness or wormwood</u>; and so it may not happen, when he hears the words of this curse, that he blesses himself in his heart, saying, 'I shall have peace, even though I follow the dictates of my heart' – as though the drunkard could be included with the sober (emphasis added) (Deuteronomy 29:17-19).

Notice here the word "bitterness" seems to be equated with "wormwood." There has been much speculation among students of Bible prophecy that the word "wormwood," when translated into the Ukrainian language, is "Chernobyl." It turns out that this is a false interpretation, but we'll leave that for another time. If you look up the word "woodworm" in the *Strong's Concordance*, here is the definition you will find:

<u>Wormwood</u> *= From an unused root supposed to mean to curse, wormwood (regarded as poisonous, and therefore <u>accursed</u>): hemlock, wormwood.*

Therefore, the first conclusion that we may draw from this pairing of the words "bitterness" and "wormwood" is that they both are characterized by **curses and being poisonous.** Do any of us really want to be cursed and have poison running through our veins? Of course not! That is reason number one that we need to reject becoming bitter as a result of having been abused. It really isn't a viable option for our lives.

The next three verses concerning bitterness come from the book of Job. We know that Job was "... blameless and upright, and one who feared God and shunned evil (Job 1:1). We will revisit Job's struggle with bitterness in Chapter Nine.

He shall never return to his house, nor shall his place know him anymore. Therefore, I will not restrain my mouth; I will speak in the anguish of my spirit; I will complain in the bitterness of my soul. Am I a sea, or a sea serpent, that You set a guard over me? (Job 7:10-12).

Here Job himself equates bitterness with anguish. The word "anguish" means, "**agonizing physical or mental pain; torment**" according to an online dictionary. Therefore, we have to ask ourselves whether not forgiving someone who has hurt us is worth having agonizing physical or mental pain and torment. Once again, the answer is definitely not! Unless one is masochistic, he or she doesn't go looking for torment. Returning to Job:

My soul loathes my life; I will give free course to my complaint, I will speak in the bitterness of my soul. I will say to God, 'Do not condemn me; show me why You contend with me. Does it seem good to You that You should oppress, that You should despise the work of Your hands, and smile on the counsel of the wicked?' (Job 10:1-3).

Now we see that Job **hates his life**. Not only does he feel removed from all sense of God's presence, he's also angry with Him. Here he expresses the awful feeling of being betrayed by God Himself. Those of us who have suffered abuse from people close to us can definitely relate to that emotion. This awful feeling will be covered more fully in Chapter Seven.

His pails are full of milk, and the marrow of his bones is moist. Another man dies in the bitterness of his soul, never having eaten with pleasure. They lie down alike in the dust, and worms cover them (Job 21:24-26).

Here Job travels from hating his life to **envisioning death**. He is full of questions about the goodness of God, and he is definitely sounding **cynical** here. He has decided that the Lord could not possibly care about mankind because he lets some die that have never "eaten with pleasure." This shows the negative course one embarks on of maintaining bitterness in one's soul. It's a pretty bleak picture, isn't it? Another consequence of holding onto bitterness is penned by King Solomon:

The heart knows its own bitterness, and a stranger does not share its joy (Proverbs 14:10).

This verse indicates that with a bitter heart one feels **alienated, isolated – just plain alone**. Pain is more bearable when we have loved ones to share some of its burden. Yet we suffer through bitterness alone; unless we decide to **poison** someone else with it who we just *know* will be on our side (see Deuteronomy 29:17-19 above). The prophet Jeremiah speaks to the loneliness of heart that accompanies bitterness:

I have become the ridicule of all my people – their taunting song all the day. He has filled me with bitterness; He has made me drink wormwood. He has also broken my teeth with gravel and covered me with ashes (Lamentations 3:14-16).

Here, Jeremiah expresses **alienation from God** and that he's feeling **punished by Him**. In today's world, we would say Jeremiah is not taking responsibility for his own feelings, not to mention that he is feeling the "double whammy" of bitterness and wormwood. Actually, considering what Jeremiah prophesied about Jerusalem, how he was constantly not believed, imprisoned repeatedly, and forced to witness the horrific judgment coming upon his own people, what he is expressing seems quite understandable.

This next scriptural example of someone feeling alienated from God and condemned by the Almighty is undeniably a description of a man undergoing **agonizing torment**:

'Repent therefore of this, your wickedness, and pray God if perhaps the thought of your heart may be forgiven you. For I see that you are poisoned by bitterness and bound by iniquity.' Then Simon answered and said, 'Pray to the Lord for me, that none of the things which you have spoken may come upon me' (Acts 8:22-24).

Here the Apostle Peter gives a stinging rebuke consistent with other verses we have reviewed. He equates bitterness with **poison**. However, the second part of the verse shows another side to Simon's bitterness. Peter is speaking about the **bondage of sin**. The fact that bitterness and iniquity are found in the same sentence shows how close they are in the eyes of the Lord. Bitterness finally results in bondage! Clearly, having bitterness in one's heart is a horrifying position in which to be. The apostle Paul gives us another characteristic of those who are bitter:

Their throat is an open tomb; with their tongues, they have practiced deceit. The poison of asps is under their lips; whose mouth is full of cursing and bitterness. Their feet are swift to shed blood (Romans 3:13-15).

Things just keep getting worse and worse! Have you ever noticed that bitter people **don't seem to be able to control their tongues**? They seem to **curse constantly**. This is an example of **poison** "under their lips." Directly after this pronouncement, the Apostle Paul links bitterness, cursing, and murder in his letter to the church at Ephesus. We shouldn't be surprised, as Jesus told us in the Sermon on the Mount that **murder begins in the heart** (Matthew 5:12-26). Continually being filled with bitterness can degenerate into someone becoming a murderer!

And do not grieve the Holy Spirit of God, by whom you were sealed for the day of redemption. Let all bitterness, wrath, anger, clamor, and evil speaking be put away from you, with all malice. And be kind to one another, tenderhearted, forgiving one another, even as God in Christ forgave you (Ephesians 4:30-32).

The way Paul describes bitterness is enough to break your heart, if you love the Lord. First, when we hold onto bitterness, we **grieve the Holy Spirit**. Secondly, look at all the other sins that are associated with bitterness. People who are quiet and tend to "stuff" their feelings would be horrified to see bitterness lumped in with the other more "flamboyant" sins of **wrath, clamor, and malice**. They would vehemently deny that they were guilty of any of these grievous sins, with the possible exception of sinning with their tongues. It's very apparent in these passages how seriously God views the sin of bitterness. In Ephesians 4:32, He gives us the only possible solution – forgiveness. We can see that it is the most powerful tool the Lord gives us to deal with the abuse we have suffered.

Pursue peace with all people, and holiness, without which no one will see the Lord: looking carefully lest anyone fall short of the grace of God; lest any root of bitterness springing up cause trouble, and by this many become defiled; lest there be any fornicator or profane person like Esau, who for one morsel of food sold his birthright (Hebrews 12:14-16).

This final verse has huge implications. We **won't see God** if we aren't pursuing peace. Part of that process involves forgiveness. I believe that this is the most serious New Testament scripture verse regarding bitterness. The first thing a root of bitterness causes is trouble with a capital "T." The second and extremely grave consequence of bitterness is that many become **defiled**. The implications of this word "defiled" cannot be too heavily stressed. This word requires a formal definition from the *Merriam-Webster Online Dictionary*:

de·file; Pronunciation: \di-ˈfī(-ə)l, dē-\; Function: transitive verb; Inflected Form(s): de·filed; de·fil·ing; Etymology: Middle English, alteration (influenced by filen to defile, from Old English fȳlan) of defoilen to trample, defile, from Anglo-French defoiller, defuler, to trample, from de- + fuller, foller to trample, literally, to full — more at FULL; Date: 14th century: to make unclean or impure: as a: to corrupt the purity or perfection of: DEBASE <the countryside defiled by billboards> b: to violate the chastity of: DEFLOWER c: to make physically unclean especially with something unpleasant or contaminating <boots defiled with blood> d: to violate the sanctity of: DESECRATE <defile a sanctuary> e: SULLY, DISHONOR ; synonyms see CONTAMINATE; de·file·ment \-ˈfī(-ə)l-mənt\ noun; de·fil·er \-ˈfī-lər\ noun.

Please look, if you will, at the synonyms of the word "defiled." **Trampled, uncleanness or impurity, debased, deflowered, contaminated, desecrated, sullied, and dishonored.** Could it get any worse? The Lord goes on to say that "many" will be defiled because of one root of bitterness. This is how interconnected we are – if I hold bitterness against you, not only will the two of us be defiled, but many around us. This verse regarding roots of bitterness contains serious implications. No devout believer would ever want their unforgiveness to affect all those they love, or are connected to, who have nothing to do with the offense. An apt analogy for "defiling many" would be like throwing a stone into a pond and watching the concentric circles that continually spread out over the water. Our sphere of influence is much greater than we think. As much bitterness as there is in the world today, we can well understand how defiled and polluted it has become.

It is a powerful thing to see the very negative physical, emotional, and spiritual results that occur when we refuse to forgive. During the process of writing this book, I felt blessed to be able to view the taping of the television program, *Jewish Voice*, hosted by Jonathan Bernis. He was interviewing an internationally renowned doctor of naturopathic medicine, nutrition, and natural therapies, Jordan S. Rubin. Dr. Rubin is known for his *New York Times* bestseller, *The Maker's*

Diet: The 40-Day Health Experience that Will Change Your Life Forever. Rubin was presenting the six keys to restoring and keeping health, and twice he repeated that when the believer refuses to forgive, the result could be the destruction of the positive effects of the other steps. In an on-line interview, Rubin summed up this concept:

> *RUBIN: And the sixth key that I've added, which is so important, is to avoid deadly emotions. Now I have been spending a lot of time researching the detrimental effects that negative emotions have, like anger, fear, anxiety, stress, and unforgiveness. I realized that when people have these negative emotions, they are contributing the same toxins to their bodies as eating junk food would. People may eat well, they may use supplements, they may exercise, they may practice advanced hygiene, but they stay angry all the time, they harbor unforgiveness, and they're vengeful. I can challenge people with a simple, practical way to practice forgiveness. I tell people when I'm sharing with them to write down a person's name that they have unforgiveness towards and then write, 'I forgive so-and-so for _____.' Forgive that person for every time that they've hurt you. Sometimes the emotions will well up, and you'll remember what they've done, but there's just something amazing about forgiveness. It's the same as if you took a 100-pound weight off your chest. When you harbor unforgiveness, it hurts you. It doesn't hurt the person you're angry with, but it literally can destroy you. As the Bible says, 'A merry heart doeth like medicine, but bitterness can rot the bones.' We need to get this off our chests.*

> *FABRY: If all of this anger and resentment and bitterness can affect our bodies, then it would be a good thing for us to get rid of it. The problem is that people don't know how to do that. In addition, simply writing a name on a piece of paper may be a volitional act, but it really has to get down into our hearts.*

> *RUBIN: That's correct. I think that... many people don't want to do it. They think they're not angry with anybody or they don't have unforgiveness. However, you would be amazed at what happens when you write down, 'My dad.' Then you say, 'I forgive him for this and this and this.' I'll tell you, God honors that, because He commands us to live in forgiveness. In addition, that simple, practical application does make a huge difference. You're forced to deal with it. God can help you. Unforgiveness is lethal to us. It's absolutely lethal. Don't bother trying to get healthy, if you are angry and resentful toward people and want [to take] revenge on them.*[3]

People listen when this next man speaks.... Well-beloved Bible teacher, Dr. Charles Stanley, makes the following point:

It is impossible to be bitter very long without affecting our bodies. More and more, medical professionals are beginning to see some kind of link between the way our bodies function and the way we think. Bitterness, anger, and other negative emotions have been associated with glandular problems, high blood pressure, cardiac disorders, ulcers, and a host of other physical ailments.[4]

One such medical professional is Dr. Archibald Hart. In his very insightful book, *Adrenaline and Stress*, he provides details of the damaging impact of living in a constant state of stress. As a devout Christian, he believes that forgiveness is one of the only ways to defuse the stress that we all experience:

The ability to forgive is, therefore, a very important stress reliever. Those who can't forgive and who harbor resentment are likely to be those who carry the greatest stress. When the mind perceives the need for revenge or defense, it keeps the alarm system at a high state of readiness – adrenaline flows abundantly![5]

Dr. Hart purports that it is this constant high level of adrenaline rushing through our bodies that causes a host of ailments. Forgiveness, on the other hand, can reverse this trend:

I doubt if a deeply forgiving person ever suffers from severe stress disease. There is something about a forgiving spirit that restores the brain's tranquility and lowers the 'fight or flight' response. Of course, anger is not the only cause of stress damage, but it certainly is a significant one. So being able to forgive those who cause us hurt can keep us free from a lot of distress.[6]

Cyril Barber and John Carter conclude that the damaging effects of bitterness are the denial of our peace and the destruction of our relationships. They claim that, over time, these effects become more severe.

Long-standing grudges become extremely corrosive to our personalities and damage our interpersonal relationships. Ultimately the repression of anger will be accompanied by mild to severe paranoia and destroy all the good that we have sought to do in our lifetimes.[7]

Wow! That's frightening to contemplate.... As to the spiritual impact of bitterness, Stanley states that we become alienated from the Lord and others, and the impact of bitterness on our Christian testimony is almost incalculable:

Bitterness also hinders our influence for Christ. What kind of a Christian testimony can we have if we are bitter toward God and toward our neighbors? How can we convincingly talk to others about the forgiveness of God when we refuse to forgive those who have wronged us? When we allow bitterness to take over our lives, that bitterness spills over into the lives of those around us.[8]

A British physician, Dr. Guy Pettitt is quite specific about the negative impact of bitterness upon us physically. The following list of Dr. Pettitt's is a sample of what occurs in the human body when we are bitter and will not forgive offenses:

Your muscles may tighten, causing postural imbalances or pain in neck, back and/or limbs.

Headaches may occur.

Muscle tension squeezes the joint surfaces together decreasing blood flow, making it more difficult for the blood to remove waste products from the cells and tissues.

It restricts the supply of oxygen and nutrients to the cells. Both these contribute to delayed and inadequate tissue repair during sleep, impairing recovery from injury, arthritis, etc.

Your teeth may clench, especially at night, contributing to dental bills for problems with your teeth and jaw joints.

Injury through inattention, accident, or violence is more likely.

The blood flow to your heart is constricted.

Your digestion is impaired.

Your breathing is restricted.

It is now being realized that your immune system functions less well.

If you have a tendency to allergy, the level at which the allergic response tends to trigger off can be reduced, so that allergic symptoms occur more frequently.

You become more vulnerable to infections, and perhaps cancer.

You feel bad, moody, irritable, and so on, and your mind is less able to see its way through problems and difficulties.

Making decisions can become harder.

You may become depressed – even suicidal.

Your creativity is reduced or even blocked.

In these and other ways, your 'stress reserves' are constantly draining away, like water from a leaky bucket.[9]

Pettitt goes on to enumerate the effects of bitterness on all types of relationships:

Stony silences.

The sweet 'Yes, dear,' which really means 'No! I cannot stand this!'

Rows [the British term for argument].

Various sexual tensions and dysfunctions.

Verbal and non-verbal abuse between adults and from adults to children, including violence, sexual, educational, spiritual and ritual abuse (<u>Note: Do you see the vicious cycle operating here?</u>).

Decreased productivity in the workplace.

Subtle sabotage of ourselves and others.

Tension, bad atmosphere or 'vibes' at home or work.[10]

I once saw a client, whom we'll call Anna, who had been deeply wounded by her sister. As noted earlier (that bitter people tend to curse a lot), Anna had one of the foulest mouths imaginable – and was unashamed of it – all the while claiming that she was serious about her faith. In a session one day, I suggested to her that it might be time to begin considering the process of forgiving her sister. I will never forget her reaction. Anna abruptly stood up, cursed and stormed out of the room (the session was nowhere near being over), exclaiming that she would **never, ever** forgive her sister! After witnessing her extreme response, I was convinced that she'd never come back. Therefore, I was utterly shocked when I called to ask whether she would come for her regularly scheduled session. Anna acted completely surprised that I would even pose such a question. Of course, she would be there, she replied, sounding puzzled as to why I was even calling.

Another example of the toll unforgiveness can take was a young male client we'll call Jason. One of his parents was Asian, the other European. They had a very volatile marriage, characterized primarily by verbal violence, and ultimately divorced. Jason's mother returned to her homeland, completely abandoning him without a second thought. Actually, he was abused in every single way at the hands of both parents and was the victim of repeated sexual abuse by acquaintances and strangers. His mother sexually abused him in covert ways, which was a huge indicator of her mental illness. The effects on Jason were profound. Though he had tried repeatedly to have a fulfilling relationship with a woman, it just did not seem possible. Although he covered it fairly well, when he became overwhelmed in life, his misogyny became evident.

Jason was so bitter toward his mother, in particular, that it literally poisoned his attempts at relationships with women. As a Christian, he definitely wanted to marry one day, but the abuse suffered at the hands of his mother resulted in him feeling that it was impossible for him every to forgive her. When I suggested working through the forgiveness process regarding the perpetrators of his sexual abuse, Jason seemed all for it. He took the booklet I offered him (which contained a very practical way to go through the forgiveness process), thanked me, and said he would call me to schedule our next appointment, as he was running late for a first date with an "incredible" woman he had met a few weeks before. Jason never returned to counseling, and to this day remains unhappily single.

In their incisive book, *Choosing Forgiveness*, John and Paul Sandford and Norm Bowen delineate eight spiritual ramifications of a believer's continued unforgiveness:

1. If we harbor unforgiveness, there is no way we can see reality – all we have is our own subjective perceptions.

The eye is the lamp of the body. If your eyes are good, your whole body will be full of light. But if your eyes are bad, your whole body will be full of darkness. If then the light within you is darkness, how great is that darkness! (Matthew 6:22-23, New International Version).

2. When we hang on to unforgiveness, our discernment becomes warped because we interpret issues from a childish point of view.

When I was a child, I used to speak as a child, think as a child, reason as a child; but when I became a man, I did away with childish things. For now we see in a mirror dimly, but then face to face; now I know in part, but then I shall know fully just as I also have been fully known (1 Corinthians 13:11, New American Standard Bible).

3. <u>*Choosing to be unforgiving causes us to fall short of the grace of God.*</u>

A man's own folly ruins his life, yet his heart rages against the Lord (Proverbs 19:3 (New International Version). See to it that no one comes short of the grace of God; that no root of bitterness springing up causes trouble, and by it many be defiled (Hebrews 12:15, New American Standard Bible).

4. <u>*When we hang on to unforgiveness, our sin comes back on us and must be dealt with again and again.*</u>

But that servant went out and found one of his fellow servants who owed him a hundred denarii; and he laid hands on him and took him by the throat, saying, 'Pay me what you owe!' So his fellow servant fell down at his feet and begged him, saying, 'Have patience with me, and I will pay you all.' And he would not, but went and threw him into prison till he should pay the debt. So when his fellow servants saw what had been done, they were very grieved, and came and told their master all that had been done. Then his master, after he had called him, said to him, 'You wicked servant! I forgave you all that debt because you begged me. Should you not also have had compassion on your fellow servant, just as I had pity on you?' And his master was angry, and delivered him to the torturers until he should pay all that was due to him. So My heavenly Father also will do to you if each of you, from his heart, does not forgive his brother his trespasses (Matthew 18:23-35).

5. <u>*Unwillingness to forgive affects our ability to confront others and to receive correction.*</u>

Reprove a wise man, and he will love you. Give instruction to a wise man and he will be still wiser. Teach a righteous man, and he will increase his learning (Proverbs 9:8-9, New American Standard Bible). Open rebuke is better than love carefully concealed. Faithful are the wounds of a friend, but the kisses of an enemy are deceitful (Proverbs 27:5-6). Like apples of gold in settings of silver is a word spoken in right circumstances (Proverbs 25:11).

6. *If we fail to forgive each other, it makes us vulnerable to attack by Satan.*

But if anyone has caused grief, he has not grieved me, but all of you to some extent.... This punishment which was inflicted by the majority is sufficient for such a man, so that, on the contrary, you ought rather to forgive and comfort him, lest perhaps such a one be swallowed up with too much sorrow. Therefore, I urge you to reaffirm your love to him. For to this end I also wrote, that I might put you to the test, whether you are obedient in all things. Now whom you forgive anything, I also forgive. For if indeed I have forgiven anything, I have forgiven that one for your sakes in the presence of Christ, lest Satan should take advantage of us; for we are not ignorant of his devices (2 Corinthians 2:5-11).

7. *Hanging on to unforgiveness creates in us the necessity to build and maintain a facade.*

Now then, you Pharisees, clean the outside of the cup and dish, but inside you are full of greed and wickedness. You foolish people! Did not the One who made the outside make the inside also? (Luke 11:39-40, New International Version). We love Him because He first loved us. If someone says, 'I love God,' and hates his brother, he is a liar; for he who does not love his brother whom he has seen, how can he love God whom he has not seen? (1 John 4:19-20). If we say that we have fellowship with Him, and walk in darkness, we lie and do not practice the truth. But if we walk in the light as He is in the light, we have fellowship with one another, and the blood of Jesus Christ His Son cleanses us from all sin (1 John 1:6-7).

8. *Holding on to unforgiveness produces physical, emotional, and spiritual exhaustion.*

Come to Me, all you who labor and are heavy laden, and I will give you rest. Take My yoke upon you and learn from Me, for I am gentle and lowly in heart, and you will find rest for your souls (Matthew 11:28-29). [11]

R. T. Kendall has also given us tremendous insight as to the spiritual implications of not forgiving:

What, then, is the result if we do not forgive? If it means that we lose our salvation, it follows that we must be saved by works. Make no mistake about it: when you forgive another person, that is a work – and it is a good work. But I would remind you that the apostle Paul said, 'For it is by grace you have been saved, through faith – and this not from yourselves, it is the gift of God – not by works, so that no one can boast' (Eph.

2:8-9). But Paul adds, 'For we are God's workmanship, created in Christ Jesus to do good works, which God prepared in advance for us to do' (v. 10). Even though we do not achieve salvation through our works, we are required to do good works, and one of those is forgiving those who have hurt us. Although we know we are saved by grace alone, there remain consequences if we choose to walk in unforgiveness. Some aspects of our relationship with God are unchangeable, but others are affected by the things that we do.

1. Salvation is unconditional; fellowship with the Father is conditional.

When we are justified before God, we are declared righteous, and that comes by faith. Anyone who transfers the trust that he or she had in their good works – and trusts what Jesus did on the cross – is credited by God with perfect righteousness. But fellowship with the Father on the way to heaven is conditional. Unconfessed sin – including unforgiveness – in our lives can block our fellowship with the Father.

2. Justification before God is unconditional; the anointing of the Spirit is conditional.

The anointing – the power of the Spirit in our lives – may ebb and flow. The Dove may come down and then flutter away for a while, but our standing before God, because of the righteousness of Christ put to our credit (Rom. 4:4-5), is permanent.

3. Our status in the family of God is unconditional; our intimacy with Christ is conditional.

We are sons and daughters of the Most High once we have been adopted into God's family. (See Ephesians 1:5.) We are as secure in the family of God as Jesus Himself is in the Trinity. Why? We have been made joint heirs with Christ (Rom. 8:17). We are saved, but our intimacy with Christ is conditional.

4. Our eternal destiny – whether we go to heaven or hell – is fixed, but receiving an additional reward is conditional.

Once we are saved, we are assured that we will go to heaven. But receiving an inheritance, a further reward, is conditional. Some may go to heaven without a reward: 'If what he has built survives, he will receive his reward. If it is burned up, he will suffer loss; he himself will be saved, but only as one escaping through the flames' (1 Cor. 3:14-15). Thank God all this is true, or there would be few, if any, ever saved! Yet having said that, totally forgiving another person is an achievable act. It can be done, and it is something you and I must keep doing. It's not enough to say, 'Well, I did it yesterday. I have paid my dues. I showed I could do it.' It is a lifelong commitment. But let no one say, 'That's beyond me!' It can be done. It may be a continual struggle, but we do have the power to overcome – and the consequences are wonderful.[12]

This has been a long chapter to wade through, but **it's almost impossible to overstate the effects of bitterness in a believer's life.** I hope that Chapters Two and Three can be a resource for readers if or when you need to counsel others about the reasons to forgive and the consequences of not forgiving.

⸺⸺

One of the deepest questions that arises when a child has been abused, and is either a believer or becomes one in later life, pertains to what our Father in heaven feels when He sees countless children being abused every day, all over the world. We can get a very good idea of what He feels from His Word, as you shall see next.

Psychological and emotional abuse is also forbidden in Scripture. Ephesians 6:4 warns fathers not to 'exasperate' or provoke their children, but to bring them up in the 'training and instruction of the Lord.' Harsh, unloving discipline alienates children's minds from their parents and renders their instructions and corrections useless. In addition, it often leads to sin against God, as it is difficult in the best of children to be angry and bitter and not sin. Parents can provoke and exasperate their children by placing unreasonable requirements on them, belittling them, or constantly finding fault, thereby producing wounds that are far worse than any physical beating can inflict. Colossians 3:21 tells us not to 'embitter' our children so they will not become discouraged. Ephesians 4:15-19 says we are to speak the truth in love and use our words to build others up, not allow rotten or destructive words to pour from our lips, especially toward the tender hearts and minds of children. – S. Michael Houdmann

God is also angry and grieved by sexual abuse, and He promises to repay for the evil that's done and to avenge any sins committed against children. True justice can be gained only through our judicial system and by allowing room for God's vengeance and judgment. – Audrey Hector

Jesus said if anyone does wrong against children ('little ones'), it would be better for him to have a millstone slung around his neck and be thrown into the sea. In other words, they will be dealt with very severely. Now you know what God thinks. – Peter's answer to Harry Stephenson's online question

And I will come near you for judgment; I will be a swift witness against sorcerers, against adulterers, against perjurers, against those who exploit wage earners and widows and orphans, and against those who turn away an alien – because they do not fear Me," says the LORD of hosts (Malachi 3:5).

For the wrath of God is revealed from heaven against all ungodliness and unrighteousness of men, who suppress the truth in unrighteousness (Romans 1:18).

Pure and undefiled religion before God and the Father is this: to visit orphans and widows in their trouble and to keep oneself unspotted from the world (James 1:27).

My defense is of God, Who saves the upright in heart. God is a just judge, and God is angry with the wicked every day. If he does not turn back, He will sharpen His sword; He bends His bow and makes it ready (Psalm 7:10-12).

When Jesus was crucified, the Maker of the universe suffered everything that Jesus suffered. The same God who suffered with Jesus suffers with all of His children. He suffered with each child, every man and woman, in the death camps. He suffers when any of His children suffer at the hands of adults. – Lewis B. Smedes.

Chapter Four

How Does the Lord Feel about Child Abuse?

It is imperative that believers know how the Lord feels about child abuse. Many perceive God as a distant, detached being somewhere "up there," who has no feelings about the incredible suffering human beings are undergoing on this earth. They wonder about whether He cares or not, when they observe all the pain inflicted on them by others that seems to go unpunished. They feel if He were a just God, He never would have allowed the abuse to occur in the first place. I will do my best, with our limited vocabulary and the confines of being a mortal, to depict accurately what the Lord feels about abuse. Answers to the questions just raised will be covered further in Chapters Six through Eight.

So how does the Lord feel, anyway? If we are created in His image, and we are told in Genesis that we are, then He must have feelings, right? That is actually correct. I believe the popular author Randy Alcorn has given us the most useful analysis of the subject.

An abundance of biblical passages show that God experiences a broad range of emotions. God commands us not to 'grieve' the Holy Spirit (Ephesians 4:30). God is said to be 'angry' (Deuteronomy 1:37), 'moved by pity' (Judges 2:18, English Standard Version), 'pleased' (1 Kings 3:10), and 'to rejoice over you with singing' (Zephaniah 3:17). Genesis 6:6 says, 'So the LORD was sorry He had ever made them and put them on the earth. It broke His heart' (New Living Testament). Since God made us in his image, we should assume our emotions are reflective of His, even though ours are subject to sin while His are not.[1]

We don't need to go very far in the Bible to find others verses illustrating God's emotions, according to Alcorn:

Now leave me alone so that my anger may burn against them and that I may destroy them. (Exodus 32:10). As a father has compassion on his children, so the LORD has compassion on those who fear him (Psalm 103:13).' In a surge of anger I hid my face from you for a moment, but with everlasting kindness I will have compassion on you,' says the LORD your Redeemer (Isaiah 54:8). As a bridegroom rejoices over his bride, so will your God rejoice over you (Isaiah 62:5). Nor does God limit his compassion to His children. He says, 'I wail over Moab, for all Moab I cry out' (Jeremiah 48:31). A passage about God's goodness and compassion contains a remarkable statement: 'In all their distress He too was distressed' (Isaiah 63:9). A form of the same word is used to describe God's people's distress as to depict God's own. Yes, our distress can involve feelings that God doesn't feel, such as helplessness and uncertainty. But clearly God intends for us to see a similarity between our emotional distress and His. The fact that the second member of the triune God suffered unimaginable torture on the cross should explode any notion that God lacks feelings. In the suffering of Jesus, God Himself suffered. No one who grasps this truth can say, 'God doesn't understand my suffering.' [2]

Okay, you say, *so God has feelings… what specifically does He feel about child abuse, and can you prove that these are truly His feelings?* Actually, I can. The immediate answer to this question lies in what Jesus Himself had to say about child abuse:

Whoever receives one little child like this in My name receives Me. Whoever causes one of these little ones who believe in Me to sin, it would be better for him if a millstone were hung around his neck, and he were drowned in the depths of the sea (Matthew 18:5-6)…. Then little children were brought to Him that He might put His hands on them and pray, but the disciples rebuked them. But Jesus said, 'Let the little children come to Me, and do not forbid them; for of such is the kingdom of heaven' (Matthew 19:13-14).

Turning again to what I consider one of the very best books written about healing child abuse by Steven Tracy, *Mending the Soul: Understanding and Healing Abuse*, we see the following Scripture verses listed as to the Lord's perspective about each type of child abuse (all verses are from the New American Standard Bible):

Condemnation of Physical Abuse

The Lord tests the righteous, but the wicked, and the one who loves violence, His soul hates (Psalm 11:5).

My son, do not walk in the way with them. Keep your feet from their path, for their feet run to evil and they make haste to shed blood. Surely, in vain the net is spread in the sight of any bird, but they [abusers] lie in wait for their own blood, they lurk secretly for their own lives (Proverbs 1:15-19).

These are six things which the Lord hates, yes, seven which are an abomination to Him: A proud look, a lying tongue, hands that shed innocent blood, a heart that devises wicked plans, feet that are swift in running to evil, a false witness who speaks lies, and one who sows discord among brethren (Proverbs 6:16-19).

Then He [God] said to me, 'The iniquity of the house of Israel and Judah is exceedingly great, and the land is filled with bloodshed, and the city is full of perversity; for they say, 'The Lord has forsaken the land, and the Lord does not see!' And as for Me [God] also, 'My eye will neither spare [abusers] nor will I have pity, but I will recompense their deeds on their own head' (Ezekiel 9:9-10).

Then he may have a violent son who sheds blood and who does any of these things to a brother... defiles his neighbor's wife, oppresses the poor and needy, commits robbery... he will not live! He has committed all these abominations, he will surely be put to death (Ezekiel 18:10-13).

<u>Condemnation and Effects of Sexual Abuse</u>

But if in the field the man finds the girl who is engaged, and the man forces her and lies with her, then only the man who lies with her shall die. But you shall do nothing to the girl; there is no sin in the girl worthy of death (Deuteronomy 22:25-26).

But the men would not listen to him. So the man seized his concubine and brought her out to them; and they raped her and abused her all night until morning, then let her go at the approach of dawn (Judges 19:25).

They ravished the women in Zion, the virgins in the cities of Judah (Lamentations 5:11).

One has committed abomination with his neighbor's wife and another has lewdly defiled his daughter-in-law. And another in you has humbled his sister, his father's daughter.... I will gather you and blow on you with the fire of My wrath, and you will be melted in the midst of it (Ezekiel 22:11, 21).

Tamar put ashes on her head and tore her long-sleeved garment which was on her; and she put her hand on her head and went away, crying aloud as she went... So Tamar remained and was desolate in her brother Absalom's house (2 Samuel 13:19-20).

Condemnation of Neglect

But if anyone does not provide for his own, and especially for those of his household, he has denied the faith and is worse than an unbeliever (1Timothy 5:8).

Condemnation and Effects of Verbal Abuse

There is one who speaks rashly like the thrusts of a sword, but the tongue of the wise brings healing (Proverbs 12:8).

A soothing tongue is a tree of life, but perversion in it crushes the spirit (Proverbs 15:4).

Death and life are in the power of the tongue (Proverbs 18:21).

Their throat is an open grave, with their tongues they keep deceiving, the poison of asps is under their lips; whose mouth is full of cursing and bitterness (Romans 3:13-14).

So also, the tongue is a small part of the body, and yet it boasts of great things. See how great a forest is set aflame by such a small fire! And the tongue is a fire, the very world of iniquity; the tongue is set among our members as that which defiles the entire body, and sets on fire the course of our life, and is set on fire by hell... But no one can tame the tongue; it is a restless evil and full of deadly poison. With it, we bless our Lord and Father, and with it, we curse men, who have been made in the likeness of God (James 3:5-6, 8-9).

Condemnation of Spiritual Abuse

There is a conspiracy of her prophets in her midst like a roaring lion tearing the prey. They have devoured lives; they have taken treasure and precious things; they have made many widows in the midst of her. Her priests have done violence to My law... Her prophets have smeared whitewash for them, seeing false visions and divining lies for them, saying, 'Thus says the Lord God,' when the Lord has not spoken (Ezekiel 22:25-26, 28).

Then Jesus spoke to the crowds and to His disciples, saying 'The scribes and the Pharisees have seated themselves in the chair of Moses; therefore all that they tell you, do and observe, but do not do according to their deeds; for they say things and do not do them. They tie up heavy burdens and lay them on men's shoulders, but they themselves are unwilling to move them with so much as a finger. But they do all their deeds to be noticed by men... But the greatest among you shall be your servant. Whoever exalts himself shall be humbled; and whoever humbles himself shall be exalted. But woe to you, scribes and Pharisees, hypocrites, because you shut off the kingdom of heaven from people' (Matthew 23:1-5, 11-13).

The Pharisees and scribes asked Him, 'Why do your disciples not walk according to the tradition of the elders, but eat their bread with impure hands?' And He said to them, 'Rightly did Isaiah prophesy of you hypocrites, as it is written: This people honor Me with their lips, but their heart is far away from Me. But in vain do they worship Me, teaching as doctrines the precepts of men. Neglecting the commandment of God, you hold to the traditions of men' (Mark 7:5-8). [3]

I close this chapter with a personal account that I believe contains a close parallel to the feelings that the Lord has about child abuse. Many years ago, I attended Church On The Way, pastored by Jack Hayford. He is known all over the world as a pastor's pastor; an author of excellence; composer of the hymn, *Majesty*; a man full of integrity, who has an exemplary walk with the Lord and walks this earth without reproach. Those are just a few descriptive phrases of our beloved "Pastor Jack." [He would hate this description – for he is a truly humble man!]

One Sunday morning, I was sitting in probably the second row of chairs. This was rather unusual for me… I typically sat more near the back of a congregation. Yet the location of my seat was no accident, because I was able to witness this entire incident up close and personal. Pastor Jack's teaching was on this very topic, "How God Hates Child Abuse" or something to that effect and was speaking in his usual informative, compelling, and touching way. All of a sudden, he stepped away from the podium and began an extemporaneous address to an anonymous congregant. Now Pastor Jack is known to raise his voice from time to time when he becomes passionate about something, and he's not embarrassed when his voice cracks due to tears from time to time. This time, however, he was displaying an emotion that I had never seen nor would see again in my time at this church – a righteous anger (similar to what Jesus displayed when he made a whip and turned over the moneychangers' tables in the Temple) that actually came out in a manner akin to a roar.

As he went on, Pastor Jack's face got redder and redder. A vein began to pulse in his forehead and he was pacing back and forth like a lion that was caged, but wanted to pounce. It appeared that it was taking every bit of self-control he had not to scream at and identify the object of his anger. I cannot possibly quote what he said that day, only paraphrase, but it went something like this: "You there in the front of the sanctuary, yes, you know who you are. At the end of the service, two ushers will come and escort you out of the building, and you are no longer welcome at Church On The Way. I know all about you and your attempts to abuse children in our Sunday School and to come on to women so aggressively. Oh yes, I know all about you! You thought you could behave in these evil ways and never be exposed. Well, guess what? You've been exposed and you're outta here, mister!"

He then returned to the podium and went on with his sermon, speaking in a perfectly calm tone of voice. You could hear a pin drop as he addressed the man and after he returned to teaching. At the end of the service, I, touched as both a therapist and survivor of abuse, turned to utter strangers and excitedly began to discuss what happened. Everyone was utterly astonished at what had happened. They were, to a person, surprised that how Pastor Jack had not chosen to call an usher up to confer with quietly about the matter and handle it discreetly, rather he had chosen to display his outrage and indignation that this man thought he could get away with any kind of abuse on *his* watch. He wouldn't stand for it!

We felt sobered, as though we had just seen the Lord break out in wrath against an evildoer… in fact, that was precisely what we observed. In his capacities as father, pastor, leader and one ultimately responsible for this sizeable congregation, he jumped right out there and grabbed the opportunity to publicly rebuke an abuser. In spiritual terms, he did represent the Lord (as a believer filled with the Holy Spirit and wielding his God-given authority to "… trample on serpents and scorpions and over all the power of the enemy").

Both the adult therapist and the child survivor parts of me were so touched and thrilled to witness what transpired that day! It exceeded my expectations of what a healthy response to child abuse would look like in the Church-at-large. I will never know exactly what Pastor Jack was referring to… evidently, the abuser was not guilty enough to be prosecuted. Perhaps Child Protective Services were called in afterward. He had the response that all children dream of when they tell an adult they've been abused. As a survivor, I experienced immense healing that day, which is an excellent example of all things working together for good.

The following Scripture, Psalm 18 (selected portions), is one of the most descriptive chapters in the Bible regarding how God feels about abuse. Granted, adults are being discussed here… but imagine these feelings magnified because of the Lord's feelings about His "little ones" (see Matthew 18 and 19):

Psalm 18

To the Chief Musician. A Psalm of David the servant of the LORD

[1] I will love You, O LORD, my strength.
[2] The LORD is my rock and my fortress and my deliverer;
My God, my strength, in whom I will trust;
My shield and the horn of my salvation, my stronghold.

[4]… The pangs of death surrounded me,
And the floods of ungodliness made me afraid.

⁵ The sorrows of Sheol surrounded me;
The snares of death confronted me.
⁶ In my distress I called upon the LORD,
And cried out to my God;
He heard my voice from His temple,
… And my cry came before Him, even to His ears.
⁷ Then the earth shook and trembled;
The foundations of the hills also quaked and were shaken,
Because He was angry.
⁸ Smoke went up from His nostrils,
And devouring fire from His mouth;
Coals were kindled by it.
⁹ He bowed the heavens also, and came down
With darkness under His feet.
¹⁰ And He rode upon a cherub, and flew;
He flew upon the wings of the wind.
¹¹ He made darkness His secret place;
His canopy around Him was dark waters
And thick clouds of the skies.
¹² From the brightness before Him,
His thick clouds passed with hailstones and coals of fire.
¹³ The LORD thundered from heaven,
And the Most High uttered His voice,
Hailstones and coals of fire.
¹⁴ He sent out His arrows and scattered the foe,
Lightnings in abundance, and He vanquished them.
¹⁵ Then the channels of the sea were seen,
The foundations of the world were uncovered
At Your rebuke, O LORD,
At the blast of the breath of Your nostrils.
²⁵… With the merciful You will show Yourself merciful;

³⁵… You have also given me the shield of Your salvation;
Your right hand has held me up,
Your gentleness has made me great.
³⁶ You enlarged my path under me,
So my feet did not slip.

> *[41] … They [the wicked] cried out, but there was none to save;*
> *Even to the LORD, but He did not answer them.*
>
> *[46] … The LORD lives and*
> *Blessed be my Rock!*
> *Let the God of my salvation be exalted.*
> *[47] It is God who avenges me… (emphasis added).*

It is my hope and prayer that in my telling you this story and citing the applicable scripture passages, you get a sense of what God feels about the abuse you suffered and the consequences in store for your abuser(s) in the event that they remain unrepentant. I firmly believe that, along with the tremendous anger the Lord feels when He sees children (or anyone) being abused, He also weeps for the pain of everyone involved. We have a High Priest who can be "… touched by the feelings of our infirmities" (Hebrews 4:15). **[To see the abuses that Jesus suffered, see Appendix C.]**

Who will distribute justice completely and perfectly when the time comes? **Even so, come quickly, Lord Jesus!**

People can become very confused when it comes to distinguishing between what forgiveness is and is not. This confusion is addressed in the next chapter, and forgiveness is clarified. We will also identify the process of healing to which forgiveness so crucial.

In forgiving, people are not being asked to forget. On the contrary, it is important to remember, so that we should not let such atrocities happen again. Forgiveness does not mean condoning what has been done. It means taking what happened seriously... drawing out the sting in the memory that threatens our entire existence. – Bishop Desmond Tutu

Forgiveness is me giving up my right to hurt you for hurting me. –Anonymous

A Christian will find it cheaper to pardon than to resent. Forgiveness saves the expense of anger, the cost of hatred, and the waste of spirit. – Hannah More

Forgiveness is not an occasional act: it is an attitude – Martin Luther King, Jr.

You will know that forgiveness has begun when you recall those who hurt you and feel the power to wish them well. – Lewis B. Smedes

Forgiveness is a gift you give yourself. – Suzanne Somers

It takes one person to forgive; it takes two people to be reunited. – Lewis B. Smedes

Forgiveness unleashes joy. It brings peace. It washes the slate clean. It sets all the highest values of love in motion. In a sense, forgiveness is Christianity at its highest level. – John MacArthur

We do not really know how to forgive until we know what it is to be forgiven. Therefore, we should be glad that we can be forgiven by others. It is our forgiveness of one another that makes the love of Jesus manifest in our lives, for in forgiving one another we act toward one another as He has acted towards us. – Thomas Merton

It is freeing to become aware that we do not have to be victims of our past and can learn new ways of responding. But there is a step beyond this recognition... it is the step of forgiveness. Forgiveness is love practiced among people who love poorly. It sets us free without wanting anything in return. – Henri Nouwen

When we forgive evil, we do not excuse it, we do not tolerate it, and we do not smother it. We look the evil full in the face, call it what it is, let its horror shock and stun and enrage us, and only then do we forgive it. – Lewis B. Smedes

The glory of Christianity is to conquer by forgiveness. —William Blake

Chapter Five

What Forgiveness Is/Isn't and the Process of Healing

One of the worst things a people-helper can do is to pressure a victim of abuse to forgive. Many people are so busy denying that they were abused as children that they will gladly leap to something "concrete" like forgiving, rather than go through the arduous and painful grief process as part of their healing. An additional complication of the "just forgive the person and move on" has been outlined in Steven Tracy's *Mending the Soul: Understanding and Healing Child Abuse*:

> *In subsequent years, I have heard abuse victims recount similar stories repeatedly, illustrating the widespread confusion in the Christian community about the relationship between forgiveness and abuse. Religious leaders and even family members are often quick to tell victims they must forgive, regardless of the circumstances of the abuse or the posture of the abuser. Sadly, insensitivity to the complexity of the biblical doctrine and ignorance of the dynamics of abuse often lead Christian leaders to inflict much additional damage on survivors of abuse.[1]*

What does Tracy mean when he speaks of the complexity of biblical doctrine about forgiveness? He clarifies that statement below:

> *In view of common misperceptions and the complexity of the issue, the best way to begin is by clarifying the nature of biblical forgiveness. One of the first problems one notes when researching this topic is that much of the religious literature implores forgiveness but never clearly defines it. It is widely known that the primary Greek verb in the New Testament used to indicate 'to forgive' is αφιημι, which in general terms conveys the idea of 'letting go.' Sadly, many Christian leaders who address forgiveness fall into the trap of oversimplification and only define forgiveness as 'letting go.' What does this*

mean for the little girl who disclosed to me that her teenage cousin had been molesting her, along with other neighborhood children, during the past year? Does it mean (as the molester's parents proclaimed) the girl and her parents should simply 'let it go' and not notify the authorities? Does forgiveness mean this family must 'let go' of their anger toward an adolescent sexual predator who brags about the number of children he has raped? Does it mean (as the extended family insists) the parents must 'let go' of their refusal to bring their daughter to family functions if the teenage molester is in atten- dance? If forgiveness doesn't necessarily mean letting go of everything, then just what is it that is let go? [2]

One of the most harmful models of forgiveness that can be communicated to survivors is one that equates "… forgiveness, trust, and reconciliation and eliminates the possibility of negative consequences for the offender."[3] Tracy goes on to give an example of this misrepresentation of biblical forgiveness:

For example, in a two-volume work that received a Book of the Year award, a respected evangelical states that, by definition, forgiveness involves a restoration of trust and a letting go of all negative emotions, including fear, anger, suspicion, alienation, and mistrust.[4]

Tracy's comment on this definition of forgiveness is right on target and needs to bring convic- tion to those who have counseled survivors in this manner:

As if this definition fails to be difficult enough for abuse victims, who have every reason in the world to fear and mistrust their unrepentant abusers, the author keeps reminding readers that if we don't forgive others, God won't forgive us. By this logic, virtually all abuse victims are damned by their inability to trust their abusers.[5]

What about the justice for which our hearts cry out? What about consequences? Can adults just do anything they feel like doing to children? Tracy notes the importance of clarifying the term "forgiveness":

It is imperative to clarify biblical forgiveness. One of the most important observations to make is that, while the Bible does describe forgiveness as the removal or letting go of a debt (Matthew 6:12), forgiveness does not necessarily remove negative consequences for the one forgiven, nor does it automatically grant trust and reconciliation. One of the clearest examples is found in Numbers 14:20-23, where God declares that he will forgive the Israelites for their rebellion, but that not one of the adults will enter the land He had promised them. More relevant for abuse is King David's sexual violation of Bathsheba and murder of her husband. Once David repented, Nathan declared that God had forgiven him and taken away his sin, and yet a series of harsh consequences was meted out by God ('I will raise up evil against you from your own household' [2 Samuel 12:11]). Similarly, when the prophet Hosea took back his adulterous wife, Gomer, by God's directive, he forgave her, but she was to remain in seclusion for two months and forgo sexual intimacy with her husband (Hosea 3:1-5). Trust is earned. Forgiving evil does not eliminate all negative consequences.[6]

Tracy goes on to reiterate that the classical Greek word αφιημι is generally defined as "to release," but that in its 125 usages in the New Testament its meaning is nuanced and cannot just be confined to "release." It is used to mean "to let go, to send away" (Matthew 13:36; Mark 4:36); "to cancel, to remit" (Matthew 18:27; Mark 2:50); "to leave" (Matthew 4:11; John 10:12); "to give up, to abandon" (Romans 1:27; Revelation 2:4); and even "to tolerate, to permit" (Acts 5:38; Revelation 2:20).[7] What, then, is Tracy's conclusion about the meaning of the word "forgiveness"?

Clearly, in defining forgiveness, one cannot simply appeal to the root meaning of αφιημι as "to let go." The only way to accurately determine the biblical meaning of forgiveness as it relates to abuse is to look at a broad range of Biblical passages that deal with forgiveness and malevolent evil and then draw pertinent principles. In doing so, one will quickly observe the complexity of biblical teaching on the subject and the inappropriateness of much of the evangelical rhetoric on forgiveness.[8]

Another problematic area is what Tracy labels "premature forgiveness of abusers." He describes it this way:

One can now see how dangerous it is for counselors or church leaders to urge prompt (and hence premature) forgiveness of abusers. This is incredibly insensitive and destructive to the victims. It can not only hinder their healing (and often strengthen unforgiveness); it can also contribute to additional abuse in the Christian community by promoting individual and corporate minimization and denial of evil... Premature forgiveness may seem to smooth things over temporarily, and it appeals to most of us who were brought up to believe that being nice was a primary Christian virtue. But it has the effect of driving anger and pain underground where they then fester like a poisonous stream.... And it has the effect of relieving the abuser of any true responsibility to examine his behavior and to change. Because premature forgiveness bypasses consequences and rehabilitation for the offender, it is, in fact, tacit permission – perhaps even an invitation – to continue the violence.[9]

The very day I was writing this portion of the book, I was utterly horrified when I saw a headline on a website that covers our local news. This story illustrates the destruction that premature forgiveness and lack of consequences and real change wreaks – for the victims, the pastors, the church, and even the perpetrator:

Phoenix dad accused of molesting daughters; 2 pastors arrested for not reporting abuse

by Jennifer Thomas

azfamily.com

Posted on July 28, 2010 at 11:31 AM

Updated Wednesday, Jul 28 at 5:34 PM

PHOENIX – Phoenix police arrested a man for allegedly molesting his two daughters and two pastors were arrested for not reporting the abuse to authorities.

According to Phoenix Police Detective James Holmes, a 16-year-old girl told a neighbor that her father had been molesting her for several years. The neighbor confronted the man, who reportedly admitted he knew what he did was wrong.

azfamily.com is not releasing the father's name to protect the victims' identities.

The neighbor and victim contacted Phoenix police officers. The teen reported at least one instance of sexual intercourse and several acts of sexual contact over nearly five years.

Detectives learned the victim's older sister, now 19 years old, had also been molested by the suspect, which caused her to move out when she turned 18.

Holmes said the suspect admitted to numerous counts of sexual abuse with both victims. On July 9, he was arrested and charged with one count of sexual abuse, two counts of child molestation and 11 counts of sexual conduct with a minor.

During interviews with the victims and witnesses, detectives learned that in 2008, the older victim told her pastors, Daniel and Laura McCluskey, that she was being touched inappropriately by her father.

Holmes said the conversation occurred at the Church on the Word at 83rd Avenue and Camelback Road in Glendale and included the two pastors, the 19-year-old victim and the suspect.

Holmes said the suspect admitted going into the victim's room at night and touching her. <u>The pastors told the victim that because the father was repentant, she should forgive him and restore their relationship</u> (emphasis added).

After this conversation, the suspect stopped sexually abusing the older victim <u>but reportedly continued sexually abusing the younger sister</u> (emphasis added).

<u>Based on the pastors' failure to report the abuse, Holmes said the younger sister continued to be sexually abused for the next one to two years</u> (emphasis added).

As mandated reporters under Arizona Revised Statutes, Homes said the pastors had a duty to report to CPS and/or law enforcement that this was occurring.

The pastors were both arrested Tuesday and booked on one count each of failure to report child abuse. [10]

Tracy goes on to list the three types of forgiveness he believes are contained in the Bible, making the term "forgiveness" more complex than first meets the eye: judicial forgiveness, psychological forgiveness, and extending grace. Once again, I would urge you to read Dr. Tracy's book yourself, as it is a comprehensive and noteworthy work on the subject of how child abuse is healed and forgiven within a Christian framework (*Mending the Soul: Understanding and Healing Abuse*).

It is imperative that we learn how to differentiate clearly between what forgiveness is and is not, as well as summarize what the process of healing looks like. Professional Life Coach Susan Stroll describes the difference:

The dictionary definition of forgiveness is 'to pardon, to waive any negative feeling or desire for punishment, being able to forgive and show mercy, the act of excusing a mistake or offense.' We are challenged in the forgiveness process when our anger and need for revenge get in the way of our sense of mercy, compassion, and kindness. Granting forgiveness does not mean that the act that was committed against you was okay, and it doesn't mean you need to continue to allow it. Forgiveness is not about reunion. Forgiveness is about acknowledgment, setting boundaries, and moving on in a positive manner. It requires that we stay in the present moment and not let our lives revolve around the past. Forgiveness is not about tolerating things that are wrong; it's not about excusing the person who did wrong against you; it's not about surrendering justice and it's not about inviting someone to hurt you again. It's about releasing ourselves from anger and releasing the feeling of [wanting to get] getting even.[11]

Rose Sweet, in an Internet article about granting forgiveness, is very specific about what forgiveness is and isn't:

Forgiveness is not letting the offender off the hook. We can and should still hold others accountable for their actions or lack of actions.

Forgiveness is returning to God the right to take care of justice. By refusing to transfer the right to exact punishment or revenge, we are telling God we don't trust Him to take care of matters.

Forgiveness is not letting the offense recur again and again. We don't have to tolerate, nor should we keep ourselves open to, lack of respect or any form of abuse.

Forgiveness does not mean we have to revert to being the victim. Forgiving is not saying, 'What you did was okay, so go ahead and walk all over me.' Nor is it playing the martyr, enjoying the performance of forgiving people because it perpetuates our victim role.

Forgiveness is not the same as reconciling. We can forgive someone even if we never can get along with him [or her] again.

Forgiveness is a process, not an event. It might take some time to work through our emotional problems before we can truly forgive. As soon as we can, we should decide to forgive, but it probably is not going to happen right after a tragic divorce. That's okay.

We have to forgive every time. If we find ourselves constantly forgiving, though, we might need to take a look at the dance we are doing with the other person that sets us up to be continually hurt, attacked, or abused.

Forgiving does not mean denying reality or ignoring repeated offenses. Some people are obnoxious, mean-spirited, apathetic, or unreliable. They never will change. We need to change the way we respond to them and quit expecting them to be different.

Forgiveness is not based on others' actions but on our attitude. People will continue to hurt us through life. We either can look outward at them and stay stuck and angry, or we can begin to keep our minds on our loving relationship with God, knowing and trusting in what is good.

If they don't repent, we still have to forgive. Even if they never ask, we need to forgive. We should memorize and repeat over and over: Forgiveness is about our attitude, not their action.

We don't always have to tell them we have forgiven them. Self-righteously announcing our gracious forgiveness to someone who has not asked to be forgiven may be a manipulation to make them feel guilty. It also is a form of pride.

Withholding forgiveness is a refusal to let go of perceived power. We can feel powerful when the offender is in need of forgiveness and only we can give it. We may fear going back to being powerless if we forgive.

We might be pressured into false forgiveness before we are ready. When we feel obligated or we forgive just so others will still like us, accept us, or not think badly of us, it's not true forgiveness – it's a performance to avoid rejection. Give yourself permission to do it right. Maybe all you can offer today is, 'I want to forgive you, but right now I'm struggling emotionally. I promise I will work on it.'

Forgiveness does not mean forgetting. It's normal for memories to be triggered in the future. When thoughts of past hurts occur, it's what we do with them that counts. When we find ourselves focusing on a past offense, we can learn to say, 'Thank you, God, for this reminder of how important forgiveness is.'

Forgiveness starts with a mental decision. The emotional part of forgiveness is finally being able to let go of the resentment. Emotional healing may or may not follow quickly after we forgive.[12]

Excerpted from *A Woman's Guide to Healing the Heartbreak of Divorce*. Copyright © 2001 Hendrickson Publishers, Inc. Used by permission. All rights reserved.

Another gifted author, Donna Neal, posted an article on the Internet simply entitled "Forgiveness." Here is what she had to say regarding what forgiveness is and isn't:

Before we delve into the subject, let's determine what forgiveness really means. Some definitions include: Merriam-Webster Dictionary: To pardon, absolve; To give up resentment of; To grant relief from payment of; Strong's Hebrew Definition: salach; To forgive: forgive, pardon, spare; Strong's Greek Definition: aphiemi; To cry, forgive, forsake, lay aside, leave, let (alone, be, go), omit, put (send) away, remit, suffer, yield up.

Perhaps it is more helpful to define what forgiveness is NOT. Forgiveness is not ignoring, disregarding, tolerating, excusing, overlooking, or closing one's eyes to the sin of another person. It is not simply letting time pass after the offense has been committed and then 'getting over it.' It is not resigning oneself to the other person's sinful actions by saying, 'Well, that's just the way s/he is and I'm stuck with her/him for life, so I'll just accept it.' It is not letting things 'roll off our backs' or agreeing to make a 'fresh start' without confronting the problem. To engage in these behaviors not only condones sin, but also perpetuates it, and as Christians, we are forbidden to do so.[13]

Now that we have seen what forgiveness is and isn't, we move on to the *process* of healing. I emphasize the word process once again, because many people think that when they begin to mourn their abuse they feel worse. **They do!** However, it is essential that they continue working on the grief, because the Lord meant for us to feel our feelings. When we ignore all our feelings, we may not feel pain, but we certainly won't experience pleasure. Dr. Sidney and Susan Simon have broken the healing process into the six distinct stages listed below:

1. <u>Denial</u>. *This is the stage in which we attempt to play down the impact or importance of painful past experiences and bury our thoughts and feelings about those experiences.*

2. <u>Self-blame</u>. *While in this stage, we try to explain what happened to us by assuming we were somehow responsible for the injuries and injustices we suffered, decimating our self-esteem as we work overtime to convince ourselves that we would not have been hurt if only we had been different or had done things differently.*

3. <u>Victim</u>. *In this stage, we recognize that we did not deserve or ask for the hurt we received. We are well aware of how we were damaged by painful past experiences, so much so that we wallow in self-pity, expect little of ourselves, indulge ourselves at the expense of those around us, or lash out at anyone and everyone who 'crosses' us.*

4. <u>Indignation</u>. *In this stage, we are angry at the people who hurt us and at the world. We want the people who hurt us to pay and to suffer as we have. Our tolerance is virtually nonexistent, and our self-righteousness is at an all-time high.*

5. <u>Survivor</u>. *Finally, at this stage, we recognize that although we were indeed hurt, we did in fact survive. Our painful past experiences took things away from us but gave us things as well. We became aware of our strengths and welcome the return of our compassion, sense of humor, and interest in matters other than the pain. We bask in the knowledge that, all things considered, we did the best we could.*

6. Integration. In this stage, we are able to acknowledge that the people who hurt us may have been doing the best they could, too, that if we are more than our wounds, they must be more than the inflictors of those wounds. With this knowledge, we can release them from prison and reclaim the energy we used to keep them there. We can put the past in perspective — without forgetting it — let go of the pain, and get on with our lives unencumbered by the emotional damage.[14]

This is quite a good description of what can take months, more likely years in many cases (mine included), to achieve. I shared with you a part of my own childhood abuse in the Introduction, and the "end of the story," with the description of my own process of healing and forgiveness work, is included in Appendix B. As for timing and healing, I believe this quote says it all:

Forgiving is a journey; the deeper the wound, the longer the journey. – Author unknown

Among former clients of mine is an incest survivor, whom I shall call "Leslie," for purposes of preserving her anonymity. Leslie came to me many years ago, as she was in great distress over the amount of weight she had gained after college. A beautiful, well-groomed, confident business-person, Leslie felt helpless in her fight against eating over her emotions. She clearly knew there was a relationship between her childhood sexual abuse and constant overeating, so that is where we began.

Leslie's biological father was never a part of her life. He chose not to marry her mother when she became pregnant with Leslie. The abuse by her stepfather began when she was nine years old. He slowly, but relentlessly, ratcheted up the abuse as she got older. ***By the time she was 17, she was forced to sleep in his bed and become his surrogate wife; because <u>when the abuse was revealed, her mother blamed Leslie</u> – and not only left her husband, but her four children in his care.***

In my opinion, the reasons Leslie survived so "well," becoming such a loving accomplished woman, were: (1) She loved Jesus with all her heart from a young age; and (2) She had the support and understanding of an adult in her life, who never gave up on her, supported her, and encouraged her to get out of the nightmare she was living in. In those days, reporting child abuse was not mandatory, and this mentor offered her the stability she desperately needed. Leslie made a formal declaration of independence, left her home to strike out on her own and go to college, and even threatened her stepfather with real mayhem, should he even begin to think about molesting her three siblings (his natural children).

Leslie was and is a courageous and admirable person, who really loved the Lord and wanted to walk with Him closely. I always felt it was a **great** privilege to work with her. As she began to relax and feel safe with me, many issues (direct results of the abuse) began to surface. She suffered from depression, anxiety attacks, fear of nighttime and the dark (being alone when her husband had to travel), severe gynecological problems, some compulsive overeating/shopping behaviors, an inability to trust God, insecurity about her appearance due to the extra weight, rage at her step-father and mother, a tendency to be a workaholic and draw her identity from her performance on the job, and an overwhelming feeling of being responsible for her younger siblings (even though they were adults by this time).

This counseling was not a "quick fix." Leslie was faithful to come to all her appointments, par-ticipate fully, do any homework assignments I gave her, and ultimately participate in a group for those with different kinds of eating disorders. In other words – Leslie was completely committed to the process of healing. However, her worst enemy (besides Satan, of course) was herself. She had unrealistic expectations about the healing process… she wanted it done yesterday! The term "to beat yourself up" was a perfect description of Leslie. Not only did she feel responsible for her siblings, but at times for the whole world. Intellectually, she knew that this was all wrong, but deep inside, as the oldest child, she believed she was at fault and needed to fix everyone and everything.

To meet or even get to know Leslie, one would never dream that she came from this back-ground. She was an extremely warm and open woman who had the ability to make people feel instantly comfortable and at home with her. She was loyal to a fault, and this got her in trouble more than once when she made herself vulnerable to untrustworthy people. When we first began to speak of forgiving her stepfather and mother, she could only bring herself to address them by their first names, feeling, as she did, so utterly estranged from them.

Whenever Leslie would "go home" for the holidays, it was a time of dread and inner conflict for her. She had been brought up in a traditional manner to "honor her parents" no matter who they were or what they had done to her. This inner tug-of-war resulted in her attending family reunions that she had absolutely no desire in which to participate. Yet her continuous care for her sisters and brother dictated that she at least attempt to coexist with her mother for a day or two during the holidays and summer vacations. Leslie never visited with her stepfather on these trips home and just barely survived encounters with her mentally ill mother (by this time, Leslie's mother had been diagnosed as having Bipolar Disorder).

As one would expect, Leslie's husband Sam (also not his real name) had a very difficult time being around her family, as they were so "crazy" and dysfunctional. He absolutely couldn't be around her stepfather for fear of becoming violent with him. He could barely tolerate being around her mother and only slightly enjoyed himself when he was with Leslie's younger brother. He was quite willing to participate in her counseling, so we began some couples' counseling to supple-ment her individual work. The word "work" seems like a feeble term to describe the process Leslie had to go through, but her desire to be whole and her love for the Lord kept her committed to the process. I only ever met her mother one time. Due to her various mental disorders, she exhibited narcissistic and histrionic behaviors during the counseling session. It became about how she had suffered… never about Leslie.

The most difficult work came for Leslie when she was trying to get pregnant ("try" being the operative word here). She had numerous, serious gynecological problems, and she and her husband had waited a long time to have children, so age was not on her side. When she did finally carry a baby girl to term, there was no containing their joy and mine. I knew this would be an extraordinary child, as she was so wanted and long hoped for. It was a difficult pregnancy, and both Leslie and Sam struggled with numerous fears as to whether they could be "good enough" parents. Sam had a hypercritical father and passive mother, which led him to have severe abandonment issues. He regularly struggled with significant insecurity and at one point became clinically depressed and anxious, to the extent that he was virtually paralyzed in getting on with life.

After experiencing the joy of their first child, Leslie and Sam began the arduous process of trying to have another – Leslie having to suffer through fertility treatments and month after month of disappointment. Her belief, which her doctor substantiated, was that she would not have had these kinds of difficulties had she not been molested. That fact made the bitterness with which she regarded her stepfather come to the surface even more. She was adamant that her daughter never be alone with him; by this time, they had reconciled to the point where she spent very short periods with him on her semi-annual treks home.

This story could go on and on, for it was a journey in every sense. Leslie never gave up in her quest for wholeness, and she was well aware of the fact that she harbored deep bitterness in her soul. She first worked on forgiving her mother, which was easier, ever since Mom had become an adoring grandmother to Sam and Leslie's daughter. Although Leslie yearned for that kind of mothering herself and knew she wouldn't ever get it, she was happy that at least her mother could give it to her little girl. Once this bond had formed, Leslie consciously gave up any hope that her mother would ever be there for her emotionally, physically, financially – in any way at all. As so often happens with the family dynamics of father/daughter incest, Leslie was her mother's mother as far back as she could recall.

She mourned this loss over time, and then turned to her stepfather. Leslie firmly believed that he had been molested as a child, and thus began her slow, but sure, development of compassion for him. Leslie was grieved that he was not saved, but competing with that feeling was her sense of massive injustice that he never had any physical consequences for abusing her. As well as escaping prosecution, her stepfather never paid a dime toward her counseling. He didn't deny that he had molested her, but never took any true responsibility for the emotional, physical, and spiritual trauma from which she suffered. The statute of limitations had run out long ago, so there was literally nothing Leslie could do, except protect her own daughter from the same fate.

Leslie and Sam struggled in their marriage was predictable, but because of the Lord in her life, Leslie could clearly differentiate between her husband and stepfather, sexually speaking. She never became a man-hater and ultimately came to the point where she was ready to write a letter of forgiveness in which she shared her Christian testimony with her stepfather. His health was beginning to fail, and she wasn't sure how much longer he would live and those factors motivated Leslie to act.

It was a breathtaking letter in its honesty with mercy woven throughout. Leslie had worked through the stages of grief and loss repeatedly during her counseling; so by the time she expressed herself to him, she felt no need to express rage or vindictiveness to him. She stated that she forgave him unequivocally and wrote of her intense desire for him to come to know Jesus as Lord. It was a remarkable event to witness, as I had been there through the entire journey with Leslie and knew exactly what it took her to write such a letter.

Her stepfather neither acknowledged nor answered the letter, but Leslie had gone into the situation without expectations of any kind of response from him. She wasn't hurt and didn't feel rejected, rather she felt a profound sense of sadness at this man's life and all that had and hadn't happened between them.

Today, Leslie still has her days when she struggles with overeating or anxiety when alone at night, but she realizes that it is a spiritual battle she faces. She walks through her days with courage and humility, depending on the Lord and having learned that He is utterly trustworthy and will never leave, hurt, or betray her.

Jesus Loves Me

Jesus loves me! This I know,
For the Bible tells me so;
Little ones to Him belong,
They are weak but He is strong.
Yes, Jesus loves me!
Yes, Jesus loves me!
Yes, Jesus loves me!
The Bible tells me so.

Jesus loves me! He who died,
Heaven's gate to open wide;
He will wash away my sin,
Let His little child come in.
Yes, Jesus loves me!
Yes, Jesus loves me!
Yes, Jesus loves me!
The Bible tells me so.

Jesus loves me! Loves me still,
When I'm very weak and ill;

From His shining throne on high,
Comes to watch me where I lie.
Yes, Jesus loves me!
Yes, Jesus loves me!
Yes, Jesus loves me!
The Bible tells me so.

Jesus loves me! He will stay,
Close beside me all the way;
He's prepared a home for me,
And some day His face I'll see.
Yes, Jesus loves me!
Yes, Jesus loves me!
Yes, Jesus loves me!
The Bible tells me so.

Words By: Anna B. Warner
Music By: Wm. B. Bradbury, Copyright Unknown

When you are feeling insecure or down, a healing thing to do is to sing this "kid's song"
and address it to the child-part of you… the Lord can use it in a very powerful way!

As we leave our definitions of what forgiveness is and isn't and the account of the healing process, a burning question remains in those who were abused as children and are stuck in recovering from the pain of the past. Their reasoning goes something like this: **"How am I supposed to trust God? After all, *He let this happen to me!*"** Read on to see how you can start to make the transition from forgiving others to trusting God.

Why did God allow such bad things to happen to me? Does God exist? Does God see? Does God care? – Heart cry of abuse survivors

My mother tried to kill me on several occasions. I remember thinking how worthless, how despicable I was to have my mother hate me this much. Even today, if someone becomes angry or upset near me, I hide. It's an automatic reaction to years of terror and hurt… a negative comment can send me into a state of self-loathing, in which her words echo in my ears years later. I used to pray at night that God would send someone to help me. Years later, someone did. – Candida Eittreim

It took me a long time to move past feeling abandoned by God. I used to ask what the h@#$ good is it being God if He cannot even prevent one child from being abused. However, I came to realize that I was viewing my situation under faulty assumptions. – Faith Allen

Because some of my abusers were "upstanding" members in the church clergy, I couldn't trust a God who seemed indifferent to my suffering and who allowed adults to abuse me. I was afraid of that kind of love, so I rejected God and the counsel of the church. – Audrey Hector

I shake my fist at God several times a week. I don't always speak in a manner most would say is reverent, and I hate it when people tell me I need to "trust" Him. And yes, you are totally right when you say that as a child I was told He would keep me safe – I bought into the whole thing as a child. I believed as a child believed, and I thought He let me down. This is something that will be hard to let go of. – Ivory

For the last 10 years, I would call myself an atheist, because I can't believe in a God who is all-powerful and all-knowing who would not intervene when children are getting hurt. That is just so hard for me to wrap my head around. – Journey

Many survivors of child abuse ask the question, "Where was God when I was being abused?" Some are unable to embrace faith because they believe God betrayed them by failing to intervene. Others believe that child abuse is proof that there is no God, because what kind of loving God would allow children to experience abuse? – Faith Allen

But what does God do as he looks down upon the evil that His children create? He should easily be able to prevent these terrible things from happening and spare the innocent victims. The fact that He doesn't means that either He is willing to allow the innocent to suffer, or He does not have the power to stop it. – Lagore

Why did You allow my alcoholic, unloving mother to retrieve me from my beloved foster parents, only to have to go through the hell of several divorces, remarriages, and many dysfunctional relationships with her? – Author unknown

Chapter Six

How Can I Possibly Trust God?
He Let This Happen to Me!

The title of this chapter reflects a practically universal question that adds a completely new dimension of suffering to the child who is abused after they have come to believe in the God of the Bible. As the abuse survivor goes on through adulthood, that question leaves a perennial ache inside their heart and increases the sense of abandonment they have already experienced. As can be seen from the quotes on the adjacent page, this pain, i.e., sadness/hurt, rapidly morphs into a simmering anger, which left unanswered, can become a raging inferno that eventually turns into the cold ashes of indifference.

Some victims of abuse, however, cannot bear to acknowledge this gut-wrenchingly honest question because of the toxic shame that they carry. They refuse to believe that they could even be slightly "mad at God" because… well, He is God, isn't He, and He might just hurl a lightning bolt down and "smite" them for being so terrible as to dare ask Him such a question! Because of denial of this very common emotion, when they have processed through all the other stages of grief sufficiently to arrive at a point of acceptance, they know something is wrong but can't quite place their fingers on what that might be. For anyone who has ever been victimized as a child (or even as an adult for that matter) and struggles to come to a place where he/she can have a close relationship with God, this scenario can present an almost insurmountable roadblock.

There are certain individuals who do not experience this anger and the resulting distrust. I can remember my counselor asking me, "Don't you blame God for not stopping your youth pastor from molesting you?" Although she looked incredulous, I could honestly answer that, no, I didn't, as I was well able to distinguish between the Lord and the fallible, frail human being who used me to meet his own emotional needs. Nevertheless, I still was unable to trust God because of my abusive father! (See Appendix B for the full account of my abuse and recovery.)

This inner cry is largely the "normal" response to the abnormal presence of abuse in one's life. I believe it is one of the devil's best weapons to keep the believer stuck in the healing and recovery process. What better way to keep the person applying Band-Aids to this enormous wound, instead of pouring oil and wine into it and binding it up as the Lord instructs in His Word? We see an example of this in the parable of the Good Samaritan in Luke 10:34: "So he went to him and bandaged his wounds, pouring in oil and wine; and he set him on his own animal, brought him to an inn, and took care of him." When a person has fallen prey to the lie that the Lord could have prevented the abuse and therefore cannot be trusted, that huge, gaping wound will stay open and raw. The following Scripture verses powerfully illustrate this condition:

My wound is incurable, though I am without transgression (Job 34:6).

Woe is me for my hurt! My wound is severe. But I say, 'Truly this is an infirmity, and I must bear it' (Jeremiah 10:19).

Why is my pain perpetual and my wound incurable, which refuses to be healed? Will You surely be to me like an unreliable stream, as waters that fail? (Jeremiah 15:18).

Your injury has no healing; your wound is severe... (Nahum 3:19).

Steven Tracy has recorded an excellent description of Satan's utilization of child abuse to corrode spiritual intimacy by applying the following "threefold strategy":

<u>Tactic</u>	<u>Internal Dialogue</u>
He uses the damage of abuse to cause victims to begin to doubt God's Word.	*'Surely the Bible doesn't teach you can't have sex with your boyfriend. After all, that's all you're good for.'*
He plays on the effects of trauma to discredit God's Word.	*'John 3:16 isn't true for you. You're too disgusting for God to love you.'*
He delights in using the evil that abuse survivors have experienced to malign God's character.	*'You can't trust God. He is either impotent or mean – or maybe both. After all, He didn't stop your father from raping you. Maybe God doesn't even exist.'* [1]

After Tracy has shown us the cognitive distortions of God that Satan uses to create distrust in Him because of a person being abused when s/he is a child, he goes on to elaborate on the theme of Satan using the abuse to create emotional distance as well:

He especially uses emotional numbing (constriction), powerlessness, shame, and a sense of betrayal as ways to disconnect survivors from God. People who are emotionally constricted have great difficulty being intimate with God (or humans) because they are shut down. Those who have a great sense of powerlessness are often afraid of God, fearing He can't be trusted. Those who are filled with shame have such a warped view of God's character that they hide from Him and cannot become intimate. Those who feel deeply betrayed are drawn to protect themselves by withdrawing; they don't trust or give themselves to others. Thus, Satan uses all of these trauma effects to keep people from understanding, loving, and trusting their heavenly Father.[2]

When we read or hear testimonies of abuse survivors, it is only natural for us to become indignant and outraged. Many victims believe that if mere human beings can feel this and are compelled to take some kind of action, how much more should their Heavenly Father have felt and acted when they were being devastated at the hands of the perpetrator(s).

I worked with a young woman I will call "Hayley" for the purposes of protecting her privacy. During our initial session, I immediately noticed her suspicious, mistrusting attitude toward me. Until she was referred to me, she had only discussed and/or worked on her issues with older men. While Hayley did have girlfriends, she always preferred the company of men, if given a choice in the matter.

During the time I worked with her, Hayley was in college, graduated, and began her career. Hayley was a brilliant young woman and excelled at whatever she put her hand to. She carried a perfect grade point average, was a gifted athlete, was excellent working with children who suffered from Autism or Asperger's Syndrome, and had a gift for working with junior high and high school students. Hayley was also a committed Christian. In spite of all this, she already had been hospitalized for her obsession with suicide and self-mutilation from the onset of our therapy.

Hayley had a very abusive childhood. Her father was mentally ill, and her parents divorced when she was quite young. Her mother was always attracted to the wrong kind of man and put her romantic relationships ahead of her children (Hayley had a sister). From the time she was quite young (around six or seven), she took care of herself and her sister, because Mom, who had sole custody, was either working or completely distracted with whoever her current boyfriend was at the time. There was no physical, emotional, or sexual abuse at the hand of either parent, but this seemingly benign, unintentional neglect of Hayley and her sister took its toll.

Hayley was definitely a child of whom any parent would be proud. She excelled at school and extracurricular activities, had many friends, was highly independent and seemed to be very mature for her age. What no one realized at the time or for years afterward was the fact that Hayley felt completely abandoned by both parents, particularly by her mother, and that condition would emerge later in her life in numerous dramatic (and traumatic) ways. In addition, no one was aware that Hayley had been sexually abused by her cousin and couldn't tell anyone. She so desperately needed affection that, even at the time, she minimized what was happening to her.

Hayley suffered from severe depression and panic attacks. Yet she covered it so well as an active leader in her church that no one realized that she was in such emotional pain until she attempted suicide the first time. Her youth pastor took her to the hospital and admitted that even with all his knowledge and experience working with young people, he was stymied as to how to help Hayley.

The diagnosis came back after her psychiatric evaluation at the hospital: Hayley had Bipolar Disorder. As if that weren't enough to contend with, it took us quite a long time to find out that she had what is called a "dual diagnosis." Hayley also suffered from Borderline Personality Disorder. The combination of the two has the potential to be lethal, and in Hayley's case, her suicidal ideation manifested repeatedly. We were constantly battling her desire to commit suicide and her addiction to cutting herself. The psychiatrists were stumped: No medication that they put Hayley on had any lasting effect in stabilizing her.

What you have just read is a condensed clinical description of Hayley's condition. As she experienced continuous, debilitating depression, she began to have serious doubts about the God she had loved so passionately. Hayley was in denial about the connection between her upbringing (or lack thereof) and her present overwhelming battle just to stay alive. Therefore, her Job-like questions were about her current condition until the youth pastor she adored moved away. Then all her feelings of abandonment, stemming from the neglect she suffered as a child, were triggered in a big way. Once again, she attempted to kill herself and was rescued just prior to succeeding.

The front Hayley was used to putting up began to slip as she became more and more depressed. She began to question the Lord as she came to grips with the despair she felt when she contemplated where she was in life. She was certain that God could not possibly love her if He allowed her to go through all these circumstances and didn't act in any way to heal her from her mental disorders. Hayley could never permanently stop the cutting and became paralyzed as she attempted to move on to professional life after she graduated from college.

In spite of her numerous emotional problems, Hayley became active in leadership of youth activities at a different church from the one she had attended as a teen. Nevertheless, she suffered from feelings of great hypocrisy about her lack of relationship with God. Hayley was full of rage toward her mother, indifferent toward her father, devastated by the loss of her former youth pastor, unable to have healthy romantic relationships, either with men or women friends. She vacillated between casual flirtations with young men and a feeling of attraction/repulsion toward the older, married men who were physically attracted to her.

Years of medical and mental health treatment didn't touch her damaged core, and the worst part of all was her love/hate affair with God. Hayley could never really accept any spiritual counsel I might give her, because she could not get past seeing me as just another mother in addition to her being so angry with the Lord. She would alternately embrace and then reject me, which not only symbolized her struggle with her mother, but her wrestling with the Lord. Hayley was unable to trust Him again, and while she paid lip service to the idea of forgiving her mother, she was thoroughly unsuccessful. Why? Because her mother had not changed in any substantial way through her suicide attempts and subsequent counseling sessions. Thus, Hayley's feelings of abandonment were simply confirmed. In all actuality, when Hayley shut down and refused to acknowledge the very normal need she had for the nurture and care of her mother as a child, she had terrible problems in opening back up. All these dynamics only solidified her struggle to believe that God was good, that He loved her, and that He would never leave her.

Below I have included excerpts of a therapeutic letter Haley wrote to her mother trying to forgive but struggling with such raw emotional pain:

Dear Mom,

Not only do I not understand our relationship, but also I don't understand my feelings pertaining to our relationship. I know that I love you. It just feels like there is a wall between us, but it is complicated because I don't want that wall to come down. Part of me wants to be close to you, but I still don't trust you. I want you to know I love you, but I have been living my own life without you for so long. Honestly, if I came to you with what I'm facing, you probably wouldn't be able to help me anyway – emotionally or literally. It's strange because I know that you're my mom, but it doesn't feel like I really have a mother. I realize that I was always kind of an independent kid anyway, but even the most know-it-all, I'll–do-it-myself kid needs guidance and love.

The more I realize that you are a victim, the less bitterness I hold toward you. However, you have made a lot of bad choices. Even the person with the worst life in the world can make good choices to change their live. And trusting Jesus to do that would almost guarantee a change. I wish that you would give up your life and live for Christ. I with that you would trust Him and let Him come into your heart and take away all the pain, guilt, and shame. It kills me because I know that He could, but it's as if you don't care or don't want Him to. I care about this so much that I've even thought about making it my last request and killing myself so that everyone I know that knows Christ will share the gospel with you. Asking you to accept Jesus would be my last wish, but it would probably only make you angry with God.

I know that you feel guilty for the way you treated us, but it wasn't right. And it really makes me mad because even though you feel guilty, you still do it. You say that you hate _____ [Mom's current boyfriend) and that he's a total jerk, but you still choose him over me. Why? Why am I not good enough? I know that you're proud of me, but I don't even care anymore. I don't even look for your approval anymore because it doesn't matter – it doesn't change anything. Now I'm stuck in this place of perfectionism and I never feel good enough for anyone or for myself, and it's probably your fault. Why are we (Hayley and her sister) always second to some jerk? In the apartment in _____, we used to be so hungry, the only food we had was what you bought for _____ (another boyfriend), and we couldn't touch it. I needed you there, and you didn't care. You didn't even know that I ran around in the middle of the night all over town when I was like nine or ten and how much trouble I should have been in for shoplifting and other things. You didn't care. We never had money for food or clothes, but if your guy ever wanted something, he got it. (Her sister) and I can't believe we even survived.

A little kid should not have to deal with what I had to. I was just a little girl and I was worried about whether or not we would have money for rent, where my next meal was coming from, how to explain to my friends why I was wearing the same socks again, or worrying about when my mommy will be home. I forgive you for everything, but that doesn't make it right. It still hurts.

I wish I could tell you that the Lord did a great healing in Hayley's life, and that she is happy and healthy at this time. While she has gone on to excel in her career, she has only continued to struggle with her emotional instability and desire to kill herself. The hopeful part of the story is that Hayley has continued to press toward emotional health in her work with subsequent counselors. Her primary issue is the toxic shame she carries about the sexual abuse. It prevents her from going any further with a fine therapist with whom she works.

Hayley's life is an extraordinary example of Satan coming in to steal, kill, and destroy a remarkable and gifted young woman. So when did his interference begin? At the time of the neglect she endured and the childhood sexual abuse she underwent. He has very nearly succeeded at killing her and has stolen a great deal from her, but I praise God that he has not and will not destroy this wonderful young woman's life. The Lord has been there all along, guiding and protecting her as she continues to work through the healing and forgiveness process.

Sexual abuse survivor Christa Sands has written an excellent book entitled *Learning to Trust Again: A Young Woman's Journey of Healing from Sexual Abuse*. Her abuse began when she was six years old. She is quite articulate about the problem of trusting the Lord when one has been abused:

Lonely and isolated in the dark pit, I longed for someone to bring me light. But everyone seemed just out of my grasp, including God. I had accepted Jesus as my Savior not long before the abuse began. Though I believed in God, I relied on my parents' faith

rather than building my own solid relationship with Him. My young mind could have deduced that God didn't love me because He 'rewarded' my profession of faith by allowing Walter to abuse me. But God protected me from totally rejecting Him in anger. Blessed with a rich heritage of faith, I had strong spiritual roots, but questions of why God permitted the abuse hung like a heavy curtain in the back of my mind. When my very life depended on receiving the love and comfort I'd heard so much about in Sunday school, I sensed a barrier between God and me. I neither felt His presence nor found His comfort. If God had turned His back on me, hope seemed impossible.... I prayed so many times, but I received no answers – at least not the way I expected. His silence was deafening. Satan whispered lies, telling me I didn't deserve God's healing and love – and I believed him. Feelings of abandonment seemed to take up permanent residence in my soul. My meager faith quickly turned to quicksand as I sank further in the pit. My doubts of God's power and love intensified into doubts of His very existence. The God I could not see became the God I could not hear or trust.[3]

As I searched the Internet for material on the inability of most abuse survivors to trust God, I came across a heart-wrenching poem that illustrates this truth more eloquently than all the case studies in the world ever could.

Inner Child

By Kate

Hello dear Jesus,
It's been a long, long time.
I hope that You still know me;
I've been hiding quite awhile.
I know that You know all things
Still, I think I should explain,
The reason I've been hiding
Is because of all the shame.
I know that I don't look so great
For meeting up with You.
But I hope You understand
I've been alone since I was eight.
You probably see the dirt marks
And smudges on my face
But it seems no matter how I try
Some things can't be erased.

They say that eyes are windows
That peer into the soul.
I'm afraid that if You look there,
You'll find it dark and cold.
I'm not sure why it is, Lord,
But You won't see any tears.
I guess they've just been locked up
Inside me all these years.
I know that limp and lifeless
Is my unruly hair.
I guess that's just what happens
When no one really cares.
And if You ask a question,
I won't have much to say.
I've found that no one really wants
To hear me anyway.
And if You care to listen,
Sit quiet and You'll hear
How hard my heart is pounding.
That's because of all the fear.
You'll notice that I wrap my arms
Around me all the time.
I do that for protection
Of the things that should be mine.
See, not so very long ago,
Without an ounce of care,
Someone took away from me
Things I never meant to share.
And if You find I tremble
When You come close to me,
It's because of all the dreadful things
That someone did to me.
Jesus I'm so sorry
If these things have saddened You.
But when I cried out to You,
You never told me what to do.
I know that in my mother's womb
You created me,
And I can't help but wonder

Is this what I was meant to be?
They say that You are everywhere,
With each and every one,
But it seems that on those dark nights
You left me all alone.
They tell me that You love me
And I suppose it's true,
But Jesus, please remember
That he said he loved me too.[4]

In summary, questioning where God was when one's abuse was happening and the resultant inability to trust Him for anything are inextricably linked and are the normal responses of the abuse survivor. When one's perpetrator is any kind of authority figure, particularly his/her father or stepfather, a child's perception of fatherhood becomes very twisted and distorted. Unless there is conscious, deliberate intervention, survivors will never know who the Lord really is and His tender, perfect parenting. You will see some of these cognitive distortions in the next chapter.

Over the centuries, there have been many misconceptions about God and His true nature. He has been misrepresented to us by legalistic religious leaders and angry earthly fathers who have, by their lifestyles, distorted His true image. – Barry and Anneliese Adams

We all need a caring human father (or an equivalent) as early as possible in our lives to help us understand what God the Father is like as a Person. Remote, indifferent, unavailable human fathers can lead us to believe that God also is detached, unconcerned, and uninvolved in the daily cares of our world. – Lambert Dolphin and David Sacarelos

But when Jesus talks about His Father, He touches issues that may be affecting us more than we realize. Maybe our problem is that His Father doesn't answer our prayers as we want Him to. Or we think of Him in terms of the human fathers we have known. Many of us have never even heard our biological father say, "I love you." Some have inherited a legacy of abandonment, addiction, and even abuse. – Mark De Haan

God is not a deceiver that He should offer to support us, and then, when we lean upon Him, should slip away from us. – Augustine

To call God "Father" means, then, that He is near to us, intimately concerned with us, fond of us, even crazy about us. He is not the distant clockmaker God of Thomas Jefferson and the Deists. This aloof God of the philosophers created the world to run by virtue of its own natural laws so that He could withdraw and occupy himself with more interesting pursuits. – Dr. Marcellino D'Ambrosio

At 20, just before I got married, Jesus took my hand. I felt safe with him, but I was afraid of His Father. He seemed a little too much like my father – distant, angry, and powerful. I rejoiced in Jesus' sacrifice for me, but I didn't let Him into my secrets. Until I had a baby, three years later, the childhood abuse stayed hidden. – Karen Rabbitt

Many of my friends had earthly fathers who have deserted them, abused them, or abused others in front of them. How do we as Christians say that God the Father is a loving and generous God who protects His children to someone who was raped by their earthly father, then deserted by him? It's a difficult task. Many of us are given such a dim view of our earthly fathers that it's hard to imagine a Heavenly Father who truly loves us. – Michael McCullough

For men or women who experienced abuse from their fathers or father figures, the problem is greatly magnified. Children develop their sense of God as a heavenly Father from their experiences with their human fathers. The Bible refers to God as our heavenly Father. So people who experienced abuse from earthly fathers find it terrifying to hear that God is a heavenly Father. – Steven R. Tracy

Chapter Seven

Distorted and Corrected Views of Father God

During the '80s, I attended a two-day conference held at a Franciscan retreat center in Santa Barbara, California. The focus of the conference was on healing for Adult Children of Alcoholics (ACAs). A former Franciscan priest turned therapist led the group of us – maybe 12 in all. This was pretty much cutting edge material; because until that point there had only been an emphasis on supporting non-alcoholic spouses, the children had not yet been addressed.

The therapist was a caring, yet no-nonsense person, all wrapped up in one. I remember the first time I shared in the group, he stopped me midway through my story, and asked, "Why do you have such a big smile on your face when you are talking about such horrible things?" That was an excellent therapeutic question, but I became so embarrassed that I didn't speak in the group again until the very end of the conference.

One of the assignments that weekend was to illustrate our concepts of God using crayons. I first had the objection (which many of us did) that I was not an artist, and I would turn out an awful picture. Our therapist said that the quality of the drawing had nothing to do with anything – that it was the ideas being externalized that mattered. So I began to draw. My one forte was drawing pictures of hands clenched as fists (looking back that is so telling). Therefore, I drew that reasonable facsimile of a huge hand in the sky holding a carrot to tantalize little me on the ground. The Lord was "dangling" the proverbial carrot, and whenever I would just about grab hold of it, He would jerk it away.

I shared with the group that I saw God as a Father who could never be pleased. Just about the time I would be close to feeling satisfied with anything I did, He would jerk the carrot away and just a little bit higher. Another way of saying this would be that I would get to a place where I thought maybe the Lord was pleased with my performance (never just in me as His daughter) only to have Him raise the bar higher.

I used the example of coming home with straight A's once when I was nine or ten, only to have my Dad comment sarcastically, "Well that's pretty good, but if you got all A/L's that would really show that you were superior to everyone else." In addition to our academic grades, we were evaluated as to our "effort and attitude," with High (H), Medium (M), and Low (L) rating. I was utterly crushed! His evaluation of my performance devastated me! Teachers just didn't score that way. They might give out an "A" with an "M" (medium effort and attitude), but A/L's... that just wasn't part of their rubric for evaluating students.

To this day, I can remember the strength of those painful feelings and coming to the realization that I could never please my father, no matter how hard I tried. My dad seemed to delight in verbally and emotionally abusing my brothers and me in sadistic ways. As a result, I began to see Father God as a sadistic sort of deity who could never be pleased. Talk about feeling hopeless, defeated, and unmotivated! In my mind, since I couldn't please my earthly father, I would **never** be able to please my Heavenly Father. I assigned other attributes to the Lord as well: He was too stern, demanding, shaming, and decidedly unsafe to ever trust with my fragile emotions. I could never "measure up" to His expectations of me, and thus my reality was that I was "unacceptable" as His child. This conclusion left me feeling hopeless and helpless.

One last point before I end this personal anecdote: I **intellectually** knew that God loved me unconditionally, but I never believed that in my heart – deep down where it really mattered. In essence, I couldn't internalize and appropriate this truth **emotionally or spiritually** so that I could begin to have a trusting relationship with my Father in heaven. The truth could not travel the so-called 18 inches from my head to my heart.

What other distortions of God do abuse victims internalize? We saw in the last chapter that victims almost universally feel abandoned by the Lord at the time of their abuse. While studying the Bible, a believer can learn that God is omnipotent (all powerful), omniscient (all knowing), and omnipresent (always present, surrounding us), but for most, the reality of the abuse negates these attributes... in fact, it seems to wipe them out altogether.

An excellent exposition on the subject of cognitive distortions of Father God is contained in the incredibly useful book, *The Steps to Freedom in Christ: A Step-by-Step Guide to Help You Resolve Personal and Spiritual Conflicts,* by Dr. Neil Anderson. I call it "incredibly useful" because I have used it with numerous clients over the years and have seen very positive results in their lives. I felt very privileged to hear Dr. Anderson speak about his book and its application. It really is life changing, and *I highly recommend it for all believers.* Dr. Anderson introduces Appendix C of his book, "The Truth about Your Father God" as follows:

Sometimes we are greatly hindered from walking by faith in our Father God because of lies we have believed about Him. We are to have a healthy fear of God – awe of His holiness, power and presence – but we no longer need to fear punishment from Him. Romans 8:15 says, 'For you have not received a spirit of slavery leading to fear again, but you have received a spirit of adoption as sons by which we cry out, 'Abba! Father!' The following exercise will help break the chains of those lies and enable you to begin to experience the intimate 'Abba, Father' relationship with Him.

Anderson then instructs his readers to work their way down the lists that follow, one by one, left to right and to read the lists aloud:

I renounce the lie that my Father God is...	I joyfully accept the truth that my Father God is...
distant and uncaring	*kind and compassionate (see Psalm 103:8-14)*
stern and demanding	*accepting and filled with joy and love (see Romans 15:7; Zephaniah 3:17)*
passive and cold	*warm and affectionate (see Isaiah 40:11; Hosea 11:3, 4)*
absent or too busy for me	*always with me and eager to be with me (see Hebrews 13:5; Jeremiah 31:20; Ezekiel 34:11-16)*
never satisfied with what I do, impatient or angry	*patient and slow to anger (see Exodus 34:6; 2 Peter 3:9)*
mean, cruel or abusive	*loving, gentle and protective of me (see Jeremiah 31:3; Isaiah 42:3; Psalm 18:2)*
trying to take all the fun out of life	*trustworthy and wants to give me a full life; His will is good, perfect and acceptable for me (see Lamentations 3:22, 23; John 10:10; Romans 12:1,2)*
controlling or manipulative	*full of grace and mercy, and He gives me freedom to fail(see Hebrews 4:15, 16; Luke 15:11-16)*

condemning or unforgiving	*tender-hearted and forgiving; His heart and arms are always open to me* *(see Psalm 130:1-4; Luke 15:17:24)*
nit-picking, exacting or perfectionistic	*committed to my growth and proud of me as His growing child (see Romans 7:28, 29; Hebrews 12:5-11; 2 Cor. 7:14)*
distant and disinterested	*intimate and involved (see Psalm 139:1-18)*

I am the apple of His eye! (See Deut. 32:9-10)[2]

The Steps to Freedom in Christ: A Step-by-Step Guide to Help You Resolve Personal and Spiritual Conflicts, Break Free from Bondage and Renew Your Mind, and Experience Daily Victory as a Child of God, **Neil T. Anderson, 2001, Regal Books: Ventura, CA. Used by permission. All rights reserved.**

It is important to note here that while survivors of child abuse may know these truths intellectually, most of them have neither been able to internalize them emotionally nor appropriate them spiritually. To really make these truths their own will take repeating and meditating on the scripture verses repeatedly. Mental Health Nurse Practitioner Juanita Ryan tells us:

The real healer of our distortions is God. God is with us as God-the-Spirit, sent to teach, comfort, counsel and heal. 'The Spirit helps us in our weakness. We do not know what we ought to pray for, but the Spirit himself intercedes for us with groans that words cannot express' (Romans 8:26). It is God's desire that we come to know Him as He is. It is God's desire to heal the distortions that cause us to hide from Him. God invites us to come into His presence and to rest in His love. May 'the glorious Father give you the Spirit of wisdom and revelation, so that you may know Him better' (Ephesians 1:17). May you come to know the God who has revealed Himself to be 'compassionate and gracious, slow to anger, abounding in love' (Psalm 103:8).[3]

Our God is faithful and will be right there to help you change when you make a total commitment to knowing and walking in the truth.

We will see how an abuse survivor can move from suffering to acknowledging God's sovereignty to being filled with hope in the following chapter.

When you and I hurt deeply, what we really need is not an explanation from God but a revelation of God. We need to see how great God is; we need to recover our lost perspective on life. Things get out of proportion when we are suffering, and it takes a vision of something bigger than ourselves to get life's dimensions adjusted again. – Warren W. Wiersbe

All born-again people are in training for rulership. Since the supreme law of that future social order, called the kingdom of God, is agape love, therefore their apprenticeship and training is for the learning of deep dimensions of this love. But deep dimensions of this love are only learned in the school of suffering. Purity is one thing, and maturity is another. The latter comes only through years of suffering. If we suffer, we shall also reign – because where there is little suffering, there is little love; no suffering, no love; no love, no rulership. – Paul Billheimer

God is doing a greater work in us, and that can only come as we learn to trust Him no matter how dark the days and sleepless the nights. And it is only as we have been through the darkness with Him that what we know with our heads slides down into our hearts, and our hearts no longer demand answers. The 'Why?' becomes unimportant when we believe that God can and will redeem the pain for our good and His glory…. When I put the sovereignty of God beside His unfailing love, my heart can rest – Verdell Davis

At the timberline where the storms strike with the most fury, the sturdiest trees are found. – *Hudson Newsletter*

Even if we may not always understand why God allows certain things to happen to us, we can know He is able to bring good out of evil and triumph out of suffering. – Billy Graham

God never allows pain without a purpose in the lives of His children. He never allows Satan, or circumstances, or any ill-intending person to afflict us unless He uses that affliction for our good. God never wastes pain. He always causes it to work together for our ultimate good, the good of conforming us more to the likeness of His Son (see Romans 8:28-29). – Jerry Bridges

The best we can hope for in this life is a knothole peek at the shining realities ahead. Yet a glimpse is enough. It's enough to convince our hearts that whatever sufferings and sorrows currently assail us aren't worthy of comparison to that which waits over the horizon. – Joni Eareckson Tada

If you have been reduced to God being your only hope, you are in a good place. – Jim Laffoon

God is the only One who can make the valley of trouble into a door of hope. – Catherine Marshall

The storms in my life have become workshops where I can practice my faith in God's sovereignty. – Jill Briscoe

Chapter Eight

Suffering, Sovereignty, and Hope

I have never forgotten Dr. James Dobson's personal account of having to participate in hurting his own son. It demonstrated to him as an earthly father, as nothing else could, what the Father feels in all of His sovereignty when He has to watch his little ones suffer and hurt. In 1993, I read the story in Dobson's poignant treatment of sovereignty, *When God Doesn't Make Sense*, and it has stayed with me all these years as a powerful illustration of our Father God's love and suffering as He maintains His sovereignty.

Dobson's son Ryan developed a terrible ear infection when he was three years old. The pediatrician treating Ryan was a brusque and impatient sort, which we don't ordinarily associate with those in the field of pediatrics. The doctor informed Mrs. Dobson that the infection itself had adhered to the eardrum and could only be treated by pulling the scab loose with a nasty-looking little instrument. He also told her that this would be quite painful for her son and that she needed to hold him down during the procedure. Apparently, Ryan understood enough of what the doctor was saying that when he attempted to insert the pick-like instrument into his ear, he screamed and broke loose. The doctor then angrily told Shirley that if she couldn't hold her son down, she'd have to call in her husband, because the procedure **had** to be done for the child to recover. I now quote what James Dobson's own description of this traumatic incident:

After hearing what was needed, I swallowed hard and wrapped my 200-pound, 6-foot-2-inch frame around the toddler. It was one of the toughest moments in my career as a parent. What made it so emotional was the horizontal mirror that Ryan was facing on the back side of the examining table. This made it possible for him to look directly at me as he screamed for mercy. I really believe I was in greater agony in that moment than my terrified little boy. It was too much. I turned him loose – and got a beefed-up version of the same bawling-out that Shirley had received a few minutes earlier. Finally, however, the grouchy pediatrician and I finished the task. I reflected later on what I was feeling when Ryan was going through so much suffering. What hurt me was the look on his face.

Though he was screaming and couldn't speak, he was 'talking' to me with those big blue eyes. He was saying, 'Daddy! Why are you doing this to me? I thought you loved me. I never thought you would do anything like this! How could you...? Please, please! Stop hurting me!'

It was impossible to explain to Ryan that his suffering was necessary for his own good, that I was trying to help him, that it was love that required me to hold him on the table. How could I tell him of my compassion at that moment? I would gladly have taken his place on the table, if possible. But in his immature mind, I was a traitor who had callously abandoned him. Then I realized that there must be times when God also feels our intense pain and suffers along with us. Wouldn't that be characteristic of a Father whose love was infinite? How He must hurt when we say in confusion, 'How could You do this terrible thing, Lord? Why me? I thought I could trust You! I thought You were my friend!' How can He explain within our human limitations that our agony is necessary, that it <u>does</u> have a purpose, that there are answers to the tragedies of life? I wonder if He anticipates the day when He can make us understand what was occurring in our time of trial. I wonder if He broods over our sorrows.[1]

It is difficult to find a church that teaches a balanced, biblical view of the suffering that all true believers in Christ will experience in their earthly lives. When I say balanced, I'm referring to the fact that most faith-based, prosperity (health/wealth) churches teach that Christians only suffer because they're living in some type of doubt or unbelief. If they are sick, depressed, spiritually oppressed, struggling financially, etc., the pastors of these churches, more often than not, will blame them for not having enough faith and/or having sin in their lives. *This is like blaming victims for the child abuse they have suffered!* The thinking goes something like this: "Well, if she beat you, you must have deserved it," or "Well, if he molested you, you must have been acting seductively." (This type of thinking is outrageous! I know of one case where a mother blamed her preschool-aged daughter for being molested by her husband. She actually believed that this tiny girl had acted provocatively with her father, thus bringing the sexual abuse on herself!)

The other extreme that teaching can take is that there is nothing but suffering to be endured in our earthly lives. There are no promises of God realized, blessings, or abundant lives to be had if one is living according to the express will of the Lord. When Jesus said, "I came that they might have life and life more abundantly," He was referring to our lives **both on earth and in heaven**. Yet in this other extreme view, life is just a series of tragedies, trauma, and deprivation. If someone happens to be physically healthy any length of time, is blessed with a comfortable lifestyle, has a healthy and well-adjusted family and/or has no serious problems within their local church, then they must be a very shallow believer indeed (so the thinking goes), one whom the devil is not attacking and who is not even slightly serious about his/her walk with God. ***Neither of these two extremes represent a truly biblical worldview!***

For staunch believers in the "name it and claim it" camp, I believe there is tremendous ignorance about what the "normal" Christian life entails. I decided to check my concordance for all the scripture verses that include the word "suffering" and look what I found! The following Scriptures – in the New Testament alone – if impressed upon those in the hyper-faith movement would probably leave them speechless or running to their pastors to give other Bible verses to refute them:

1. *So they departed from the presence of the council, rejoicing that they were counted worthy to suffer shame for His name (Acts 5:41).*

2. *For I will show him how many things he must suffer for My name's sake (Acts 9:16).*

3. *...and if children, then heirs—heirs of God and joint heirs with Christ, if indeed we suffer with Him, that we may also be glorified together (Rom. 8:17).*

4. *For I consider that the sufferings of this present time are not worthy to be compared with the glory which shall be revealed in us (Rom. 8:18).*

5. *And if one member suffers, all the members suffer with it; or if one member is honored, all the members rejoice with it (1 Cor. 12:26).*

6. *Now if we are afflicted, it is for your consolation and salvation, which is effective for enduring the same sufferings that we also suffer. Or if we are comforted, it is for your consolation and salvation (2 Cor. 1:6).*

7. *For we do not want you to be ignorant, brethren, of our trouble that came to us in Asia: that we were burdened beyond measure, above strength, so that we despaired even of life (2 Cor. 1:8).*

8. *And I, brethren, if I still preach circumcision, why do I still suffer persecution? Then the offense of the cross has ceased (Gal. 5:11).*

9. *As many as desire to make a good showing in the flesh, these would compel you to be circumcised, only that they may not suffer persecution for the cross of Christ (Gal. 6:12).*

10. *For to you it has been granted on behalf of Christ, not only to believe in Him, but also to suffer for His sake (Phil. 1:29).*

11. *I know how to be abased, and I know how to abound. Everywhere and in all things I have learned both to be full and to be hungry, both to abound and to suffer need (Phil. 4:12).*

12. *For, in fact, we told you before when we were with you that we would suffer tribulation, just as it happened, and you know (1 Thess. 3:4).*

13. *… which is manifest evidence of the righteous judgment of God, that you may be counted worthy of the kingdom of God, for which you also suffer (2 Thess. 1:5).*

14. *For to this end we both labor and suffer reproach, because we trust in the living God, who is the Savior of all men, especially of those who believe (1 Tim. 4:10).*

15. *For this reason I also suffer these things; nevertheless I am not ashamed, for I know whom I have believed and am persuaded that He is able to keep what I have committed to Him until that Day (2 Tim. 1:12).*

16. *Yes, and all who desire to live godly in Christ Jesus will suffer persecution (2 Tim. 3:12).*

17. *My brethren, take the prophets, who spoke in the name of the Lord, as an example of suffering and patience (James 5:10).*

18. *Is anyone among you suffering? Let him pray (James 5:13).*

19. *For this is commendable, if because of conscience toward God one endures grief, suffering wrongfully (1 Pet. 2:19).*

20. *For what credit is it if, when you are beaten for your faults, you take it patiently? But when you do good and suffer, if you take it patiently, this is commendable before God (1 Pet. 2:20).*

21. *But even if you should suffer for righteousness' sake, you are blessed (1 Pet. 3:14).*

22. *For it is better, if it is the will of God, to suffer for doing good than for doing evil (1 Pet. 3:17).*

23. *Beloved, do not think it strange concerning the fiery trial which is to try you, as though some strange thing happened to you (1 Pet. 4:12).*

24. Therefore let those who suffer according to the will of God commit their souls to Him in doing good, as to a faithful Creator (1 Pet. 4:19).

25. Do not fear any of those things which you are about to suffer. Indeed, the devil is about to throw some of you into prison, that you may be tested, and you will have tribulation ten days. Be faithful until death, and I will give you the crown of life (Rev. 2:10).

There is enough material there for a whole other book. Those with a victim mentality or martyr complex would dwell solely on these verses to the exclusion of Scriptural passages speaking of blessings in the life of the believer and enumerating the thrilling promises of God! One other example of not rightly dividing the Word of God would be the idea that a Christian is not suffering consequences because of foolish choices they have made; instead, they interpret their suffering because they are being "persecuted for righteousness' sake."

So how do we obtain a balanced viewpoint regarding suffering, God's sovereignty, and hope? Certainly, the Bible is our first source for truth with respect to these subjects. We can then turn to the enormous amount of wisdom that has been recorded over the centuries by those who have suffered, dug in, weathered the storms, and come to a place of hope again through their faith in an ultimately good God. An excellent treatment of this subject is contained in *When God Weeps: Why Our Sufferings Matter to the Almighty,* by Joni Eareckson Tada and Steve Estes.

When we speak of child abuse, we address suffering in the same breath – that is, child abuse is synonymous with suffering. Everyone involved and all who are touched by the act(s) of abuse suffer terribly. Chapter One contains the definitions of the different types of child abuse. All who have ever experienced any sort of child abuse, if they are not in denial about it, can attest to the suffering that is implicit in it and the prolonged, if not lifelong, suffering afterward. We have seen that we must be honest with others, the Lord, and ourselves when we are victimized by abuse if we ever expect to be healed. When you read the accounts of abuse survivors in Appendix B, you will be astounded and marvel at the depths of suffering these people endured, yet survived and healed from in large part due to forgiving their abusers.

Dr. Lynda Hunter has some profound insights as she describes universal suffering in her book, *God, Do You Care? Trusting God through the Storms*:

'Disruptive moments'… can be defined as enduring pain, misery, or difficulty. Suffering disrupts our inner tranquility through emotional, physical, mental and spiritual circumstances. Suffering brings pain, separation, and incompleteness. It can make us powerless and mute and push us toward hopelessness and despair. Suffering can maim, wither, or cripple the heart. Suffering affects every aspect of our experience as human beings and unites people from every walk of life into a common experience of pain, irrespective of race or language, wealth or poverty, learning or virtue. You can't know the right person or have the right things to avoid pain. Pain can't be bought or sold.[2]

The most comprehensive treatment of suffering, God's sovereignty, and hope that I have found in my research was published just last year. In Randy Alcorn's If *God Is Good: Faith in the Midst of Suffering and Evil*, he examines these subjects tirelessly… relentlessly. I would recommend this volume to all Christians, but probably only those who are scholarly and interested in philosophy and theology would read every chapter. There is powerful truth present throughout the book, because Alcorn consistently returns to the Word of God for wisdom and explanations to some very daunting and complex questions. Here is an example Alcorn gives that captures how we react to God when we suffer:

While teaching a seminary course on the theology of Heaven, I met Randy Butler, a pastor, who told us about his teenage son's death three months earlier. Randy took the class on Heaven so he would understand what Kevin, who was both his son and best friend, was experiencing. After the class Randy said, 'For twenty years, God gave me a perfect life, family, and ministry. Then Kevin died, and nearly every morning, for three or four months, I screamed questions at Him. I asked, 'What were You thinking?' And, 'Is this the best You can do for me?' And finally, 'Do You really expect me to show up every Sunday and tell everyone how great You are?' In the silence I began to hear the voice of God… then, without any announcement, when I became silent, God spoke to my soul. He had an answer for each of my three questions.'[3]

Alcorn then goes on to a comprehensive rendition of suffering and evil in the world as it affects Christians. Here are is an excerpt pertaining to God's sovereignty and its reach:

<u>God's sovereignty gives Him ownership and authority over the universe.</u> God's sovereignty is the biblical teaching that all things remain under God's rule and nothing happens without either His direction or permission. God works in all things for the good of His children (see Romans 8:28). [Note: This is what is known in movie reviews as a 'plot spoiler.' See Chapters Eleven through Fourteen for how Romans 8:28 relates to trust.] These 'all things' include evil and suffering. God doesn't commit moral evil, but He can use any evil for good purposes. 'Dominion belongs to the Lord, and He rules over the nations' (Psalm 22:28). Because He has absolute power, no one, including demons and humans who choose to violate His moral will, can thwart His ultimate purpose…. 'In Him we were also chosen, having been predestined according to the plan of Him who works out everything in conformity with the purpose of His will,' wrote Paul (Ephesians 1:11). 'Everything' is comprehensive, allowing for no exceptions. God works even in those things done against His moral will, to bring them into conformity with His purpose and according to His plan. God can and will redeem the worst thing that ever happens to His child.[4]

Believers have defined and described God's sovereignty in different ways down through the centuries. One theologian described it as follows:

Sovereignty does not mean God can do anything. It means God can do anything that is not contradictory to His nature. God is never surprised by the events of life. He is sovereign over all decisions that respect or reject Him as God. The sovereignty of God does not dispel or eliminate my human responsibility and right of decision. In his rewrite of Axioms of Religion, Hershel Hobbs states, 'The holy and loving God has the right to be sovereign. With reference to God, sovereignty means that without the counsel or consent of anyone outside Himself, God acts in accord with His nature and will to accomplish His benevolent and redemptive purpose.' This definition should draw us to God as our loving and wise Creator, Redeemer and Father. J. I. Packer goes so far as to say, 'The recognition of God's sovereignty is the basis of our prayers... every time we pray is to confess our own impotence and God's sovereignty.'[5]

At this point, a biblical dictionary definition is helpful as we seek to understand God's sovereignty:

I. *Biblical usage of the word 'sovereignty' in reference to God. A. Old Testament - Heb. word malku - 'king, kingdom, reign, royalty' Ps. 103:19 - 'the Lord has established His throne in the heavens; and His sovereignty rules over all.' Dan. 7:27 - 'the sovereignty, the dominion, and the greatness of all the kingdoms under the whole heaven will be given to the people of the saints of the Highest One; His kingdom will be an everlasting kingdom, and all the dominions will serve and obey Him.' 1. Heb. word malku is best translated 'kingdom' in all cases. Other three usages of malku in Dan. 7:27 are thus translated. 2. Heb. word adonai - 'Lord' may express concept of sovereignty. B. New Testament - Greek word dunastes - 'ruler, official' from dunamis - 'power'. I Tim. 6:15 - 'He is the blessed and only Sovereign, the King of Kings and Lord of Lords.' (KJV – Potentate) 1. Greek word dynasts is best translated 'ruler' (cf. Luke. 1:52). 2. Greek word kurios - 'Lord' may express concept of sovereignty. C. 'Sovereignty' is not necessarily a Biblical word, but a theological concept. D. Other Scriptures cited to express concept of sovereignty. I Chron. 29:11, 12 - 'Thine, O Lord, is the greatness and the power and the glory and the victory and the majesty, indeed everything that is in the heavens and the earth: Thine is the dominion, O Lord, and Thou doest exalt Thyself as head over all. Both riches and honor come from Thee, and Thou dost rule over all, and in Thy hand is power and might; and it lies in Thy hand to make great, and to strengthen everyone.' Rev. 19:6 '... the Lord our God, the Almighty, reigns.' Rev. 19:16 - 'King of Kings, and Lord of Lords.'*

II. Defining the concept of 'sovereignty.' A. English word usage 1. Etymology - Oxford Etymological Dictionary of the English Language. a. Late Latin - super-anum - 'chief above'. b. Middle French - soverain - 'princely'. c. Old English - souerein - 'supreme, chief, principal.' 2. Dictionary definition - Webster's Collegiate Dictionary. a. supreme power, dominion. b. undisputed ascendancy, dominance. c. unlimited extent, absolute. d. autonomy, independence, absolutely free. e. superlative quality, excellent. f. unqualified, unmitigated, unconditional. 3. Synonyms - Roget's Thesaurus. Supremacy, superiority, ascendancy, all-powerful, all-sufficient, irresistible, overwhelming, authority, jurisdiction, absoluteness, mastery, control, reign. D. Venturing a definition of 'sovereignty'. 1. God is 'over all' and 'above all' - 'God is on the top rung of the ladder.' 2. God is absolute, autonomous and independent. 3. God is omnipotent and Almighty. 4. God is the authority who acts out of His inherent perfect character. 5. God is the authority who acts out of His inherent absolute authority. Authority = Gk. exousia - 'out of being.' 6. God is Lord of Lords and King of Kings - I Tim. 6:15.[6]

Another definition found in an Internet article, "The Sovereignty of God in History" by John Deffinbaugh, has some scripture verses that illuminate this oftentimes difficult-to-grasp concept:

Virtually all Christians give at least verbal assent to the doctrine of the sovereignty of God. There are simply too many texts that teach this truth to deny it: The LORD has established His throne in the heavens, and His sovereignty rules over all (Psalm 103:19). But our God is in the heavens; He does whatever He pleases (Psalm 115:3). For I know that the LORD is great, and that our Lord is above all gods. Whatever the LORD pleases, He does, in heaven and in earth, in the seas and in all deeps (Psalm 135:5-6). The meaning of sovereignty could be summed up in this way: To be sovereign is to possess supreme power and authority so that one is in complete control and can accomplish whatever he pleases. A number of similar definitions of sovereignty can be found in books on the attributes of God: 'The dictionaries tell us that sovereign means chief or highest, supreme in power, superior in position, independent of and unlimited by anyone else.' Furthermore, His sovereignty requires that He be absolutely free, which means simply that He must be free to do whatever He wills to do anywhere at any time to carry out His eternal purpose in every single detail without interference. Were He less than free He must be less than sovereign.[7]

Jerry Bridges has the following discussion of the sovereignty of God (he calls it "providence") in his classic book, *Trusting God: Even When Life Hurts*:

I have developed a definition that I can more easily remember: <u>God's providence is His constant care for and His absolute rule over His creation for His own glory and the good</u>

of His people. Again, note the absolute terms: constant care, absolute rule, all creation. Nothing, not even the smallest virus, escapes His care and control. But note also, the twofold objective of God's providence: His own glory and the good of His people. These two objectives are never antithetical; they are always in harmony with each other. God never pursues His glory at the expense of the good of His people, nor does He ever seek our good at the expense of His glory. He has designed His eternal purpose so that His glory and our good are inextricably bound together. What comfort and encouragement this should be to us. If we are going to learn to trust God in adversity, we must believe that just as certainly as God will allow nothing to subvert His glory, so He will allow nothing to spoil the good He is working out in us and for us. [8]

Bridges goes on to emphatically state his conclusions as to the matter of God's sovereignty:

God is in control; He is sovereign. He does whatever pleases Him and determines whether we can do what we have planned. This is the essence of God's sovereignty, His absolute independence to do as He pleases, and His absolute control over the actions of all His creatures. No creature, person, or empire can either thwart His will or act outside the bounds of His will.... Confidence in the sovereignty of God in all that affects us is crucial to our trusting Him. If there is a single event in all of the universe that can occur outside of God's sovereign control then we cannot trust Him. His love may be infinite, but if His power is limited and His purpose can be thwarted, we cannot trust Him. You may entrust to me your most valuable possessions. I may love you and my aim to honor your trust may be sincere, but if I do not have the power or ability to guard your valuables, you cannot truly entrust them to me. [9]

When you begin to grasp the magnitude of God's sovereignty and other aspects of His character, e.g., omnipotence, omnipresence, omniscience, immutability, etc., there will be light at the end of the tunnel for you as you heal from childhood abuse. That little bit of light will begin to grow and expand until it has become hope. The following author makes a distinction between modern-day usage of the word "hope" and its biblical counterpart:

What is hope? Is it a wishy-washy maybe or a kind of unsure optimism? The modern idea of hope is 'to wish for, to expect, but without certainty of the fulfillment; to desire very much, but with no real assurance of getting your desire.' In Scripture, according to the Hebrew and Greek words translated by the word 'hope' and according to the biblical usage, hope is an indication of certainty. 'Hope' in Scripture means 'a strong and confident expectation.' Though archaic today in modern terms, hope is akin to trust and a confident expectation. By its very nature, hope stresses two things: (a) futurity, and (b) invisibility. It deals with things we can't see or haven't received or both.... For example, we do not see the justifying work of God, the imputation of Christ's righteousness to our account... the indwelling of the Holy Spirit when we are saved, or our co-union with Christ. We believe this to be a reality, but this is a matter of our hope. We believe in the testimony of God in the Word and hope for the results in our lives. In summary, hope is the confident expectation, the sure certainty that what God has promised in the Word is true, has occurred, and or will in accordance with God's sure Word.[10]

The difference between the modern usage of "hope" and the biblical one is also validated by the *Merriam-Webster Online Dictionary* definition:

Etymology: Middle English, from Old English hopian; akin to Middle High German hoffen to hope. Date: before 12th century, intransitive verb 1: to cherish a desire with anticipation <hopes for a promotion>; 2 archaic: TRUST transitive verb 1: to desire with expectation of obtainment; 2: to expect with confidence: TRUST. synonyms see EXPECT.— hoper noun; — hope against hope: to hope without any basis for expecting fulfillment.

I will conclude this chapter with a personal anecdote about a season of my life when I encountered hope in a way that pushed my faith up several levels. For a period of about two years in the late '90's, I suffered horribly with gastro-esophageal reflux disorder (GERD). GERD is now a disorder that afflicts thousands of people, and in its most severe form can lead to esophageal cancer. The doctors tried many medications to give me relief and continued to increase the dosage to what one pharmacist called an alarming level. This was my first experience with chronic pain. It was not disabling from the standpoint of my having to take a leave of absence from my private practice; however, my ability to concentrate and really to be of assistance to my clients was severely diminished.

The diagnostic tests for GERD felt worse than the disorder itself. I had to repeat one of these ghastly tests because the doctors couldn't believe how high my acid levels were (the test involved a nurse placing a tube up my nose, down my throat, into my stomach that had to remain in place for 24 hours – a tortuous medical experience. You get the picture! Even with the results of these tests, the gastric surgeon whom I finally got in to see refused to perform a surgery that held great promise for those who suffered from severe GERD, called a *laparoscopic fundoplication*. At that point, I became quite depressed, as I felt there was no hope that I would ever feel any better. As a formerly healthy person, I really didn't have any idea how to cope with the chronic pain.

One fast-forward will make the outcome of my story more meaningful. I now study Hebrew with others who want to be able to read and translate the Bible in its original language. In 1997, that idea never even crossed my mind.

When I would cry out to God in my hopelessness, I began to "hear" a strange word in my spirit. It didn't mean anything to me, but I was often aware of it floating around in my head when I was first waking up. The syllables sounded like "ha-teek-va." It sounded somewhat Hebraic to me, so I decided to look it up in a Hebrew-English dictionary at a Barnes & Noble one day. Since I knew absolutely no Hebrew at this point, this was a challenge in and of itself!

When I finally found the word, I was astounded! The "Ha" part was the word for "the." The dictionary entry read as follows, "Tikvah (הוקת) is the Hebrew word for hope." My spirit soared that my loving Father God would put that Hebrew word in my heart! (We just learned that 'hope' means confident expectation of the Lord's intervention on our behalf.) Not only that, but the dictionary entry went on to say that "Hatkivah" was the name of Israel's national anthem. At that point, I was completely blown away. Here is the translation for "Hatkivah":

As long as in a Jewish breast
The soul's stirring has not ceased
The eye for longing will not rest
Until it gaze on Zion in the east
Our ancient hope will not perish
Hope from ages long since past
To live free in the land we cherish
Zion and Jerusalem at last.

Even as I write to share the Lord's intervention in my life with you, my eyes fill with tears. The goodness and the love of God are so real to me – my desire is that they will become that real to you as well. Now, for the end of the story.

(At this point, nothing had changed in my circumstances, but now I had **hope**!) Prior to this particular challenge of physical suffering, I had had the tremendous privilege of touring Israel twice and loved to collect what is called "Judaica" – books, papers, objects, art, jewelry, etc., having to do with Jewish people or Judaism. I was in my local Christian bookstore one day a couple of weeks after my discovery of the word "hope" in Hebrew (Hatkivah), and I came upon a gorgeous music box with a menorah on the cover. The box almost looked like stained glass, with its detailed etching and gorgeous colors.

I turned the box over to see what song it played and was in absolute awe to see that it was none other than "Hatkivah." I almost burst out sobbing right there in the store, because it was such incredible confirmation that one way or another I was going to get relief from the pain. To have such a beautiful reminder of the hope that the Lord gave me in such a time of suffering continues to bless me to this day. The music box resides in my office, and I frequently wind it up and play it as a memorial to how good the Lord was then, now, and always will be. Sure enough, shortly after finding the music box, I also found a gastroenterologist who referred me to a surgeon. This wonderful doctor agreed that the surgery was indicated and would very likely relieve my symptoms all together. I went ahead, had the surgery, and was *pain-free* afterwards… **only a mighty and sovereign Lord would arrange all those circumstances to let me know He loved me and was working on my behalf even when things looked so hopeless.**

I hope this anecdote has blessed you. God is not a respecter of persons, and what He did (and does) for me, He will do for you. You can have real hope for healing from the deep wounds of your child abuse.

Forgiving others kicks off this wonderful process of healing. It's time to implement what you have been reading about until now. You are starting down the road to freedom. Keep going, my friend – it's well worth all the effort it in the end!

Many times, you have to go through the entire [forgiveness] process more than once. You get through it the first time, and you feel okay, but then later, you find yourself angry about it, either because someone else brought it up or something unrelated reminded you of it. It's okay to have to work through the process again because each time you do, you learn something different about it and yourself. – Dawn Ellis-Lopez

So with my in-laws I asked God to help me to forgive them – to really forgive them so that should they want to see me again I would be able to respond. This took several months of prayer (and yes, it's best not to rush) before I felt ready to let go and ask God to bless them. – Anonymous

We live in an age of instant gratification. Nowadays, it seems like everything's got to be faster than fast, from Internet speeds to communicating via tweets. But there's no such thing as high-speed forgiveness. Genuine forgiveness takes time. It's a healing process. And depending on the gravity of the transgression against you, it could take a very long time at that. – Julian Burke

1. Understand what forgiveness is not. 2. Understand that it is often unwise to forgive face to face. 3. Select a time and place when you can be alone for a season of time. 4. Pray and ask the Holy Spirit to bring to your mind all the people you need to forgive and the events you need to forgive them for. 5. Make a list of everything the Holy Spirit brings to your mind, even if it seems trivial to you. 6. Take two chairs and arrange them facing each other. Seat yourself in one of the chairs. 7. Imagine that the first person on your list is sitting in the other chair. Disclose everything you can remember that the person has done to hurt you. Do not hold back the tears or the emotions that accompany the confessions. 8. Choose by an act of your will to forgive that person once and for all time. You may not feel like being forgiving. That's all right. Just do it and the feelings will follow. God will take care of that. Do not doubt that what you have done is real and valid. 9. Release the person from the debt you feel is owed you for the offense. Say, "You are free and forgiven." 10. If the person is still a part of your life, now is a good time to accept the individual without wanting to change aspects of their personality or behavior. 11. Thank the Lord for using each person as a tool in your life to deepen your insight into His grace and conforming you to the image of His Son. 12. Pray. This is a suggested prayer to pray as you "talk" to each person: Because I am forgiven and accepted by Christ, I can now forgive and accept you, _____, unconditionally in Christ. I choose now to forgive you, _____, no matter what you did to me. I release you from the hurts (take time to name the hurts), and you are no longer accountable to me for them. You are free. 13. When you have finished praying through the hurts you have suffered, pray this prayer of faith: "Lord Jesus, by faith, I receive Your unconditional love and acceptance in the place of this hurt, and I trust You to meet all my needs. I take authority over the Enemy, and in the name of Jesus, I take back the ground I have allowed Satan to gain in my life because of my attitude toward _____. Right now I give this ground back to the Lord Jesus Christ to whom it rightfully belongs.' – Dr. Charles Stanley, *The Gift of Forgiveness*

Chapter Nine

Implementing the Steps of Forgiveness

It's time to get down to what we call "brass tacks." Everything we have covered up to now has been very important background information. Without this backdrop, the command that Jesus gives us to forgive seems completely unreasonable and impossible to walk out. The first "brass tack" I address here is making the choice to forgive. Even the world now uses the phrase "make choices" to indicate that people have freedom to choose how they act in life. At least once a week, a client and I will discuss their past, usually in terms of he/she "made some bad choices back then that are still influencing my life today."

The principle just identified is that choices (good or bad) lead to consequences (good or bad). This is actually an immutable law cited repeatedly in the Bible, e.g., what a man sows that shall he also reap, the wages of sin is death, because you have eaten from the tree, cursed is the ground for your sake; in toil, you shall eat of it all the days of your life, etc. I also frequently see *the consequences of parents not enforcing consequences...* they have very disobedient, not too appealing children. In Chapters Two and Three, we saw the consequences of choosing to forgive or choosing to remain bitter and unforgiving and observed weighty consequences either way a person decides to go.

I was never particularly fond of the Nike slogan, "Just do it!" I've always thought that it was rather simplistic, and that there were many legitimate reasons why people could not always "just do it." The older I get (and hopefully my grey hairs are the reflection of my obtaining some godly wisdom), the more I see that, in fact, this expression is quite biblical. I have also learned that saying, "I can't" is actually tantamount to saying, "I won't." I have become aware (many times painfully so!) of the numerous choices that other people and I make every day in every part of our lives.

If you have decided that you are making the choice to forgive, we now come to "brass tack" number two: When do you plan to act on this decision? Is it now (as soon as possible), or is it more nebulous (somewhere along the line I'll get to it when I'm ready)? Part b of "brass tack" number two reflects my having learned a tough lesson in life that I now impart to you: Guess what? **You'll never be ready!** I am convinced that whether we have been redeemed or not, this is possibly the easiest spiritual discipline to procrastinate practicing. For one thing, we may be bogged down with many misconceptions about what forgiveness is and isn't. Since you have read Chapters Two and Three, you don't have that reason to put it off any longer.

Another factor involved here is that, as human beings, we tend to embrace pleasure and reject pain. The forgiveness process is painful and messy, and it is just easier to put the whole thing off indefinitely. Besides that, holding on to our sense of outrage and righteous indignation makes us feel powerful, when forgiving often leads to our feeling quite vulnerable – initially, at least.

We now move on to the final "brass tack" – number three. Okay, *I'm ready to just do it*, you say. But how? Maybe you have tried to forgive one or more people in the past and been unsuccessful. I have found Neil T. Anderson's booklet, *The Steps to Freedom in Christ: A Step-by-Step Guide to Help You Resolve Personal and Spiritual Conflicts, Break Free from Bondage and Renew Your Mind, and Experience Daily Victory as a Child of God,* to be the most helpful guide to me personally in making the choice to forgive become a reality. Once again, I will quote extensively from this jewel of a guide that I wish Christians everywhere would really sink their teeth into, so to speak, so they could become free in Jesus! That's been my objective as a mental health professional all these years – to see the captives freed and filled with righteousness, peace, and joy.

Dr. Anderson makes the whole process very practical. If you are a person who needs structure and likes a systematic approach to things, Anderson is your man. He gives a prayer that you are to pray aloud to start the process:

Dear Heavenly Father,

I thank You for the riches of Your kindness, forbearance, and patience toward me, knowing that Your kindness has led me to repentance. I confess that I have not shown that same kindness and patience toward those who have hurt or offended me. Instead, I have held on to my anger, bitterness and resentment toward them. Please bring to my mind all the people I need to forgive in order that I may now do so. In Jesus' name, amen.[1]

Anderson continues by instructing you (and me, actually, since forgiving is a lifetime discipline, which is why I include myself so often in this book) to list the names of people on a separate sheet of paper who have come to your mind after praying that prayer.[2] He then makes two profound points that are crucial as you formally start the process:

Often we hold things against ourselves as well, punishing ourselves for wrong choices we've made in the past. Write 'Myself' at the bottom of your list if you need to forgive yourself. Forgiving yourself is accepting the truth that God has already forgiven you in Christ. If God forgives you, you can forgive yourself Also, write down 'Thoughts Against God' at the bottom of your list. Obviously, God has never done anything wrong, so we don't have to forgive Him. Sometimes, however, we harbor angry thoughts against Him

because He did not do what we wanted Him to do. Those feelings of anger or resentment against God can become a wall between us and Him, so we must let them go (emphasis added).³

Anderson goes on to enumerate what forgiveness is and is not. Although it would seem this distinction has already been discussed exhaustively in Chapter Five, he writes in a unique, concise, and thoroughly practical manner that has made things very clear and straightforward. It has been incredibly useful to me, as I have learned to practice the discipline of forgiving others who have abused me. Anderson just seems to hit on every point that we really are hung up on when we work on forgiving others:

1. <u>*Forgiveness Is Not Merely Forgetting (Note: Please, let him explain before blindly rejecting his use of this phrase.).*</u> *People who want to forget all that was done to them will find they cannot do it. Don't put off forgiving those who have hurt you, hoping the pain will one day go away. Once you choose to forgive someone, then Christ can come and begin to heal you of your hurts. But the healing cannot begin until you first forgive.*

2. <u>*Forgiveness Is a Choice, a Decision of Your Will.*</u> *Since God requires you to forgive, it is something you can do. Sometimes it is very hard to forgive someone because we naturally want revenge for the things we have suffered. Forgiveness seems to go against our sense of what is right and fair. So we hold on to our anger…. But we are told by God never to take our own revenge (see Romans 12:19). Let God deal with the person. Let him or her off your hook…. By forgiving, you let the other person off your hook, but he or she is not off God's hook. You must trust that God will deal with the person justly and fairly, something you simply cannot do….He tells you to forgive others for your sake. Until you let go of your anger and hatred, the person is still hurting you. You can't turn back the clock and change the past, but you can be free from it….*

3. <u>*Forgiveness Is Agreeing to Live with the Consequences of Another's Sin.*</u> *You are going to live with those consequences whether you like it or not, so the only choice you have is whether you will do so in the bondage of bitterness or in the freedom of forgiveness. No one truly forgives without accepting and suffering the pain of another person's sin. That can seem unfair, and you may wonder, 'Where is the justice?' The Cross makes forgiveness legally and morally right. Jesus died once for all our sins. Jesus took the eternal consequences of sin upon Himself…. We, however, often suffer the temporary consequences of other people's sins. That is simply a harsh reality of life all of us have to face. Do not wait for the other person to ask for your forgiveness.*

Remember, Jesus did not wait for those who were crucifying Him to apologize before He forgave them.

4. *Forgiveness Comes from Your Heart. Allow God to bring the painful memories to the surface, and then acknowledge how you feel toward those who've hurt you. If your forgiveness doesn't touch the emotional core of your life, it will be incomplete. Too often, we are afraid of the pain, so we bury our emotions deep down inside us. Let God bring them to the surface so He can begin to heal those damaged emotions.*

5. *Forgiveness Is Choosing Not to Hold Someone's Sin Against Him or Her anymore. It is common for bitter people to bring up past issues with those who have hurt them. They want the other people to feel as badly as they do! But we must let go of the past and choose to reject any thought of revenge. This doesn't mean you continue to put up with the future sins of others. God does not tolerate sin and neither should you. Don't allow yourself to be continually abused by others. Take a stand against sin while continuing to exercise grace and forgiveness toward those who hurt you. If you need help setting scriptural boundaries to protect yourself from further abuse, talk to a trusted friend, counselor or pastor (emphasis added).*

6. *Forgiveness Cannot Wait Until You Feel Like Forgiving. You will never get there. Make the hard choice to forgive even if you don't feel like it. Once you choose to forgive, Satan will lose his power over you in that area, and God will heal your damaged emotions. Freedom is what you will gain right now, not necessarily an immediate change in feelings.*

Now you are ready to begin. Starting with the first person on your list, make the choice to forgive him or her for every painful memory that comes to your mind. Continue until you are sure you have dealt with all the remembered pain caused by that individual. Then work your way down the list in the same way.

As you begin forgiving people, God may bring to your mind painful memories you've totally forgotten. Let Him do this even if it hurts. God wants you to be free; forgiving those people is the only way. Don't try to excuse the offender's behavior, even if it is someone you are really close to. Don't say, 'Lord, please help me to forgive.' [Note: Until I read this book that was the way I always prayed when working on forgiving someone.] He is already helping you and will be with you all the way through the process. Don't say, 'Lord, I want to forgive...' because that bypasses the hard choice we have to make. Say, 'Lord, I choose to forgive....' For every painful memory you have for each person on your list, pray aloud:

Lord, I choose to forgive _____ *(name the person)*
for _____ *(what he/she did or failed to do), which*
made me feel _____ *(share the painful feelings).*

After you have forgiven each person for all the offenses that came to your mind, and after you have honestly expressed how you felt, conclude this step by praying aloud:

Lord, I choose not to hold on to my resentment. I thank You for setting me free from the bondage of my bitterness. I relinquish my right to seek revenge and ask You to heal my damaged emotions. I now ask You to bless those who have hurt me. In Jesus' name, amen.[4]

The Steps to Freedom in Christ: A Step-by-Step Guide to Help You Resolve Personal and Spiritual Conflicts, Break Free from Bondage and Renew Your Mind, and Experience Daily Victory as a Child of God, Neil T. Anderson, 2001, Regal Books: Ventura, CA. Used by permission. All rights reserved.

I will always be grateful for the obedience of Neil Anderson in putting together this small, but very powerful, volume: *The Steps to Freedom in Christ.* It has made such a difference in my life and the people I know who have worked it all the way through. ***I cannot emphasize enough how much every person reading this book needs to get a copy of*** <u>***The Steps to Freedom in Christ.***</u> ***You may be bound in so many areas of which you have no conscious awareness.***

I had a female client we'll call Muriel. She is one of a handful of clients I have had who worked through Anderson's book thoroughly and completely. When we reached the chapter on forgiveness, she commented that she really couldn't think of anyone that she held anything against and denied that she felt any resentment or bitterness toward anyone. That was a **first** for me to hear from a client, so I gently reminded Muriel of the life events that had hurt her, which she had shared with me as we went through her personal history.

After I identified three or four people from Muriel's past whom she realized she had not forgiven, she went home to work on her list of bitterness toward people who had hurt her, both when she was a child and as an adult. We had prayed that the Holy Spirit would bring to mind anyone she was forgetting. She subsequently came in with a list *six pages long* (and her handwriting was small!) of the people who had wounded her, what they had done, and how she felt about it. That was the most dramatic example for me of how good, earnest believers repress and gloss over their pasts without bothering to examine whether they have any unforgiveness in their hearts.

One matter that Anderson does not address is that you can pray these prayers once, feel better, go on your way, and later on, the feelings of hurt and anger can/will come up repeatedly. The feelings may feel identical in intensity to when you prayed these forgiveness prayers initially. I tell clients that forgiveness is a process, and the peeling an onion analogy is apt here. Whenever one begins to peel the onion layers, the process can seem endless – so many layers! The worse the offense (and we know that child abuse most often leaves lifelong scars), the more layers of pain there are to be forgiven.

In addition, when that abuse continues into adulthood (which is frequently the case), there are new offenses for which to forgive the abuser and decisions to be made as to whether or not to stay in an active relationship with this person. [**Note: We have now seen several authors who strongly advise the need for protecting yourself from ongoing abuse.**] An unknown author really captured the onion-peeling process:

> *Recovery is like an onion;*
> *You peel away layer by layer,*
> *Each section bringing you*
> *Closer to clarity.*
> *Along the way, you cry a lot,*
> *But when you finally reach*
> *The center, the core,*
> *You'll find it's really sweet.*

A survivor of horrendous child abuse, Stormie Omartian (see Appendix B for her story), had this to say about the onion:

> *Getting free from our past doesn't happen overnight. It took me years to become completely free. After finally getting free of layer after layer of unforgiveness toward my mother, I found that I also harbored deep resentment toward my dad for never rescuing me from her insanity. That unforgiveness was so deeply buried in me that I was not even aware of it until I asked God to show me if it was there. Once I was set free of that, I came to a place of peace and productivity I had never before experienced.[5]*

I have experienced this dilemma "up close and personal" as the saying goes. While my childhood sexual abuse was over and had long been dealt with thoroughly, forgiven, and healed, my father continued to abuse my brother and me as adults. Because we loved him so, we were always striving to have that close relationship that was denied us in the past. I once read that as long as we are alive, we never get over trying to get the love and approval of our parents. The reason that principle has stuck with me is that I see it played out every day in my coaching practice.

After my father became sober, he initially changed into a kinder, more understanding person. Then little by little, the abuse started again – he became a dry drunk. I believe that was so for two reasons: (1) He had never surrendered his heart to the Lord; and (2) He had never explored, grieved, and healed from the abuse and abandonment that he suffered as a child.

My father made his amends to my mother, brothers, and me, according to A.A.'s Twelve Steps. For a brief time, my brothers and I began to experience great improvement in our relationships with him. However, he remained a bitter man, and as he aged, he began to slip back into old behaviors. What was different was now our spouses joined us as objects of his verbal and emotional abuse. What was tricky about the whole thing was that the abuse was intermittent, so the good times were really good and the bad times just as painful as when we were children. Thus not only had I been implementing the forgiveness process (as new memories surfaced), but I now had to deal with present-day abuse. Since the damage done was severe and affected all aspects of my life, I definitely peeled that onion a very long time. (To read more about this process, go to Appendix B, where I recount my own story.)

Dr. Sandra Wilson identifies the dichotomous thinking that characterizes many Christians regarding the nature of forgiveness in her powerful book, *Released from Shame*. There are many books written about shame, but they can be "New Age-y" or humanistic in their solutions to the problem. I would heartily recommend this book to any believer who struggles with the intense shame that comes with child abuse, because I had the privilege of meeting Dr. Wilson at an *American Association of Christian Counselors* seminar, and she is living proof that healing and forgiveness of childhood trauma is possible:

> ***People who use all-or-nothing thinking tend to assume that forgiveness must either be an event or a process. Forgiveness is both. Forgiving begins with an initial, purposeful commitment of our wills in which we 'set sail' for forgiveness. But even after sincere commitments, we can be blown temporarily off course by painful memories or other violent emotional storms. During these storms, we may feel confused, discouraged or guilty if we misunderstand the nature of forgiveness. It's important to remember that only God forgives perfectly. The rest of us have to keep working at it with continual recommitment.[6]***

In the quotes at the beginning of this chapter, we read that Dr. Charles Stanley identified 13 steps to forgiveness in his book, *The Gift of Forgiveness*. If you examine these steps, you'll find that they are very similar to those that Anderson lists. We even see that slogan "Just Do it" in step eight. The primary difference between the two processes is that Stanley uses the so-called empty chair technique (which can be very powerful – I have used it with many clients) and that the forgiveness is "once and for all time." You have just read how, in my experience, that does not always play out practically when one is processing deep wounds.

I like the way Lewis B. Smedes handles the layers-of-the-onion question as he relates it to Matthew 18:22:

What Jesus said about forgiving seventy times seven had nothing to do with putting up with things until the seventy times eighth offense. He was telling us not to make forgiveness a matter of numbers. He was talking about healing our memories of a wound that someone's wrong etched in our cemented past. Once we have stopped the abuse, we can forgive however many times that it may take us to finish our healing.[7]

I have one other personal anecdote that applies to implementing forgiveness. This was an amazing turn of events that demonstrated the Lord's sovereignty over everything (Chapter Eight) and His ability to redeem what seemed to be a disaster. This story is an exception to the rule of dealing strictly with child abuse, but its pertinence to the process of forgiveness is unquestionable.

During my last year of graduate school before becoming a Marriage and Family Therapist, I was training at a Christian counseling center. My supervisor, Angela, as I'll call her, was unabashedly emotional (she blamed that on her being partly Italian), very competent at what she did, an excellent teacher, and a devout Christian. I was such a raw recruit, so wet behind the ears that I followed every instruction she uttered in detail. I was thrilled that the Lord had moved me into this wonderful place. I was the envy of my classmates, because although I received a small amount of compensation, I was the only one of us therapists-in-training who had a paid position.

I never knew much about her childhood, but she had been abused in every way possible during her marriage (she was now divorced), and that type of relationship rarely exists without the victim being abused as a child. I did know she had been sexually abused when she was young and continually fought a losing battle with her weight. Angela was short in stature and morbidly obese.

So what happened? For the first several months that I worked there, I was shy and kept to myself. I didn't interact with the rest of the staff therapists, because when I was at the agency I was either busy seeing client or doing the endless paperwork that just goes with the territory. I would rush in and out of the office, because while I was carrying a full load of classes at school, I also had quite a few clients to see. I only had one more semester to go and then I would graduate.

There was one woman who worked there with whom I began speaking on an increasingly frequent basis. Aggie (not her name) was a very soft-spoken, kind woman, but when she needed to confront someone, she could be quite tough. Angela observed over time that Aggie and I were getting close, and it bothered her. I was in a particularly fragile state at that point, as my brother was fighting his losing battle with AIDS and his overall state of health was deteriorating rapidly.

I began to experience a lot of pressure on all fronts. School was demanding, my brother was getting worse, and Angela was attempting to keep Aggie and me apart. She could be a controlling woman, and she simply didn't like our relationship and was trying every way she knew to discourage it. The environment became so uncomfortable at the agency that I decided I would need to look for a new placement.

Just prior to my giving notice, my brother died. I was devastated and only returned to the agency one time when I knew Angela wouldn't be there to return the necessary materials. She sent a lovely spray of flowers and appeared to accept that the reason I left was due to the trauma of my brother's death. On the other hand, Aggie subsequently departed with open hostility on both women's parts. Angela accused Aggie of corrupting me, as if I were some impressionable child (I was 35 at the time). My theory was that Angela felt jealous of our closeness and hurt at being excluded.

Aggie and I continued our friendship long after we both left the agency. However, I didn't see Angela for at least five years after my departure, and that relieved me no end. I felt as though I had "kind of" forgiven her, but the thought of even casually running into her somewhere would provoke severe anxiety on my part.

Over the years, Aggie and I attended several counseling conferences together. When well-known Christian psychologists Drs. John Townsend and Henry Cloud traveled to our locale to present a conference on "Making and Maintaining Boundaries," wild horses couldn't have kept us away. So whom should we see the first day of the conference? There was Angela looking as uncomfortable as we both felt. We passed each other without a word – talk about awkward... yikes! This encounter ruined things at the conference for me, because I was so uncomfortable with having seen her and fearful of running into her again.

Fast-forward another five years. I had not seen Angela any other time after the conference, which was just as well, so my thinking went. Aggie and I had been very close friends over the last 10 years. She was quite distraught over the looming specter of my husband's and my move to Arizona. We were on a countdown actually, there were only about two months left before our move.

One night, I was having a late dinner with my mother at a local coffee shop. She had already eaten, so she was only interested in a piece of pie for dessert and this restaurant was famous for their exquisite pie. We got all the subtle and not-so-subtle-signals that the shop was about to close down, so we paid the bill and left.

As my mother and I were leaving the restaurant, out of the corner of my eye I saw a woman going in about five minutes before closing time. The parking lot was not well lit, and while I noticed this woman, I certainly wasn't scrutinizing her. Mom and I were immersed in some kind of fascinating conversation and so lingered outside just a few minutes. We hugged goodbye and she drove away, but I was a little slower at starting up my vehicle to leave – a 1980's Toyota truck. While I enjoyed driving it, I was always somewhat nervous when backing up due to my poor depth perception and the inevitable blind spot that existed even with three mirrors at my disposal.

As I slowly backed up, there was a thump and I felt a sickening feeling in the pit of my stomach. I rolled down my window while leaning across the front seat to retrieve my registration and proof of insurance. Suddenly I heard a strangely familiar voice, well, shriek really, and there she was – Angela in all her Italian glory – yelling that I had run into her – not her *car*, but her *body*. She was already threatening to sue me for every penny I had. When I turned to face her, I froze. We were rendered speechless at the sight of each other.

"Is that you, Angela? I managed to inquire in a quivering voice. She nodded, and then broke into a huge smile as she recognized me instantly. I followed up by questioning if she were hurt, but she laughed and replied, "No, not really… you barely tapped me, but you did have a pretty broad target, after all… " (acknowledging her loss of the battle of the bulge). We both descended into giggles at the thought that for 10 years, we had not spoken to one another, and now the Lord had taken extreme measures to heal the relationship– I had to literally run into her! The anxiety of all those years spent avoiding her dissipated in an instant. I got out of the truck, and we stood and talked, and talked, and talked. It was getting so late that we finally agreed to meet for lunch later that week. When we did, we had a marvelous discussion, forgiveness was asked and granted on both parts, and we tried to catch up on a decade of each other's lives.

The night of our "run-in," I could swear I almost heard what I was sure was a thundering chortle from the skies. Only the Lord Himself could have arranged for us to have met and reconciled in this way! Afterward I moved and never heard from her again, but that's all right – a complete healing took place then, and I know I will see her again one day when we all see Jesus. How's that for "forced" forgiveness? All I know is – it's one for the books!

It is now time to move on to the connection between forgiving others and trusting God. Why have I coupled the two and exactly how are they related? Just turn the page and you'll find out.

By forgiving others, we free ourselves spiritually and emotionally. Forgiveness is an act of our own personal will in obedience and submission to God's will, trusting God to bring emotional healing. – Author unknown

When we fail to take responsibility for ourselves, we not only hurt other people, but we also are not trusting God for what He has brought into our lives. Either way, we are rejecting reality. We are rejecting what is true about what God has brought into our lives, and we are rejecting our feelings about it. And that is not faith. In essence, faith is trusting God with every aspect of our lives, both the difficult things and the comfortable things. It is good for us to go to that frightening and alone place and to feel our feelings. When we jump to solutions too quickly, bypassing our pain, we miss an opportunity to trust God. He brought us here, and we must trust Him here, where He meets and cares for us. – Nancy Scott

Joseph's brothers hated him so much that they plotted his murder. Instead, they sold him as a slave to some Ishmaelite traders. In Egypt he gained the favor of Pharaoh, who gave him a position of responsibility second only to that of the king. During a famine, his brothers came to him for food, not realizing who he was. When Joseph finally identified himself, he spoke this assuring word to them: "Do not therefore be grieved or angry with yourselves because you sold me here; for God sent me before you to preserve life" (Gen. 45:5). Later he said to his brothers, "But as for you, you meant evil against me; but God meant it for good, in order to bring it about, as it is this day, to save many people alive" (Gen. 50:20). – R. W. De Haan

And I am confident that we as children of God will be able to look back over our lives someday and say, "All of this worked out for good." Job could say, "Though He slay me, yet will I trust in Him" (Job 13:15). That is the kind of faith in God we need, friend. We know that He is going to make things work out for good because He's the One who is motivating it. He's the One who is energizing it. – J. Vernon McGee

Trust in God's promises comes to light in obedience to His commands…. It is therefore a contradiction in terms to say that we acknowledge Christ's rule in our lives if we do not submit to His word…. There is no distinction in the Bible between knowing God or Jesus as our "Savior" and knowing Him as our "Lord." Saving faith always expresses itself in obedience (James 2:21-24). – Scott Hafemann

It's amazing how people can affirm that God is a God of order and absolute precision in everything He does in the natural world, yet believe He unconcerned about the moral world. The scientist in the laboratory operates on the basis that his chemical mixtures are not going to violate a known truth and blow the building to bits. The astronauts who blast off into space count on the absolute immutability and accuracy of scientific laws. If God is a God of law and order in the natural realm, He's not going to say, 'Oh, just do your own thing. Believe anything you want.' Such inconsistency is absurd! – John MacArthur

Chapter Ten

How Forgiveness Unlocks the Door to Trust

What is it that connects the forgiveness process with being able to trust the Lord? I hope that you now understand that when you are obedient and forgive those who have abused you, you will experience numerous blessings that accompany that submission to the Lord. When we have processed and grieved our childhood losses, we come to a place of acceptance of what has happened to us and can begin to see hope for the future.

You have also seen how distorted views of Father God are a direct result of childhood abuse, and that your mistaken notions of who He is are like an enormous block wall that prevent you from trusting in and experiencing intimacy with Him. As you choose to forgive in obedience to Christ, a funny thing begins to happen. All the emotional energy that has been directed at your abusers can now be directed to coming to know who our Father God really is.

Summary: By forgiving others, we free ourselves spiritually and emotionally. Forgiveness is an act of our own personal will in obedience and submission to God's will, trusting God to bring emotional healing.[1]

If we embrace the fact of God's sovereignty, the door is unlocked and we can begin to take those small, halting steps toward trusting Him in all things. Did I say all things? Remember the "plot spoiler" in the last chapter? It was the conclusion we can reach about God's trustworthiness that is encapsulated in one of the most powerful and oft-quoted verses in the entire Bible – Romans 8:28. Let's examine that verse in a few translations:

> *And we know that all things work together for good to them that love God, to them who are the called according to His purpose. (KJV)*

> *And we know that all things work together for good to those who love God, to those who are the called according to His purpose. (NKJV)*

And we know that God causes all things to work together for good to those who love God, to those who are called according to His purpose. (NASB)

We are assured and know that [God being a partner in their labor] all things work together and are [fitting into a plan] for good to and for those who love God and are called according to [His] design and purpose. (Amplified Bible)

And we know that in all things God works for the good of those who love Him, who have been called according to His purpose. (NIV)

And we know that for those who love God all things work together for good, for those who are called according to His purpose. (English Standard Version)

And we have known that to those loving God all things do work together for good, to those who are called according to His purpose. (Young's Literal Translation)

Ray Pritchard makes an astute observation and then draws a conclusion that is quite pertinent with respect to trusting God:

Did you catch the difference there? In the King James version, God is way down at the end of the phrase. In the other... versions, God is at the beginning. It is partly a question of text and partly a question of grammar. There is nothing wrong with the traditional versions, but the modern translations bring out a proper emphasis.... We will never properly understand this verse as long as we put God at the end and not at the beginning.... In reality, God is there at the beginning and He is there at the end and He is at every point in between (Romans 8:28). Romans 8:28 is the New Testament equivalent of Joseph's great affirmation of God's sovereignty.... His overruling providence and His everlasting, immutable faithfulness, when he declared to his brothers (who had attempted to kill him)... 'And as for you, you meant evil against me, but God meant it for good in order to bring about this present result, to preserve many people alive' (Gen. 50:20).[2]

We are now going to take Romans 8:28 apart and examine each of its primary phrases by using the wisdom contained in Bible commentaries going back to the 18th century, beginning with commentary writer James Denny's passage on "we know":

The words 'we know' are used about thirty times as the expression of the common knowledge of the saints of God as such.... We know Romans 8:28-30 is true because we know God and He has said it. His word is trustworthy and that guarantees His promise. Indeed, His character rests upon it. We know because we know Him. We know not by looking at the events of our lives but by knowing our God. There are so many things we don't know. We don't know why babies die or why cars wreck or why planes crash or why families break up or why good people get sick and suddenly die. But this we know – God is at work and He has not forgotten us…. The comforting truth of Romans 8:28 is based especially on God's sovereignty. If all things work together for good (all events, all circumstances, all trials, all happenings, etc.), then it follows that God must be over all things and must control all things. This is not fearful fatalism and determinism. This is the wonderful fact that an all-wise, all-loving, just God is in complete control of all things! [3]

The Christian's heart cry when they go through tragedy, trauma, and testing remains: What does the phrase "all things" really mean? John MacArthur writes that

<u>All things</u> is utterly comprehensive, having no qualifications or limits. Neither this verse nor its context allows for restrictions or conditions. <u>All things</u> is inclusive in the fullest possible sense. Nothing existing or occurring in heaven or on earth 'shall be able to separate us from the love of God, which is in Christ Jesus' (Rom. 8:39). Paul is not saying that God prevents His children from experiencing <u>things</u> that can harm them. He is rather attesting that the Lord takes all that He allows to happen to His beloved children, even the worst things, and turns those things ultimately into blessings…. No matter what our situation, our suffering, our persecution, our sinful failure, our pain, our lack of faith in those things, as well as in <u>all</u> other <u>things</u>, our heavenly Father will work to produce our ultimate victory and blessing. The corollary of that truth is that nothing can ultimately work against us.[4]

As we continue to pursue this path of understanding to Romans 8:28, we examine the phrase "work together." MacArthur adds that

<u>sunergeo</u> (is the Greek word) from which is derived the English term <u>synergism</u>, the working together of various elements to produce an effect greater than, and often completely different from, the sum of each element acting separately…. Contrary to what the King James rendering seems to suggest, it is not that things in themselves work together to produce good. As Paul has made clear earlier in the verse, it is God's providential power and will, not a natural synergism of circumstances and events in our lives that causes them to work together for good… No matter what happens in our lives as His children, the providence of God uses it for our temporal as well as our eternal benefit, sometimes by saving us from tragedies and sometimes by sending us through them in order to draw us closer to Him…. God uses the evil of sin as a means of bringing good to His children. That would have to be true if Paul's statement about 'all things' is taken at face value. Even more than suffering and temptation, sin is not good in itself…. Yet,

in God's infinite wisdom and power, it is most remarkable of all that He turns sin to our good. The Lord uses sin to bring good to His children by overruling it, canceling its normal evil consequences and miraculously substituting His benefits....[5]

Now we come down to where the rubber meets the road. How is the word "good" used in Romans 8:28? Ray Pritchard explains '**good**' by asking the poignant questions that most, if not all, Christians will have during their walks with the Lord:

Is Paul saying, 'Whatever happens is good?' No. Is he saying that suffering and evil and tragedy are good? No. Is he saying everything will work out if we just have enough faith? No. Is he saying that we will be able to understand why God allowed tragedy to come? No. What, then, is he saying? He is erecting a sign over the unexplainable mysteries of life – a sign that reads 'Quiet. God at work.' How? We're not always sure. To what end? Good and not evil. That's what Romans 8:28 is saying.... Our danger is that we will judge the end by the beginning. Or, to be more exact, that we will judge what we cannot see by what we can see. That is, when tragedy strikes, if we can't see a purpose, we assume there isn't one.... God has predestined you and me to a certain end. That certain end is the '<u>good</u>' of Romans 8:28. That certain end is that we might be conformed to the likeness of Jesus Christ... <u>God is not committed to making you healthy, wealthy and wise.</u> He is committed to making you like His Son, the Lord Jesus Christ. And whatever it takes to make you more like Jesus is <u>good</u>... Paul emphasizes that in all of the ups and downs in the believer's life there is an overarching, albeit not always obvious, eternal purpose for good which God is always providentially orchestrating behind the scenes (emphasis added).[6]

The next phrase that bears examining is "them (or those) that (who) love God." To whom is this phrase referring? C. H. Spurgeon has the following explanation:

In regard to 'them that love God'... there are many things in which the worldly and the godly do agree, but on this point there is a vital difference. No ungodly man loves God in the Bible sense of the term. An unconverted man may love a God, as, for instance, the God of nature, and the God of the imagination, but the God of revelation no man can love, unless grace turn him from his natural enmity towards God. And there may be many differences between godly men; they may belong to different sects, hold very opposite opinions, but all agree in this, that they love God: (1) As their Father, they have 'the Spirit of adoption, whereby they cry Abba Father;' (2) As their King, they are willing to obey Him; (3) As their Portion, for God is their all; and (4) As their future inheritance. Note the association of love for God and obedience to Him. Jesus reiterates this important association declaring that... 'He who has My commandments and keeps them, he it is who loves Me; and he who loves Me shall be loved by My Father, and I will love him, and will disclose Myself to him.' (John 14:21).[7]

⌘

At this point, it's important to recap where we've come from and where we're going. When you have worked or are working on forgiving those who abused you, you are being completely obedient to the Lord. You are showing your love for Jesus by keeping His commandments. This is the key to appropriating Romans 8:28. We don't simply believe in God; we love Him and show that by being obedient. This is not a work that earns us salvation... but a natural result of loving God and living His way.

⌘

As we conclude our study of Romans 8:28, we want to know what Paul means when he uses the term "called according to His purposes." John MacArthur has a helpful note explaining that

The call spoken of... is sometimes referred to as the 'general call' (or the 'external' call) – a summons to repentance and faith that is inherent in the gospel message. This call extends to all who hear the gospel. 'Many' hear it; 'few' respond... Those who respond are the 'chosen,' the elect. In the Pauline writings, the word 'call' usually refers to God's irresistible calling extended to the elect alone (Rom. 8:30-note) – known as the 'effectual call' (or the 'internal' call). The effectual call is the supernatural drawing of God which Jesus speaks of in John 6:44.... The 'chosen' enter the kingdom only because of the grace of God in choosing and drawing them.[8]

Finally, we will see what is meant by God's "purpose," according to the Bible commentaries:

Job learned through much trial the truth about God and testified... 'I know that Thou canst do all things, and that no purpose of Thine can be thwarted (or stopped).' (Job 42:2).... Purpose (4286) (prothesis [word study] from pró = before, forth + títhemi = place) means to plan in advance and comes to mean that which is planned or purposed in advance. Purpose means an intelligent decision, which the will is bent to accomplish. God has two purposes, our good and His glory and ultimately, He will make us like Jesus Christ! Furthermore, His purpose is certain to succeed! And it is well that we remember that the purposes of God are the most important reality in one's spiritual life. God's purpose is to make His children like His Son, and He will succeed....

Professor E. C. Caldwell ended his lecture, 'Tomorrow,' he said to his class of seminary students, 'I will be teaching on Romans 8. So tonight, as you study, pay special attention to verse 28. Notice what this verse truly says, and what it doesn't say.' Then he added, 'One final word before I dismiss you – whatever happens in all the years to come, remember: Romans 8:28 will always hold true.' That same day, Dr. Caldwell and his wife met with a tragic car-train accident. She was killed instantly, and he was crippled permanently. Months later, Professor Caldwell returned to his students, who clearly remembered his last words. The room was hushed as he began his lecture. 'Romans 8:28,' he said, 'still holds true. One day we shall see God's good, even in this.' [9]

Unless you specifically undertake a Bible study on the subject or your pastor ever teaches on Romans 8:28 in this way, this chapter contains one of the most detailed expositions of this verse that you will come across. This has been necessary to connect your obedience in forgiving abuse to the process of coming to trust the Lord.

It is readily apparent to me how the Lord has used all the tests and trials of my life to fulfill this undeniable tenet of Scripture. Early on as I began to counsel people, I realized that the Lord was going to bring good out of the abuse I had endured to help others, not from any position of superiority, but as one who had been there. It got to the point that there wasn't any issue a client or student could present that I could not relate to in the least or that the Lord hadn't helped me walk through at one time or another. The "good" that came out of my childhood abuse is explained quite clearly in 2 Corinthians 1:3-5:

Blessed be the God and Father of our Lord Jesus Christ, the Father of mercies and God of all comfort, who comforts us in all our tribulation, that we may be able to comfort those who are in any trouble, with the comfort with which we ourselves are comforted by God. For as the sufferings of Christ abound in us, so our consolation also abounds through Christ.

As we proceed in our journey, we have come to a "watershed moment." The following chapter's title, *What Does Trust in God Look Like?*, was a therapeutic expression that I only recently incorporated in my coaching practice – i.e. what does _____ look like? I suppose it still feels a little foreign on my tongue, as I haven't used it many times when working with clients. However, it's really an excellent question, as most abuse survivors really have no idea what constitutes trusting God. When I gave a bit of my own story in the Introduction, I alluded to how stymied I was when trying to understand trust in God. I understood the phrase intellectually but hadn't the faintest idea what trusting God was experientially speaking. I remember the day I actually looked up the word 'trust' in the dictionary and purchased my first book about trusting God, because I just couldn't internalize the concept. Let's move forward to see what trusting God actually does look like.

Jesus appears to be holding out His hand to us even as He calls us. He tells us He will provide a bridge over the chasm if we will abide in Him. We hear His words, but such language is strange to us, sounding like the dialects of many who have used us or consumed us and then left us along the highway, exposed and alone. We pull back. Many of us return to Vanity Fair and mortgage our heart to purchase more of what is religiously or materially familiar. A few of us arouse our spirit and take a step toward the chasm. – Brent Curtis

God is doing a greater work in us, and that can only come as we learn to trust Him no matter how dark the days and sleepless the nights. And it is only as we have been through the darkness with Him that what we know with our heads slides down into our hearts, and our hearts no longer demand answers. The why becomes unimportant when we believe that God can and will redeem the pain for our good and His glory…. When I put the sovereignty of God beside His unfailing love, my heart can rest. – Verdell Davis

While the Lord calls me to be wise and discerning, He reminds me often that His discernment cannot dwell in a cynical, distrustful heart. With Him, there is no hidden agenda and no ulterior motive. His gifts are free for the taking, but I cannot take these gifts if my hands are already full of my own weapons of self-protection. Therefore, He asks me to lay down the shields that I have forged for protection and to pick up the shield of faith in their place. He asks me to take Him at His Word. – Katherine Walden

When a train goes through a tunnel and it gets dark, you don't throw away the ticket and jump off. You sit still and trust the engineer. – Corrie Ten Boom

True faith is trusting the sovereign God even when we don't understand. – Hank Haanegraff

Prayer is an act of faith. Just by praying to God, you are declaring your trust in Someone other than yourself. Your faith is increased as you pray and watch how God answers your prayers. God says in Jeremiah 33:3, 'Call to Me and I will answer you, and I will show you great and mighty things, which you do not know.' God is awesome in power, and there is never a time when He is not beside you. He is faithful and holy – Charles Stanley

Calmness is the way we show that we are trusting in God. – Author unknown pointless.

Job losses, cancer, stock market crash, car problems, stress… seems like there's always a long list of things that have gone wrong or things we don't like. Our first reaction when something goes wrong is to worry and be afraid. We think things aren't going to work out. We don't believe God will do what He says, so we freak out. Trusting God shouldn't be difficult, but for some reason, it's a tough thing to do. There's a really good sign that says 'I will handle all your problems today, God.' If we can stop our own fears and worries and let God take care of things, He will work things out. – Sally Knitter

Chapter Eleven

What Does Trust in God Look Like?

Since you have read this far, you know that a dictionary definition of each term of significance precedes any discussion of that term... well, nothing has changed! The following definition of the word "trust" is from *The American Heritage® Dictionary of the English Language*:

Trust (trŭst) n. 1. Firm reliance on the integrity, ability, or character of a person or thing. 2. Custody; care. 3. Something committed into the care of another; charge. 4. a. The condition and resulting obligation of having confidence placed in one: **violated a public trust.** *b. One in which confidence is placed. 5. Reliance on something in the future; hope. 6. Reliance on the intention and ability of a purchaser to pay in the future; credit. 7. Law a. A legal title to property held by one party for the benefit of another. b. The confidence reposed in a trustee when giving the trustee legal title to property to administer for another, together with the trustee's obligation regarding that property and the beneficiary. c. The property so held. 8. A combination of firms or corporations for the purpose of reducing competition and controlling prices throughout a business or an industry. trust·ed, trust·ing, trusts. v.intr. 1. To have or place reliance; depend:* **Trust in the Lord. Trust to destiny.** *2. To be confident; hope. 3. To sell on credit. v.tr. 1. To have or place confidence in; depend on. 2. To expect with assurance; assume:* **I trust that you will be on time.** *3. To believe:* **I trust what you say.** *4. To place in the care of another; entrust. 5. To grant discretion to confidently:* **Can I trust them with the boat?** *6. To extend credit to.*

[Middle English truste, *perhaps from Old Norse traust, confidence; see deru- in Indo-European roots.] trust'er n. Synonyms: trust, faith, confidence, reliance, dependence. These nouns denote a feeling of certainty that a person or thing will not fail.* Trust *implies depth and assurance of feeling that is often based on inconclusive evidence:* 'The mayor vowed to justify the trust the electorate had placed in him.' Faith *connotes unquestioning, often emotionally charged belief:* 'Often enough our faith beforehand

in an uncertified result is the only thing that makes the result come true' (William James). *Confidence frequently implies stronger grounds for assurance:* 'Confidence is a plant of slow growth in an aged bosom: youth is the season of credulity' (William Pitt). *Reliance connotes a confident and trustful commitment to another:* 'What reliance could they place on the protection of a prince so recently their enemy?' (William Hickling Prescott). *Dependence suggests reliance on another to whom one is often subordinate:* 'When I had once called him in, I could not subsist without dependence on him.'

It is relevant to take note of the different words for "trust" in Hebrew. These definitions come from Jeff Benner's article, "Biblical Word of the Month – Trust," found on his *Biblical Hebrew E-Magazine.*[1]

חסה *(chasah, Strong's #2620)*
Psalm 18:2. The LORD [is] my rock, and my fortress, and my deliverer; my God, my strength, in whom I will trust *(KJV). This word has the meaning of 'to lean on someone or something.' If you are hiking with a group of your friends and you sprain your ankle, you are going to lean on one of your companions to help you out of the wilderness. God is the One that we lean on when things get tough. We can also lean on our friends and family for support as well.*

בטח *(betach, Strong's #982)*
Psalm 56:4. In God I will praise His word, in God I have put my trust*; I will not fear what flesh can do unto me (KJV). This word has the more concrete meaning of 'to cling.' A related word, avatiyach (#20), is a melon that clings to the vine. Even though the melon is huge, just as our problems seem to be, the vine is very small. We may not see God, but He is our strength, the One who nourishes us just as the vine nourishes the melon.*

יחל *(yachal, Strong's #3176)*
Isaiah 51:5. My righteousness [is] near; My salvation is gone forth, and Mine arms shall judge the people; the isles shall wait upon Me, and on Mine arm shall they trust *(KJV). This word is usually translated as hope but it does not mean to wonder if something will happen and 'hope' it does, but to 'know' that something will happen in the future. We do not hope that God will protect us; we 'know' He will. In the above passage, the concrete image of holding onto God's arm for support can be seen, but the word arm (zeroah) is a Hebraic euphemism (using one word to mean something else) for 'strength.' This passage is saying that the people will know that God's strength will save them.*

אָמַן *(aman, Strong's #539)*

Psalm 78:22. Because they believed not in God, and <u>trusted</u> not in His salvation… (KJV). The word aman means to 'be firm.' When setting up a tent, you always choose 'firm' soil to drive in your tent pegs so that when the wind blows, the tent pegs will not be pulled out of the ground collapsing your tent (see Isaiah 22:23 where the word aman is translated as 'sure'). This word is the verb form of the word 'amen.' When we say 'amen,' we are literally saying I stand firm on this prayer.[1]

<u>That's all fine and well</u>, you say, *but what <u>does trusting God actually look like?</u> <u>Enough with the definitions, already. This isn't helping in any tangible way!</u>* You're absolutely right… definitions only appeal to your intellect and haven't yet traveled the so-called 18 inches down to your heart. I really get that. That was my struggle for many years and an issue with which my clients and I grapple regularly. You also may be laboring with the problem described by Deborah Kern in her excellent new book, *Learning to Trust God*:

You may have always believed 'all things work together for good' and other Scriptures that help us to trust, but at this moment the pain of your circumstances is overwhelming any past knowledge of God's goodness. You may be struggling with unanswered questions, anger and bitterness. Give God an opening by saying, 'God, I want to trust You and feel close again, but I just can't Please. Help me.' Allow God to bring peace and healing back into your wounded soul.[2]

There was an exercise used regularly in what once were known as "Sensitivity Groups." Sensitivity Training (or T-groups as they were called in Europe) and Encounter Groups were big in the '70's. My father, a high-level manager in the aerospace industry, was actually forced to participate in this training by his company. It was the closest thing he had to any kind of counseling at the time. It was on-site group therapy – the goal was to make people more aware of each other and the effect their words and actions had on others. Initially, he would come home and regale us with humorous examples of required activities. After a while, he got very serious, almost down, about the group and didn't discuss it at the dinner table anymore. The exercises were definitely getting to him. I cannot remember him ever referring to the "trust exercise."

A caricature of the "trust exercise" can be seen in a recent "Geico gecko" commercial, in which the boss (a gigantic being compared to the gecko) wants to turn around and fall into the gecko's arms. The gecko says in his Australian accent, "Oh, dear!" The observer knows that the gecko will be flat as a pancake in seconds. On a 1980's television series, *One Day at a Time*, during the opening credits/theme song, a trust exercise scenario was shown each week. One of the female co-stars was supposed to be falling into the slick/heart-of-gold handyman's arms, but he didn't catch her – and of course, she fell backwards on to the floor! Although this was a humorous element of the sitcom, it also was a real exercise used for years in therapy circles to test a client's ability to trust his fellow group members.

It's safe to say that almost everyone demonstrates trust daily as s/he goes about his or her routines in life. Who consciously worries that when they sit in a chair it will collapse under them? An old chair at my Grandfather's house actually **did** collapse when my brother went to sit in it, so he wouldn't think this was too funny... actually, no, he has a terrific sense of humor and has sat on chairs hundreds of times since then with no trust issues! When most people walk through the doors of their home, they don't think the roof is going to cave in on them. Of course, that also happens sometimes, but it is extremely rare, and something we don't give much mental airtime to.

We depend on the laws of gravity every day and rarely contemplate what would happen if they just ceased altogether. When we go to sit down in our cars and shut the doors, we don't expect them to come crashing off the car in our hands. The list goes on and on.

Yet when it comes to trusting our Creator... the One who flung billions of galaxies into space, we get somewhat queasy and simply can't rely on Him, because we were abused at the hands of those we trusted. Our distorted images of God (covered in Chapter Seven) also contribute in a significant way to our inability to trust the Lord. In many cases, we made silent, inner, conscious, or unconscious vows never to trust any authority figures again and/or that the only one we could depend on to take care of us was ourselves. I now know that I made both those vows unconsciously as I was growing up. The inner vows interfere in our interactions with teachers, bosses, law enforcement officers, pastors, etc. in a huge way. They will convince us that we have to fill those aching, painful voids ourselves – meet our own needs – leading to multiple obsessions and addictions.

James Blanchard Cisneros has given us this excellent "word picture" about trust vs. mistrust:

Why is it that we have more faith that the pieces of a puzzle made by a company in Taiwan will all fit together than we have that the pieces of our life that are presented to us by God will fit together? One person chooses to put like pieces together first, while another chooses to put the edges of the puzzle together first, but neither individual ever really doubts that the puzzle will somehow fit perfectly. The edges in and of themselves probably have little to do with the main image or idea of the puzzle, yet without them, the puzzle is incomplete. In the beginning, some pieces, even when they fit perfectly together, might not help you to understand what the puzzle is about; only in its completion can you appreciate the parts that at first seemed insignificant and pointless.[3]

What does trust in God look like? Trust looks like the cover of this book.

Whenever I see toddlers fast asleep in their fathers' arms, I think of trust. All kinds of chaotic, even traumatic, things can be happening all around these children, but they know their daddies will take care of everything. When fathers throw their toddlers into the air and catch them, then the children giggle and want "more" or "again" – this is a picture of trust.

Even as we have been examining why people who were abused as children can't trust, we can look to other children as our example for trust. When one is growing up in a reasonably healthy family, their very first stage of development (according to Erik Erikson's child development theory) is "trust vs. mistrust." When babies cry, they're attended to and their needs are met in a reasonable fashion, according to the theory they will develop trust. However, if anything disturbs that process, and the infants' needs aren't met, they begin to see the world as a threatening, definitely unsafe, place. In an article entitled, "The Developmental Stages of Erik Erikson," Arlene F. Harder describes the first stage of development:

> **Stage One, Infancy: Birth to 18 Months – Ego Development; Outcome: <u>Trust vs. Mistrust</u>; Basic Strength: Drive and Hope.** *Erikson also referred to infancy as the Oral Sensory Stage (as anyone might who watches a baby put everything in her mouth) where the major emphasis is on the mother's positive and loving care for the child, with a big emphasis on visual contact and touch. If we pass successfully through this period of life, we will learn to trust that life is basically okay and have basic confidence in the future. If we fail to experience trust and are constantly frustrated because our needs are not met, we may end up with a deep-seated feeling of worthlessness and a mistrust of the world in general. Incidentally, many studies of suicides and suicide attempts point to the importance of the early years in developing the basic belief that the world is trustworthy and that every individual has a right to be here. Not surprisingly, the most significant relationship is with the maternal parent, or whoever is our most significant and constant caregiver.*[4]

I have been told stories by both my parents as to what I was like as an infant and toddler. My mom has often told me that when she would go to church and leave me in the nursery, I absolutely would not stop crying until she came to pick me up at the end of a service (separation anxiety with a capital "S"). In those days, there were no screens in which a number for your child could be surreptitiously flashed a couple of times during a service to let you know he/she was in distress (or the nursery teacher was about out of her mind!).

The services were generally an hour long, and I would cry the entire hour. Obviously the caregivers weren't doing anything to me, but I would not be comforted until my mommy showed up and made the world right again. In addition, when she and my father were going out for the evening, I would cling to her skirt and make it difficult for her to leave. My apologies, Mom! I also displayed a tremendous level of stranger anxiety and would try to hide underneath her skirts when around someone I didn't know. However, I knew that my Mom met those early needs very well. So why was I so distrustful? Enter Dad.

Only a few years ago, my father told me that the reason he didn't pick me up and cuddle me as an infant was that I would scream whenever he came near me. That made my therapist mind suspicious and threw it into overdrive! What was going on that I would react to him that way? I've never gotten an answer to that question, but when I told Mom, she laughed ruefully and said that that was just an excuse of his for being a distant parent. One thing I do know for sure... I have very few memories of my dad being physically demonstrative in showing me affection. I strongly believe that I was afraid of him, on some level, most of my life. I refer you once again to Appendix B for my story of abuse/healing/forgiveness.

Jesus informed us that it was only as we became childlike (not childish) that we would enter the Kingdom of heaven: "Assuredly, I say to you, whoever does not receive the kingdom of God as a **little child** will by no means enter it "(Mark 10:15 and Luke 18:17).

It only makes sense that however trusting and secure you were as a child would have a profound impact on the way you respond to God as an adult. I'm so grateful to the Lord that *it doesn't have to stay that way,* as we are about to learn.

We come, in our trust, unto God, and the moment we so embrace Him, by committing our total being and eternity to Him, we find everything is transformed. There is life in us from God. – Horace Bushnell

I realize anew that, just as we must learn to obey God one choice at a time, we must also learn to trust God one circumstance at a time. Trusting God is not a matter of my feelings but of my will. I never feel like trusting God when adversity strikes, but I can choose to do so even when I don't feel like it. That act of the will, though, must be based on belief, and belief must be based on truth. – Jerry Bridges

Though He slay me, yet will I trust Him. – Job 13:15

Your level of trust is directly related to how well you know God and His Word. To trust God, you must know Him; and if you truly know Him, you will trust Him. You'll trust Him because He is totally trustworthy. In order to accomplish change in your life, you need to retrain your mind to think according to God's patterns. You must know and believe what His Word says about Him. – Dr. Ed Delph

All thought, cleverness, knowledge, talent and gift – which the world superstitiously worships – must be set aside in order to enable one to trust the Lord wholly. – Watchman Nee

Assurance grows by repeated conflict, by our repeated experimental proof of the Lord's power and goodness to save; when we have been brought very low and helped, sorely wounded and healed, cast down and raised again, have given up all hope and been suddenly snatched from danger and placed in safety; and when these things have been repeated to us and in us a thousand times over, we begin to learn to trust simply by the Word and power of God, beyond and against appearances: and this trust, when habitual and strong, bears the name of assurance; for even assurance has degrees. – John Newton

Faith is a reasoning trust, a trust that reckons thoughtfully and confidently upon the trustworthiness of God. – John Stott

Learning to trust God seems to require learning to stop relying on yourself so much. It means radical change at our core. Most of us don't like change of any kind, much less surgery on our core self. Surgery hurts; it incapacitates and can even make us howl with pain. God, the divine Surgeon, is worth trusting. He loves us more than we can know. His wounding seems grievous, but it restores us to wholeness. If you find yourself under His knife, be still and learn to trust Him. You *will* laugh again. – Seth Barnes

Trust God or worry. Those are the two choices you have in every situation. Trust God and be at peace. Worry and experience stress. Your choices are that simple, and you will make your life as peaceful or stressful as you choose to make it. Trust God and be at peace. This is all that is asked of you. – James Cisneros

Chapter Twelve

Learning to Trust God

Is trusting God something you actually can learn to do? Absolutely! The point that must be reiterated is that the Lord does not ask us to do something that is impossible. He gives us the grace to carry out whatever it is He asks of us.

One of the most common issues I have dealt with over the years with Christian clients is the so-called "18 inches between the head and heart." **It is so very frustrating to know intellectually that God loves you with an everlasting love and not be able to feel it in the least.** I am not advocating that our walk with the Lord be based on feelings, but down through the centuries there had to be more than just intellectual awareness of His magnificence, glory, and infinite love for people to be willing to be martyred for Jesus' sake!

A believer can have studied theology, memorized Scripture, prayed unceasingly, attended church faithfully, even fasted and prayed – and not have any inner sense of intimacy with God. One can know all the Lord's character traits – His Omnipotence, Omnipresence, Omniscience, Sovereignty, Immutability, Holiness, Truth, Love, Righteousness, Purity, etc., etc. – and still not really know Him. However, if you're reading this book and have gotten this far, I am **certain** that you know and love the Lord. Yet for all the reasons we have been learning about, including: (1) how abuse results in distorted ideas about God; (2) how trauma can leave someone emotionally numb; (3) how child abuse breaks its victims' hearts and spirits; (4) how victims feel abandoned and betrayed by the Lord, and so on, trusting God can seem like a daunting, if not downright impossible, undertaking.

Is there any way that instructions on trusting the Lord could be given and followed successfully? The answer is a resounding "yes" when abuse survivors want to go on in their spiritual journeys, pressing toward intimacy with God Himself! He wants that with us **even more than we do.** At the risk of sounding sacrilegious, my experience in this area has led me to think of trusting God as a skill one can master over a lifetime — a muscle, as it were, which can be worked and strengthened until it is working at maximum capacity.

A concrete example would be helpful here. Adult children of an alcoholic parent(s), called ACAs in recovery circles, are notorious for either being: (1) completely mistrusting of others and unwilling to confide anything of a personal nature to another person; or (2) inappropriately, and without boundaries, trusting of complete strangers, willing to confide all their deep, dark secrets to anyone in one sitting. That's why people who don't seek professional counseling often have been known to tell "everything" to bartenders, hairstylists, or barbers! ACAs find themselves, as far as the trust scale, on these two extremes. They can even vacillate between the two, confusing themselves and others.

What is the standard counsel given to ACAs concerning trust? That they take relationships slowly. They need to start by sharing one bit of harmless information about themselves (harmless in that if the other person leaked this information no harm would be done). Depending on how the "candidate" for trust responds to this information, e.g., they are interested and want to know more, ignore the confidence and only talk about themselves, or run out and tell the first person they meet, the ACA can determine if it is wise, safe, and desirable to go forward and confide something else about themselves. If the response they receive is favorable, then they are instructed to share something just a little more personal about themselves and, once again, evaluate the potential friend's response. If, once again, the way this potential new friend acts is positive, the ACA can go a bit further. This process can continue until an intimate relationship has developed.

To follow up on that analogy, the way that trust is built with God operates according to the same principle (although His perfection and ultimate trustworthiness makes it a very rough comparison). You can come to know peoples' character by how they respond in numerous situations over a certain length of time. Similarly, as we trust the Lord with a seemingly small thing and find Him trustworthy, we trust Him with something of more import. We are not testing the Lord; rather He is revealing His character with each incidence of our attempt to trust Him. He doesn't get angry with us, for He knows the immense amount of pain we are dealing with, specifically, and the frailty of human beings, in general.

The late Ruth Graham, widely loved and admired by the Body of Christ, described the learning to trust God process in an eloquent way:

We would take a step or two, then another. All of our senses would be awake. We were listening, looking, feeling for the slightest hint of a break in that ice. And thick ice does groan and creak, although those sounds don't necessarily mean it will break. We would take those first steps, wondering if the ice would hold. After a few more steps, we would become more confident and take several more, maybe in quick succession this time. The more the ice proved solid, the wider our steps would fan out and the bigger our skating area would become. I have discovered that walking with God works this way. Each time you venture a step with God and find Him to be trustworthy, you become more willing to take another step. Then another. As He secures your steps, it becomes easier to commit. Pretty soon, you realize you're on the journey. You're discovering God's trustworthi-

ness. You're living with Him in relationship.... It takes willingness to walk forward and discover God, but to grow in relationship with Him will require something more – that we trust His direction and step out. Taking the first baby steps out on the ice is one thing. But we want to get across the pond. We do that step by step. As we understand God's direction, we act on what we've discovered. We engage what we've learned.[1]

An Australian Internet blogger, from the Anglican Media Sydney, has given us some very practical ways to learn how to trust the Lord:

The Bible often emphasizes how God can be trusted in a way that human beings can't. That doesn't mean it will necessarily be easy for us to trust God, but it does mean that we should try not to allow human failings to rob us of the comfort of God's dependability. Sometimes we need to pray, like the man in Mark's gospel who was let down by Jesus' disciples and so struggled to trust Jesus Himself: 'I believe; help my unbelief!' Learning to trust God comes by getting to know His trustworthy character and track record of faithfulness to His promises. So it helps to read from the Bible regularly and to look for reasons to trust God. Read through one of the four gospels, for example, and notice how the writers often quote from the Old Testament to show that God's promises are being fulfilled in Jesus. Or read Exodus or Joshua in the Old Testament, and notice how God keeps His promises and rewards His people's trust. In the Psalms, the writers are often calling on God to help them because God has helped them in the past.[2]

Let's review what we know about trusting God. We need to simply look at our lives and observe how many things we already trust. We need to observe little children and see how it is they trust their parent(s) so much when they're not being abused. We need to trust God with something little and observe His trustworthiness. After that, we need to trust God in another situation and observe how He answers, and so on. We need to become very familiar with His Word, so we can learn about His magnificent character.

We need to get to know all we can about God's sovereignty and goodness, mankind's utter depravity, and the enemy of our souls. Why? So we can learn to discern what is going on in our circumstances that can't be seen by the naked eye, so to speak (i.e., we need to become very familiar with Romans 8:28 and know what it is and isn't saying – see Chapter Eight for a refresher).

We need to talk with God – notice the word "with." Many talk to Him, or even at Him, listing all their requests and then when finished just go on to another activity. Like any other relationship, we need to **listen** as well as **speak.** We can hear His voice and not lose our minds (a common fear)! We find assurance of our ability to hear the Lord in the Word of God: *For He is our God, and we are the people of His pasture, and the sheep of His hand; Today, if you will hear His voice...*

(Psalm 95:7); To Him the doorkeeper opens, and the sheep hear His voice; and He calls His own sheep by name and leads them out (John 10:3); And they will hear My voice; and there will be one flock and one shepherd (John 10:16); and My sheep hear My voice, and I know them, and they follow Me (John 10:27).

We need to know the promises of God and believe that He will "make good on them." **We need to know that He isn't mad at us and won't reject us, as the following Scripture verses demonstrate (<u>rejection</u> is usually up there in the top five fears of those who have undergone abuse):**

1. *... to the praise of the glory of His grace, by which He made us accepted in the Beloved (Ephesians 1:6).*

2. *All that the Father gives Me will come to Me, and the one who comes to Me I will by no means cast out (John 6:37).*

3. *Are not two sparrows sold for a copper coin? And not one of them falls to the ground apart from your Father's will (Matthew 10:29).*

4. *Then He said to them, "What man is there among you who has one sheep, and if it falls into a pit on the Sabbath, will not lay hold of it and lift it out? (Matthew 12:11).*

5. *What do you think? If a man has a hundred sheep, and one of them goes astray, does he not leave the ninety-nine and go to the mountains to seek the one that is straying? (Matthew 18:12).*

6. *And I give them eternal life, and they shall never perish; neither shall anyone snatch them out of My hand (John 10:28).*

These verses show such **tenderness** on the Lord's part. One other special verse for those who have been victimized and are having difficulty trusting God is, **"A bruised reed He will not break and a smoking flax He will not quench"** (Isaiah 42:3). Our most feeble steps toward Him bring joy to His heart, and He will never be critical, squashing our attempts like so many bugs underfoot.

This may sound a bit clichéd, but when I am having trouble trusting God, I start to practice gratitude. I focus on the most basic things that I am thankful for (salvation in the Lord Jesus Christ, being able to have a Bible, my husband, other immediate family, some wonderful friends, a roof over my head, food in my belly, clothes to wear, transportation, a satisfying career, etc., etc. When I have been terribly depressed, I have even had to get down to the essentials such as eyes that see, ears that hear, legs that hold me up, hands that are typing this manuscript, etc. This I call "encouraging myself in the Lord" as did David in 1 Samuel 30:6. That was a colorful event in David's life. When he and his soldiers came back to Ziklag, found the town burned and the women and children gone, David was definitely in trouble. His "loyal" comrades-in-arms wanted to stone him. Yikes!

Another thing I like to do when I'm feeling low is to review all the times God has intervened on my behalf over the course of my life. The Lord frequently told the Israelites to make a memorial here, build an altar there, or write the vision down as soon as possible. Why? Because we're so quick to forget His marvelous works on our behalf. Our Creator knows that when we review these events, our faith is immediately strengthened!

I am inspired by what Tom Stewart has to say about trusting the Lord:

God alone is worthy of our trust. 'God is not a man, that He should lie; neither the son of man, that He should repent: hath He said, and shall He not do it? Or hath He spoken, and shall He not make it good?' (Numbers 23:19). The true believer does not ask why he should trust God; instead, he asks, 'How can I trust God more fully?' The Apostle Paul understood that his faith was strengthened, when he approached his divinely allowed 'necessities' as being for 'Christ's sake' (2 Corinthians 12:10). 'Therefore I take pleasure in infirmities, in reproaches, in necessities, in persecutions, in distresses for Christ's sake: for when I am weak, then am I strong.' This indicates that Paul knew that his necessities were actually opportunities to trust God.[3]

So what conclusions has Stewart drawn about trusting God that would differ from what many of us are being taught in the Church today?

Trusting God is akin to breathing for true Christians. 'For in Him we live, and move, and have our being' (Acts 17:28). The LORD Jesus Christ is worthy of our trust. 'Worthy is the Lamb that was slain to receive power, and riches, and wisdom, and strength, and honor, and glory, and blessing' (Revelation 5:12). If we would only combine the necessities of our circumstances with the Spirit-led discoveries of who God is and how He will fulfill our needs, then we would avail ourselves of the opportunity to trust Him more. If we can understand, by God's Spirit, what the Apostle Paul knew about the necessity of our 'infirmities,' then we would also 'glory' in the opportunities for His grace – i.e., His character and promises – to supply our every need. <u>This would only cause us to trust Him more.</u> 'And He said unto me, My grace is sufficient for thee: for My strength is made perfect in weakness. Most gladly therefore will I rather glory in my infirmities, that the power of Christ may rest upon me' (2 Corinthians 12:9, emphasis added).[4]

I often tell clients who are experiencing difficulty trusting the Lord that if He has taken care of them up to this point, and He changes not (is immutable), why would He just stop now? That makes sense to them as a reason to trust Him. One of my life verses is James 1:17, "Every good gift and every perfect gift is from above, and cometh down from the Father of lights, with whom is no variableness, neither shadow of turning" (KJV).

Why this verse? Because when everything around is changing constantly and things seem to be completely out of control, we abuse survivors can panic. This particular verse was special from the time I was in the eighth grade. I had been asked to read the Scripture passage for the morning church services. Hence, I stood in front of a good-sized congregation and read the passage of James that contains this verse, with shaking knees, dry mouth, and clammy palms.

Another reason this verse is so pertinent to abuse survivors is that many suffered with an abuser who was emotionally volatile and could change his or her mood or mind in seconds. **It is so wonderful to me that our Lord does not change and never will.** This attribute of God is called "immutability." The *King James Version Bible Dictionary* definite immutability as follows: "Refers to unchangeableness; the quality that renders change or alteration impossible; it also means invariableness."

Deborah Kern, in her practical and profound book, *Learning to Trust God*, gives the following reassurance to believers who are learning to trust the Lord in all things:

> *Our initial reactions to circumstances are not a measure of our ability to trust. God. It's how we deal with them. It's what we do with the emotions that threaten to engulf us. It's what we do with this impatience as time continues to drag on. It's what we do with our faltering hopes and shattered dreams. In all things, we must come to God. The attitude and emotions we initially bring with us are not important. It only matters that we trust Him enough to come to Him. When we do, God is able to help us. He will give us the ability to let go of the fear and the anger. He will help us pull our eyes away from the overwhelming circumstances and He will give us grace to keep going.[5]*

Kern has many meaningful things to say in her book. She makes the following very pointed assertion:

> *It is important to realize that you'll never be happy as a Christian until you learn to trust God. External circumstances will rule your life and your emotions. You'll never get past your own childish perception of things and you'll always hold back from submitting to God in all. The path you walk will be formed by outside circumstances and littered with the problems you will create. God's desire for our lives is that we have a secure and trusting relationship with Him. Accepting Christ as Savior is only the first step. From that point on, we gradually learn to trust in God. Each step progresses us further along.*

It's a process, and the steps involved are sometimes difficult, and sometimes long and labored, but always guided by our heavenly Father.[6]

In a very down-to-earth manner, Kern continues to describe the struggle that we have really trusting the Lord when we've just recently been wounded by someone close to us:

Oh, it is definitely hard to think of any good that can come when we are struggling with painful emotions, hurting and angry at people who have wronged us! Maybe as you are reading this, your insides are knotting up and your fist is unconsciously clenching.... This anger and bitterness has kept you from even wanting God to bring good from it. Somehow, that seems like giving in. Yet, at some point, you are going to have to make the choice to let go of the bitterness and lament and accept God's role in your circumstances. Healing for you may begin when you accept that God did allow it into your life and He does want to use it for good. No matter how bad it seems, God can redeem it. But He can only do that when you turn to Him in acquiescence to His sovereignty in your life.[7]

I love Deborah Kern's personal example of watching her daughter learn to jump into a swimming pool, forced to weigh her trust for her mother against the great fear of the unknown. Following is an excellent illustration of our struggle to trust the Lord:

We taught our children to swim at a very early age, and although our son Matthew took to the water like a little duck, Jula was more hesitant. Each step in the process of getting her 'waterproofed' seemed to be a major production, such as the day she learned to jump into the water. I can still picture her standing on the edge of the pool trying to get the courage to jump in...

Nervously, she hopped from one foot to the other her blond pigtails bouncing up and down as she would start to jump, then stop herself, over and over again.

Standing in the water, I held out my arms and tried to coax her, 'Come on Jula, jump! I'll catch you!'

She looked over at her brother, confidently jumping in all by himself, and then back at me standing in the water.

'Come on, honey!'

The expression on her face was easy to read as she wavered back and forth: Do I really want to do this? It looks like fun, but will she catch me? Will I go under? *Her instinctive fears of the unknown struggled with her desire to please me and do what her brother was doing.*

'You can do it!' I urged.

She crouched down again, her eyes growing big as she determined to really do it this time. She moved to jump and then tried to stop herself, but it was too late. Over the side she came, arms flailing and legs kicking. As I reached out and caught her, she grabbed me and held on tight.

'See? Wasn't that fun?' I asked. She laughed nervously and looked over to see if her brother had been watching. Gently, I bobbed up and down in the water with her and then walked around for a moment.

Then I sat her back up on the side of the pool and said, 'Let's do it again.' Her face fell and she started squirming and looking around. She didn't cry or say anything, but her reluctant expression still spoke volumes. What? Wasn't once enough?

But when she glanced over at Matthew, happily jumping in the water and crawling out to do it all over again, her expression changed again and she moved a second time to the edge. She started hopping up and down, just like before, trying to work up her courage. She was probably still thinking, Okay, so she caught me once, but will she catch me again?

She struggled with it while I persuaded, 'Come on Jula. I'm right here. It was fun, wasn't it?'

Finally, with one last peek at Matthew, another look of determination came across her face. She leaned forward and hurled herself into the water and into my waiting arms. Soon she was climbing out on her own and running over to the side to jump into my arms over and over, laughing excitedly and hugging me each time I caught her.

It's scary, isn't it, to throw ourselves into the unknown, to place our lives into another's care – to 'trust' someone? We instinctively hold back all or part of ourselves in those kinds of situations.

The Hebrew root word for 'trust' suggests 'to fling oneself off a precipice.' What a great word picture for our relationship with God! At times, it really does seem like we are flinging ourselves into the unknown, believing in a God who can't be seen or heard, choosing to embrace a belief that says God is good in spite of all the evil we see around us.[8]

Following is an amazing, faith-building story that clearly illustrates one of my client's challenges in trusting the Lord. Elena, as we'll call her, had an alcoholic father who walked out on her mother and abandoned her and her siblings. She was sexually abused by two different men. Her mother and sister (both of whom she was very close to) suffered horribly from terminal diseases and died while still young.

As is so typical with survivors, Elena married an emotionally unavailable man who was an alcoholic/addict. This man used to pour out such outrageous emotional abuse and deprivation on her and their children that I called him "my father times two." She hung in there for over 20 years with him, all the while hoping and praying he would change and become the husband she wanted and the father her children needed.

Because Elena had abandonment issues from her childhood, separation/divorce from her husband didn't seem like a viable option to her. As he got worse, she would take the children, leave, and find separate living quarters. However, she never wanted her kids to have to feel what she did, as far as the loss of a father, so she would invariably return to her husband and the cycle of abuse would begin all over again.

Elena most definitely suffered from battered woman's syndrome, though her husband never laid a hand on her (so like my father). He had beaten her down emotionally to the point that she simply could not see making it on her own. It was not until one night when her husband was drunk and raging (she described his face was downright demonic), that he finally hit their son. That's when he crossed the line; the police were called in, he was arrested, and Elena obtained a restraining order.

From the beginning of this separation, which ultimately culminated in divorce, Elena had financial problems. An intelligent and capable woman, she brought home a substantial paycheck. However, her husband's compulsive spending had ruined their credit and there was almost nothing held in reserve (for retirement, college for the kids, the proverbial rainy day, etc.). Between just the normal cost of living and paying exorbitant attorney fees (a result of her soon-to-be-ex husband wanting to punish her in divorce as he had in the marriage), there just was never enough money to be coming out "in the black."

As Elena's and my work progressed, she went from the survivor stage (just getting through every day was a challenge) to her life settling down into a somewhat predictable routine. Yet it didn't make any substantial difference that she and her husband were living in different homes, for they still needed to interact regarding their children. Since this was the case, her ex-husband then he took every single opportunity to demean, manipulate, reject, and frighten Elena.

Because of this continuing abuse, we began to concentrate on helping Elena to set boundaries with her husband and to trust God for His provision, though her financial status worried her daily. Although Elena had worked extremely hard at her company for over two decades, her reputation was damaged for the following reasons: (1) A strong "good ole boy" network existed that saw her as a threat, undermining her at every turn; and (2) The fact that her husband had worked there as long as she and had dragged both their names through the mud on many occasions.

Thus, when Elena applied for promotion to a higher position, her expectations were nearly nonexistent. Because the company advertised the position within and without, **somewhere in the neighborhood of 3,000 people applied for the position.** I guess the fact that the Lord does take care of His children makes the end of the story predictable, yet it was anything but while it was happening. Here she was in a financial crisis, and her current supervisor was taking his time about submitting her application – it ended up being submitted the last day applications for the position were being accepted.

You got it! **Elena was the employee selected out of those 3,000 people and hired for the position!** Only a sovereign Lord could see Elena's faithfulness all those years she was being abused. She loved Him and did everything she could to be the best wife, mother, daughter, sister, worker, and witness for Jesus possible. Somewhere, deep in my spirit, I knew she was going to get the job. Therefore, my encouragement all along was for her to trust the Lord, that He would never fail in taking care of her and her children. **This has to be the most dramatic vindication by the Lord I've ever seen. My level of faith shot through the roof as I witnessed God's direct intervention on Elena's behalf!**

In learning to trust God, those of us who have ever had fears of abandonment need to meditate on a few relevant Bible verses:

Be strong and of good courage, do not fear nor be afraid of them; for the LORD your God, He is the One who goes with you. He will not leave you nor <u>forsake</u> you (Deut. 31:6).

And David said to his son Solomon, "Be strong and of good courage, and do it; do not fear nor be dismayed, for the LORD God—my God—will be with you. He will not leave you nor <u>forsake</u> you (1 Chron. 28:20).

For we were slaves. Yet our God did not <u>forsake</u> us in our bondage, but He extended mercy to us in the sight of the kings of Persia, to revive us, to repair the house of our God, to rebuild its ruins, and to give us a wall in Judah and Jerusalem (Ezra 9:9).

For the LORD loves justice, and does not <u>forsake</u> His saints; they are preserved forever, but the descendants of the wicked shall be cut off (Psalm 37:28).

I will bring the blind by a way they did not know; I will lead them in paths they have not known. I will make darkness light before them, and crooked places straight. These things I will do for them, and not <u>forsake</u> them (Isaiah 42:16).

When my father and my mother <u>forsake</u> me, then the LORD will take care of me (Psalm 27:10).

He [God] Himself has said, I will not in any way fail you nor give you up nor <u>leave</u> you without support. [I will] not, [I will] not, [I will] not in any degree <u>leave</u> you helpless nor <u>forsake</u> nor let [you] down (relax My hold on you)! [Assuredly not!] (Hebrews 13:5, Amplified Bible).

... and behold, I am with you <u>all the days</u> (perpetually, uniformly, and on every occasion), to the [very] close and consummation of the age (Matthew 28:20, Amplified Bible).

Are you assured that the Lord will never leave or forsake you – that He will be with you all the days of your life? If not, read, re-read, and try to memorize those verses until they become part of you. I love the following poem and quote:

> *Trust Him when dark doubts assail thee,*
> *Trust Him when thy strength is small,*
> *Trust Him when to simply trust Him*
> *Seems the hardest thing of all.*
> *Trust Him, He is ever faithful,*
> *Trust Him, for His will is best,*
> *Trust Him, for the heart of Jesus*
> *Is the only place of rest.*
> *Author unknown*

———— ❈ ————

> *The writer of these pages knows what it is*
> *to hang on the bare arm of God,*
> *and he bears his willing witness*
> *that no trust is so well warranted by facts,*

or so sure to be rewarded by results,
as trust in the invisible, but ever-living God.
Charles. H. Spurgeon

So what will be the result of all this grueling spiritual work in your life? Read on, my friend... **the best is yet to come!**

He who trusts in the Lord, mercy shall surround him (Psalm 32:10).

O taste and see that the Lord is good: blessed is the man that trusts in Him (Psalm 34:8).

Trust in the Lord with all your heart and lean not on your own understanding. In all your ways acknowledge Him, and He shall direct your paths (Proverbs 3:5-6).

Blessed are all they that put their trust in Him (Psalm 2:12).

God is our refuge and strength, a very present help in trouble. Therefore we will not fear, though the earth be removed, and though the mountains be carried into the midst of the sea, though the waters thereof roar and are troubled, though the mountains shake with the swelling thereof (Psalm 46:1-3).

The Bible mentions many benefits of trusting in God. Here are just a few of those benefits: 1. Happiness: Proverbs 16:20; 2. Spiritual 'Fatness' or Health: Proverbs 28:25; 3. Safety: Proverbs 29: 25; 4. Mercy: Psalm 32:10; 5. Deliverance: Psalm 22:4-6; Help: Psalm 28:7; 7. Rejoicing: Psalm 5:11; 8. Refuge: Psalm 62:8; 9. Salvation: Isaiah 12:2; 10. Guiltless: Psalm 34:22; 11. Peace and Strength: Isaiah 26:3 -4; and 12. No Fear: Psalm 56: 3- 4. – Absolute Bible Study

If we will put our trust in the Lord, we'll be like a tree that is planted by the water that sends out its roots by the stream (Jer. 17:7-9). Such a person is like the tree by the water. God provides an endless source of blessing and strength, flowing all the time, no matter what happens in life. Just as the tree can develop roots to reach along the banks to take full advantage of all the water, so a person could develop spiritual roots to reach out and receive all the blessings that God is wishing to give to them. At times when God comes close, they know it and are able to be close to Him, to spend time with Him and enjoy Him. They do not rely on themselves for survival and blessing, but on the One who gives them their water, their nourishment, their blessings. – Tom Higgins

His ways are not our ways, and we must be willing to trust that He does truly know best. Isaiah 55:9 says, "For as the heavens are higher than the earth, so are My ways higher than your ways, and My thoughts than your thoughts. Trust is a decision. Make that decision today! – Mrs. Charles E. Cowman

Trust in the Lord, and do good; dwell in the land, and feed on His faithfulness. Delight yourself also in the Lord, and He shall give you the desires of your heart. Commit your way to the Lord, trust also in Him, and He shall bring it to pass. He shall bring forth your righteousness as the light, and your justice as the noonday. Rest in the Lord, and wait patiently for Him; do not fret because of him who prospers in his way, because of the man who brings wicked schemes to pass. Cease from anger, and forsake wrath; do not fret – it only causes harm (Psalm 37:3-8).

Trust and obey, for there's no other way, to be happy in Jesus but to trust and obey – Daniel Towner

Chapter Thirteen

Blessings for Believers Who Forgive Others and Trust God

Out of believers' desire to keep up with the times, the Contemporary Christian Music movement was born. I don't have anything against our modern worship choruses – what I do have a problem with is that most churches have virtually retired all their hymnals and maybe, once in a great while, they will have one hymn sung in a worship service. *We are being robbed of such a rich heritage of wisdom and insight as to how to live the Christian life!* The knowledge and wisdom contained in those hymn never become obsolete.

As I pen these words, there is one hymn that just keeps running through my mind: *Trust and Obey.* Therefore, I decided to do a little research on the historical background of the hymn:

John H. Sammis (1846-1919) gave up his life as a businessman and part-time YMCA worker to study for the ministry. He was ordained a Presbyterian minister in 1880 and then served at several pastorates. In his later years, Sammis taught at the Bible Institute of Los Angeles. Daniel B. Towner (1850-1919) was music director for several well-known churches and schools, including the Moody Bible Institute. He published several music books and wrote the music for many well-loved hymns, including <u>At Calvary</u> and <u>Only A Sinner Saved By Grace.</u> In 1887, just following an evangelistic meeting held by Dwight L. Moody, a young man stood to share his story in an after-service testimony meeting. As he was speaking, it became clear to many that he knew little about the Bible or acceptable Christian doctrine. His closing lines, however, spoke volumes to seasoned and new believers alike: 'I'm not quite sure. But I'm going to trust, and I'm going to obey.' Daniel Towner was so struck by the power of those simple words that he quickly jotted them down, then delivered them to John Sammis, who developed the lyrics to <u>Trust and Obey.</u> Towner composed the music, and the song quickly became a favorite. It remains popular with hymn singers today.[1]

Trust and Obey

1.   *When we walk with the Lord in the light of His Word,*
What a glory He sheds on our way!
While we do His good will, He abides with us still,
And with all who will trust and obey.

Refrain:
Trust and obey, for there's no other way
To be happy in Jesus, but to trust and obey.

2.   *Not a shadow can rise, not a cloud in the skies,*
But His smile quickly drives it away;
Not a doubt or a fear, not a sigh or a tear,
Can abide while we trust and obey. (Refrain)

3.   *Not a burden we bear, not a sorrow we share,*
But our toil He doth richly repay;
Not a grief or a loss, not a frown or a cross,
But is blessed if we trust and obey. (Refrain)

4.   *But we never can prove the delights of His love*
Until all on the altar we lay;
For the favor He shows, for the joy He bestows,
Are for them who will trust and obey. (Refrain)

5.   *Then in fellowship sweet, we will sit at His feet,*
Or we'll walk by His side in the way;
What He says we will do, where He sends we will go;
Never fear, only trust and obey. (Refrain)

Daniel B. Towner, 1887, Copyright: Public Domain

Dr. Sandra Wilson has an insightful comment to make about this hymn as it relates to her emotional healing in her powerful memoir, *Into Abba's Arms: Finding the Acceptance You've Always Wanted*:

When I was a child, I learned to sing the gospel song "Trust and Obey." And for most of my faith life, I thought the primary challenge was to obey. Well, I've changed my mind. Like the Galatians [Note: Wilson is referring to Paul's discussion with the Galatian church about the law and grace, Galatians 2:16; 3:6-14; 5:1-8], many of us may find it easier to trust our own abilities to obey religious laws than to trust God's grace-filled, non-abandoning love. Perhaps faith means, in part, entrusting ourselves to God's promise never to abandon those who abandon themselves to Him. And based on our knowledge of God's character and experience of His perfect love, He calls us to obey, not so that He will love us more, but so that He can bless us more (emphasis added).[2]

We've come to the end of a very long journey…. As stated throughout, for most abuse survivors, the process of healing, forgiving others, and trusting God can take decades. Even the ability to trust the Lord for everything can take believers who weren't abused as children a lifetime to attain. As the world grows darker and the Second Coming of Jesus draws nigh, the necessity of trusting the Lord for everything in our lives is only increasing exponentially. Those who can't trust will be overcome by anxiety, which then leads to fear, which then leads to terror.

As Jesus tells us in Luke 21:25-27: "And there will be signs in the sun, in the moon, and in the stars; and on the earth distress of nations, with perplexity the sea and the waves roaring; **men's heart failing them from fear and the expectation of those things which are coming on the earth,** for the powers of the heavens will be shaken (emphasis added)." To translate that into medical terms, because of all the things happening in the time just preceding Jesus' Second Coming, the numbers of people who suffer heart attacks will spiral hopelessly out of control!

However, we who trust the Lord can take heart! Dr. Ed Delph and Alan and Paula Heller list the blessings of trusting God in their book, *Learning to Trust Again*:

1. *Trusting God releases His power in your life.*
2. *Trusting God releases His blessings and goodness to you.*
3. *Trusting God releases victory to your life by establishing you in conflicts.*
4. *Trusting God creates inner joy and brings happiness to your life.*
5. *Trusting God produces endurance… and preserves you in hard times.*
6. *Trusting God releases His lovingkindness toward you.*
7. *Trusting God stops you from seeking after idols in your life.*
8. *Trusting God delivers you from the wicked.*
9. *Trusting brings God's help in times of sorrow.*
10. *Trusting God produces a Spirit-led, Spirit-bred, and Spirit-fed life.*
11. *Trusting God draws you near to God.*
12. *Trusting God gives you courage to declare His works.*
13. *Trusting God helps you to take courage.*
14. *Trusting God overcomes the negative effects of uncertainty.*
15. *Trusting God keeps you in a safe place.* [3]

Therefore, when you have accomplished the difficult work outlined in this book, you will be one of the blessed ones who will experience the Kingdom of God, which is **righteousness, peace, and joy in the Holy Spirit** (Romans 14:17). This is the legacy left by Jesus for all obedient and trusting believers. Thank God that He doesn't require us to be all finished (we won't be!) before we start to experience that righteousness, peace, and joy.

As if these blessings aren't enough, you will enjoy an **intimacy with God**, which is so incredible that the following two verses in the New Testament contain the only words that can begin to describe it:

But as it is written: 'Eye has not seen, nor ear heard, nor have entered into the heart of man the things which God has prepared for those who love Him (1 Cor. 2:9).

Now to Him who is able to do <u>exceedingly abundantly</u> above all that we ask or think... (Eph. 3:20, emphasis added).

Please don't let Satan convince you that you have been disqualified from these promises and blessings because of whatever sin in your life you are struggling with – that is an enormous lie! Continue to read and know that the Lord has no favorites – that He wants to bless you just as much as He wants to bless others that you think are more "worthy" than you. That's just another lie.

What does this life in the Kingdom of God, right here on Earth, look like? For most of you reading this book, these are just pretty words that have little to do with your everyday lives. With the pain and shame that remain in survivors' souls, **righteousness** sounds like a quality only Jesus and a precious few others possess.

In fact, however, if you have been born again, this attribute was imputed to you at the time of Jesus' death, burial, and resurrection. What does "imputed" mean? We find the following definition in the *Holman Bible Dictionary*:

<u>Impute, Imputation</u>: Setting to someone's account or reckoning something to another person. God reckoned righteousness to believing Abraham (Genesis 15:16). This means that God credited to Abraham that which he did not have in himself (Romans 4:3-5). This does not mean that God accepted Abraham's faith instead of righteousness as an accomplishment meriting justification. Rather, it means that God accepted Abraham because he trusted in God rather than trusting in something that he could do. Similarly, drawing from Psalm 32:1-3, Paul stated that only God can forgive sin. Those who are forgiven are not regarded as wicked since the Lord does not impute to them their iniquity. Instead, these are considered or reckoned as children of God (Romans 4:7-8, Romans

4:11, Romans 4:23-24). The imputation of righteousness lies at the heart of the biblical doctrine of salvation. This righteousness is seen in Christ who purchased redemption. God grants righteousness to those who have faith in Christ (Romans 1:17; Romans 3:21-26; Romans 10:3; 2 Corinthians 5:21; Philippians 3:9). This righteousness imputed or reckoned to believers is, strictly speaking, an alien righteousness. It is not the believer's own righteousness, but God's righteousness imputed to the believer.[4]

What can we conclude from this definition? That we need never worry about trying to be "righteous" on our own again. It is a supernatural attribution at the time of salvation. It is important to know that when God looks at you, He doesn't see your "filthy rags' righteousness." No, He sees you clothed with the spotless, dazzling white robe of righteousness that you were dressed in when you were born again.

The Lord tells us in Isaiah 61:10: "I will greatly rejoice in the Lord, my soul shall be joyful in my God; for He has clothed me with the garments of salvation, He has covered me with the robe of righteousness, as a bridegroom decks *himself* with ornaments, and as a bride adorns *herself* with her jewels." In other words (now please catch this): **When the Father looks at you, He doesn't see your sinfulness; He sees Jesus in you! So from now on, whenever Satan, the accuser of the brethren, comes and tries to shame you with any sins you have committed in the past, which you have confessed and repented of, you can tell him to get lost, because you're clothed in Jesus' righteousness. You know what? He has to leave you alone, right then and there!**

———— ∞ ————

Some time ago, I began seeing a client we'll call Bonnie. Bonnie had a very abusive and neglectful childhood. Her biological father was never in her life, and her mother communicated in many ways that she didn't want Bonnie. She was actually raised by her grandmother, who belittled and criticized her constantly and punished her by shutting her in closets for long periods of time. Bonnie's levels of anxiety knew no bounds, understandably so. She was, however, the first client I had ever seen who was so shame-based that she had a very difficult time believing in her own salvation.

We worked on it and worked on it, seemingly to no avail. Finally, one day out of the clear blue (or so it seemed to me), Bonnie announced that she had read a little book given to her by a pastor from her church and became convinced that she was saved. We were both thrilled! The point of relating Bonnie's story is to show the difficulty some abuse survivors have with embracing basic doctrine about their salvation and the impasse they come to in their attempts to trust Father God. This woman told me repeatedly how much she loved Jesus but was terrified of the Father. In her case, it has been, and continues to be, a long process to overcome these distortions and replace them with the truth of who our Father God really is!

—⊗⊗⊗—

We need to continue to examine definitions of biblical phrases. Nearly all believe they know what **peace** is, but do they really, in the context of God's Word? Peace is defined in the *Collins English Dictionary* as follows:

peace [pi ː s] n. 1. a. the state existing during the absence of war. b. (as modifier) peace negotiations. 2. (modifier) denoting a person or thing symbolizing support for international peace. 3. (often capital) a treaty marking the end of a war. 4. a state of harmony between people or groups; freedom from strife. 5. law and order within a state; absence of violence or other disturbance (a breach of the peace). 6. absence of mental anxiety (often in the phrase peace of mind). 7. a state of stillness, silence, or serenity (at peace). a. in a state of harmony or friendship; b. in a state of serenity; c. dead (the old lady is at peace now); hold or keep one's peace (to keep silent). (Law) keep the peace (to maintain or refrain from disturbing law and order); make one's peace with (to become reconciled with); make peace (to bring hostilities to an end); vb; (intr) Obsolete except as an imperative to be or become silent or still [from Old French pais, from Latin pāx].

Jeff Benner has dug into the ancient meanings of Hebrew words and can offer quite a bit of insight. Following is his definition of **peace** (shalom):

שלום *When we hear the word peace, we usually associate this with meaning an absence of war or strife, but the Hebrew meaning of the word shalom is very different. The verb form of the root word is shalam and is usually used in the context of making restitution. When a person has caused another to become deficient in some way, such as a loss of livestock, it is the responsibility of the person who created the deficiency to restore what has been taken, lost or stolen. The verb shalam literally means to make whole or complete. The noun shalom has the more literal meaning of being in a state of wholeness or with no deficiency. The common phrase Shalu Shalom Yerushalayim (Pray for the Peace of Jerusalem) is not speaking about an absence of war (though that is part of it) but that Jerusalem (and by extension all of Israel) is compete and whole and goes far beyond the idea of 'peace.'[5]*

In my studies of Bible translations, I have found that the fullest possible meaning of the word "**peace**" is contained in the *Amplified Bible:*

And God's __peace__ [be yours, that tranquil state of a soul assured of its salvation through Christ, and so fearing nothing from God and content with its earthly lot of whatever sort *that is, that <u>peace</u>] which transcends all understanding, shall garrison and mount guard over your hearts and minds in Christ Jesus (Phil. 4:7).*

Who were chosen and foreknown by God the Father and consecrated (sanctified, made holy) by the Spirit to be obedient to Jesus Christ (the Messiah) and to be sprinkled with [His] blood: May grace (spiritual blessing) and <u>peace</u> be given you in increasing abundance [that spiritual <u>peace</u> to be realized in and through Christ, freedom from fears, agitating passions, and moral conflicts] (1 Peter 1:2).

In an Internet article entitled "The Nature of the Divine Blessings of Grace and Peace," J. Hampton Keathley, III identifies the different types of **peace** that will accompany the believer who trusts God:

<u>The Peace of Reconciliation, Peace with God</u>. It may refer to the peace of salvation where man is brought into a right relationship with God through faith in Christ (Rom. 5:1; Gal. 6:12-16). In Ephesians 2, Christ is seen as the peacemaker (Eph. 2:14-18).

<u>The Peace of Fellowship, the Peace of a Conscience Void of Offense</u>. This is the personal peace which God gives to the individual through fellowship with the Lord, through walking in concord with God with all known sin confessed and turned over to God's grace and knowledge of all things (1 John 1:9; 3:19-21; Gal. 5:22; 1 Tim. 1:5; Acts 24:16).

<u>The Peace of Assurance, the Peace of God</u>. This is the peace that comes from being confident of God's supply: that God is in control. This is the peace that settles our nerves, fills our mind, and allows us to relax even in the midst of uproar around us (Phil. 4:6-9; Gal. 5:22; Ps. 119:165; Pr. 3:13-17).

<u>The Peace of Harmony, Peace with Others</u>. This is the peace of unity and oneness in the Body of Christ; oneness of mind and purpose (Eph. 4:3; Phil. 2:2-4; 1 Thess. 5:13). God reaps a harvest of peace where there are believers sowing and watering their minds with the Word. But Satan, the agent of disunity and strife, seeks to reap a harvest of discord through hurt feelings, unwillingness to forgive, and selfish ambition when people refuse to operate on the principles and promises of the Word (1 Cor. 2:6-11; Mark 9:34, 50; Phil. 2:1-4).

<u>The Peace of Pronounced Blessing</u>. Refers to the wish and prayer for spiritual and physical prosperity, security, and safety for others (John 20:19, 21, 26).[6]

Keathley goes on to enumerate the spheres in which the peace of God exists in our lives if we have been born again:

(1) The <u>peace</u> of eternal security with the assurance of our salvation.

(2) The <u>peace</u> of good conscience, of no known sin unconfessed.

(3) The <u>peace</u> of knowing God's will, of God's direction.

(4) The <u>peace</u> of knowing that God will supply.[7]

I hope by this time you are beginning to see the incredible **blessings** that are heaped on us when we process our grief over abuse, forgive the abuser(s), and learn to really trust the Father with our lives. In the Beatitudes, when Jesus tells us that we are **blessed**, I find the *Amplified Bible*'s meaning of the Greek word for "**blessed**" inspiring:

<u>Blessed</u> (happy, to be envied, and spiritually prosperous, with life-joy and satisfaction in God's favor and salvation, regardless of their outward conditions) are the poor in spirit (the humble, who rate themselves insignificant), for theirs is the kingdom of heaven!

<u>Blessed</u> and enviably happy (with a happiness produced by the experience of God's favor and especially conditioned by the revelation of His matchless grace) are those who mourn, for they shall be comforted!

<u>Blessed</u> (happy, blithesome, joyous, spiritually prosperous with life-joy and satisfaction in God's favor and salvation, regardless of their outward conditions) are the meek (the mild, patient, long-suffering), for they shall inherit the earth!

<u>Blessed</u> and fortunate and happy and spiritually prosperous (in that state in which the born-again child of God enjoys His favor and salvation) are those who hunger and thirst for righteousness (uprightness and right standing with God), for they shall be completely satisfied!

<u>Blessed</u> (happy, to be envied, and spiritually prosperous with life-joy and satisfaction in God's favor and salvation, regardless of their outward conditions) are the merciful, for they shall obtain mercy!

<u>Blessed</u> (happy, enviably fortunate, and spiritually prosperous – possessing the happiness produced by the experience of God's favor and especially conditioned by the revela-

tion of His grace, regardless of their outward conditions) are the pure in heart, for they shall see God!'

Blessed (enjoying enviable happiness, spiritually prosperous with life-joy and satisfaction in God's favor and salvation, regardless of their outward conditions) are the makers and maintainers of peace, for they shall be called the sons of God!

Blessed (happy and enviably fortunate and spiritually prosperous in the state in which the born-again child of God enjoys and finds satisfaction in God's favor and salvation, regardless of his outward conditions) are those who are persecuted for righteousness' sake (for being and doing right), for theirs is the kingdom of heaven!

Blessed (happy, to be envied, and spiritually prosperous, with life-joy and satisfaction in God's favor and salvation, regardless of your outward conditions) are you when people revile you and persecute you and say all kinds of evil things against you falsely on My account (Matthew 5:3-11).

Once again, I feel the need to admonish you not to "freak out" at all the things Jesus is instructing you to do enumerated above. God's work in us takes place over a lifetime – this is known as the sanctification process. In addition, we have His ironclad promise to us that we can be "... confident of this very thing, that He who has begun a good work in you will complete *it* until the day of Jesus Christ (Phil. 1:6). Another reassuring verse along these lines is, "He who calls you is faithful, who also will do it (1 Thess. 5:24). Finally, we have this declaration: "Now to Him who is able to keep you from stumbling, and to present you faultless before the presence of His glory with exceeding joy... "(Jude 1:24).

All right, what about joy? Most people probably assume that they know the meaning of the word "joy," but we have discovered the depth of the meaning of words in the Bible, which often goes beyond a mere dictionary definition. For instance, most people think "joy" and "happiness" are synonymous, which they aren't! The *Merriam-Webster Online Dictionary* gives the definition below:

Joy - *noun* \\'jȯi\\Definition of *JOY 1. a:* the emotion evoked by well-being, success, or good fortune or by the prospect of possessing what one desires: DELIGHT. *b:* the expression or exhibition of such emotion: GAIETY. 2. a state of HAPPINESS or felicity: BLISS. 3. a source or cause of DELIGHT. — *joy·less\\-ləs\\ adjective;— joy·less·ly adverb; — joy·less·ness noun;* Examples of *JOY:* 1. Their sorrow turned to *joy.* 2. I can hardly express the *joy* I felt at seeing her again. 3. Seeing her again brought tears of *joy* to my eyes. 4. The flowers are a *joy* to behold! 5. What a *joy* it was to see her again. Origin of

***JOY* Middle English, from Anglo-French *joie,* from Latin *gaudia,* plural of *gaudium,* from *gaudēre* to rejoice; probably akin to Greek *gēthein* to rejoice First Known Use: 13th century.**

It is always valuable to find out what noted Bible scholar John MacArthur has to say in a discussion about the biblical definition of joy:

We live in a sad world – a world of despair, depression, lack of fulfillment, and dissatisfaction. Man defines happiness as an attitude of satisfaction and delight based upon present circumstances. He relates happiness to happenings and happenstance. It is something that can't be planned or programmed. Biblical joy consists of the deep and abiding confidence that all is well regardless of circumstance and difficulty. It is something very different from worldly happiness. Biblical joy is always related to God and belongs only to those in Christ. It is the permanent possession of every believer – not a whimsical delight that comes and goes as chance offers it opportunity. A good definition of joy is this: It's the flag that flies on the castle of the heart when the King is in residence. Only Christians can know true and lasting joy…. Joy is a gift from God that is mixed with trials. In fact, joy is most evident in the midst of trials. A believer's joy remains in spite of sadness, sorrow, or difficulty.[8]

That brings us to the biggest blessing of all because of forgiving others and trusting God: intimacy with God Himself. Many people equate intimacy with sexual intercourse, which is certainly one aspect of it, but it is so much more. "Intimate" is defined in the *Random House Dictionary* as follows:

in·ti·mate; ˈɪn tə mɪt; *Spelled [in-tuh-mit] –adjective; 1630s, 'closely acquainted, very familiar,' from L.L. intimatus, pp. of intimare 'make known, announce, impress,' from L. intimus 'inmost' (adj.), 'close friend' (n.), superl. of in 'in.' 1. associated in close personal relations:* **an intimate friend.** *2. characterized by or involving warm friendship or a personally close or familiar association or feeling:* **an intimate greeting.** *3. very private; closely personal:* **one's intimate affairs.** *4. characterized by or suggesting privacy or intimacy; warmly cozy:* **an intimate little café.** *5. (of an association, knowledge, understanding, etc.) arising from close personal connection or familiar experience. 6. engaged in or characterized by sexual relations. 7. (of clothing) worn next to the skin, under street or outer garments:* **intimate apparel.** *8. detailed; deep:* **a more intimate analysis.** *9. showing a close union or combination of particles or elements:* **an intimate mixture.** *10. inmost; deep within. 11. of, pertaining to, or characteristic of the inmost or essential nature; intrinsic:* **the intimate structure of an organism.** *12. of, pertaining to, or existing in the inmost depths of the mind:* **intimate beliefs.**

By now, you're probably saying to yourself, I can't take even one more definition – I'm burned out on dictionaries! I totally get that; however, there's just one more word and its definition that we absolutely **must** deal with. However, this one is qualitatively different from all the other definitions.

There's hardly been anything to really laugh about in this book – we're dealing with such serious and painful subjects, but finally (in the next to the last chapter, yet!) there is something humorous in our study of the rewards of forgiving others and trusting God. When researching a biblical definition of intimacy with God, the very first thing you will find out is that the Hebrew word for "to know" is (are you ready?) none other than "yada." <u>Yes, as in "yada, yada, yada" of the hugely popular *Seinfeld* television series!</u>

That this incredibly significant biblical word has the connotation of "Yeah, yeah, you've told me enough about this already… get to the point!" is completely opposite from its actual meaning in Hebrew. On one website, the commentator made the following point: "It [the word 'yada' on *Seinfeld*] refers to people being redundant, monotonous, or verbose. It is also used as a fill-in-the-blank phrase for details that are either unimportant or obvious to everyone. That is how most of us have come to know the term 'yada.' Here is the **actual** definition of the Hebrew word for "to know":

<u>Original Hebrew word:</u> יָדַע yada; phonetic spelling: (yaw-dah'). The biblical Old Testament word for knowing God means the following: to know God means to perceive; to learn to understand; to recognize; to believe; to accept His claims; to conform; to be willing to perform or live; to see or experience.[9]

The exposition of the word "yada," i.e., the detailed description or discussion of the word, seems as though it is infinite on the Internet. I had so much information to sift through that I narrowed the field to descriptions of "yada" which are pertinent to establishing what true intimacy with God looks like. Kevin Dedmon has valuable insight on the subject:

'Yada' in the Old Testament means to 'know' in five distinct dimensions. The first dimension of yada is to know something or someone in complete detail. It means to study, analyze, or investigate something until you know something or someone completely. How much more of God is there to know? How many of us have a complete revelation of His nature, personality, attributes, and ways? How many of us have read the same scriptures over and over for years, and then had a truth jump out at us that we had never seen there before? The second dimension of yada is to know something technically. It is to know how something works technically. It is part of the wisdom that Paul was praying for in Ephesians 1:17. It is not just knowing that something does work, but also how it works. Wisdom is knowing how something works in all of its aspects. A lot of people know about God, but how many actually know God so well that they know the intricacies of how He operates, the keys that unlock His presence in our lives?

Yada is not just knowing the details about God, but also knowing His ways, as Moses prayed in Ex. 33:13, 'If you are pleased with me, teach me your ways so I may know you (yada) and continue to find favor with you.' Yada is being able to understand God's ways, so that we can take out of Him what we need, as well as putting back into Him the things He desires from us to further our relationship. The third dimension of yada is to know God by personal experience. A lot of people know about God, but God wants us to know Him through encounters in which we personally experience His presence. The fourth dimension of yada is to have a face-to-face encounter. It is one thing to encounter God's goodness expressed in physical healing, forgiveness, intervention, provision, or blessing, but God desires an up-close and personal face-to-face encounter. Our heavenly Father does not desire an absentee relationship with His children in whom He just sends the things we need and desire from afar. No, His desire is to reveal himself to His children every day. The fifth and final dimension of yada is sexual intimacy. Some may even say that this fifth dimension cannot be fully experienced until a person has comprehensively satisfied the first four dimensions. The aim of yada is intimacy. God's desire is to have a comprehensive, personal, face-to-face, intimate encounter with each one of us. God wants to yada with us every day.[10]

In the following quote, the author of the commentary is demonstrating that in Proverbs 3:6, translating "yada" as acknowledge doesn't begin to describe the intensity of what a truly intimate relationship with the Lord is like:

The verb 'yada'(to know) exhibits a wide array of meanings in biblical Hebrew.

Nahum Sarna writes: In the biblical conception, knowledge is not essentially or even primarily rooted in the intellect and mental activity. Rather, it is more experiential and is embedded in the emotions, so that it may encompass such qualities as contact, intimacy, concern, relatedness and mutuality. Other reference works support this judgment. 'To know God is to be in right relationship with Him, with characteristics of love, trust, respect, and open communication. When yada refers to God, explains another, it denotes an 'intensive involvement... that exceeds mere cognitive relationship.'

Of King Josiah, God said through his prophet: 'He judged the cause of the poor and needy; then it was well. Is not that what it means to know Me? Yahweh demands' (Jer. 22:15, 16; NRSV). Such comments clarify the close link in Proverbs 3:5-6 between trusting and knowing God. To 'know God' is to have a vital relationship with Him, one characterized by faithfulness, and rooted in love, confidence, and profound, enduring regard. Trust and knowledge are integral and inseparable aspects of such a relationship. To 'know God' in all one's ways is to act in a manner that ennobles that relationship, that solidifies it, that promotes its welfare and shows that one cherishes it above all else (1 Chron. 28:9). It is to rely on God, to trust the rightness of His ways and seek to be guided by them in every circumstance. To thus 'know God' pleases Him (Jer. 9:24; 22:16; Hos. 6:6; Ps. 36:10).[11]

It is helpful to know the Greek counterpart to the Hebrew "yada." On one website, the similarities and differences were noted:

The Greek words 'oida' and 'ginosko' are used in the New Testament. They have wider meanings as the Hebrew word 'yada,' but in the context that they are used in the New Testament, they also have the following additional meaning: to know 'ginosko' God means [the following]: to believe and accept Jesus, to know Jesus is to know God, to know Truth, and to respond in faith. [12]

Another source paints the following picture as to what intimacy with the Lord – that "yada" knowing – consists of:

To know God thus includes a wide range of mental, emotional, and experiential knowledge. The fruit of this intimacy includes love, reverence, obedience, honor, gratitude, and deep affection. We come to know Him as sovereign Ruler, Master, Parent, Brother, Friend, Savior, and Lawgiver. We would never know this mixture of admirable qualities and authority without getting close to Him. They compel us to yield to Him with all of our hearts while we strive to obey and glorify Him.[13]

There is a beautiful song that captures the essence of the "yada" way of knowing Jesus, as well as the blessings of forgiving others and trusting God (righteousness, peace, and joy, as seen earlier in this chapter). The composer/lyricist explains why it is such a powerful song. Note that to really "yada" Jesus, we will share in the fellowship of His sufferings and become like Him in His death. **(Moral of the story – there is no such thing as cheap grace, and we must count the cost of following Him!)**

Knowing You

By Graham Kendrick

This song comes from words penned by the Apostle Paul while in jail, awaiting execution. It touches the head and heart of the follower of Jesus Christ, because it lifts up our best Friend as the most important "thing" in our lives.

But whatever was to my profit I now consider loss for the sake of Christ. What is more, I consider everything a loss compared to the surpassing greatness of knowing Christ Jesus my Lord, for whose sake I have lost all things. I consider them rubbish, that I may gain Christ and be found in Him, not having a righteousness of my own that comes from the law, but that which is through faith in Christ – the righteousness that comes from God and is by faith. I want to know Christ and the power of His resurrection and the fellowship of sharing in His sufferings, becoming like Him in his death, and so, somehow, to attain to the resurrection from the dead (Philippians 3:7-11, NIV).

All I once held dear, built my life upon,
all this world reveres and wars to own,
all I once thought gain I have counted loss,
spent and worthless now compared to this.

Knowing You, Jesus, knowing You.
There is no greater thing.
You're my all, You're the best, You're my joy,
my righteousness, and I love You, Lord.

Now my heart's desire is to know You more,
to be found in You and known as Yours,
to possess by faith what I could not earn,
all surpassing gift of righteousness.

Knowing You, Jesus, knowing You.
There is no greater thing.
You're my all, You're the best, You're my joy,
my righteousness, and I love You, Lord.

Oh, to know the pow'r of Your risen life,
and to know You in Your suffering,
to become like You in Your death,
My Lord, so with You to live and never die.

Knowing You, Jesus, knowing You.
There is no greater thing.
You're my all, You're the best, You're my joy,
my righteousness, and I love You, Lord.

Knowing You, Jesus, knowing You.
There is no greater thing.
You're my all, You're the best, You're my joy, my righteousness;
You're my all, You're the best, You're my joy, my righteousness;
You're my all, You're the best, You're my joy, my righteousness;
and I love You, Lord.

Lyrics and Music Copyright 1993 Make Way Music

In the last exposition of "yada" that I quote from a Bible study online, we are given the true "nuts and bolts" of what it means to be intimate with the Lord:

God wants us to talk to Him about and involve Him in all aspects of our life, and have a lifestyle of prayer and talking to Him. Hearing God's voice is the most important part of our prayer time with Him. Good communication and learning to hear His 'still, small voice' is essential to knowing God and His attributes, His ways, His will, and His plans. When you love someone, you want to know them more and more. It takes time and effort and desire and determination in order to get to know God... it is a lifelong process and a heart attitude... make knowing God your main desire and pursuit – nothing will please Him more. The more you know Jesus the more you will love Him and trust Him, and delight in Him, and follow and obey Him. God wants you to 'pour out your heart to Him,' whatever it is you are feeling and going through, because He deeply cares for you. Note how David would be completely honest with God in some of the psalms (e.g., Psalm 13 and 22). God is always truthful with us, and He wants us to be truthful with Him.[14]

To use "yada" Seinfeld's way, at this point you're probably saying, "Yada, yada, yada" – enough with the definitions already!"

Once more, I believe that Deborah Kern has an eloquent explanation describing what happens to us in God's presence (intimacy):

It is in God's presence where we exchange our understanding for His.

It is in His presence where we pour out our emotions of fear, distrust, hurt and anger, and receive back His ability to find contentment in the middle of a storm, and peace in the midst of crisis.

It is in His presence where the principles we have read in His Word are made a part of us as He reveals to us how they apply to our lives and our situations.

It is in His presence where we begin to release ourselves into His hands and allow Him to direct our lives and bring good into every circumstance.

It is in His presence where we begin to fathom His great love for us.

It is in His presence where we become aware of His concern for every detail of our lives.

It is in His presence where we acknowledge God as Lord of our lives and learn that we can trust Him.

It is in His presence where we stop leaning upon our own understanding and begin to lean upon His.[15]

Intimacy, then, revolves around allowing God to love and talk to you. As you forgive others and learn to trust God based on His character, a dialog will happen quite naturally. Doesn't He tell us that we will recognize His voice?

But you do not believe, because you are not of My sheep, as I said to you. My sheep hear My voice, and I know them, and they follow Me. And I give them eternal life, and they shall never perish; neither shall anyone snatch them out of My hand (John 10:26-28).

And when He putteth forth his own sheep, He goeth before them, and the sheep follow Him: for they know His voice. And a stranger will they not follow, but will flee from Him: for they know not the voice of strangers (John 10:4-5, KJV).

You never would have read this far if you didn't want all that the Lord has for you! In the final chapter, you will learn how to hear His voice and know without a doubt that it is the Lord Himself speaking to you!

To have God speak to the heart is a majestic experience, an experience that people may miss if they monopolize the conversation and never pause to hear God's responses. – Charles Stanley

I think it's good to make sure if the voice you hear is God's – but in my experience it's been very obvious and I'll attempt to explain. Let me say first that it's not easy to explain this via the written or spoken word – but I'll try. One thing I've noticed is that the thoughts come fast when God speaks to me. I mean it's like a flood. I've used the term 'download.' I'm probably a little slow but it's hard to keep up! And there has been NO doubt. One particular time it was so obvious that God had spoken because I was so energized. I was ecstatic! The thoughts that came were not mine – it was an understanding of grace – which I had asked for. I never really understood grace. After that experience, I did. I can't really explain the feeling – but trust me when I say that you will know when God speaks to you! – Robert Pedersen

Why is it important that you are with God and God alone on the mountaintop? It's important because it's the place in which you can listen to the voice of the One who calls you the beloved. To pray is to listen to the One who calls you 'My beloved daughter,' 'My beloved son,' 'My beloved child.' To pray is to let that voice speak to the center of your being, to your guts, and let that voice resound in your whole being. – Henri Nouwen

There is not in the world a kind of life more sweet and delightful than that of a continual conversation with God. – Brother Lawrence

Prayer is not monologue, but dialogue; God's voice is its most essential part. Listening to God's voice is the secret of the assurance that He will listen to mine. – Andrew Murray

Prayer at its highest is a two-way conversation – and for me the most important part is listening to God's replies. – Frank C. Laubach

If you had asked me a few years ago if I ever heard God speak to me, I would have given a nebulous response. I have never heard a Charlton Heston-type bass voice booming out of the clouds. Nevertheless, over the years, I have occasionally discerned the Spirit's inaudible voice speaking in my thoughts. Better, higher, and wiser thoughts than my own thoughts, these gentle impressions on my heart encouraged or admonished me in ways that drew me nearer to heaven. – Sandra Wilson

I want to encourage you to accept God's invitation to hear Him in everyday life. It will be the most fascinating journey that you ever embarked on! It will take you to places you never dreamed and have you doing things you never thought possible. Hearing God's voice will be the most joyful sound you have ever heard… even though you may never hear an audible sound! Each day ask Him to order your steps and you will find yourself hearing things that leave you speechless. – Kathi Pelton

Chapter Fourteen

My Sheep Know My Voice

We often make the process of becoming intimate with the Lord more complicated than it actually is…. Terri Guillemets made the following observation. "Some stand on tiptoe trying to reach God to talk to Him - you try too hard, friend - drop to your knees and listen to Him, He'll hear you better that way."

I don't know about you, but I don't enjoy one-sided relationships – at the very least, I don't get close to other people when they only want to talk about themselves, don't want to let me talk about myself, and/or only seem to listen to what I have to say in response to what they've been saying. That might sound selfish, but I don't think so…. I believe that relationships need to be reciprocal to thrive. Why should we think our relationship with God is any different? Dr. Sandra Wilson shows the connection between building intimacy with friends and with the Lord, in her book, *Into Abba's Arms: Finding the Acceptance You Always Wanted:*

> *Spending time with God in solitude, experiencing the reality of His presence, and cultivating inner quietness create the condition in which we can hear Him more clearly. And as we share our hearts with God and hear Him share His heart with us, our relationship grows deeper, closer. More real…. That's how friendships work.[1]*

Complete healing of the deep wounds of child abuse can happen when we truly get to know God as our Father, according to Dr. Wilson:

> *In the same way, our heavenly Father wants us to know more than how to practice spiritual habits. He wants us to know Him – His faithful heart and His non-abandoning love. As children and/or adults, some of us have experienced betrayal of trust, abandonment, and insecurity about our place of belonging in relationships. Therefore, it is within relationships that we can begin to experience trustworthy love and secure belonging. Healthy human relationships with faithful spouses, caring friends, godly counselors, and wise*

pastors can help. I know because I have had all of them<u>. But we will never experience</u> <u>*life-transforming healing from abandonment, the ultimate acceptance we crave, or a*</u> <u>*rock-solid sense of secure belonging apart from an intimate, heart-heart relationship*</u> <u>*with Him (emphasis added).²*</u>

Four foundational Bible passages give us the confidence to approach our Abba Father:

'I will be a Father to you, and you shall be My sons and daughters,' says the Lord Almighty (2 Cor. 5:18).

For you did not receive the spirit of bondage again to fear, but you received the Spirit of adoption by whom we cry out, 'Abba, Father' (Rom. 8:15).

And because you are sons, God has sent forth the Spirit of His Son into your hearts, crying out, 'Abba, Father!' Therefore you are no longer a slave but a son, and if a son, then an heir of God through Christ (Gal. 4:6-7).

Let us therefore come boldly to the throne of grace, that we may obtain mercy and find grace to help in time of need (Heb. 4:16).

What I want to share now are personal examples of how I have become intimate with the Lord. Please bear in mind that I have been walking with the Lord in a committed way for just over 25 years. So what I will be relating to you took place over two and a half decades – **no way does this happen overnight!** Several years ago, it occurred to me that I might be able to "hear" the Lord's voice apart from the traditional ways I had been taught (which are the mainstays of any solid believer's walk with God, i. e., through one's own Bible study, Bible teachers, and the counsel of respected elders in the faith).

I had read Frances Roberts' devotional *Come Away My Beloved* and all her other books repeatedly over the years, and what the Lord had spoken to her yielded enormous blessings in my life (see Bibliography). I love their personal tone, as the books primarily are in the first person – the Father Himself is speaking. Here is a pertinent excerpt about the difficulty we have in trusting God and what to do about it:

My presence is experienced not by how you feel, but how you believe. It is your trust that brings you near to Me. I am always with you, as I promised I would be. Your awareness of My presence is in proportion to your confidence in Me. If you find it difficult to trust, then LOVE Me. Love bridges every gap and leaps over every mountain. It is the ultimate cure for every ill.[3]

A relevant section regarding forgiveness follows:

Mercy is the grace of the forgiven. It is possible to give only that which has been received. The man who has not accepted his own forgiveness cannot extend forgiveness to his brother. It is the nature of mercy to be gracious. Grace forgives and in so doing unlocks the self-condemned from his prison of guilt. This law operates between God and man and between man and his brother. What you loose on earth, said Jesus, shall be loosed in heaven; and likewise, what you bind on earth shall be bound in heaven. Any resentment harbored toward a brother is a binding force upon his soul.... Many a saint has lost communion with his Heavenly Father and forfeited inner peace because of hate, resentment, and unforgiveness, even when these thoughts have been concealed in the innermost recesses of his heart.[4]

A final excerpt from Frances Roberts' *Make Haste My Beloved* shows the Father's exquisite tenderness as He deals with us:

My mercy flows in the stream of all your woes, My Child. No obstacle within yourself can restrict My grace. I love you when you cannot love yourself. I forgive you while you are still repenting. I am blessing you while you are still pleading for mercy. I am not thwarted by your unperfected expression. I use many vessels while they are struggling with their failures; for in their conscious sense of need, they are more yielded to Me than they who think themselves to be without flaw.[5]

Thus, even though I felt intimidated and very unsure of myself, one morning after I had read the Word and prayed, I just put pen to paper and decided to see what would happen. I've never heard the audible voice of the Lord, and since I am a literary sort of person, it seemed like a good idea to journal it. It is significant to note at this point that nobody told me to do this... I hadn't read or been taught about writing it down (except for Frances Roberts' books). Looking back, I now realize that our Teacher, the Holy Spirit, was the One who dropped the idea into my spirit and was drawing me.

Until that point, I had been too wounded to want to hear from God.... I was just sure He would be angry with me and disappointed with my "performance" as a Christian. Therefore, by the time I ventured out into this unknown territory, I had enough emotional healing so that the idea of the Lord speaking to me wasn't foreign, mystical, or frightening.

I did everything possible to quiet myself internally, simply be still, and wait and see what would happen. Was I in for a surprise! It turns out that the Lord is speaking to us all the time (except, of course, when we're talking to Him). Because we so seldom stop to really listen for His still, small voice, we miss the glorious ways He reveals Himself, in addition to the wisdom and insight He wants to impart. However, the most important things He wants to communicate are **His love, healing, warmth, tenderness, mercy, acceptance, and encouragement – so that we never have to feel terrible insecurity or fear of abandonment again.**

I simply began writing the thoughts and impressions that came to me. Although many people are concerned that they'll hear Satan speaking to them, because of reading Roberts' books, I was familiar with what the Lord's voice sounded like. My biggest obstacle was in believing that it actually was the Lord communicating with me and not just my own wishful thinking. Ah, but He had the ready answer for that! Being an avid reader all my life and having been a professional editor, I have a fairly large vocabulary. So what did the Lord do? He began to throw in words that I simply wouldn't use in ordinary conversation.

An example of this was one time when He said, "Your path will be strewn with blessings." "Strewn?" I know what the word means, but I can safely say I don't use it in everyday communication. Once in a while, I might think of "strewn" as an overwhelmingly messy surface that has items scattered all over it, but in association with "blessings," I don't think so! Another word our Father used was "assay." I had an idea what that meant, but I had to go to the dictionary just to make sure. This was just one way He let me know that, without a doubt, it was His voice I was hearing/writing! The other way I just knew it was the Lord was that He would throw in Bible verses that I was familiar with, but had never memorized. I readily confess that memorization is not one of my strong suits, and as I am studying Hebrew currently, my lack of skill in this area has been borne out time after time.

I was filled with awe that the Creator of the Universe would talk **to me** (gulp!) when I would settle down and listen. I also felt incredibly grateful that He was continually healing me of the wounds that I still carried, despite the consistent love of a husband and other family members, many years of counseling, and what was in the pages of practically every Christian self-help book known to man (and here, I am not exaggerating!). I desperately wanted to go higher and deeper in my walk with Him… really know (yada) Him… but at the same time, I was stuck because of my hurts and fears.

When I began listening to my Abba, He would speak to me in short sentences – simply – as one would to a child, which makes sense! The entries in my journal might be a couple of short paragraphs at the most. Here is the first message I received from the Lord (which just seemed to flow out of my pen). In my journal, I labeled it "First words of the Lord while waiting on Him":

My Child, I am doing a work in you. Heed not the voice of man. Rest in Me. I AM gracious unto you. Your needs will be met and your desires satisfied. Know that I am God, the all-sufficient One. Look to Me always. I love you, My Child.

The two words showing me that these weren't just my own thoughts were "heed" and "unto." I don't talk like that! Here is later sample:

Daughter, I am your shield. Look not unto man, for he can never satisfy fully. Wait in My presence, for there you will find peace and rest. Direct your energies toward loving Me. I will never disappoint you, My Child. My Living Water will flow over you, refreshing and completing you. This is My way; walk ye in it… again I say, you will never be disappointed. You are unutterably precious to Me, My little one. I love you with an everlasting love. Praise Me for this and all the other blessings you receive from My hand. Come to Me with your deepest hurts and regrets. I will restore, heal, and bless you, My precious Child.

Again, when I analyzed this for "authenticity," the same distinction between my thoughts and the Lord was shown. I don't use the words "unto," "ye" or "unutterably." I'm also sure I never would have thought to, much less, actually call myself "precious." My deep-seated emotional pain was addressed by Him in the last sentence. These may sound like small things, but they were enough to let me know He was speaking. I also noted the relatively simple tone He used when speaking, and the tenderness with which He addressed me as "My little one." These were all things I desperately needed to hear and receive from Him.

Dr. Wilson describes one of her first "close encounters" with the Lord where she "heard" His voice:

For example, one morning I was meditating on the truth that God the Son allowed Himself to be temporarily but truly overcome (He really died). He did that so He could overcome the sin and death that would – without Him – eternally overcome us. As I murmured my stunned appreciation, I 'heard' these words [Note: and she wrote them down as she heard them]: 'You are just beginning to get an inkling of what I mean when I say I love you. I mean, I really love you! You matter to me. Those times when you are most enthralled – most moved with love for me – are but a dim reflection of how much I love you. I love you enough to let you walk away from Me so that when you return – and you will, as you know – you will experience even more of My love. And no matter how wonderful, how loving and merciful you come to know that I am, I am far more."[6]

These times of hearing the Lord never failed to be a balm to my soul – soothing, uplifting, and edifying words. As time went on, the length of the entries increased and I neither paused nor hesitated – the words came to me in a way that simply flowed naturally. In the opening quotes, Robert Pedersen referred to the process as "downloading." Here is one other entry that shows the increasing length of the messages I received and the upward pull that He was exerting to bring me into more intimacy with Him. It is evident in this entry that I had been hurt over something that had happened (probably in my counseling practice), and that as I became discouraged over it, I withdrew from His presence. Examining the word in retrospect led to that conclusion. I must have told the Lord in prayer that I missed our times together.

O My Daughter, strive to please no one but Me. Make Me your heart's desire, and all other things shall fall into place. Come beside the still waters, and I will restore and refresh you. You are exhausted and starving from not feeding on My Word. I love you, dear one, and have missed you too. Know that I will never leave you or forsake you. Don't leave Me for long periods of time, for it harms your soul more than you know. Eliminate non-essentials, and focus on Me. You will never regret the way your time is spent. Lo, I come quickly, and verily the time is short indeed. Be my mouthpiece and speak into the lives that I have given you. Hesitate not; go in the boldness I will give you each time you lean in utter dependence upon Me. For I desire to bless you with seeing the release of the captives and the healing of the brokenhearted. You must not care about the opinions of others; it is My opinion that is most important. Again I say, go boldly and you will not be disappointed. Shine in the dark places; shine with the light of forgiveness and grace. I AM that I AM that I AM your God who provides for and takes care of you. I seek to bless you in all that you do, in your going out and your coming in.

Lo… verily? Once again, not words I am inclined to use. However, by this time I needed no convincing that this was my Abba, my Papa, my true Daddy speaking to me. His voice had an unmistaken ring of authority; His words were always encouraging and uplifting and His love for me evident. **This simple practice did more to heal me, over many years, than anything else did.** As I continued, the messages increased in length. I was astonished at how much the Lord had to say to me and how profound the messages were!

Before we venture into other areas involved in hearing the Lord's voice, I will leave you one more example of His speaking to me. Over the years, I have accumulated easily a book's worth of words that the Lord has spoken to me. They have many different themes and are always unique in some way. Some are general and some very specific. There is one common element to every message that the Lord has given me: they each contain a line or two that definitely reassures me that He loves me and will never leave me… that is a constant.

O My beloved one, praise Me, My Child. Praise Me when it is most difficult to do so. For I revel in any child of Mine who trusts Me enough to praise Me when all around them is darkness or confusion. When you praise Me, I will be a Light in your darkness and confusion will cease and be replaced by peace.

I AM well pleased with you, My Daughter. You have learned to distinguish between the precious and the vile. You are trusting Me more and more. You are forgiving as I forgive. Your heart of compassion is like Mine – it is broken with the pain of others. This is a gift, My Child, though it brings great pain to you at times. Don't ask to have a thing changed as far as this heart of compassion, because I formed you for this very purpose – to shed abroad the glory of God, My love for the broken ones, My encouragement to those who are discouraged, and to bring My healing to the brokenhearted. You were created for this, and you will continue in this capacity.

I AM removing all hindrances from your life. Yes, I AM opening doors that heretofore have been slammed shut in your face. I AM removing your defects, My chosen vessel. You have become soft and pliable in My hands, and I AM fashioning you into a vessel of beauty, a golden cup holding the pure water of My Word with which to set others free. Be not dismayed at how long it has taken you to get to this point. I can use all the broken fragments of your tests and trials to the point that you will always understand deep within the suffering and sorrows others are enduring.

Continue to relinquish any layers of unforgiveness that remain toward those who have offended you. You have tasted freedom in the Spirit and found it to be good. As you release others from their sins against you, you become like Me. That is the point of refining – your surface reflects My image as it has been polished.

It is time to launch out into the deep where unfamiliar territory awaits you. You have not walked this way before, and I will equip you with the skills and strength to press on through. I say 'press on' because you will meet with much opposition from the enemy. He will attempt to deter, distract, and destroy in whatever ways he can. But you are becoming a victorious overcomer – a strong tree with deep roots from which you draw your nourishment. You will not be uprooted by the strong winds of opposition. You will only become more deeply rooted in My Word and Me, so that it will be impossible for the enemy to bring you down.

Continue to allow Me to refine your character, increase your integrity, and form you into the image and likeness of My Son. You must no longer struggle against whatever comes in your life, for you have come to realize recently that I really do use everything in your life for your good (Romans 8:28).

To read more of the words the Lord has given me, please see Appendix F. Note that any of these "rhema" words of the Lord must line up with Scripture. If they contain anything that contradicts the Holy Bible (logos), they must be discarded immediately. Below is the Wikipedia description of what the difference is between the two types of words:

Some modern usage distinguishes rhema from logos in Christian theology, with rhema at times called 'a word from the Word,' referring to the revelation received by the reader from the Holy Spirit when the Word (logos) is read. In this usage, 'logos' refers to Christ. In this modern usage, Logos is the 'Word of God,' Jesus Christ, the subject from Genesis to Revelation. Rhema is the revealed Word of God, as an utterance from God to the heart of the reader via the Holy Spirit, as in the Gospel of John '... the Holy Spirit, whom the Father will send in My name, will teach you all things and will remind you of everything I have said to you.' In this usage, rhema refers to 'a word that is spoken when the Holy Spirit delivers a message to the heart, as in the epistle to the Romans. Consequently, faith comes from hearing the message, and the message is heard through the word of Christ (rhematos Christou) and in the gospel of Matthew: 'Man does not live on bread alone, but on every word (rhema) that comes from the mouth of God.'[7]

So what distinguishes the Father's voice from Satan's voice and your own inner voice, sometimes called "self-talk"? In their excellent primer on the subject, *Listening Prayer: My Sheep Hear My Voice*, Dave and Linda Olson give us ways to distinguish one from the other:

The names God allows Himself to be called in the Scriptures tell us much about who He is and what He will do. For example, God is love. He refers to Himself in the Word as a Father, a Friend, a Companion, our Creator, and a Giver of good gifts. God wants to build a relationship with you, as a close friend. He wants you to trust Him. He wants only good for you. He made you and sees you as having tremendous potential. How will you feel when you hear His voice? You will feel rested and peaceful. You will feel at home and comforted.... You will feel special, empowered, and courageous. You will feel that you have received the same reception the prodigal son received. You will feel loved. God's voice affects you like a cool mountain stream. It feels restful, and it refreshes and invigorates you.

The Scriptures call Satan the adversary, the evil one, a spoiler, a destroyer, a thief, the accuser of the brethren. He wants to destroy our relationship with the Father. He wants to ruin our relationships with other people. He wants to spoil our joy. Satan's voice may make you feel slimed, defeated, isolated, hopeless, helpless, cynical about life, full of despair, or mesmerized. You may feel you have to take matters into your own hands. Satan's voice sounds like Las Vegas looks: glittery and garish. You feel a hypnotic pull

170

toward it; you feel a bit mesmerized. There is often a sense that you have lost your will, a feeling that you can't stop what you are doing. This voice tempts you to make quick, rash decisions. Satan tries to make you feel uncomfortable about going to God in prayer. He tries to cause you to doubt your forgiveness. He uses discouragement. He appeals to our pride and need for revenge.

The self-talk voice is the voice of your flesh. It is what you say to or about yourself all day long. This voice speaks from insecurity. The self-talk voice echoes the teachings, values, and cultural standards of this world, rather than the attitudes and values of God. Self-talk is driven by our need to be accepted and acceptable. Your critical self-talk voice will speak convincingly when you are feeling particularly unlovely, unlovable, or full of self-hatred. This voice is often destructive, filled with despair and feelings of helplessness. The person who listens to this voice will feel drained of energy or motivation. The self-talk voice makes you feel demoralized, insecure, and full of self-hate. It drives you to judge yourself inaccurately: either elevated too high or brought down too low. You may feel that you can never measure up.[8]

I once was debating with a client over whether he was hearing Satan's voice or self-talk. We concluded that for the beginner, it is enough to know that it's not God's voice. Mature believers need to have their ears fine-tuned to be able to discern exactly who is speaking so they can fight a good fight in spiritual warfare.

Mark and Patti Virkler have written several books that contain real and practical ways to "hear" the voice of the Lord resulting in conversation as a two-way street. In their compelling and inspiring work, *Four Keys to Hearing God*, they quote Charles Finney as he describes believers who have intimacy with God through hearing His voice:

[They] love the Scriptures intensely because they testify of Jesus. They search and devour the Scriptures because they tell them who Jesus is and what they may trust Him for.... They do not stop short and rest in this testimony; but by an act of loving trust [they] go directly to Him, to His person, thus joining their souls to Him in a union that receives from Him, by a direct divine communication, the things for which they are led to trust Him. This is certainly the Christian experience.... The error to which I call attention does not consist in laying too much stress in teaching and believing the facts and doctrine of the Gospel, but consists in stopping short of trusting the personal Christ for what those facts and doctrine teach us to trust Him and satisfying ourselves with believing the testimony about Him, instead of committing our souls to Him by an act of loving trust.[9]

The Virklers speak of the simplicity of hearing God's voice (which with a little help from Satan makes it feel impossible):

We are going to make something that has been very hard, very simple. I [Mark] could not hear God's voice for the first ten years of my Christian life, and now I have spent 30 years teaching the Body of Christ how to do so. It is as simple as quieting yourself down, fixing your eyes on Jesus, tuning to spontaneity, and writing! And <u>all</u> Christians can do it! <u>You</u> can do it! Jesus <u>promised,</u> 'My sheep hear My voice' (John 10:27). So you <u>can</u> hear His voice. His voice sounds like spontaneous thoughts that light upon your mind, especially as your heart is fixed on Him. And you <u>can</u> do this <u>every day</u> as part of your morning devotions. You can live out of His voice all day, by simply seeing Him alongside you (He is Immanuel, God with you) and staying tuned to spontaneity all day long. The Bible calls this abiding in Christ (see John 15:4) or 'praying without ceasing' (1Thes. 5:17, emphasis added).[10]

Mark Virkler goes on to relate his experience:

After going to Bible college, becoming an ordained pastor, and closely questioning people who professed to hear from God, I still didn't know what His voice sounded like. Their favorite answer seemed to be, 'You know that you know that you know.' Well, that didn't help me because I didn't know, and that is why I was asking them! It appeared to me that my 'relationship' with Jesus was quite thin. I couldn't hear Him. I couldn't see Him, and I couldn't feel Him. It sure seemed more like a theology about Jesus than a relationship with Him. Through a full year of my life devoted to focused prayer and research, the Lord taught me four simple keys that unlocked the ability for me to discern the voice of God within me. Now, whenever I need or want to hear from God, I can – as long as I use all four of these keys. I have traveled worldwide teaching what I have learned, and the four keys have worked in every culture, every circumstance, and every age group. God's people can recognize His voice, just as He promised! Very simply stated, the four keys to hearing God's voice are:

<u>*Stillness:*</u> *Quiet yourself so you can hear God's voice.*

<u>*Vision:*</u> *Look for vision as you pray.*

<u>*Spontaneity:*</u> *Recognize God's voice as spontaneous thoughts that light upon your mind.*

<u>*Journaling:*</u> *Write down the flow of thoughts and pictures that light upon your mind.[11]*

I highly recommend the books mentioned above to help you as you choose to seek more intimacy with Father God. Again, for those who need structure, they are excellent guides to an unfamiliar practice and provide a sense of spiritual safety with the guidelines included therein.

—∞∞∞—

What are some other ways to know that our Abba speaks with us? One of the amazing ways He has chosen, in His grace, to speak with me is what I would call the use of "confirming Scriptures." When I am not spending the dedicated blocks of time that hearing His voice requires, the Lord will speak to me in a different way. Instead of the longer and more detailed e-mail-type-of-communication I just described, this way of hearing the Lord is more like receiving texts in its brevity. Let me explain.

A couple of totals are critical in understanding the miraculous nature of this way of hearing the Lord's voice. There are 1,189 chapters in the entire Bible. I am not a gambler, nor am I particularly knowledgeable about probability, odds, etc. In order to write this section, I even consulted an online mathematician. He helped me to understand how statistically unlikely this is to happen once, not to mention repeatedly! I recognized that this was simply another way our God of infinite variety lets me know that He is always there and how much He loves me.

So what is this alternative way of hearing God's voice? Very simply, within the space of 24 hours, the Lord will impress upon me to read a certain chapter of the Bible. This can be any of the 1,189 chapters – a reading from the Torah; historical records of the Israelites and their relationships with the Lord; major or minor prophets; Psalms or Proverbs; Gospels, Acts, Epistles, or the Revelation of Jesus. Within the **next 24 hours**, I will hear or read a verse or verses from **this identical chapter from a completely different source!**

For example, either I will be impressed on my own to read a chapter, or I'll first come across it in one of the three online daily devotionals that I receive. Then, quite independently of that, I will come across **the identical chapter**, for example, being quoted on a radio station; in a Christian magazine or book I am reading; in my online browsing; on a brochure or newsletter; or any other independent source that I just "happen to stumble" upon. This happens more days than not each week. Every time it happens, I become overwhelmed inwardly with the Lord's incredible love, attention to detail, and how miraculous this way of His speaking is to me... and I don't use the word "miraculous" lightly.

As I was researching what the odds of 1 in 1,189 represented, I just "happened" to find the following article on the Internet. See the marvelous ways God works? David Appelman, the creator of *FanGraphs*, wrote the following description of exactly the same odds of 1 in 1,189 in a word picture I could grasp:

The other day I attended an Orioles game and just like every other baseball game I've been to in my entire life, I didn't catch a foul ball. I didn't catch a home run ball either, but that would have been impossible where I was sitting. While I was watching a few lucky fans snag souvenirs, I wondered what my chances of catching a foul ball actually were. Doing some quick back of the envelope calculations, I figured there were maybe 30 balls a game hit into the stands, and maybe around 30,000 fans at each game. If that were the case, about 1 in every 1,000 fans would walk away with a foul ball/home run. In reality, there were 120,946 foul balls and home runs during the 2005 season and 74,915,268 fans in attendance that same year, which ends up being about 1 in every 619 fans end up with a ball. This is probably better than the actual odds since not all foul balls are hit into the stands. If we were to say half of all foul balls were hit onto the field and the other half hit into the stands then the odds jump to 1 in 1,189 (emphasis added). Finally, there are some places in a stadium where you couldn't possibly catch a foul ball, and other places where you'd likely increase your chances, making that 1 in 1,189 hardly 100% accurate, but good enough for a rough estimate. Odds are, the only way I'll be getting a baseball at a game is at the souvenir stand.[12]

I found that pretty amazing since it gives us a visual representation of what the odds are of me "hearing" or reading the same single chapter of the Bible from disparate sources, within 24 hours. The Lord has done this so many times that whenever it happens, He and I smile broadly, and I dance around the room when He and I are alone. I realize people will try to argue this gift away, but I know (yada) that this is the Lord, even as it is confirmed by the statistical odds. I feel loved and secure when the Lord confirms Himself and His words to me repeatedly.

The day after I wrote this chapter, the Lord spoke to me this way. During the short time that I had for conversing with the Lord, I used the old "just open the Bible randomly and see what you get" method. I went directly to Job, Chapter 42. In my continuing research for this book, I have consulted with at least 50 Christian books that contain quite a variety of subjects. I was returning to some highlights I had marked in *Experiencing the Father's Love: Learning to Live as Sons and Daughters of Our Heavenly Father,* by Os Hillman. Here we go – roughly four hours after reading this chapter at home (and that was all I read in the Bible that day), I turned to the following passage in Hillman's book:

Job concluded God was not love because he attempted to understand his calamities from one viewpoint – his. We are incapable of understanding all the ways of God. Faith requires us to trust that there are things we will not fully comprehend in this lifetime. Job discovered this in the last chapter of Job: 'I have heard of You by the hearing of the ear, but now my eye sees You. Therefore, I abhor myself, and repent in dust and ashes' (Note: Job 42:5). He didn't need to understand God; he needed to see God face to face. He needed to understand his issue was with Satan, not God.[13]

I had **no way of knowing** that I would read this particular chapter that day, as I was supposed to be sitting in a Bible Study studying "The Jewish Roots of our Faith" where we have been studying Bible prophecy about the End Times. I overslept and missed the Bible Study, thus the spontaneous reading of Job, chapter 42. Although I knew I would be doing research that same day for this chapter, there are any number of books from which I could be quoting. This is how I know that this phenomenon is not random or coincidental – rather it's my Abba speaking to me while emphasizing a biblical principal [i.e., in the mouth of two or three witnesses, a matter is established (Deuteronomy 17:6 and 2 Corinthians 13:1)]. Here were my two witnesses confirming that the Lord was speaking to me, and **I did absolutely nothing to bring them to my own attention!**

With respect to this method of the Father's communication with me, whenever this happens, I once again become convinced that the Lord indeed has each of our hairs numbered and knows the name of each star He has created. Another analogy would be that found in Luke 12:7: "Are not five sparrows sold for two copper coins? And not one of them is forgotten before God" or Matthew 10:29: "… not one of them falls to the ground apart from your Father's will." I read the following statement on a website: "Currently there are over 150 million house sparrows throughout the continental 48 states of the United States."[14] Okay, that's just addressing one country (minus two states) in the world. Could we possibly calculate even the approximate number of worldwide?

These are all examples of the incredible kind of detail that is employed by our Father with respect to creation. As I continued my research on this subject, I determined that there are 774,746 words in the entire Bible.[15] The following example proved beyond a doubt that my Father really wants me to know He is in charge and has everything under control.

One day, Father God brought the name "Oreb" to my attention in Isaiah 10:26: "And the LORD of hosts will stir up a scourge for him like the slaughter of Midian at the rock of Oreb; as His rod was on the sea, so will He lift it up in the matter of Egypt." I make it a practice frequently to pray Psalm 83 over Israel. Therefore, within the same incredible timeframe as always, the Lord had me read this strange name again: "Make their nobles like Oreb and like Zeeb, Yes, all their princes like Zebah and Zalmuna" (Psalm 83:11). It turns out that this name is only in the Scripture seven times. So what are the odds that out of the 774,746 words in the Bible that I would come upon a word twice within the space of 24 hours that is used only seven times? It makes my brain hurt just thinking about it! I would definitely need a mathematician to figure this one out. **The Lord certainly goes to great lengths to show us His love in ways that let us know how much He is concerned about every detail of our lives!**

I think the most dramatic "word" that I have received occurred during the last week I was writing this book. I was listening to a CD by Marty Goetz (an incredible Messianic Jewish pianist/vocalist; look him up; order one of his albums; and I can **guarantee** you won't be sorry). The song being played and sung was his musical version of Psalm 23. The song wasn't even over when, as I was cleaning my desk, I came upon some decorative "coins" that I got at a woman's luncheon at least a year ago. The first one I looked at (mind you, **while the song was still playing**) had the words, "The Lord is my Shepherd," on its front. That one just "blew me away!" (to use an expression from the seventies). When something like this happens, I know the Lord is virtually shouting at me. This only happens when I am spiritually "hard of hearing" and haven't yet gotten the significance of something spiritually. He certainly got my attention this time, so I've been meditating on Psalm 23 and a shepherd's job description (which can be found in Phillip Keller's *A Shepherd Looks at the 23rd Psalm*).

Perhaps the most personal way the Lord ever spoke to me was via a human being at an extremely critical time in my life. It involved the pastor of my church, while we were on a tour of Israel. As excited as I was to be on the trip, I was experiencing profound depression and a feeling of hopelessness, certain that I could never "measure up" to what I then perceived as the Lord's standards for me. I felt great shame over some things I had done, and I was way too scared ever to confess them to anyone else but someone who absolutely **had** to keep my confidence. On the second day of the trip (we were on a cruise through the Greek Isles to visit biblically significant sites on our way to Israel), I summoned up all the nerve I had, approached Pastor Ezell, whom I barely knew, and asked if I could have some time to speak with him about personal matters.

In what proved to be a devastating response, Pastor Ezell replied that now was not the best time for me to be seeking his counsel, as there was a lot going on for him as shepherd of our large group on tour. He advised me to disembark, go ahead with my friends and enjoy sightseeing with them and touring the island, and ask to speak with him later.

I instantly felt crushed…. In some intangible way, I all but gave up, shutting down emotionally as never before. Inwardly I vowed that I would not ask him to speak again later – that I would never attempt any personal contact again. I felt so incredibly vulnerable even asking him to talk and took his answer so personally that any hope I had left drained away. After that, I rapidly descended into a deep pit of rejection and bitterness. Thinking that the entire trip was ruined, I decided to simply avoid him the rest of the time and try to salvage whatever I could from being in the Holy Land.

A couple of days later, when our group was returning to their cabins, stuffed from a huge luncheon buffet and given some free time, Pastor Ezell approached me and asked if I would like to talk. I was shocked and actually could feel all the rejection and bitterness I had within begin to melt away. Anticipating the relief of just venting about my hopeless life, I followed him to a comfortable room on the ship and began pouring out what was lodged so deeply in my heart.

After I made my confessions and tearfully expressed my hopelessness, Pastor Ezell suddenly and unexpectedly asked me, "Were you ever molested?" I could barely catch my breath as I answered affirmatively, wondering, *Boy, can this guy read minds or what?* After telling me about my history of abuse, I was amazed as he showed me connections between what had happened to me as a child and the chaos of my current emotional state. As we wound up our discussion, Pastor Ezell instructed me to call the church office when we got home and schedule some counseling sessions with him.

While looking down and away from him, I whispered, "I feel so ashamed of what I've done and telling you about everything… what must you think of me?" I will never forget what happened next. He tipped my chin up so that I had no choice but to look at him and then answered the cry of a wounded soul. **"Well, you know what? I just love you more, because now I know you more."**

What??? I stared at him, at first uncomprehendingly, but then with the dawning awareness that a sizeable part of my deep emotional wounds had been healed right then and there. **In that moment, Pastor Ezell became Abba Father Himself. It was no longer the human being that I was hearing, rather the Lord was speaking directly through him – imparting His grace, mercy, and love to me in a way that male authority figures never had before.** A gigantic chunk of the monolith of shame, which was ever present in my life, broke off and vanished. Although I would continue working on shame issues over the years, that was an unforgettable day of receiving the Lord's healing.

A few years ago, Abba reached out to me and I was able to receive what was to bring much greater intimacy between us. One night I couldn't sleep and had gone to the family room in our home to just commune with the Lord. The enemy, accuser of the brethren that he is, began listing recent spiritual failures and, in taking me back to my early adulthood, brought up shortcomings and failings (aka sins) that I had already **confessed, repented of,** and **put under the Blood of Jesus**.

As I spiraled downward in complete freefall, I landed in a horrible place of regret, condemnation, and despair. I thoroughly reviewed how differently my life had turned out from what I felt was an early calling to full-time Christian service. The comparison trap beckoned – I couldn't stop thinking that if I had been brought up in a different setting, with a believing father who had encouraged me to follow Jesus, I might have turned out to be a better daughter of the King. I might have truly been able to bring glory to His name. I began comparing myself with Christians who had excelled in their walks (singers, Bible teachers, missionaries, etc.) and despised what I now saw as my pathetic, anemic testimony.

Overall, it was the kind of mental spiritual attack that the devil specializes in – overwhelming believers with memories of sin, regrets, and emotional pain over their entire lifespan. As I felt myself falling into an abyss of sorts, I distinctly "heard" His still, small voice begin to speak. In His ineffable way (no way to really put this into words), Abba Father let me know that He knew all the desires I had had as a Christian youth and that He understood my feelings of sorrow and shame over the way I had "turned out." He went on to say that even though **I hadn't become who I thought I was supposed to be,** that He was making something beautiful out of the marred, chipped, broken vessel that I believed myself to be. He also let me know that He was pleased with me and would continue to mold, shape, and refine me into that vessel of honor that I so passionately wanted to be.

By far the most valuable truth He imparted to me that night was that He loved me just the way I was – that if I never changed one iota that His love would not diminish for me. Though I had never voiced the question, deep in my heart I had often agonized over how He could love me – in fact, why did He love me? His reply brings tears of joy whenever I think about it:

I love you because you are Mine – you are My precious Daughter, and I don't need reasons to love you. My love for you has not been, nor will ever be, more or less, than it is right now. Nothing you do or don't do has any bearing on My love for you. You can stop performing for Me any time now, because you don't need to earn My love! Just bask in the infinite love that I have for you. Hear Me once again: I love you just because you are Mine.

Our Father God feels that way about each one of His sons and daughters. If you will simply become quiet and still before Him, I can **guarantee** that you will hear the same message, but it will be in a unique form that speaks directly to your heart. The way He chooses to communicate these unalterable facts to you will likely be completely different from mine, Frances Robert's, Sandra Wilson's, Mark Virkler's, or anyone else who testifies that when they hear God's voice, healing does bring joy unspeakable and full of glory into our souls (1 Peter 1:8).

Afterword

You absolutely owe it to yourself to read the accounts of child abuse survivors as far as the process of forgiveness they went through and the healing that obedience in this realm produced (**Appendix B**). As I note at the beginning of the appendix, these accounts could make up a stand-alone volume. The abuse reported by the survivors is shocking, heinous, inconceivable, devastating, horrific, revolting, etc., etc. The evil perpetrated against innocent children is palpable as one reads the accounts. However, if the abuse was **all** that was described, reading it would just make you feel outraged, indignant, and deeply depressed. The reason for choosing to include these particular survivor accounts lies in their incredible illustrations of the power of forgiveness and subsequent healing of wounds from abuse that seems unforgiveable.

I cannot recommend the survivors' books highly enough, as I only included excerpts that were applicable to this book. The account of my own abuse and forgiveness process is lengthy, but I want nothing from my life story that might validate other survivors' abuse, aftereffects, and healing process to be off limits. I also want to comfort, encourage, bring hope (hatkivah), and inspire readers. One of my favorite Bible passages showed me a piece of the "all things work together for good" puzzle in my life (and will most likely be in yours as well):

> *Blessed be the God and Father of our Lord Jesus Christ, the Father of mercies and God of all comfort, who comforts us in all our tribulation, that we may be able to comfort those who are in any trouble, with the comfort with which we ourselves are comforted by God. For as the sufferings of Christ abound in us, so our consolation also abounds through Christ (2 Cor. 1:3-5).*

I have been able to comfort others with the comfort I received countless times. It is a beautiful thing to be able to say with Joseph: "**But as for you, you meant evil against me; but God meant it for good, in order to bring it about as it is this day, to save many people alive**" (Gen. 50:20). Our sovereign Lord can turn anything with which our abusers and Satan intended to harm us into a spiritual, sometimes even natural, victory for us.

Although I have compared myself many times with other, more mature believers, I have come to the point of saying I would not choose to be anyone else in this world other than myself. That isn't **self-esteem** talking; rather it's **Christ-esteem**. I am happy with who I have become in Christ Jesus. Although details of all our stories differ, the process of healing from child abuse is the same for everyone. We know that God is not a respecter of persons – He doesn't play favorites – therefore what He has done and continues to do for me, He will do for you!

On the question of self-esteem, I struggled for years to come to a balance between secular humanistic psychology and the basic doctrinal tenets of Christianity. The underlying philosophies completely contradict one another! The idea of unlimited human potential (and that all we need was to have our self-esteem levels raised) and the biblical doctrine that we must take up our crosses and follow Jesus – dying for Him on a daily basis as we crucify the flesh – just didn't mesh.

In his incisive and hard-hitting book, *The Culture of Excess: How America Lost Self-Control and Why We Need to Redefine Success*, J. R. Slosar makes the following observations:

> *Fortunately, the do-it-now and feel-good-about-yourself movement has been challenged. In the early 1990s, psychology had an active debate about the self-esteem movement that had resulted in approximately 30 U.S. states enacting more than 170 statutes promoting self-esteem in schools. Many notable psychological researchers pointed out research showing that gang leaders, terrorists, and extremely ethnocentric people all had higher than average self-esteem. In addition, young males with higher than average self-esteem were more likely to engage in sexual activity at an earlier age than would be considered appropriate or desired. On the flip side, psychological research showed that those with low self-esteem were not prone to violence. The noted researcher Roy Baumeister, who acknowledges 'probably publishing more studies on self-esteem than anybody else,' reports in 1996, 'The enthusiastic claims of the self-esteem movement mostly range from fantasy to hogwash.' Most notable is his summation: 'My conclusion is that self-control is worth ten times as much as self-esteem.*[1]

Hmmm... isn't that interesting? Self-control – a fruit of the Holy Spirit! When Don Matzat came out with a book entitled, *Christ-Esteem: Where the Search for Self-Esteem Ends,* the proverbial light bulb switched on in my mind. Why would I give my clients the mixed message that they were great people and thus lift their self-esteem, yet simultaneously communicate that we are sinners saved by grace and need to die to our flesh to be conformed to Christ's image? The book title alone answered that particular conundrum that causes conflict in the heart of every conscientious Christian counselor. Please see Appendix D for more on this subject of vital importance to the Body of Christ.

Ah, but I digress. You might be frustrated that I keep using words like "continuing," "process," "lifelong." *Not very encouraging*, you're thinking, *I need my healing... like yesterday*! That's quite understandable.... **The good news is that I do believe survivors reach the point in their lives where they are whole!** That's one good thing about grief: it has an end to it! The process of sanctification, however, does not. By definition, it takes place over the lifespan. Although you will bear the scars of abuse on your body and in your psyche, they will no longer be painful to the touch. Our High Priest Jesus still bears the physical scars of His torturous abuse right now and will for all eternity.

As far as healing goes, we are told in the Word of God that while we are walking around in these mortal bodies, things will happen in our lives that will really hurt. Along with our need for additional healing at those times, we will need to forgive those who offend us. Remember what Martin Luther King, Jr. said? **"Forgiveness is not an occasional act: it is an attitude."**

It's very helpful if you can think of that catchy little slogan that used to be on bumper stickers: "Please be patient with me – God isn't finished yet!" as a truth that, when accepted, makes the trials and tribulations that we all go through more comprehensible. We really are Christians under construction!

On a different note, the danger of reconciling with an unrepentant abuser has been stressed repeatedly throughout this book. If the offending party believes he/she has done nothing wrong, he/she will keep right on doing it, in one form or another. Those of you who were physically abused by someone, now, oftentimes by virtue of your size alone, can prevent that from continuing, but often the abuser will simply switch over to emotional/verbal abuse. I make the following statement boldly and unapologetically:

<u>I don't believe the Lord calls His children to abuse!</u>

In other words, the days when a woman might be receive pastoral counsel to continue to live with a battering husband are past (at least in 99 percent of cases, hopefully). If a person who is constantly criticizing and belittling you is confronted with that fact and doesn't slow it down or eventually stop, my core belief is that it is absolutely permissible with the Lord for you to step back from the relationship temporarily or permanently. The Lord I serve doesn't call us to be punching bags in any way for anyone (with the exception of our brothers and sisters who are imprisoned and being persecuted for their faith).

During the time I wrote this book, a member of my father's family re-entered my life after a period of separation and started their emotional abuse all over again. It definitely hurt and got me down for a while, but with Abba's love plus the understanding and support of family and friends, I can definitely say I am healed from their abuse. I got the "opportunity" to forgive once again and put into practice things about which I was writing.

It is my fervent hope and earnest prayer that you will be touched and inspired by what you have read – inspired enough to start the process yourself. As the saying goes, "There's no time like the present!" What will be the ultimate result? You will be able to pray the following and mean it with all your heart:

Abba, I surrender my will and my life to You without any reservation and with boundless confidence, for You are my loving Father. (Prayer by Brennan Manning)

Appendix A

Are You Born Again? If Not, You Can Be!

By J. C. Ryle

This is one of the most important questions that could be asked. Jesus Christ says, *"Except a man be born again, he cannot see the kingdom of God"* – John 3:3.

Are you born again?

It is not enough to reply, "I belong to the church; and I suppose I am." Thousands of nominal Christians have none of the marks and signs of being born again which the Scripture has given us.

Would you like to know the marks and signs of being born again? You may know those six signs and marks of being born again as given in the first epistle of John.

First of all, John says, *"Whosoever is born of God doth not commit sin;" and again, "Whosoever is born of God sinneth not."* – I John 3:9; 5:18 (KJV).

A man born again, or regenerate, does not commit sin as a habit. He no longer sins with his heart and will and whole inclination, as an unregenerate man does. There was probably a time when he did not think whether his actions were sinful or not and never felt grieved after doing evil. There was no quarrel between him and sin; they were friends. Now he hates sin, flees from it, fights against it, counts it his greatest plague, groans under the burden of its presence, mourns when he falls under its influence, and longs to be delivered from it altogether. In one word, sin no longer pleases him, nor is even a matter of indifference; it has become the abominable thing which he hates. He cannot prevent its dwelling within him. If he said he had no sin, there would be no truth in him (1 John 1:8). But he can say that he abhors it, and the great desire of his soul is not to commit sin at all. He cannot prevent bad thoughts arising within him, and shortcomings, omissions, and defects appearing, in his both words and actions. He knows, as James says, that *"In many things we offend all"* (James 3:2). However, he can say truly, and in the sight of God, that things are a daily grief and sorrow to him, and that his whole nature does not consent unto them.

I place this mark before you. What would the Apostle say about you? **Are you born again?**

Secondly, John says, *"Whosoever believeth that Jesus is the Christ, is born of God"* – 1 John 5:1 (KJV).

A man born again, or regenerate, then, believes that Jesus Christ is the only Savior by whom his soul can be pardoned; that He is the divine person appointed by God the Father for this very purpose, and that beside Him there is no Savior at all. In himself, he sees nothing but unworthiness, but in Christ he sees ground for the fullest confidence, and trusting in Him he believes that his sins are all forgiven. He believes that for the sake of Christ's finished work and death upon the cross, he is reckoned righteous in God's sight, and may look forward to death and judgment without alarm. He may have his fears and doubts. He may sometimes tell you he feels as if he had not faith at all. But ask him whether he will rest his hopes of eternal life on his own goodness, his own achievements, his prayers, his minister, or his church, and see what he will reply. Ask him whether he will give up Christ, and place his confidence in any other way of religion. Depend upon it; he would say that though he does feel weak and bad, he would not give up Christ for all the world. Depend upon it; he would say he found preciousness in Christ, suitableness to his own soul in Christ, that he found nowhere else, and that he **must** cling to him.

I place this mark before you. What would the Apostle say about you? **Are you born again?**

Thirdly, John says, *"Every one that doeth righteousness is born of Him"* – 1 John 2:20 (KJV).

The man born again, or regenerate, then is, a holy man. He endeavors to live according to God's will, to do the things that please God, to avoid the things that God hates. His aim and desire is to love God with heart and soul and mind and strength, and to love his neighbor as himself. His wish is to be continually looking to Christ as his example as well as his Savior, and to show himself Christ's friend by doing whatsoever Christ commands. No doubt, he is not perfect. None will tell you that sooner than himself. He groans under the burden of indwelling corruption cleaving to him. He finds an evil principle within him constantly warring against Grace, and trying to draw him away from God. But he does not consent to it, though he cannot prevent its presence. In spite of all shortcomings, the average bent and bias of his way is holy, his doings are holy, his tastes holy, and his habits holy. In spite of all this swerving and turning aside, like a ship beating up against a contrary wind, the general course of his life is in one direction toward God and for God. And though he may sometimes feel so low that he questions whether he is a Christian at all, he will generally be able to say with old John Newton, "I am not what I ought to be, I am not what I want to be. I am not what I hope to be in another world, but still I am not what I once used to be, and by the Grace of God I am what I am."

I place this mark also before you. What would the Apostle say about you?

Are you born again?

Fourthly, John says, *"We know that we have passed from death unto life, because we love the brethren"* – 1 John 3:14 (KJV).

A man born again, or regenerate, then, has a special love for all true disciples of Christ. Like his Father in heaven, he loves all men with a great general love, but he has a special love for those who are of one mind with himself. Like his Lord and Savior, he loves the worst of sinners, and could weep over them; but he has a peculiar love for those who are believers. He is never so much at home as when he is in their company. He is never as happy as when he is among the saints and the excellent of the earth. Others may value learning, or cleverness, or agreeableness, or riches or rank, in the society they choose. The regenerate man values Grace. Those who have most Grace, and are most like Christ, are those he most loves. He feels that they are members of the same family with himself. He feels that they are his fellow-soldiers, warring against the same enemy. He feels that they are his fellow travelers, journeying along the same road. He understands them, and they understand him. He and they may be very different in many ways in rank, in station, in wealth. What matter? They are Jesus Christ's people. They are his Father's sons and daughters. Then he cannot help loving them.

I place this mark also before you. What would the Apostle say about you? **Are you born again?**

Fifthly, John says, *"Whatsoever is born of God overcometh the world"* – 1 John 5:4 (KJV).

A man born again, or regenerate, does not make the world's opinion his rule of right and wrong. He does not mind going against the stream of the world's way, notions, and customs. "What will men say?" is no longer a turning point with him. He overcomes the love of the world. He finds no pleasure in things which most around him call happiness. He cannot enjoy their enjoyments: they weary him: they appear to him vain, unprofitable, and unworthy of an immortal being. He overcomes the fear of the world. He is content to do many things which all around him think unnecessary, to say the least. They blame him: it does not move him. They ridicule him: he does not give way. He loves the praise of God more than the praise of men. He fears offending Him more than giving offense to man. He has counted the cost. It is a small thing with him whether he is blamed or praised. He is no longer the servant of fashion and custom. To please the world is quite a secondary consideration with him. His first aim is to please God.

I place this mark also before you. What would the Apostle say about you? **Are you born again?**

Sixthly, John says, *"He that is begotten of God keepeth himself"* I John 5:18 (KJV).

A man born again, or regenerate, is very careful of his own soul. He endeavors not only to keep clear of sin, but also to keep clear of everything that may lead to it. He is careful about the company he keeps. He feels that evil communications corrupt the heart, and that evil is far more catching than good, just as disease is more infectious than health. He is careful about the employment of his **time:** his chief desire about it is to spend it profitably. He is careful about the **friendships** he forms: it is not enough for him that people are kind and amiable and good-natured; all this is very well; but will they do good to his soul? He is careful over his own daily habits and behavior: he tries to recollect that his own heart is deceitful, the world full of wickedness, and the devil always laboring to do him harm; and, therefore, he would fain be always on his guard. He desires to live like a soldier in an enemy's country, to wear his armor continually, and to be prepared for temptation. He finds by experience that his soul is ever among enemies, and he studies to be a watchful, humble, prayerful man.

I place this mark also before you. What would the Apostle say about you? **Are you born again?**

Such are the six great marks of being born again. Let everyone who has gone so far with me, read them over with attention, and lay them to heart.

I know there is a vast difference in the depth and distinctness of these marks in different people. In some they are faint, dim, feeble, and hardly to be discerned. In others, they are bold, sharp, clear, plain, and unmistakable, so that any one may read them. Some of these marks are more visible in some, and others are more visible in others. It seldom happens that all are equally manifest in one and the same soul. All this I am quite ready to allow.

But still after every allowance, here we find boldly painted six marks of being born of God. Here is an inspired Apostle writing one of the last general epistles to the Church of Christ, telling us that a man born of God **does not commit sin, believes that Jesus is the Christ, does righteousness, loves the brethren, overcomes the world, and keeps himself.** I ask the reader to observe all this.

Now what shall we say to these things? What can they say to those who hold that regeneration is only an admission to outward church privileges; I am sure I do not know. For myself I say boldly, I can only come to one conclusion. That conclusion is that only those persons are born again, who have these six marks about them, and that all men and women who have not these marks are not born again. And I firmly believe that this is the conclusion to which the Apostle wished us to come. **Reader, have you these marks? Are you born again?**[1]

—⊸∝∝∝⊷—

If you have read this section and believe you are **NOT** born again and want to be, please read the following prayer aloud with all your heart (which is quoted from Rick Renner's wonderful book, *Paid in Full: An In-Depth Look at the Defining Moments of Christ's Passion*):

Lord, I can never adequately thank You for all You did for me on the Cross. I am so undeserving, Jesus, but You came and gave Your life for me anyway. I repent and turn from my sins right now. Jesus, I receive You as my Savior, and I ask You to wash away my sin by Your precious blood. I thank You from the depths of my heart for doing what no one else could do for me. Had it not been for Your willingness to lay down Your life for me, I would be eternally lost.

Thank You, Jesus, that I am now redeemed by Your blood. You bore my sin, my sickness, my pain, my lack of peace, and my suffering on the Cross. Your blood has cleansed me from my sin and washed me whiter than snow, giving me right standing with the Father. I have no need to be ashamed of my past sins, because I am now a new creature in You. Old things have passed away, and all things have become new because I am in Jesus Christ (1 Corinthians 5:17).

Because of You, Jesus, today I am forgiven; I am filled with peace; and I am a joint heir with You! Satan no longer has a right to lay any claim on me. From a grateful heart, I will faithfully serve You the rest of my days!

If you prayed this prayer from your heart, something amazing has happened to you. No longer a servant to sin, you are now a servant of Almighty God. The evil spirits that once exacted every ounce of your being and required your all-inclusive servitude no longer possess the authorization to control you or to dictate your destiny.

As a result of your decision to turn your life over to Jesus Christ, your eternal home has been decided forever. HEAVEN is now your permanent address.

God's Spirit has moved into your own human spirit, and you have become the 'temple of God' (1 Corinthians 6:19). What a miracle! To think that God, by His Spirit, now lives inside of you! I have never ceased to be amazed at this incredible miracle of God in my own life. He gave me (and you!) a new heart and then made us His home!

Now you have a new Lord and master, and His name is Jesus. From this moment on, the Spirit of God will work in you and supernaturally energize you to fulfill God's will for your life. Everything will change for you now – and it's all going to change for the best! [2]

Appendix B

Accounts of Abuse Survivors Who Chose to Forgive

*I*n this appendix, I have included both first-person accounts and biographical articles written about people who have survived child abuse, trauma, torture, and atrocities... and have chosen to forgive. These people are speaking from different religious perspectives, e.g., Jewish, Christian, New Age, Buddhist, etc., as well as from the standpoint of atheism. To a person, they agree on the fact that healing could not come unless they had at least a willingness to forgive. I have also included my own account of the abuse I suffered, the process of healing, and the path of forgiveness I chose.

Warning:

These survivor accounts may contain triggers. For those just beginning to deal with memories of abuse, I would recommend NOT reading this appendix. Definition: An abuse trigger is an emotional or physical reaction to something in the present that is connected to your past abuse. When you are in the midst of a trigger, you may not be able to distinguish the past from the present. You may have images or memories of the abuse. A trigger can be anything from a certain smell to someone touching a certain part of your body. If you are currently in therapy to heal from child abuse, show this book to your therapist before reading this appendix.

Important Note:

As carefully spelled out in Chapter One, please do not compare your abuse to any of these survivor accounts. Many people will be intimidated by reading Holocaust survivors' accounts of the abuse they suffered and their process of forgiveness. I included them for many reasons, the most important of which is to show how freeing forgiveness is for anyone. Please keep in mind that any and all kinds of abuse result in horrible damage to a child, and it never just "goes away" as we wish it would. Many people who "only" suffered emotional and verbal abuse will say that they wish their abusers would have beaten them... that the more "subtle" abuse results linger far longer than physical abuse. This is not to minimize physical abuse – just an exhortation that whatever kinds of abuse you or a loved one endured have produced lasting, deep wounds that can seriously hinder an unbeliever's desire to be born again or a believer's walk with God.

This appendix could actually be a standalone book. However, my intention is that many survivors' accounts of the process of forgiveness be inspirational and illustrative of the process of healing. I urge you to purchase any or all of the books being quoted here – hopefully these excerpts will simply whet your appetite and make you want to know the rest of the story.

Anne

I have been on a road, a journey for much of my life. Looking to find a way to discover peace, a place where my feet are on the ground and my face tipped up to the sun.

I was raped as a child, following the death of my father, by someone in my family. It happened many times over many years. It has come close to destroying me and killing my faith in life and living. But yet it hasn't destroyed me, it hasn't managed to tip the balance of life into the red.

For me this road is about reconciliation and choice. The reconciliation is not [necessarily].... with the person who hurt you, because often as in my case, that is not possible, but there is also a need for reconciliation with yourself. I have a yearning, a calling towards peace. And hatred towards another or towards myself is not going to lead me towards peace. I have had to learn to forgive myself for not telling anyone, for not saying no, for not getting help. I have had to learn not to hate myself, my body and my history for not giving me the tools to stand firm and know that I have a right to be alive.

As for the person who did this to me, I can honestly say that my overwhelming feeling is compassion. To wound someone like that can only be done by someone who hates themselves, who has no respect for themselves and who is suffering deeply. He has great wounds himself and that is why he did what he did. The road to feeling this has been long and at times, my fear and anger toward him and myself have been overwhelming. I have battled with self-harm, suicidal yearnings, self-loathing and still now, in order to combat those feeling, I have to actively choose to turn away from those mechanisms that I used to survive.

The biggest turning point has been realizing I have a choice in how I respond to how I feel. I do not have to indulge those feelings of loathing, self-hatred or powerlessness. If I have no choice in those feelings then ultimately I will not recover. Whereas if I can choose where to place my focus and my attention then I find I have more options, more chance of healing. I cannot change what happened to me but I can change my response to it.

My ultimate aim would be to help in understanding so that people who have harmed others do not go on to do it again. And in that capacity I would very much want to be involved in what you are doing. Hatred and anger will only breed hatred and anger. Ultimately that is why what happened to me happened.

I have written to people on death row for 10 years now and I have come to see so clearly in the relationships I have built up that none of us are the sum total of the best, or the worst, thing we have ever done. I have written to one particular man now for all of those 10 years; he was convicted of rape and murder and yet we still have found a way of letting both our humanity shine through. I would say that for both of us it has been ultimately a deeply healing thing.

So much of my life is now healed; I am happily married with children. So much is happy and my face is mostly tipped up towards the sun. And that is lovely. The bits that are still sore I am learning to live alongside and find reconciliation with. I do not fight them anymore but we are learning to live with each other. I am learning over and over, as I did as a child, to choose life, to choose saying yes and to choose to love. It has been so hard to get here, so hard to find a way to choose to live again but so worthwhile.

http://theforgivenessproject.com/visitor-stories/annes-healing-following-childhood-rape/

Stormie Omartian

Where Stormie Omartian Finds Her Power
By Tim Stafford

(Stormie) Omartian grew up with an abusive mother. The family was poor, and Omartian often went to bed hungry. When she was a little girl on a remote Wyoming ranch, her mother would lock her in a closet and leave her for hours. She also beat her and cursed her. Her father, a quiet and gentle soul, was too passive to defend her. They had no neighbors. The little girl would make up poems and stories to entertain herself.

Ultimately, Omartian's mother would be diagnosed as schizophrenic, though she was never hospitalized. Her daughter, an only child until she was 12, believed her mother hated her.

The family moved to Southern California, where her father ran a gas station and later worked at Knott's Berry Farm. Omartian felt ashamed of her home. She believed herself ugly and unlikable. In junior high school, she tried to commit suicide. In high school, she compensated for her shaky confidence by joining student government and participating in school plays. She always got good grades. While studying music at UCLA she began to work in Hollywood. Soon she was singing, dancing, and acting on one TV show after another. Yet she grew even unhappy. "No matter what glamorous and wonderful things happened to me," she says, "I still saw myself as ugly and unacceptable."

She used drugs and practiced occult religions. Relationships with a variety of men, married and unmarried, led to illegal abortions. She had panic attacks wherever she worked. She entered a brief and loveless marriage. Deeply depressed at 28, she began to plan her suicide.

That was when a friend talked her into visiting a young pastor, Jack Hayford. He gave Omartian three books to read: C. S. Lewis's *The Screwtape Letters*, the Gospel of John, and a book on the Holy Spirit. When they met again, Hayford invited Omartian to commit her life to Jesus. "I left the office feeling light and hopeful, though I didn't know what it all meant," she later wrote.

Omartian had almost no church background. She knew nothing about Christian living. Furthermore, she soon discovered that her problems had not gone away. But she had incredible motivation to grow. "She had been so wounded and bruised, so injured, she was broken at all points," Hayford remembers. "Yet she was remarkably gifted, with a ready heart and a quick mind. There was childlikeness in Stormie's heart toward God that she has always maintained."

Even though she fell in love with Hayford's church, The Church on the Way, Omartian continued to struggle with depression. Even after marrying Michael and quitting show business, she had daily thoughts of suicide. A church counselor, Mary Anne Pientka, believed that a spirit of oppression was involved. She suggested three days of fasting, followed by a careful regimen of confession and prayer. "When we prayed, that depression lifted," Omartian says. "It was the most amazing thing. I had no idea that could even happen. I felt the depression lift and I thought, 'Okay, this is amazing, this is like taking an aspirin, and you get rid of your headache.' I was assuming it would be back in the morning.

"But the next morning I woke up and it was still gone. And the next day, it was still gone. And the next, and the next, and the next. I tell you, if I wasn't a believer before, I was then. I was never so shocked. I tell you, it wasn't my faith. It was a demonstration of God's power, and I really had nothing to do with it. I was so amazed. That changed my life."

Omartian knows that some people need thoughtful counseling as well as prayer. Some people need medical attention. A chemical imbalance requires drug therapy, she says. Omartian also knows that not all our prayers get answered as we prefer. "For example, I've always prayed that my kids would be safe, that they wouldn't be in an accident." But her children did have accidents. "You shouldn't get mad at God if he doesn't answer exactly the way you prayed it," she explains. "He heard you. Just trust Him."

This article first appeared in July 2004 issue of *Christianity Today*. Used by permission of Christianity Today International, Carol Stream, IL 60188.

Account from Stormie's book on her process of forgiveness:

Another important key was forgiveness. Forgiving others, especially my mother, became something I had to deal with daily. I confessed forgiveness for her in the counseling office and thought I had taken care of it until the very next time I saw her. Then all the old feelings of hatred, frustration, bitterness, and anger came forth like a flood, and along with them came their partners, defeat and low self-esteem.

"God, I forgive my mother," I confessed daily whether I felt like it or not. "Help me to forgive her completely." I knew without a doubt that harboring unforgiveness would keep me from the wholeness and blessing God had for me, and that it would make me sick physically. I knew I could never be completely whole as long as I had any unforgiveness. I had to keep working on it. It was during this time I learned that forgiveness doesn't make the other person right, it makes you free.

God was faithful to answer my prayer, and forgiveness for my mother developed in me to such a point that I was eventually able to see her as God made her to be and not the way she was. I saw how the traumas of her life had misshaped her, and how she, like I had been, was a victim of her past.... I saw her like I had never seen her before, and instead of hating her I felt sorry and began praying for her healing.

——⁂——

Over the next few weeks, I began to see clearly that I did indeed harbor unforgiveness toward my dad for never once coming to my rescue when I was a child. He never let me out of the closet. He never pulled my mother off my back. He never once protected me from her insanity. I had been let down by the one person who was my protector, my covering. The unforgiveness I harbored was unconfessed because I had never allowed myself to consciously think angry thoughts toward him.... The more this problem was exposed, the more it became apparent that we weren't talking about simply unforgiveness and anger. We were talking about rage – rage toward my dad. Because of this rage and unforgiveness, I had grown up to distrust all male authority – not all men, but only those in authority over my life, such as my pastor and my husband.

I confessed my unforgiveness for Dad, and as I did.... it unleashed a torrent of emotion unlike any I'd experienced in adult life. I recognized it as the pain I had felt as a small child locked in a closet with no one to help me.... I was sure it wasn't the only thing that leads to mental imbalance, but I knew for certain that a sound mind cannot exist with deep unforgiveness and rage. There is a direct tie between forgiveness and wholeness (emphasis added).

....

After I forgave Dad, I could see how much he really did love me. He never showed it openly because he was not comfortable doing that, but his love was there just the same. I discovered that even though a parent may love a child deeply, unless the child perceives that love he won't feel loved.

Stormie Omartian, *Stormie: A Story of Forgiveness and Healing* (Eugene, OR: Harvest House Publishers), 1986. Used by permission. All rights reserved.

Kari

Kari witnessed repeated abuse of her younger sister at the hands of her uncle when they were both small children. Not long after, her mother entered a physically violent relationship with her stepfather who has also sexually abused his biological daughter.

I met my now fiancé and just knew he was "the one." You know how you meet someone and they ask, "What type of guy/girl do you typically go for?" Well he asked that and I declined to answer because after what seemed to be a lifetime of being let down, I didn't need someone trying to live up to a definition undefined. Does that make sense?

Someone trying to live up to the fairytale that doesn't exist, I mean my mom was supposed to be my mom. As in ideally a nurturing, protecting, and loving person of their child, when in all reality she was the mom that she knew. Not the mom by the books. All I required was that he didn't drink beer and try to kiss me, etc. The stench of my mom's husband's breath haunts me to this day.

We fell in love and… my newfound boyfriend was now what school was to me then: an escape. Willingly, we had sex before he knew of the abuse. We were coming from Orlando, I had wandered into the thoughts somehow, and I folded like a chair.

He immediately pulled over on the interstate, heard me out, held me so close, and felt my pain. He was absolutely disgusted and never wanted to meet him, declaring that if he did he'd confront him. I made him promise not to; he agreed but said he'd never shake his hand though. I had, at the point of meeting my fiancé, just come to know that I had to heal to move forward. I have forgiven my mom and her husband although they don't know it….

http://thesolsurvivor.blogspot.com/

Faith Allen

It has taken me years to come to terms with issues surrounding forgiveness. The abuses that I suffered as a child ran much deeper than a simple grudge over a property dispute. It has taken me years to overcome the severe damage that my abusers inflicted upon my body, soul, and spirit. I was unable to forgive them until I worked through many other issues, including honoring my emotions associated with all that I had endured.

I define forgiveness much differently than society does. Society uses pat sayings like "forgive and forget" that are simply not possible. How can I possibly "forget" being severely traumatized? The trauma happened, and it cannot be undone. Society also equates forgiveness with reconciliation, which takes away the abuse survivor's power because she needs the abuser to take action toward reconciliation, and many abusers have no interest in doing so. I have found that reconciliation is not necessary in order to forgive, because forgiveness is a gift that I give myself and has nothing to do with the other person.

Forgiveness is a choice rather than a moment. It is a series of choices to stop nursing your bitterness toward your abuser and, instead, use the freed-up energy toward healing yourself. You need do nothing externally for this to happen, and you certainly do not have to have contact with your abuser to accomplish this.

Each time you focus on your bitterness toward your abuser, no matter how legitimate your grievance is, you are choosing to keep yourself "wed" to your abuser. You continue to think about him, and you feed the negativity inside of yourself. When you do this, you continue to give your abuser power over your life. You also choose to continue hurting *yourself* because it is you, rather than your abuser, who suffers from the bitterness you are nursing.

When you choose to stop nursing the bitterness, you stop putting energy into your "relationship" with your abuser. You stop thinking about your abuser, and you free up that energy toward healing yourself. In time, you will find yourself becoming indifferent toward your abuser.

While hatred and love are polar opposites, they both involve investing energy into another person. The true opposite of love is indifference because you stop thinking about the other person altogether.

I do not like to use the term "forgiveness" because of all of the associations that society places on this term. Instead, I like to call this process "letting go." By letting go of the bitterness, I was able to heal myself. My abusers' lives were not affected as I moved from hating them to letting go, but the healing I experienced in letting go of the bitterness was immense. Letting go was a gift that I gave to myself, and I needed nobody else to take action for me to make that choice.

I suffered enough as a child. Through letting go, I ended my suffering for good. I took back my power by choosing to let go of the past and focus on my present.

http://www.associatedcontent.com/article/501051/forgiveness_and_adult_survivors_ of.html?cat=17

Peter Loth

I grew up in communist Poland after WWII. My "Matka" (Mama) loved me and did all she could to provide food and shelter for the two of us. The city of Torun, where we lived, had been bombed out; some of the buildings were empty shells. Only the ancient cathedrals and the thick castle walls, built in the 11th century, remained. Matka and I lived for a while, like so many others, in the underground sewer system. With very little left above, we were at least safe and warm. We ate whatever we could find – cats, mice, insects, anything!

My first memory is of men taking me by force away from Matka. I cried and kicked and they answered with their fists. I was taken to an orphanage where 30-40 German children were kept in one room. The Russians and Poles had such hate for the Germans for what they had done during the war that now they vented their anger on these young ones. The orphanages had no beds, one bucket for a potty, one bucket to hold the food (slop) for all of the children. During the day, we were used as slave labor in the coal mines. At night, we were used for the pleasures of the Russian soldiers and the people who ran the orphanage. Fortunately, Matka's brother was an officer in the Polish army. Many times, he rescued me from the orphanage only to see me taken again and returned there weeks later.

There was one girl at the orphanage I will always remember. This girl had a yellow star on her shirt. She would comfort me after I had been abused. She would hold me and tell me "It's OK, God loves you." One night, the Russian soldiers came to the door and dragged me to the train station. I could hear a noise like a "pop." As we got there, I could see a pile of bodies – children's bodies. One by one, the Russian soldiers took each of the German children, put a pistol to their head, and shot. I saw my friend – the girl with the star – shot in the head and thrown on the pile. When I was to be next, I heard Matka cry out to the Russian officer and I saw her open her dress to him. The officer yelled out a command and I was pushed away – able to go home with Matka. The Russian followed us home to our apartment. (Matka had sold her body to save my life.)

When I was six years old, in one of the orphanages on Christmas, I couldn't take any more pain – I tried to kill myself. Truly, it was only an angel of God who saved me. For a few years after that, Matka and I were able to live in a room in the castle wall. How I loved that place! I would lie on the deep windowsill and stare out at the Vistula River, dreaming of faraway places. Between times spent at the orphanages, my friends and I would cross the river to the old fort and play with swords we had found, pretending to be medieval knights.

Matka had been a circus performer and was friends with a band of gypsies. They loved me and told me that when I turned 14 they would take me to travel with them. How I longed for that day! I would be able to live free. On my birthday, I was so happy! I knew that Matka had given her blessing to this – knowing that it would be the best thing for me. Instead, Matka came to me, with tears in her eyes. She held a paper in her hand and told me that she was not my real mother. My real mother was in West Germany and I would have to leave Poland and go to her. I felt such anger at Matka, such betrayal! I ran from the birthday party and went to hide at the fort across the river. For days, I stayed there. My friends knew where I was and brought me food and water. Finally, I returned.

Before I was able to leave for Berlin, I went through months of interrogation by the Russian KGB, months of rifle beatings due to the fact that the papers detailing the facts about my true Mother had come from a U.S. Army base in Germany. For 16 months, the Russians would not let me go because they thought I must be a spy knowing someone in the U.S. Army. I was a 14-year-old kid!

I finally went through Checkpoint Charlie from East Berlin to West Berlin. Freedom? Not quite. I finally met my real mother, Mama – she spoke only German and English, I spoke Polish and Russian. It was difficult. I hated her. How could she have left me and gone on to freedom herself? Mama must have seen the hurt and all the questions in my eyes. She unbuttoned her shirt and showed me her back – it was covered with scars. She showed me her breasts – they were mutilated. On her forearm, a number had been tattooed. I understood the pain and abuse she had taken, but I had no understanding of who had done it or why. I wept and embraced my Mama.

Mama had married an African American G.I. in West Germany and had two little girls with him. How I loved my sisters. We transferred to the U.S. to Georgia – in 1959. I was verbally and physically abused from both sides – the whites and the blacks. I was thrown out of the white schools and thrown out of the black schools. Once again, I was caught in the crossfire of hate.

My stepfather became abusive to my sisters. Unable to help them, I would go to my room and cry myself to sleep. One night I could take it no more, I attacked my Father with my fists. He came after me with a chain and beat me severely. I ran to the window, jumped out, and ran away. Many times during the next forty years, I tried to find my mother and sisters. I had even joined the US Army, hoping to find them through the military bases. All I found was more discrimination.

I learned to block out my past; I learned to lie to avoid the pain. When people would notice my accent and ask where I was born, I would tell them "Greenland." In 1988, my wife and I were attending a Charismatic Catholic Church in Miami, Florida. We loved what we felt at that church. The church held a retreat for men called "The Emmaus Retreat." It was a powerful weekend of ministry and contemplation.

During a quiet time while I was praying outside in the rose garden there, I saw the face of Jesus before me. When I looked into His eyes, He took me on a journey to my childhood. In His eyes, I saw flashes – pictures – of my past: getting beaten in The South by the whites and blacks; 1958-59 and the hate I had received in Germany for being a Pole; then to Poland – flashes of the years in the orphanages, living in the sewer, seeing the executions of children and adults, the hunger; I saw Matka taking me in her arms from my Mama; then I saw myself as a baby lying on a table, taken from my mother, and doctors were performing procedures on me; then He took me to my mother's womb – it sounds strange – but I could feel my mother's pain as she was beaten and abused, and I could feel myself cringe in my tiny body.

Then I felt happiness and peace in the womb and I knew it was the first few months. The Lord told me that He loved me and that He had been with me through all of my life. I wept and promised to follow Him and be true to Him all the days of my life.

As I learned to surrender different areas of my life to God, I finally surrendered my mother and my sisters whom I had not seen for so many years. I told the Lord "You know where they are. Please keep them safe. If you want me to find them, You do it." Months later, I received a phone call – "Are you Peter? This is your sister, Barbara. Are you a Christian?" My 2 sisters were fine – Mama had died that March, the month I had prayed the prayer of surrender. The three of us had a reunion shortly thereafter and they told me that Mama had been in a concentration camp, that she had Jewish blood on her mother's side. I couldn't believe any of it. I contacted the Red Cross to investigate for me and it was confirmed – with the date of her arrest and the "prisoner number" which had been tattooed on her arm. She had been arrested while 2 months pregnant with me. I was shocked – I had been born in a concentration camp!

I started feeling the stirrings of God that I was to go back to Poland to face it all. Again, God in His gentle ways gave a confirmation – a man came to me and said that the Lord was going to use me in a great way. He said that God had showed him that I was to go back to Poland to be healed – without this healing, I would not be able to minister to others. He then furnished the tickets for our trip to Poland.

In Poland, we went to Stutthof Concentration Camp. My heart was filled with pain. As we walked to the gas chamber, the ovens, I could feel the pain of the thousands of people who had walked there so long ago. In the barracks were pictures of the Nazi officers who had worked the Camp. I heard the audible voice of God, "Piotrusu. Piotrusu. Piotrusu. You have to do something for Me. Go down on your knees in front of each picture and forgive them." I said, "I can't do it." The Voice said, "You have to forgive them before I can forgive you." As I fell to my knees and forgave each one, I felt so different. I felt as if all of the things I had suffered in my life had been for a purpose – to give God the glory. I had a joy that I had never felt before – a freedom in my spirit. I have been given a revelation that we must learn from this recent past. It is a foreshadowing of what will come in the future. We must restore His Commandments, especially the first two Commandments, if we are to be able to survive. If we surrender our lives to Him, trust His provision, and worship His Holy Name, He will weave the pieces of our lives together – as horrible and painful as they appear to be – into a beautiful picture revealing His mercy, forgiveness, and unconditional love.

http://www.forerunnerministries.org/Media.aspx

Account from Peter's book on his process of forgiveness:

After this [Peter's healing experience during the Emmaus Retreat], I was a changed man. I fully accepted the fact that God was in control of my life. I had finally learned that when I was in control, things never turned out right. Of course, there were times here and there when I would try to take that control back, but I knew deep down that if I wanted or needed answers, the only one who could provide them was God.

"God," I cried out, "Please help me. I don't know what to do or where to turn. All this information is too much for me. And yet, it isn't enough. I don't know anything about my past really. I don't know who I am or why I'm even here."

I lifted my head from the table and looked upward.

"I just feel like I should have died a long time ago. I should have died with those people in the concentration camp. I should have died with Star that night! I shouldn't be here... why am I still here?"

The house was silent, but in the stillness, I suddenly had an answer.

Go back to the beginning.

I stood up from the table, my headache dissipating. Yes! I had to go back to the beginning. I had to return to the place I was born. I knew I would find the peace I was looking for within the gates of my initial imprisonment.

….

After driving another 430 kilometers, we entered the town of Sztutowo, Poland. I knew the concentration camp had to be somewhere within the town limits. We drove around, looking for any sign of the place, but we couldn't find anything. I noticed a little drugstore in the distance, so I pulled up and ran inside to ask directions.

…..

On the sign of the road, hidden behind some branches, was a large sign bearing the name: STUTTHOF.

I lost it.

I could hardly see through all my tears. I was a mess, but somehow I managed to pull in the drive and park in the little parking lot.

….

I sobbed even more. This was where it all began. Where my life took a turn for the worse, right at the very beginning.

We sat in the car for a few moments before getting out. Val shoved a few tissues in my direction, and I cleaned off my face. I couldn't sit any longer. I had to face my past.

….

I marched through the gates, barely stopping to glance at the surroundings. My tears turned to anger. I could feel all the hatred I had ever experienced in my life begin to simmer below the surface. I couldn't let it out, though. Not here. Not now. I had to be strong for my family.

To my right was the commandants' headquarters. The building was large and beautiful, with big open windows and tall pillars. It looked like a summer villa for getting away from the world. The building's past, however, was not pretty. While doing research on the camp, I had come across a picture of Hitler's right-hand man, Himmler, standing in front of this very building. Nazi flags hung from the pillars behind. The picture made me sick to my stomach.

So I turned to my left, instead. Before me was a small, rickety wooden barrack. I walked in and saw the pile of thousands of shoes that had been stolen from the prisoners who lived and died in the camp. As I stared into the midst of the gray mass, one pair caught my eye. It was clearly a pair of baby's shoes. I choked on my tears, nearly gagging.

If the men responsible for the deaths of these innocent people were still alive, I knew I could kill them myself. They deserved to die for the horrific pain and anger I was feeling.

....

We walked along the grounds some more, noticing the bombed-out barracks alongside those that were still standing. Inside each remaining barrack was information regarding the history of the camp and the various medical procedures that were carried out within its gates.

As we entered one of the barracks, I noticed a little table with various metal tools lying on it. I read the blurb of information about the contents and found that it was where abortions were carried out. Almost every child born at Stutthof was murdered. Those who were allowed to survive were taken for experimental treatments to the hospital in Tiegenhof... I must have been one of those children.

I rushed through the rest of the barracks, barely reading any of the material. My adrenaline was pumping, and I had to move. I had to do something with the anger.

As we made our way out of the barracks and into the far end of the field, we found ourselves in front of a gas chamber. To the right of the gas chamber was another larger building that housed several ovens, which were used to burn the dead bodies of the camp's prisoners. My blood went cold. Somehow, I had managed to avoid these as a baby. But why? Why was I saved and not others? Why me?

I had to get out of there. I was wrong for coming in the first place. What had I been thinking? Why did I think I would gain any answers by coming to such a wretched place?

"We've got to go!" I called to my family as they were still taking in the scene before them.

They hurried toward me.

"What's the matter?" Val asked.

"I can't be here anymore."

"But, don't you want to try to get any records?"

"What's the point?" I yelled.

"We drove all this way. I thought that's what you wanted."

"I can't be here, Val! This place is evil. I can't be in this place!" I yelled, storming ahead of the rest of them.

I knew she was right, though. If there was any chance that the camp did have documents for me, I had to at least try.

....

I skimmed the sign.

"The office is closed on Mondays. It will be open again tomorrow." Forget it. I knew this was a waste of time. I wish I never came here.

I swiftly turned around and marched down the steps and out the gate. I didn't look back. I wanted out of that place. If I never saw it again, I would be a happy man.

....

The next morning we drove back to Stutthof. This time, we knew exactly where it was located and exactly what to expect. None of us was very excited to be returning, but after talking more

200

with Val the night before, I realized that it was the whole point of our trip to Europe. I was going to learn something. I could sense it.

....

"I think I need to look around once more before going to the records office," I told my family, who nodded in understanding.

....

The first barrack was full of panoramas and maps of what the camp looked like when the Nazis were in control. Stated in detail were the strategies behind the Nazis' desire to destroy the world's Jewish population. As I walked from one barrack to the next, the information became more specific, detailing what went on at Stutthof. I learned that Stutthof was one of the largest soap-making factories of all the camps. The soap was not of ordinary design – it was made from the body fat of those who perished within the walls of the camp.

My anger from the previous day resurfaced as I continued reading. I wanted to see the people's faces who could run such a facility. I wanted to give them exactly what they deserved. How could anyone despise human life so much that they could actually manufacture and use soap made out of human bodies?

I left the stuffiness of the barracks, though I knew there was still more to see, and stepped out into the fresh air. I wasn't sure if we had made the right decision to come back....

I took a deep breath and stepped inside the dark building. Before me was a maze of dioramas and poster boards. As I walked among them, they began to lead me farther into the darkness that was my past. There were pictures of starved children and scarred women. There were pictures of the camp being liberated. There were pictures everywhere.

Suddenly I stopped short. On the poster board in front of me was the face of Max Pauly, the head commandment of Stutthof.

Sandy and Phil seemed to fade into the background, as I stood face-to-face with the man who had destroyed my life. I stared into his vacant eyes, hoping to find some reason for his choosing to hurt so many. I received no answer.

I wanted to hurt him. I wanted to tear down that picture and rip it to shreds. He was the reason I suffered. This man was responsible for everything I had endured.

As I looked around, I noticed that to the right of him were pictures of his subordinate commandants. Looking at each, I cursed their names and wished them to the worst confines of hell imaginable. I wanted them to be suffering for every ounce of pain I – or any of their victims – felt while living and dying at the camp.

All the hatred I had ever felt in my life would never equal the amount of hatred I felt standing before those pictures.

And then I heard a voice.

"Piotrusiu, Piotrusiu, Piotrusiu."

For a moment, I wasn't sure what I heard. Was that my own voice in my head?

And then again, from nowhere, I heard the voice.

"Forgive them. Get down on your knees and forgive them."

No, I knew that Voice clearly. I knew I would never think to actually forgive the men I held responsible for the destruction of my childhood. Only God would be so bold as to ask me to forgive these evil men.

"I can't! Why should I? They don't deserve my forgiveness," I screamed on the inside. There was no way I would ever forgive these men. I hated them too much.

Then, in words much bolder and clearer, I heard God say:

"Forgive them or I cannot forgive you."

I was stunned. What could that possibly mean? How could I be lumped in the same category as these men?

"Forgive me?" I asked. "But what did I do? I'm the victim. I was the one who suffered. Why would I need forgiveness?"

"You broke one of My commandments, Peter. 'Thou shalt honor thy mother and father.' Did you honor your mother?"

I never expected that answer. I never in a million years would have realized the depth of my sin toward my mother, but in that moment, it came crashing over me.

I broke down in tears. He was right. I hadn't honored my mother. I had hated and despised her for abandoning me as a child. I didn't understand then the pain she must have endured for my sake. I was probably alive because of her sacrifices.

....

I knew in that moment that I had to forgive my mother for the abandonment I had felt all of those years.

I never felt so utterly convicted in my entire life. I didn't deserve forgiveness, just as these men didn't deserve forgiveness. Yet, God was offering it to me.

"Lord, You are right. Please forgive me for not loving my mother the way I should have loved her. Please, please forgive me for all the times I cursed her name and wished she were dead. Forgive me for not understanding until this very moment my own sin. I've been placing blame left and right, but my hatred is no different from these men."

Then, broken before the Lord, I fell to my knees before the pictures of Max Pauly and Paul Werner Hoppe, one of the other commandants of Stutthof.

I could barely get the words out, but they finally came.

"I forgive you."

A wave of emotion swept over me like nothing I've ever felt in my life, but I kept going. I knelt before the next picture and said the same.

"I forgive you."

Each time I knelt before another picture of a commandant and said those words, I felt more weight lift off me. The words came easier with each picture I knelt before.

I'm not sure how many men and women I forgave that day. But when I finally stood up, all of the anger, hatred, and tension I had been carrying my entire life seemed to have melted away.

I could breathe. I was able to stand before those men and know that they could no longer affect me. The hatred I had felt toward them would no longer have a hold on me. For the first time in my life, I was truly free.

I lifted up my arms before God and thanked Him for His gift of freedom. The answer I had been searching for didn't come from any document. My identity was in God. Sure, I still had questions about my past, but finding the answers to those questions wasn't going to help me discover who I was. I was completely clear on that now. I was God's child, and no one could ever convince me otherwise.

I was so full of gratitude and complete happiness that I began humming a praise song to God. I was aware of no one around me. It was just me and my Father. And He deserved all the praise that was in me.

....

After his visit to Stutthof Concentration Camp, Peter returned to the United States a changed man. The hatred he felt toward all those who had wronged him began to slowly melt away with the help and guidance of God.

Peter Loth with Sandra Kellogg Rath, *Peace by Piece: A Story of Survival and Forgiveness.* **(Longwood, FL: Xulon Press, 2008). Used by permission. All rights reserved.**

Salimata Badji-Knight

Salimata Badji-Knight, 37, was brought up in a Muslim community in Senegal, where she was circumcised at the age of five. She moved to Paris when she was nine, and has spent most of her adult life campaigning to prevent the practice of female circumcision in African cultures. She now lives in Dorset.

I was five when the women from my village said we were going into the forest. There was a whole group of us girls aged between five and 16; we were happy because we thought we were going for a picnic. But it wasn't a picnic. Even more than the pain and the crying, I remember the shock of realizing that they'd tricked us. I knew they had cut something from me, but I didn't know what. The women were kind in their way, giving us sweets and nice food; it was their way of asking for forgiveness. But it was also their way of seeking revenge – repeating a crime that had been done to them.

Only later, when I was a teenager, did I realize exactly what had happened. We had been circumcised, supposedly to make us cleaner and to stop us having boyfriends. For my parents it was like preparing me for marriage – they were doing it for my own good and I accepted this because circumcised Muslim women have stature and respect. Later, when I came to live in Paris, it was a big shock to discover that this was not something that happened to everyone. I was horrified to see Senegalese girls being told they were going on holiday to Africa, when in fact they were being taken back to be circumcised. For my mother it was a normal part of her culture, and in Paris, she secretly had three of my younger sisters circumcised.

I was full of rage and was determined to stop this brutal practice. I started to talk to anyone who would listen: the social services, doctors, the police and other Africans living in Paris. For a long time I blamed all the women in my community who had united to do this to me, and I blamed all the men for standing by and allowing it to happen. I blamed my mother because she condoned it, and my father because he had never been there to stop it.

When I discovered that most people believe circumcision to be a terrible wrong, I felt suicidal. Circumcision takes away your identity and your dignity. It was only when I became a Buddhist and stopped viewing myself as a victim that I stopped feeling unworthy. Out of rage came compassion, and the realization that this was not my mother's fault, nor the fault of the women who had done this to me. They were simply blinded by tradition.

If I'd held on to all that anger and blame, I'd be dead by now. But my anger has had great results, because it has made me fight to stop this practice. I now work with a campaign ground called Forward, and I speak at schools both in the UK and France. When I first met my husband, I told him not to expect me to be sexually driven. "If I say no I mean no," I said firmly. He is a very patient man and has great respect for me.

Today my three sisters work with me to stop the practice of circumcision. Even my mother now understands that it's a violation of human rights. And before he died six years ago, I was able to have a good talk with my father. I opened my heart to him and explained how female circumcision could affect you physically and mentally. He cried and said that no woman had ever explained the suffering to him. Then he apologized and asked for forgiveness. The next day he called my relatives in Senegal and told them to stop the practice. As a result, a meeting was cancelled and 50 girls were saved.

http://theforgivenessproject.org.uk/stories/page/60/

Calvin Sandborn

Today, Calvin Sandborn thinks fondly of his father, something he still finds odd, because he hated him when he was alive. Calvin Sandborn is a professor of environmental law and the legal director of the University of Victoria Environmental Law Clinic. He is the author of *Becoming the Kind Father: A Son's Journey* (New Society, 2007).

Dad was an angry, hard-swearing, tattooed man's man. He'd been an Alaska bush pilot, but by the time I came along, he was a California travelling salesman, drinking himself to death. When I was two, he got drunk and threw my empty crib across the bedroom. When I was 12, he challenged my brother to a fistfight. He routinely shouted at us in front of our friends. By the time I was 13, I wished he would die.

And then he did. I thought that my wish had killed him, and for the longest time I couldn't forgive myself. I was scared to death I would damage someone else.

But four decades on, I've forgiven myself for hating him. More difficult, I've somehow forgiven myself for the Dad-like fury I inflicted on my own family.

To my surprise, as I became kinder to myself, I formed a more rounded picture of Dad. His anger had its reasons. His father died young, leaving him with a stepfather who favored his own kids. When Dad was 14, his preacher grandfather hauled him in front of the congregation and viciously denounced him for teaching other kids the Charleston.

Humiliated, Dad ran away from home and joined the carnival, growing up on the road with hardened carnies. In middle age, his sales job was crushing. He was a brilliant man with a Grade 8 education, reduced to knocking on doors and imploring merchants to buy advertising promotions like imprinted pens and squeeze coin purses.

But Dad's biggest problem was that he never got in touch with his own pain, never learned how to process his feelings. Like many men, he believed the lie that "Big boys don't cry," so he refused to seek out friends and instead turned his pain into anger.

The anger kept shameful sorrow at bay. Swigging vodka straight from the bottle, he forced us to cry his tears.

This was the Dad I hated. But a funny thing happened after I forgave him. A different Dad returned from the shadows, borne by a flood of memory. I found myself recalling the times when he didn't drink.

It was evening at the river. I was five, and Dad was still young and strong. We were camping in the California Coast Range. Although I couldn't swim, I had wandered down to the river after dinner and paddled an inner tube out to the middle of the big dark pool. I lay back in the inner tube, gazing at the cliff that loomed above on the other side of the water.

Suddenly I slipped through the middle of the tube, and I was in the water, struggling. I sank into the cold dark water. As I resurfaced, I could see Dad running down the beach, tearing off his shoes and plunging powerfully into the river. Then I was under again, swallowing cold water, sinking into blackness.

....

Then I felt myself being pushed powerfully to the surface, as Dad rose like a sea lion below me. I gasped the air and was saved.

But he had swallowed water, too, and began to cough and struggle himself. "Dad!" I cried in a panic. He sank below me, and I again fell back into the black waters, gulping and sputtering, stepping on his head. As we sank, the murky yellow light of the world receded into darkness, with no sound but my thundering heartbeat.

I felt his hands grip my calves and place my feet firmly on his shoulders. Then, as in the game we'd often played, he drifted down and bounced back up from the river bottom, thrusting me to the surface. And then his tattooed arm was around my chest, towing me to safety. Keeping my face above the water, he coughed, then murmured, "It's OK, Cal. It's OK."

Finally, we staggered on to the sandy beach. As I stood gasping, shivering and crying, he hugged me to his heaving chest. Then he went to the trailer to get a towel and wrapped it around me. Later, as he heated hot chocolate on the Coleman stove he did the unusual — he sat me on his lap. After a while, he turned the Giants game on the radio, and we sipped hot chocolate while the sun sank behind the cliff.

At the end of his life, I think Dad, like me, had forgotten that day. He forgot his goodness. I wish that, when he ruminated on his failures, he had been able to remember the good things. I wish that, when he thought of his years of unemployment, his bankruptcy, the jalopies he drove, his failed marriages, his destructive anger, that he had been able to recall that day on the river. Most of all, I wish he'd had a kind father to remind him of the good things about himself – his sense of humor, his charm, his ability to spin a story for a crowd, his compassion for the unfortunate, his intelligence, his ability to make a day's outing with a young boy into an exciting adventure.

I wish someone had told him that he did not have to be a Man of Steel, that it was OK to be sad.

I wish he had understood that he was no different from any of us, a mixture of good and bad.

I wish he had realized that he could be forgiven, and that he could forgive.

The fact was, he didn't have to die alone in the Country of Resentment. There was room for him in the Country of Love.

http://theforgivenessproject.org.uk/visitor-stories/calvin-sandborn%e2%80%99s-story-of-forgiving-his-father/

Rose Price

I am a survivor of Hitler's Holocaust. My family, which lived in a little city in Poland, was warm and caring. We looked out for one another. My relatives lived within walking distance of each other, so if it rained and you ducked into the nearest house, you were always in the home of a cousin or an aunt or uncle.

My upbringing was very Orthodox. My mother instilled in me that Judaism was life. I never knew a difference between a high holiday and a low holiday. A holiday was a holiday. Every Shabbat (Sabbath) was even celebrated as a holiday… When Hitler took power, change came quickly. The Germans invaded in September 1939. One day at school shortly after the invasion, all the Jewish students were called up to the front of the classroom. With a guard standing nearby, our teacher told us, "Don't come back to the school anymore because you are Jews." I was ten and one-half years old. We were all absolutely devastated.

The next thing the Germans did was throw us out of our home and force us to live in a ghetto. They took the whole town of Jews and put us on one street.

My sister, who is two years older, and I were among the first to be sent away. We were on our way to visit our grandmother when the Germans grabbed us and put us to work in the ammunition factory.

It was a horror because we went from a warm house into freezing conditions and from a loving, hugging, kissing family to a man constantly beating us with a whip. For a while, we went back to our parents in the evenings. But one day, instead of letting us return home, they marched us into the woods. That summer I had been in the woods gathering mushrooms, blueberries, and raspberries. Now I was confined to a prison camp in those same woods.

It's unthinkable what those people did to us. It's almost indescribable. In the morning, they woke us up when it was still dark. We had to go outside, no matter what the weather was, and line up five deep for them to count us.

We worked a full day at the factory. I operated a machine that stretched out a piece of aluminum from a quarter of an inch to the length of a rifle bullet. I had to grease it, feed it, and take away the shells.

Before the invasion, my biggest responsibilities were to go to school, learn, come home, help my mother with the housework, do some gardening, and watch out for my younger sister. Now I was being told that either I learned how to work that machine or I would die. And I had to learn quickly.

I cried for a while, until one day I just couldn't cry anymore because I didn't have any tears left. That happened after the city was evacuated and I knew I would never again see my parents or my family. That was my last day of crying for 25 years.

At first I would still pray. I would get up in the morning and say the Modeh Ani and during the day, I would say the Shema and just pray to God. One day I prayed that God would send my mother because I was hungry and homesick. I needed a mother's hug instead of the beatings. I wanted to take a bath because I was covered with dirt and we didn't have soap. I prayed and nothing happened. When my prayers were not answered, I concluded that there was no God.

I was transferred from one concentration camp to another until I was sent to Bergen-Belsen and then Dachau. It's hard for me to believe that I lived through such horror. Such horrible, horrible things happened at Bergen-Belsen. We were tortured. We were put in a field and forced to dig sugar beets out of the almost frozen ground with our bare hands. I remember my hands bleeding badly.

We had many difficult experiences in the camps. One stands out as particularly cruel. I was working in the field one day digging up sugar beets and by then I was more like a zombie because I had been in these conditions for several years. I decided I was going to steal a sugar beet and eat it. I was determined that my belly was not going to hurt that night.

All we used to receive was a quarter-of-an-inch thick piece of bread—it was 80% sawdust— and a cup of coffee. That was our food for 24 hours. Obviously, this was barely enough food to exist on, let alone to sustain someone working in the extreme cold.

When the guard caught me, I got such a bad beating that even today when I talk about it I can still feel the cat-o'-nine tails on my back and on my face and around my body and the punishment of hanging by my hands—all because I stole a sugar beet.

The cold weather alone killed many of us because we were not dressed properly. We would have to stand in line for hours, no matter how deep the snow was, half-naked and without shoes.

One time while we were lined up, we were completely undressed for an experiment to see how long it would take our blood to freeze. To this day, when I am in cold weather, and my toes and fingers go completely numb, I remember that time when my body started to freeze. The only reason I survived the experiment was because several people fell on top of me and their bodies kept me warm.

I had made up my mind that I would survive the same day that I had said there was no God. When I did survive, I took full credit. Later, I realized it had to have been the Lord.

But there were days when I thought I wasn't going to make it. When we were on our way to Dachau, our train was bombed. As we ran into the woods to get away from the train, I thought to myself, "That's it. I've made enough bullets. Let them use the bullets on me." Death looked better than life.

One time when I was still in a camp in my own hometown, I was walking across the field with somebody, and I smiled. For the offense of smiling, the Germans put me in a sewer tank for 24 hours. I had to stay on my toes to keep from drowning. I was no more than 12 years old at the time.

Another difficult time was when my sister, who was in the same camp, got typhoid fever. She was my last living family member, and I didn't think I could go on if I lost her too. The guards came in periodically to check for those who were sick. Then they would take them outside and leave them to freeze. I laid on top of my sister to protect her and when they asked people to lift up their hands to show they were healthy, I put my hand up in place of hers.

Twice, I was selected to be shot. Both times when the guards unlocked the chain, I ran away. The second time I ran into a guard. I was running so hard I bounced off him. But he didn't see me. It could only have been God. If he had seen me, he would have shot me himself. I looked up at him and then fled into a wooded part of the camp.

When we were finally liberated in May 1945, I was full of unforgiveness for what I had been through. I hated the Germans with a passion. The unforgiveness literally poisoned my body, causing me to need 27 operations.

I was looking for somebody who would be willing to drop a bomb on Germany and Poland. I had lost all of my family except my sister and one aunt—nearly 100 relatives.

After I was released, I came to America and got married and had children. As much as I hated God, I became active in the traditional synagogue. My children needed to learn about Judaism, but I couldn't teach them because I was dead inside. Socially, I was the best Jew. I was active in helping to build the Hebrew school. I even worked my way up to become president of the sisterhood.

If someone had asked me back then, "Do you believe in God?" I would have said, "No." Even today, many rabbis don't believe in the Bible and very few believe in God. But I believed in maintaining my Jewish identity and tradition

One day my teenage daughter came to me and said the worst thing I could imagine. She said, "Mommy, I believe in Jesus Christ, and He is the Jewish Messiah."

I nearly had a heart attack. I told her what Jesus Christ did to her family and why she didn't have many aunts and uncles. The Nazi guards had told me over and over that because I killed Jesus Christ, He hated me and put me into the camps to kill me.

When I was seven or eight years old, I was hit in the head with a crucifix by a priest in Poland for the "crime" of walking on the sidewalk in front of his church.

So for my daughter to believe in Jesus Christ was death. I threw her out. I couldn't have this enemy living in my house. When my husband went to the house where she was staying to check on her, he became a believer too. The house was used as an outreach to Jewish people.

My younger daughter was still going to a private Hebrew school. But somehow, I knew that she had secretly become a Messianic believer, and I beat her for it, even though I don't remember doing it.

[Note: This article continues with the process of Rose Price coming to know Yeshua (Jesus) as her Messiah – being born again. For the sake of brevity, I have deleted most of the account. I would highly recommend her book and the video about her life referenced at the end of these two accounts.]

Shortly after that encounter, I went to a dinner at Arthur DeMoss' house. Mr. DeMoss was a wealthy Christian businessman who would open his home once a year as an outreach to Jewish people. He asked me if I would mind if he prayed for me. I told him, "I don't care if you stand on your head. It's your house."

Instead of standing on his head, he started to pray. Jews never close their eyes in prayer, but all of a sudden, I closed my eyes and said a very simple prayer: "God of Abraham, Isaac and Jacob, if it's true, if He who they are saying is Your Son and You have a Son and He is really the Messiah, okay. But, Father, if He isn't, forget that I talked to you." That was the first prayer I had prayed since 1942. I felt the biggest stone rolling off my back. For the first time since the war, I cried and I felt so clean. I knew He was real and I made Him my Messiah.

When Holocaust survivors get angry with me today because I am a Messianic Jew, I just show love to them because I know how they feel. I've been there. I don't argue with them.

One day I got a call from Sid Roth. A friend of his, a pastor from a large church in Berlin, had just called him to say, "We're going to rent the largest coliseum in Berlin, the one that Hitler used for his meetings, and we're looking for Messianic Jews to take part in the events we have planned."

Sid said, "I have the perfect person," meaning me. But when he called me, I refused.

....

I finally surrendered. I went with my husband and four other believers. Many more came later. It was, as I said, a six-month struggle. I had people pray and fast for me.

This was a big event. A number of prominent Christians were there including Pat Robertson, Demos Shakarian, and Pat Boone.

When I walked into that coliseum, the one where Hitler said the Nazis would rule the world for a thousand years, it was jam-packed with young Germans. A number of them had stars of David, Jewish stars, around their neck. Israeli flags were waving.

When I saw the American leaders, some of whom I knew, and I saw the German people wearing stars of David and mezuzahs, I thought, *It's impossible.* Then I thought, *What am I doing here? Lord, what do You want from me? Get me out of here. I don't want to speak German. Am I doing this right or am I telling the Germans and the world that it's okay to go kill Jews?* These thoughts tormented me until I spoke.

On Sunday, they called me up to speak. I don't remember saying the things that were printed. I don't remember speaking on forgiveness. But after I finished my talk, some people came up to me who were the last people on the face of this earth that I wanted to see. They were ex-Nazis. Apparently, I had asked for any ex-Nazis to come up and be prayed for and be forgiven. I don't remember saying it, but here they were asking me to forgive them. Could I forgive them face-to-face as I had from the podium?

That's when I realized that I had spoken on forgiveness. One of those who had come forward was a guard from Dachau. He had been in charge of punishment. When he came and identified himself, my body shriveled up in pain as he knelt down. He was pleading with me to forgive him.

I am a believer, but people cannot comprehend what I experienced in Dachau and Bergen-Belsen. They cannot imagine the hell I went through. It was only by the grace of God that I was able to forgive those who came forward, because Rose Price could not forgive them for the atrocities I went through as a child.

As I was ready to leave Berlin, one of the ex-Nazis with whom I had prayed for forgiveness came up to me. He said that after I had prayed with him he had his first night's sleep since the war.

Another time I was in Germany again and I realized I was not far from Bergen-Belsen. I knew that I had to go back. Once and for all, I had to bury Bergen-Belsen. I had a Swedish couple with me, Susan and Gary, and a German man named Otto—all believers.

I had to ask a guide for the location of the main gate. I didn't recognize it because the barracks had all been burned. But I knew if they put me where the main gate had been, I could find where the barracks had stood. I was amazed that even today no grass grows where the electric wires were located. No matter how many times they plant grass, it does not grow.

The guide gave me a list of the names of those who had been at Bergen-Belsen and I found my sister's and my name on the list. We were on the last transport out from Bergen-Belsen to Dachau. After that, all those who remained died of typhus.

I cried and I wept. At one point, I was hollering at Bergen-Belsen, "You died, but I survived! I am here! I survived!"

While I was hollering, I started to pray for the salvation of the country and that the German people would learn of the Messiah's love and forgiveness.

At one point I asked, "Lord, how can I pray that prayer at this cemetery where so much happened to me, so much that is indescribable?"

As I was praying, the German man [guide] became hysterical. I went over to him to hug him and he said, "How can you pray for us when we did that to you? My family was involved with this. We put you here. How can you? Show me the strength. Show me the strength."

Then he asked for forgiveness and the four of us just kept on crying and praying for one another and for the German people.

If you feel you cannot forgive someone, you cannot hate anyone more than I hated the Germans. I lost my stomach. I had 27 operations before I went to Berlin.

Hate has an address in your body. Love cannot dwell in the body with hate. When I finally gave up all the hate and love started coming in, something happened inside my body. I didn't have pain anymore. I haven't had an operation since 1981 because the Lord has taken all that poison out of me.

Nobody knows the pain you have gone through and nobody knows the pain I went through. But there is no excuse for hate. You have to forgive. You have to give up the hate.

It's not even up to you to have the strength to forgive. You cannot do anything in your own power. You have to go to the Lord and the Lord will give you the strength.

http://www.theythoughtforthemselves.com/pages/chapters/3.php

Account from Rose's book on her process of forgiveness:

"I can't speak of forgiveness," I said to Charlie. "Not after everything that was done to me and my family in the country."

I went to the leader of our congregation and told him what was being asked of me. "Everyone wants me to go – Sid, Charlie, my kids – but I don't think I can go and talk about forgiveness when I really don't forgive the Germans for what they did to me and to the people I loved."

"But Rose," he said, "Consider the other side for a moment. What if you do go? And what if you can forgive? Think of the healing that would begin to take place in you!"

I still couldn't imagine it. My anger and bitterness over my stolen childhood and the murder of my family were attached to me in a peculiar way. If I thought about our suffering, my muscles tightened up and acid churned in my stomach. It was unpleasant, but familiar. It was my defense against the painful recollections.

In January, I received a letter from Volkhard Spitzer, a pastor in Berlin who was organizing "Berlin for Jesus," asking me personally to come.

The next six months were a battle. Every day I prayed, and every day I felt deep inside me that I should go to Germany, but I refused to give in to that instinct. "God of Abraham, Isaac and Jacob. You know what was done to me there. Please, don't make me go back. Anywhere but Germany, Lord. Please, anywhere else!"

....

Walking through the terminal to the plane was perhaps the longest mile of my life. "Why am I doing this?" I kept saying out loud and to myself. "I swore I'd never go back there." Poor Charlie [her husband] bore the brunt of my anxiety. "This is your fault," I said to him as we found our seats on the aircraft.

....

I figured I should actually determine what I was going to say to the thousands of Germans who were coming to this rally. I drew up an outline. "First I'll tell them what they did to me, my family, my people. Then I'll ask them how they could do such a thing." But I couldn't get past that point to the forgiveness part.

....

When we landed, I forced myself out of my seat into the aisle and to the door of the plane. I didn't look out the window. When we disembarked, I froze. Charlie and the others didn't realize I wasn't with them and so for a moment, I was alone in the corridor. I stood there, rigid as other people maneuvered around me. My feet refused to move. Suddenly I was there again; the cattle car doors opening, the darkness, the selection upon arrive, the screaming as loved ones were separated from each other, the crematoria.

When my husband and the others realized I wasn't with them, they ran back to me. But terror had gripped my heart and they had to drag me down the corridor to a chair. A man came up to us and said he was a doctor. As soon as I heard those words in German, I snapped, "Get him away from me! I've had enough of German doctors! Don't let him touch me!"

But no words escaped my lips. I was screaming in silence. Finally, I was able to shout: "Get away from me!"

My friends asked an airline agent if we could board the plane ahead of the other passengers. On board, someone gave me a drink and spoke to me in English. The memories receded, and I was not back in the camps, as I had been a moment before. The plane engines revved and we sped down the runway and took off like a bird for Berlin.

....

Sunday came at last and we all went to Olympic Stadium, the great complex that Hitler built for the 1936 Olympics to serve as a showpiece for Teutonic superiority. It was here that an African-American, Jesse Owens, won six gold medals, piercing Hitler's theory of a German master race. And it was here, in 1981 on Reconciliation Day, the high point of the week, that a Jewish woman slated for extermination was to speak about love and reconciliation to about 37,000 Germans.

....

I don't remember my name being called. I was suddenly aware that I was at the podium with thousands of upturned faces staring at me. I gripped my Bible and my notes.

I opened my mouth to tell those Germans what they'd done. Let me tell them of the "lagerarrest," the prison bunker where executions or flogging and other tortures were carried out routinely. Let me tell them of Dr. Rasher's Block 5, specializing in high pressure and exposure experiments, or Professor Shilling's experiments infecting prisoners with malaria. Let me tell them of the SS-Economic Administrative Main Office, an innocuous name for a bureau charged with ordering and overseeing the construction of gas chambers.

On the plane, I'd scribbled an outline of what I would say. It was all here on a piece of paper. Yet I could not find the words to speak.

These German faces were spread out expectantly before me like poppies in a vast field waiting to be mowed down. And yet thoughts of revenge boiled inside me: "If only I had a machine gun, I could wipe out at least the first three rows."

I turned to my friends in the front row. "I need you to pray for me," I said aloud...My stomach was churning and my body was visibly shaking. I prayed, "God give me strength. Let me see you, not the Nazis." Then, as I looked out over the crowd, I could swear I saw Hitler's face.

Then suddenly, a woman ran up the aisle toward me screaming and waving and pointing. A security guard grabbed her but she continued to shout and point.

And then everyone, the entire crowd, thousands of people were also shouting and waving and pointing in the same direction. They were on their feet, cheering and I turned to see what they were looking at.

They were pointing to my right where the large Olympic torch was burning. Beyond it, the American and Israeli flags fluttered in the wind. That Israeli flag was planted smack in the middle of Olympic Stadium where Hitler had proclaimed the thousand year Reich would be cleansed of Jews.

And beyond it in the sky, I saw the most beautiful rainbow I'd ever seen. It was a double rainbow, and it intersected to form a cross. I have never seen anything like it before or since.

I knew then that God was there with me, and I knew that I could go on. I held the paper with my prepared remarks, but when I spoke, none of that came out. Instead, as I listened to my own voice, I heard words of compassion, not condemnation. It was like listening to someone else speak, and the message was one that only God could have given me.

Nothing in me wanted to forgive or forget what had happened to me. But I realized I was speaking of forgiveness and understanding. "Not you sitting here," I told them, "but another generation of Germans fell under a doctrine of hate and death. The German nation – the most educated and advanced in the world in medicine, science and art – became the world's worst murderer."

I looked down at this sea of faces, most much younger than I, and shared some of the things that had happened to me in the camps. Then I said, "But God's love is such that He forgives even all that. He forgives your country. He forgives you. And He loves you. He loves you so much that He was willing to be tortured and killed to prove it. And if He can forgive me in my rebellion and you in yours, then I can forgive you too. By His grace, I forgive you. I thank God that I'm here in this place, and I forgive you completely."

I sat down and bowed my head. I could hear the pastor at the podium crying. When he spoke he said, "Rose, Rose, look at the people!" I looked up and saw them all on their feet cheering. The pastor asked me to go back to the podium, but I couldn't. I raised my eyes to the heavens and spoke to my God. "I didn't want to do it, Lord, but once again, you sustained me."

But as it turned out, this had not been my last test. When I opened my eyes, I saw six men coming down the aisles, one by one. They approached the stage and said they were all ex-Nazis. They asked me to come down and to forgive them as I had from the podium.

This was one testing of my faith I had never imagined. I had just uttered words of forgiveness to thousands; it was far more difficult to stand face-to-face with one ex-Nazi and to forgive him.

Yet that is what I did. I climbed down the steps, not realizing what I was doing. I stood on the stadium floor and looked at the first man, and spoke words of forgiveness that I knew I could not have spoken the day before.

Another man approached me and said he used to be a guard at Dachau. He knelt in front of me and asked me to forgive him. Even then, I was tempted to break his neck. "I could kill just one," I thought. But as my hands moved toward him, I heard myself say, "Did you ask Jesus to forgive you?"

"Yes," he answered. I couldn't postpone his peace. I forgave him for what he had done to my family and me.

The rest of the day seemed a dream. The speakers and the music lasted well into the evening. Floodlights came on. I sat there between my two cops listening to others share their stories, letting myself be moved and healed, feeling bitterness evaporate in the same place where it had once rained down.

Rose Price, *A Rose from the Ashes: the Rose Price Story* (San Francisco, CA: Purple Pomegranate Productions, 2006).

Nancy Richards

Review of Nancy's book on Amazon.com: Heal First, THEN Forgive, April 13, 2006
by "crochetlover"

Nancy Richards offers a fresh face to the concept of forgiveness in her book *Heal and Forgive: Forgiveness in the Face of Abuse*. It deserves a closer look from anyone struggling with recovery from childhood abuse.

A woman who runs a ministry for adult daughters of controlling and abusive families recommended I take a look at Richards' work when I shared with her my own journey. I ordered it last week and found it so absorbing I finished it in just over two hours.

Ms. Richards walks us through her own brutal childhood, one that we discover began at birth, and became exacerbated after her father died and her mother remarried a man who was extremely cruel and sadistic. We learn about the literal joy he took out of beating Nancy and her brothers, how he ripped everyone apart with his words and would look for anything he could find to perpetrate the terror he inflicted. Worse yet are the ways we learn this man is able to influence Nancy and her siblings to turn on each other and how she becomes the household scapegoat.

Eventually Nancy leaves home to marry and start a family of her own. We learn her family of origin does not improve, take responsibility or offer amends for their past behavior. Instead, her mother proceeds to divorce and remarry several abusive men in succession, and continues to promote blaming Nancy for all the "family's" problems, to the extent that she convinces everyone Nancy is crazy and to side against her.

Ms. Richards attempts this whole time to forgive her abusers. After all, aren't we all taught to leave the past behind, forgive other's wrongs, and be family no matter what? Don't they tell us that unless we do these things, we won't heal?

But in the course of her efforts she finds the opposite – she is unable to heal. To the contrary, the harder she tries, the more pain she feels, the greater her resentments, and the more abuse her family of origin is able to heap on her.

In Nancy's quest to figure out why this isn't working, she comes across an understanding therapist and several books from psychological and spiritual perspectives that turn our culture's traditional concept of forgiveness upside down. She learns that perhaps the solution for her is to NOT forgive in the way she has been led to believe, that the whole idea of making peace while overlooking the evil of abusive behaviors is in fact self-defeating and self-destructive. Nancy realized that she must think first of her own needs, to protect herself and her own family.

The end result is that Ms. Richards ends up "divorcing" her mother, which also causes an unfortunate loss of relationships with other family members, including her brothers. As of the publication, she had not spoken to any of them in twelve years.

She also decides to stop working on forgiving them, and start focusing on her recovery and her daughters. It is these actions in themselves that allow healing to flow into her life, and eventually, she is able to find TRUE forgiveness.

I found this book to be very powerful in both the story it had to tell and in the message it had to give. I have followed a very close path in my own life; the parallels between her family's behavior and mine were eerie. I too have had to "divorce" my family of origin and in the process lost relationships with other relatives and even some family friends. So to read such a similar story to mine was incredibly validating.

On a spiritual level, I also found Nancy's story and her sharing of some resources regarding forgiveness to be a relief. Like myself, Ms. Richards is a Christian, and she includes pieces of wisdom from others within that vein who support a different concept of forgiveness and do so from a Christian perspective. As someone who felt torn over whether my choices broke the commandment to honor my mother and father, this book served as a valuable resource to help me reconcile this area of my life.

I cannot recommend this book enough for anyone who is struggling with a family of origin that is broken due to unmended abuse. I also believe anyone who is a friend or loved one of someone recovering from childhood abuse will find this book beneficial for understanding the survivor's struggle to find healing and, yes, forgiveness.

http://www.amazon.com/Heal-Forgive-Forgiveness-Face-Abuse/
product-reviews/1577331583/ref=dp_top_cm_cr_acr_txt?ie=UTF8&showViewpoints=1

Account from Nancy's book on her processes of healing and forgiveness:

At some point in most abuse survivor's healing journey, he or she faces the question of forgiveness. Are there some abuses too atrocious to forgive? Is it possible, or even healthy, to forgive someone who has never asked to be forgiven, someone who has never acknowledged any wrongdoing, and someone who continues to practice the same abusive behaviors?

All too often, well-intentioned people ask us to forgive and forget. For decades, I heard from friends, relatives, therapists, and fellow Christians that I needed to forgive my abusers in order to heal. This advice – and the attempts I made to forgive before I'd learned to exercise personal boundaries – left me open to further injury and damaged me deeply. When I finally mustered the courage to buck societal expectations, not to forgive and to put my own healing and well-being first, I achieved a level of healing that I never thought was possible. My period of not forgiving created the space necessary to achieve the greatest emotional growth of my life. Wow!

Sometimes it is necessary to place a moratorium on forgiveness until healing has taken place. This affords us the opportunity to 1) validate our stories with sympathetic listeners, 2) express our anger in appropriate ways, 3) mourn our losses, and 4) protect others and ourselves from re-injury. After many years of militantly not forgiving, I was both shocked and surprised to find that the unintentional by-product of this healing was – ironically – forgiveness.

At that time, I realized that the old adage, "Forgive and Heal," was backwards. For me, it was "Heal and Forgive!" If I only knew then that adequate healing had to come first, it would have saved me a great deal of time and pain. So now, I shout it from the roof tops "Heal first, THEN Forgive!" How then do we heal?

Validation

Our greatest opportunity for healing comes from the offender. When the person who harmed us is willing to offer restitution, we are truly blessed. This means the wrongdoer must be willing to acknowledge the harm he or she caused us, offer a genuine apology, demonstrate a willingness to restore what was taken and change abusive behavior. However, because of the chronic nature of abuse, most victims do not have their abuse acknowledged by the offender. Still, validation is key. When we do not receive acknowledgment from the person who harmed us, we need to have our abuse acknowledged by other individuals, so we feel as if justice has been served.

For me, justice came in the form of supportive friends, a therapist, and support groups who stood by me during my 14-year estrangement from my family. Each time someone validated my experiences, I became stronger and clearer about what happened to me and the effect it had on my life. For most survivors, abuse is our only reality. Even if we are aware of our childhood abuse, we often live in denial about the effect the abuse had on us until another party bears witness to our trauma. Support and validation from others dissolved my isolation and gave me the necessary strength to journey forward to the life I deserved.

Anger

Forgive and forget. Anger corrodes. Only through forgiveness can you heal. *These often heard statements usually instill within us a sense of urgency that implies we must forgive immediately. Yet healing and forgiveness are a process.*

It is important to note that for most survivors, it isn't anger that holds us back from forgiving – it is fear. I was afraid that if I forgave, I would be hurt again.

Anger has its place. We can't deal with our fear until we deal with our suppressed anger.

It wasn't until I received validation from other people that I found appropriate ways to discharge my rage. I gave myself permission to be constructively angry – to use my anger as an aid in moving forward – until the hurt no longer felt present. Expressing anger in the company of trusted confidantes gave me the sense of not being alone, and validated that I had a right to my anger.

There is an important distinction between a) perpetuating anger by raging at the individuals who harmed us, and b) releasing pent-up anger in safe environments apart from the individuals who caused the harm. Bringing my injuries "into the light" and acknowledging my anger in the safety of supportive individuals brought me the emotional freedom necessary to find a measure of peace.

Mourning

Discharging my anger freed me to honor my pain and mourn my substantial losses.

Protection

An important and often overlooked aspect to healing is that of protecting others and ourselves from further harm. In order to heal, we must be free from the anxiety of re-injury. Boundary issues are common in abusive family systems. When a child's body, heart, and soul are routinely violated, her life is constructed in the absence of boundaries. Forgiveness must go hand in hand with learning to set and maintain clear, respectful boundaries (emphasis added).

Each survivor has her own individual timetable that must be honored. As long as I carried unhealed wounds, forgiveness would have to wait. Healing requires a great deal of time, self-

examination, hard work, and pain. Yet, I have learned that once an adequate amount of healing has been accomplished, forgiveness becomes a viable opportunity.

Forgiveness doesn't mean that we "excuse" offensive behavior; it doesn't mean forgetting or even trusting the person who harmed us. Nor does it require us to "let go" of our safety. Rather, for me, forgiveness meant healing enough to let go of resentment and find peace.

Nancy Richards, *Heal & Forgive: Forgiveness in the Face of Abuse* (Nevada City, CA: Blue Dolphin Publishing, 2005). Used by permission. All rights reserved.

Eva Mozes Kor

At the age of ten, twins Eva and Miriam Mozes were taken to Auschwitz where Dr. Josef Mengele used them for medical experiments. Both survived, but Miriam died in 1993 when she developed cancer of the bladder as a consequence of the experiments done on her as a child. Eva Kor has since spoken explicitly about her experiences at Auschwitz and founded The C.A.N.D.L.E.S Holocaust museum in Indiana where she now lives. In 2003, the museum was destroyed in an arson attack, believed to be by white supremacists.

Miriam and I were part of a group of children who were alive for one reason only – to be used as human guinea pigs. During our time in Auschwitz, we talked very little. Starved for food and human kindness, it took every ounce of strength just to stay alive. Because we were twins, we were used in a variety of experiments. Three times a week we'd be placed naked in a room, for 6-8 hours to be measured and studied. It was unbelievably demeaning.

In another type of experiment, they took blood from one arm and gave us injections in the other. After one such injection, I became very ill and was taken to the hospital. Dr Mengele came in the next day, looked at my fever chart and declared that I had only two weeks to live. For two weeks, I was between life and death, but I refused to die. If I had died, Mengele would have given Miriam a lethal injection in order to do a double autopsy. When I didn't die, he carried on experimenting on us and as a result, Miriam's kidneys stopped growing. They remained the size of a child's all her life.

On January 27, 1945, four days before my 11th birthday, Auschwitz was liberated by the Soviet army. After 9 months in refugee camps I returned to my village in Romania to find that no one from my family had survived

Echoes from Auschwitz was a part of my life but I did not speak publicly about my experiences until 1978 after the television series *The Holocaust* was aired. People would ask me about the experiments but I couldn't remember very much, so I wanted to find other twins who were liberated with me. I wrote to newspapers asking them to publish an appeal for other survivors of Mengele to contact me. By 1980, I was sending out 500 letters a year – but still no response. In desperation, one day I decided to start an organization in which I would make myself President.

People are always impressed if they get a letter from a president, and it worked. Finally, I was able to find other twin survivors and exchange memories. It was an immensely healing experience.

In 1993, I was invited to lecture to some doctors in Boston and asked if I could bring a Nazi doctor with me. I thought it was a mad request until I remembered that I'd once been in a documentary that had also featured a Dr. Hans Münch from Auschwitz. I contacted him in Germany, and he said he would meet with me for a videotaped interview to take to the conference. In July 1993, I was on my way to meet this Nazi doctor. I was so scared, but when I arrived at his home, he treated me with the utmost respect. I asked him if he'd seen the gas chambers. He said this was a nightmare he dealt with every day of his life. I was surprised that Nazis had nightmares, too, and asked him if he would come with me to Auschwitz to sign a document at the ruins of the gas chambers. He said that he would love to do it.

In my desperate effort to find a meaningful "thank you" gift for Dr. Münch, I searched the stores, and my heart, for many months. Then the idea of a forgiveness letter came to my mind. I knew it would be a meaningful gift, but it became a gift to myself as well, because I realized I was NOT a hopeless, powerless victim. When I asked a friend to check my spelling, she challenged me to forgive Dr. Mengele too. At first I was adamant that I could never forgive Dr. Mengele, but then I realized I had the power now... the power to forgive. It was my right to use it. No one could take it away.

On January 27, 1995, at the 50th anniversary of the liberation of Auschwitz, I stood by the ruins of the gas chambers with my children – Dr. Alex Kor and Rina Kor – and with Dr. Münch and his children and grandchild. Dr. Münch signed his document about the operation of the gas chambers while I read my document of forgiveness and signed it. As I did that, I felt a burden of pain was lifted from me. I was no longer in the grip of pain and hate; I was finally free.

The day I forgave the Nazis, privately I forgave my parents whom I hated all my life for not having saved me from Auschwitz. Children expect their parents to protect them, mine couldn't. And then, I forgave myself for hating my parents.

Forgiveness is really nothing more than an act of self-healing and self-empowerment. I call it a miracle medicine. It is free; it works and has no side effects.

I believe with every fiber of my being that every human being has the right to live without the pain of the past. For most people there is a big obstacle to forgiveness because society expects revenge. It seems we need to honor our victims, but I always wonder if my dead loved ones would want me to live with pain and anger until the end of my life. Some survivors do not want to let go of the pain. They call me a traitor and accuse me of talking in their name. I have never done this. Forgiveness is as personal as chemotherapy – I do it for myself.

http://theforgivenessproject.org.uk/stories

Account from Eva's book on her process of forgiveness:

In 1993, I traveled to Germany and met with a Nazi doctor from Auschwitz, Dr. Münch. Surprisingly, he was very kind to me. Even more surprising, I found that I liked him. I asked him if he knew anything about the gas chambers in Auschwitz. He said that what he knew had been fueling the nightmares he lived with every single day. He went on to describe it, saying, "People would be told they were taking a shower and to remember their clothes hanger number, and to tie their shoes together. When the gas chamber was fully packed, the doors closed hermetically and sealed. A vent-like orifice opened in the ceiling, dropping pellets like gravel to the floor. Somehow, the pellets operated like dry ice and turned to gas. The gas began rising from the floor. People tried to get away from the rising gas, climbing on top of one another. The strongest people ended atop a pile of intermingled bodies. When the people on the top of the pile stopped moving, that was when I knew, from looking through a peephole and watching it all, that everybody was dead." Dr. Münch signed the mass death certificates; there were no names on them, just that there were two thousand or three thousand dead people.

I told Dr. Münch that this was very important information, for I had not known that the gas chambers worked that way. I asked him if he would come with me to Auschwitz in 1995, when we would be celebrating the fiftieth anniversary of our liberation from the camp. I further asked him to sign an affidavit about what he had said and seen and done, and to do it at the site of all those killings. He said that he would love to.

So I returned from Germany, and I was so glad that I would have an original document witnessed and signed by a Nazi – a participator, not a survivor and not a liberator – to add to the historical collection of information we were preserving for ourselves and for future generations. I was so grateful that Dr. Münch was willing to come with me to Auschwitz and sign that document about the operation of the gas chambers, and I wanted to thank him. But what does one give a Nazi doctor? How can one thank a Nazi doctor?

For ten months, I pondered this question. All kinds of ideas popped into my head until I finally thought: "How about a simple letter of forgiveness from me to him? Forgiving him for all that he has done?" I knew immediately that he would appreciate it, but what I discovered once I made the decision was that forgiveness is not so much for the perpetrator, but for the victim. I had the power to forgive. No one could give me this power, and no one could take it away. That made feel powerful. It made me feel good to have any power over my life as a survivor.

I began writing my letter and came up with several versions, working through a lot of pain. Concerned about my spelling, I called my former English professor to correct my letter. We met a few times and she asked me to think about forgiving Dr. Mengele, as well. At first, I was shocked, but later I promised her that I would, for I realized that I had the power even to forgive the Angel of Death. "Wow," I thought, "It makes me feel good that I can do that. I have that power and I am not hurting anyone with it."

We arrived in Auschwitz in January 27, 1995. Dr. Münch signed his document. Then I read my own personal statement of forgiveness, and I signed it.

Immediately I felt that a burden of pain had been lifted from my shoulders, a pain I had lived with for fifty years: I was no longer a victim of Auschwitz, no longer a victim of my tragic past. I was free. I also took that moment to forgive my parents, whom I had hated all my life for not protecting us from Auschwitz, for not saving us from growing up as orphans. I finally understood that they had done the best that they could. I also forgave myself for hating my parents in the first place.

Anger and hate are seeds that germinate war. Forgiveness is a seed for peace. It is the ultimate act of self-healing.

I look at forgiveness as the summit of a very tall mountain. One side is dark, dreary, wet, and very difficult to climb. But those who struggle up and reach the summit can see the beauty of other side of the mountain, which is covered by flowers, white doves, butterflies, and sunshine. Standing at the summit, we can see both sides of the mountain. How many people would choose to go back down on the dreary side rather than stroll through the sunny flower-covered side?

I have given over 3,000 speeches throughout the world, written two books, and contributed three chapters in three other books. I hope to teach young people the life lessons I have learned through all my pain and everything I have been through and survived: 1. Never ever give up on yourself or your dreams, for everything good in life is possible. 2. Judge people on their actions and the content of their character. 3. Forgive your worst enemy and forgive everyone who has hurt you – it will heal your soul and set you free.

When I look back on my teenage years, I would never have believed that anyone would want to listen to me or that I would have anything important to say. So I am saying to you, whoever is reading this book, to remember: never ever give up. You can survive and make your dreams come true.

And I would like to end with a quote from my Declaration of Amnesty read at the fiftieth anniversary of the liberation of Auschwitz:

"I hope, in some small way, to send the world a message of forgiveness, a message of peace, a message of hope, a message of healing. Let there be no more wars, no more experiments without informed consent, no more gas chambers, no more bombs, no more hatred, no more killing, no more Auschwitzes."

Eva Mozes Kor and Lisa Rojany Buccieri, *Surviving the Angel of Death: The Story of a Mengele Twin in Auschwitz* (Terra Haute, IN: Tanglewood Publishing, Inc., 2009). Used by permission. All rights reserved.

Anna (England)

Anna and her brother (both from the UK) were sexually abused by their father for many years. He denies the abuse ever happened. As an adult, Anna cut off all contact with her father but in 1998, she decided to get back in touch with him and has continued to dialogue across their irreconcilable differences. Tragically, in 1999, Anna's brother committed suicide.

I was sexually abused by my father from when I was 3 until I was 12. I only survived the abuse by dissociating – my body stayed present my conscious mind split off and 'forgot.' But when my son was 3, I began to recover my memories and in the end decided to confront my father. He denied the abuse and continues to do so. I survived the remembering by splitting in a different way – I stopped all contact with my father.

At least that is the situation from my perspective, from my father's perspective it looks very different:

Out of the blue comes a false accusation of childhood sexual abuse, first from his daughter and then from his son. They cut off from him completely and deny him access to his grandchildren. He is reported to Social Services and questioned by the police. His son sends vindictive letters to him, his second wife and to members of his local community. He is afraid that he may lose his job, his second family and his place as a respected member of church and community. His son commits suicide, and he is blamed and not allowed to go to the funeral.

Reconnecting with my father has not been an easy journey. For a long time I focused on my rage. I wanted revenge, to punish, even to kill. I made my father wholly bad, "Other." But I wasn't able to cut myself off totally. I began to grieve that this abuse was done to me not by a stranger, but by someone who also loved me, and I loved him.

I first decided to get back in touch with my father after a 5 Rhythms Dance Workshop at which I realized I was trapped by the past and unable to move beyond feeling a powerless victim. That first meeting was a very positive experience. I told my father I had not changed what I believed, only what I was choosing to do with it. I was no longer a helpless victim, I made choices, I set boundaries and I spoke directly about my experience of the abuse – all things that were not possible as a child.

I invited my father to speak from within his belief system and asked him to allow me to do the same. I told him I knew that not all of what happened between us when I was a child was bad and that I also want to acknowledge the good bits. I suggested going for a walk and he agreed. Walking, we began to explore ways of communicating across our irreconcilable differences and have been doing so ever since.

Over the last eight years, fighting to establish the truth of what happened between us in the past has become less important to me than what happens now and in the future. At first when I started speaking out about my abuse, it was very important to me to be believed. Now I am less concerned about establishing my truth and more interested in how to relate positively across our irreconcilable differences. I spent a long time hating my father, now I am finding more creative ways to relate to him beyond the victim/perpetrator polarity. Making the shift beyond feeling a helpless victim of an unchangeable abuser is an awesome experience and has been personally healing, both psychologically and spiritually.

In addition, when I am aware that this most private of oppressions between father and daughter is also part of a much bigger picture and that all of these issues relate not only to sexual abuse, but also to all of the abuses that we perpetrate in the world, I feel less alone and more inspired to create something meaningful from my traumatic experiences that will also be healing for the world. I hope that together we can find new ways of resolving our conflicts that do not perpetuate cycles of revenge and violence, whether those conflicts are with our friends and family or carried out in our names by our political leaders or in the names of our spiritual traditions.

It is not an easy step to go beyond the polarity of victim and perpetrator; we tend to act as if the innocent and the guilty are totally separate. But victim and perpetrator, good and bad, co-exist within each of us. My father was a good son to my grandmother, he is a well-respected member of his local community and he was both a good and an abusive father. Suicide bombers may also be good sons and fathers and well-respected members of their local communities.

Forgiveness is an interesting concept in relation to my father. I think forgiving is an on-going process, which comes and goes and develops over time rather than something that can be achieved once and for all (emphasis added). He says he has forgiven me for all the upset I have caused him by my "false accusation." Can I forgive him for something he denies? The answer is both no and yes. What my father did to me and to my brother is unforgivable, but I no longer need him to admit it or to pay for it in some way. I have reached a new place, a place beyond my painful history and toward a more sustainable future both for myself in my personal relationships and, I hope, for the world.

http://theforgivenessproject.org.uk/stories/page/28/

Henri Landwirth

Henri Landwirth survived five concentration camps to live the American Dream. Arriving in the United States at the age of twenty-one with $20 in his pocket, he went on to a successful 50-year career in the hotel business, always mindful of improving the lives of those in need. He has established six philanthropic organizations: The Fanny Landwirth Foundation, The Mercury 7 Foundation, Give Kids the World, Dignity-U-Wear, Memories of Love, and the Gift of Life in America Foundation.

Holocaust survivor Henri Landwirth doesn't really want to talk about the Holocaust.

He'd rather point people to the DVDs and books about his life.

"It's in there," he'll say.

Still, about once a week, he stands in front of auditoriums full of students and tells his story over and over. He recently agreed to speak at 48 high schools and middle schools in Duval County this year and next. Tonight, St. Johns County residents will get their chance to see him at Flagler College.

He'll tell the audience anything they want to know. But the truth is, he wishes he didn't have to bring it up.

"It's still hard for me to talk about," he said. "I live with it at night. Sometimes I cannot sleep."

But week after week, he retells the horrors that many people call unspeakable.

He still gets emotional. Every time.

"Most of the survivors cannot go to schools anymore," he said. "But I feel a duty to the generations that I go and see. I really feel it's very necessary."

He tries to bring the Holocaust alive in the eyes of middle school students. Many, like the middle schoolers he went to see earlier this month, sometimes can't yet appreciate what's in front of them.

In the halls, students talked about "The Holocaust Guy" as adults herded the chatting groups into the auditorium. Girls waves at friends. Adults ssh-ed.

"I have a lot of things to tell you," Landwirth said to the students, kids about the age he was when a Nazi soldier stormed into his house, put a gun to his father's head and demanded to know where their money was.

"In a few years, no one will see any survivors anymore. I am one of the few left. So listen to me; please listen to me."

He tried to cram all the lessons he learned in five years of Holocaust and 81 years of life into one speech.

"If you cannot forgive, you cannot love. And you're angry," he said. "Please, I beg you. Forgive each other. I also beg you to stop hating each other. Now, go home and tell your parents you love them."

He let the students ask questions, and conversation spread out faster than a spilled barrel of oil when someone asked something silly or when Landwirth dropped a fact, like that he was in the camps from the age of 13 to 18.

Landwirth would have to speak louder into the microphone wired to the stage.

"How did you get your tattoo?" one girl asked.

"You want to see it?"

"YES!" The crowd cheered, as if it was a prize he was hiding behind a curtain.

"You want to see my name, my name for five years?" he asked.

"YES!"

There was chatter as he unbuttoned the cuff of his shirt and rolled up his sleeve.

The kids gasped as they saw it, close to the elbow on his inner arm, a blue label unreadable from the crowd.

"That was my name: B4343," he told a silent audience, his arm stretched out. "It wasn't Henri. It was B4343. We were treated like animals."

There was a quiet as he continued.

Landwirth told them about the underground camp, where he didn't see sunlight once while working in an ammunitions plant. Even with typhus, he somehow was one of 300 survivors out of 3,000 workers.

He told them he ate a small slice of bread and some watery soup every day.

He told them how he slept on bedsprings, using his shoes as a pillow.

He told them about being orphaned and alone and a prisoner in his teenage years.

But the most important thing he had to tell them, he said, was about what happened within him after the Holocaust.

"One day I just forgave the Germans," he said. "As soon as I did that, the hate that I had for them went away."

Bystanders are the real enemy, he said. And the roots of the Holocaust are the same as the roots of bullying, of judging one another by how they look.

"Too many of us have been bystanders," he said.

At the end of the speech, students waited past the bell to hug Landwirth. Really, he needed the hugs as much as the students want to give them.

Students grabbed their friends who missed the presentation and dragged them in the door, pointing, "That's him."

"Oh, I want to hug him," said one girl.

On the way out, her friend said, "This was the best day ever."

http://staugustine.com/stories/032008/news_txt01_004.shtml

Account from Henri's book on his process of forgiveness:

Terrible things can move a person toward faith or away from faith. It depends on the individual.

I was young and strong and able to work, so I was separated from my sister and my mother. I feared for their safety, and for the first time in my young life, I felt truly apart, disconnected and alone.

I wondered why a loving God would allow the Holocaust to happen. Where was God when we needed Him? I certainly didn't feel God's presence during my first experience with deportation. In fact, I was feeling something quite different, a kind of nervous fear that found its way permanently into my heart. Maybe we really were alone. What if it did not matter how loud our screams echoed? What if the number of dead grew to the thousands? The tens of thousands? God forbid, the millions. What if the world knew what was happening and did not care? What if sane men and women around the world knew what Hitler was trying to accomplish and shrugged their shoulders over steaming dinner, and thought such death and destruction of the Jews may not be such a terrible thing?

Worst of all, what if God did not exist?

Where does a heart truly broken, a spirit hopelessly abandoned, find hope? What exists within a human being that allows for survival amidst such devastation? It must be God. We might not know it, or believe it, when we are in the middle of the fire, but it must be God. Who else could it be?

. . . .

When I left Czechoslovakia, I was still angry, still kind of crazy. Little thoughts bothered me. I thought of the Germans who didn't actually participate in the camps but who let them happen by their silence. I felt a tremendous hatred for all Nazis.

Now that the war was over, they were on the bottom of the stick instead of holding it against us. As I wandered, I picked fights with former Nazis and Nazi supporters. I beat them up because of who they were. This hatred grew as the months passed and became the foundation of my third life, my life of vengeance.

Walking along a river between towns, I came upon a German boy dressed in the uniform of the Hitler Jugen, Hitler's organization for children. He wore black leather pants and shirt. He was proud of himself, I could tell that. I blocked his way. It was just him and me.

I asked the boy if he was a good Hitler Jugen, and I could see in his eyes that he was scared. I told the boy to take off his uniform. I wanted to hurt him in some way. I told him to strip naked or I was going to kill him. Those were my words: "Take off your clothes or I'm going to kill you!" He realized that I was serious. I was so angry, I think if he had refused, I would have actually killed him with my bare hands. He took off everything but his underwear. I told him to take them off, too. I took all his clothes and I threw them into the river. Then I held him by the neck, and a strange thing happened. I stopped wanting to hurt him. I told him to run. I started to yell at him in German. He was very afraid. And he ran.

I watched the Hitler Jugen run away until he was out of sight. I watched him but thought about myself. What I had done to him hadn't made me feel better; it made me feel ashamed. I did not want to become what I despised. Any fate was better than turning into one of them.

———— ✇ ————

[It would be many years before he could say he forgave the Germans, but he had turned compassion's corner. The healing had begun (Excerpt from Love & Hate: The Story of Henri Landwirth by Bill Halamandari, self-published no copyright, 2007.)]

Survivors remember those who committed the crimes. Their faces are never too far away. If I want to, I can close my eyes and picture their faces. Most of us can. Not enough night exists to banish them from our memory, not enough time has passed to allow them to slip away.

I'm sure many of the executioners were sadists who enjoyed what they were doing. Others did it to survive themselves. Still others used the excuse that they had to follow their orders or be thrown into the ovens. When I think of all the people who committed these crimes, I do not feel hatred anymore. There isn't forgiveness, but there is no longer hatred. [Note: Do you see the process of forgiveness here?] Those who were torturers and murderers and liars will pay the price for it. No man can escape that.

....

To try to be a caring person takes too much positive energy to waste time with hatred and vengeance. I try to live my life in the present. I worry about things I must do today, and I think about the plans for tomorrow. But I try not to live too much in the past.... What good can come of it? I leave my hatred to the past. There is no room in my life for it. I pray every day to focus on the living, to give to others today. I want to have peace in my life. To help others and be peaceful. If I can achieve this, that is enough for any man.

....

What people should realize is that most of us would have done anything for vengeance. We would have killed. If I had seen the men from the death camps, it would not have taken me a second. I would have tortured them and killed them. This is not a good thing to know about yourself.

But facing the truth is important. This period helped me get rid of all the anger and bad thoughts that had consumed me. I found some peace with myself and the world around me.

There is no life-affirming value when a person keeps hatred and anger in his heart. Only bad things can come from such thoughts. It is possible to take that hate and anger, every drop of it, and change it into love and caring. Once a survivor can reach that point, he will be on the way to a better, more fulfilling life. No matter how cruel the past has been to you, today can be a happy time. Just for today, let yourself enjoy life. Instead of hating, reach out to your brother or sister and help them. Kindness makes all the difference, both to the person receiving it and the person giving.

I still have certain strong feelings; they are not hate, but feelings with conviction against the terrible things that took place in Germany. [Note: Here we see more processing.]

Henri Landwirth with J. P. Hendricks, *Gift of Life* **(Self-published, no copyright, 1996).**

———❊❊❊———

[Note: Somewhere along the way, between 1996 and 2006, Henri made a conscious choice to forgive the abuse and the losses he had suffered at the hands of the Nazis. I have researched as much as possible on the subject, and all I came up with was that he had chosen to forgive along the way. His biographer made the following statements]:

———❊❊❊———

Henri had lived in hell. He had seen the worst humanity had to offer and yet he chose to answer with the best. Where there was abundant reason for anger, hate, and bitterness, there was only love, forgiveness, joy, and – yes – gratitude. How was this possible? I wondered. How do you get from hell to humanity? How do you get love from hate? I would spend 20 years trying to answer those questions.

....

Henri has always had an innate sense of what can be done. The tragic death of a fifteen-year-old boy at a high school near his home in March of 2006 made him wonder what more he could do to fight the forces of darkness.

The boy had committed suicide. While no one knows for sure why this child chose to end his life, racism was believed to be a contributing factor. A black boy in a predominately-white rural school, he was constantly subjected to racial slurs and mocked by his peers.

After the boy's death, the school was rocked by a series of race-related incidents. Concerned about the escalating violence, the principal invited Henri to speak to the student body, hoping his story might cause students to think about the consequences of their actions.

Henri told them how hate had nearly destroyed his life. He talked about the five years of torture and brutality he had endured at their age, his desire for vengeance, and the miracles that followed his forgiveness. He urged the students to make love not hate the focus of their lives. And he asked them to practice forgiveness.

"If you cannot forgive, you cannot love fully," he said, "and life without love is nothing.'

The following day, an English teacher at the school gave her students a pop quiz. "I have never done anything like that following an assembly," she said, "but there has never been an assembly like that one."

To her surprise nearly every student made eighty percent or above on the quiz. Inspired by the students' response, Henri cancelled plans for a vacation and began seeking engagements at local high schools, hoping to teach tolerance, forgiveness, and compassion.

....

Emily [Henri's granddaughter] is twelve years old, the youngest. "They killed your mother and father," she says. "If you hadn't survived we wouldn't be here. How could you forgive the Germans?"

228

"I had to," Henri says. "I couldn't live any other way. The lesson we must learn from the Holocaust is that evil is real. It has existed since the inception of man, and will continue until mankind is extinct. That is why we must talk about what happened in the concentration camps. People have to understand where hatred leads."

Halamandaris, Bill, *Love & Hate: The Story of Henri Landwirth* (Self-published, no copyright, 2007).

Dave Pelzer

Biography of Dave Pelzer
By Callista Meyer

Facing death at the hands of his mother, Dave Pelzer has survived one of the most extreme cases of child abuse in California's history. Dave's mother was mentally disturbed and alcoholic, making the child's life horrendous until the ripe age of 12 when he was finally saved and placed in foster homes until reaching 18 years of age. Continuing his courageous journey of life, Dave was determined to make himself a better person regardless of what obstacles entered his path.

The abuse Dave suffered began around the time he began attending public school. When Dave and his siblings were caught misbehaving, Dave most often received the punishment. This punishment began with banishment to the corner of his room but soon escalated to include being shoved against a mirror and forced to say "I am a bad boy" repeatedly with his mother's addiction to alcohol beginning. Soon Dave's father also discovered the joys of alcohol and while he did not engage in the abuse, Dave's father also did not try to stop it.

Dave's mother continued punishing him by pummeling his head, forcing him to perform household duties instead of watching television and once she even burned his arm over the gas stove. Dave tried to stall his mother's punishments until someone else came home but quite often, this was nearly impossible. Being refused food, Dave often stole food from the school cafeteria to survive. Unfortunately, Dave was caught stealing one day and the incident reported to his mother. Dave's punishments then escalated to include only to be referred to as "The Boy" and he was told not to speak or look at anyone.

Dave was forced to perform the household chores and then be hidden in the basement. Soon he was forced to sleep in the garage with no blankets or pillows. The abuse only got worse as Dave began to grow older. He was forced to eat from his brother's soiled diapers, locked in the bathroom with a mixture of ammonia and bleach to breathe in the hazardous fumes and his mother managed to choke him hard enough that at school he was unable to breathe due to the swelling.

Life was indeed horrendous for this young boy, with no one noticing that the abuse was occurring until Dave was 12 years old, and a teacher at school noticed that he had no skin on his arms because he was forced to soak them in ammonia. Several teachers put their own jobs on the line to help save this poor boy from suffering by contacting the police. This phone call literally saved Dave's life.

The next six years, Dave spent in and out of various foster homes where he began to learn how to lead a normal life and heal from his many years of suffering. At the age of 18, Dave was able to leave foster care and enlisted in the U.S. Army. Dave was chosen by the Army to refuel the secretive SR-71 Blackair while in midair. Dave served actively and on a rigorous schedule, but he still found time to volunteer with the community. Dave received the California Volunteer Award in 1990. Eventually, the pain was overcome and Dave learned to forgive his parents and began to advocate for abused children. During this time, Dave also published numerous books, including *A Child Called It* and *A Man Named Dave*. His very first novel was nominated for a Pulitzer prize. In total, Dave has written and published six novels of which four were on the *New York's Times Bestseller's List* simultaneously.

Dave promotes resilience, service to mankind, personal responsibility and growth, as well as having faith in humanity. Dave came from a very poor home life suffering at the hands of his own mother but overcame this abuse with the help and assistance of others and has become one of the world's living proofs that you can overcome abuse and you are not alone!

http://www.helium.com/items/1186060-child-abuse-dave-pelzer (by Callista Meyer)

Account from Dave's book on his process of forgiveness:

I nodded. As I stood in front of Mother, my eyes scanned her every feature, in the vain hope of finding the person I had worshiped as a tiny child – the person I had so longed to love me. Yet, as I closed my eyes, I could not give Mother the humanity I gave to total strangers. With all the compassion I could muster, I swallowed hard before saying, "Go in peace."

....

"No!' I lashed out, pointing my finger in her face. Raising my voice, I could feel my legs shudder. "Don't you even... don't you spoil it. Not after all you've done. This is not one of your little games that you can manipulate. You have... no one, nothing left. Just stop it! For once put away your bullshit and do what's right, for God's sake!" I pleaded, on the verge of tears. "I swear to you, with all of my honor, I wish you no pain, no suffering. I only wish you peace." I paused, as my chest seemed to heave. Calming myself, I said in a controlled voice. "That's all I can... that's the best I can do."

Mother's eyes tried to bore right through me. After a few moments, her intensity softened. I slowly shook my head back and forth. Without saying the words, I mouthed, "I can't. I can't do that."

With a nod, Mother showed that she understood. Perhaps she had thought that by calling me during her emotional state, I would rush over and anoint her with forgiveness. To my own dismay, and after a lifetime of constantly proving my worthiness to others, I did not – I could not – forgive Mother.

....

Stopping in front of me, Stephen [David's son} asked, "Do you forgive her? I mean, your mom?"

Kneeling down, I held him by his shoulders. "Absolutely. Somehow, some way something made my mom the way she was. Back then, when she was raised, she was not allowed to talk about things that might appear to be negative. I don't think she had anyone to turn to, to really help her deal with whatever it was that troubled her.

....

Now, standing alone beneath God's creation, I closed my eyes, relaxed my body, and inhaled as much air as my lungs could hold. I could almost recapture the scent of Mother's perfume and Father's shiny jet-black hair and beaming smile, as I recalled that evening so long ago. Opening my eyes, I found the north star and muttered, "Rest in peace. May God Almighty grant you both eternal peace. Amen."

Dave Pelzer, *A Man Named Dave: A Story of Triumph and Forgiveness* (New York, NY: The Penguin Group, 2000).

Hanneke Coates

Hanneke Coates was born just before the Second World War on the island of Java in the Dutch East Indies (now Indonesia). After Pearl Harbor and the invasion of the Japanese, she spent three and a half years of her childhood in one of the 300 or so concentration camps around the Archipelago, which held mostly women and children. Husbands and fathers were sent to work on the Burma railway line or in camps around Japan.

We were constantly moved from one camp to another, or from one end of a camp to another end, often in boarded up train carriages, without seating, lavatories, food or drink. My final camp was the notorious Tjideng camp, which housed around 10,000 women and children and where food was very scarce (half a coconut shell with rice and water-lily soup once a day). Water and sanitation were almost non-existent and medical supplies very scarce since Red Cross parcels were withheld by the Japanese. The most lasting effect of those three and a half years in captivity was the constant and total humiliation the Nipponese inflicted on us. We were constantly screamed at, punished by withholding the little food we had, publicly humiliated by having hair hacked off with blunt knives and lashed at by the long whips the Japanese soldiers carried in their boots. We were expected to bow to our captors whenever they came into sight. Many times, we were herded on the parade ground and for hours on end made to stand in the burning hot tropical sun or in the middle of the night while having to bow to our oppressors. By the end of the war, many hundreds of thousands of women and children had died through malnutrition, tropical diseases and lack of medication. I was one of the lucky ones.

After my nursing training, I married and had three children. The humiliation of the early years of my life had a direct influence on my relationship within my marriage and for many years, I was subjected to domestic violence, more humiliation and great unhappiness. The camp years had "conditioned" me to be humiliated in later life. After almost 40 years of marriage, my partner simply moved out one day after having broken yet more bones. Domestic violence is now a recognized syndrome and both the local police and my own Church were a constant source of support. It was through attending a Christian divorce recovery course that I first learned to deal with my traumas through forgiveness.

Forgiveness does not have to mean that we have to be "matey" with those who have abused us. I have learned that life is about choices. Betrayal is something others do to us, but bitterness is something we do to ourselves. If we do not forgive, we lose the joy of living. When we forgive, we release peace and restoration to the forgiven as well as to ourselves.

http://theforgivenessproject.org.uk/visitor-stories/page/4/

Nonna Lisowsakaja Bannister

The Secret Holocaust Diaries is a haunting eyewitness account of Nonna Lisowskaja Bannister, a remarkable Russian girl who saw and survived the unspeakable evils of World War II. For half a century, she kept her story secret while living a normal American life. She locked all of her photos, documents, diaries, and dark memories in a trunk. Late in life, she unlocked the trunk first for her husband, and now for the rest of the world.

Nonna's is a story of suffering, torture, and death, but also a story of incredible acts of kindness that show the ultimate triumph of faith and love over despair and evil. *The Secret Holocaust Diaries* is in part a tragedy, yet an unforgettable true story about forgiveness, courage, and hope. – Tyndale House Publishers

http://secretholocaustdiaries.com/

Account from Nonna's book on her process of forgiveness:

Preface

Though similar to other memoirs of the war and the Holocaust years, Nonna's account provides a rare glimpse into the life of a girl who was born to a wealthy family in the Ukraine, experienced great suffering in Stalin's Soviet Union and eventually lost her family and her own freedom at the hands of Nazi Germany. It is a story with unusual significance as one of the few firsthand accounts of a girl from a once-privileged family, who fell into the ranks of the Ostarbeiter – the primarily Ukrainian "Eastern laborers" transported to Germany during the war as slave labor under Adolph Hitler's regime. The fact that she not only survived such turmoil and tragedy but also moved on through faith in God to forgive those who took away so much makes her story all the more remarkable.

Introduction

The events described in the following pages were written from my diaries and notes that were transcribed from the four to six languages in which I had written them – starting when I was nine years old. I have translated the poems and thoughts and scripts into English. I have worked on keeping these all together since 1942, when Mama and I left our homeland and were sent to Germany, where we were to be slave labor. In these notes, I kept a record of all the terrors, atrocities, and the new life into which we were thrown. Throughout these ordeals, I never forgot my grandmother and the rest of my family, which had been torn apart and ultimately destroyed.

....

I am compelled to write this story because I was a witness to many events that took place then and because I am the only survivor of my entire family.

....

There were times when I would think about my family that I had lost, and I would think about how close and loving we had been. However, I just could not bring myself to inflict my sad memories on my husband and my still-young children. I did not want anything to interfere with the happiness that we had, and certainly when the children were growing up, my only concern was to protect them from anything that would leave them with depressing impressions. I wanted so very much to create a healthy and happy environment for all of them.

....

How can one tell the story, especially write the story, without knowledge of the writer? The story is so real and so full of horrors. How can I describe the things that I have seen and felt and that made me the sole survivor of my family – all the troubled times and horrors and terror that surrounded all of us? It is difficult for me to put my thoughts into proper perspective, especially since my English vocabulary is somewhat limited.

Though I have lived in America for forty-seven years, I still find it difficult to express my thoughts properly. I have yet another problem, which is that I have allowed myself to forget the languages I knew so well when I came to this country. I spoke six languages very well, and most of my notes and some of my poems, which I wrote between nine years old and nineteen years old, were written in the Russian, Ukrainian, Polish, Latvian, and German languages.

....

Most of my writings were about my mother, father, and my brother, Anatoly. I also became very close to God Himself, and my writings were full of expressed feelings toward faith in God and His mercy on me. I felt very close to God, and I felt that He had chosen to keep me alive for a very definite purpose. So I put into writing all my feelings – as best I could – and all that I had learned about God from my dear grandmother and my parents.

Three Miles Closer

[According to Nonna's later note, the new house was probably more like eight miles closer to the Great House than were they had been before – only three miles away from it.]

It was a large house with a big foyer and several large rooms, even though it looked more like an office building or a post office than it did a home. Mama got Papa situated in the bed, and we started a fire in the stove to warm up the room.... We settled down to try to make Papa as comfortable as possible. Papa was still very calm and talked to Mama and me, telling us not to be bitter at the Germans – that they were doing what they had been told to do.

....

Amazingly, through the whole ordeal, as horrible as it was for Papa, he had remained the same gentle and kind person he had always been. For him, there was always a reason for any situation (no matter how horrible it was), and he would forgive anyone for what was done to him. At times, it would infuriate me the way he would defend the actions of those who had unjustly hurt him.

"They could not help themselves and did what they did to protect themselves from the unknown," *Papa would say.*

To me, it was a simple act of cruelty and sadism.

....

I sat for a long time just watching Papa, when suddenly an incredibly peaceful feeling came over me. It was almost as though I was surrounded by a dozen angels or something. I looked at Papa, and I saw an expression on his face that was not there a few minutes before – he looked as though he smiled. His lips were not moving, but I thought I heard him say, "It is all right now, and I am happy." I leaned over closer to his face and whispered, "Papa, are you awake?" But there was no motion, and for the first time, I noticed his chest was not moving. I stood up and slowly started to walk backward without taking my eyes off of Papa until I was out of the kitchen. I felt like I needed some fresh air.... I started walking around a small tree in the deep snow. I kept going in circles, and I kept chanting, "Papa is happy! Papa is happy!"

Afterword: Did It Really Happen?

Just as we read and believe in the great God Himself and Christ, who we believe was crucified for the cause of salvation of all who were created by God, we must not forget what happened to those who were tortured, tormented, and murdered by the hands of evil men. They (the victims) did not commit any crimes except that they were born and were just there in those troubled times. As the philosopher Santayana forewarned, "Those who cannot remember the past are condemned to repeat it!"

However, I believe forgiveness is important. It is to forgive, as God teaches us, but never forget – rather, to apply the truth to our lives in such a way that we do not repeat our sins over and over again. If we learn our lessons from the Word of God... and if we believe in His Word as God's Word, we shall also be aware of all that happens while we are in His world.

Since we cannot turn back, but live our lives now and tomorrow and after, we need to be aware of evil things, which may always be with us until death. Death comes quickly, and we all will die sooner or later. But it is the life after death that fills us with great hope, and we should never be afraid of dying. However, if we learn how to survive even when we are faced with death, we become stronger and can live until God is ready to take us into eternity.

Appendix A: Life with Nonna as told to the editors by Henry Bannister, Summer 2008

Henry Bannister met Nonna in 1951, after her ship from Germany arrived in New Orleans, Louisiana. They married shortly after her arrival in America, and their marriage lasted fifty-three years and fifty-three days.... Henry and Nonna had three children.

Nonna was an intelligent, lovely woman. She was beautiful physically, emotionally, and spiritually. As brutal and horrifying as they were her experiences in German-occupied Russia and subsequently in Germany in the midst of the Holocaust only deepened Nonna's faith in God. This faith saved her from the bitterness many Holocaust survivors developed after the war's end. Love and compassion ruled Nonna's heart. With God's help, she forgave those who purposely hurt her, as well as those – both Russian and German – who so cruelly slaughtered her family.

Nonna was a loving and faithful wife, mother, and grandmother during her marriage of more than five decades. When she decided to tell Henry about her Holocaust experiences – a few years before she died – she spoke without hatred, bitterness, or anger. She held on to her grandmother Feodosija's deep faith in God, and until her last years she regularly worshiped in church. She was baptized in the Russian Orthodox church as a child and worshiped there; after the war, she became Baptist through the influence of American Baptist missionaries in Germany. The Napoleon Avenue Baptist Church of New Orleans, Louisiana, sponsored her emigration to the United States, and she worshipped in Baptist churches thereafter. Nonna also remembered her father's words about forgiving others. She forgave much, and her forgiveness kept her from a long life built on bitterness and revenge seeking.

Nonna Bannister with Denise George and Carolyn Tomlin, *The Secret Holocaust Diaries* (Carol Stream, IL: Tyndale House Publishers, Inc., 2009). Copyright © 2009 by NLB Partners. Used by permission.

Petrica Danut Chereches

For two years, Petrica Danut Chereches, 14, has been a resident at St. Laurence's Hospice for children with HIV/AIDS: a Romanian hospice run by the British-based charity, Children in Distress. At the age of five, he was placed in one of the squalid orphanages that made the headlines in 1989, after Ceausescu's fall from power. It was at this orphanage that Petrica contracted HIV. He has recently been reunited with his mother, Violeta Toma.

Petrica

A year ago, I was reunited with my mother for the first time in eight years. When I was little, she moved away from the district where the orphanage was and we lost touch. She probably thought I was dead, because children with HIV were not expected to live. When I moved to St. Laurence Hospice, an address was found for my mother.

A meeting was arranged for her to come and visit me at a children's holiday home, not far from where she lived. But I still had a bad feeling about her. I couldn't understand why she'd abandoned me and why, when I'd begged her to take me home, she had refused. I was only five years old. Poverty isn't a good enough reason to abandon your child.

I had written a letter to give to my mother asking her these questions, but when we met, I couldn't give it to her because I could see how happy she was to have found me. Her face was full of love and regret. So instead, I just asked, "Why didn't you take me home when I asked you to?" She told me that she hadn't been able to: she had my older sister to look after and there was no money. I accepted her answer. I had to. How could I judge the difficulties of her life at that time? Now that I have seen her again, I forgive her. I can't hold on to the past, because the past is over and I want us to have a future together. I want to have a little part of my mother. And to have that little part, I need to forgive. Like this, we may be able to become close again.

Violeta

When I remarried, my daughter stayed with me while Petrica, who was then five, went to live with his father. I had no idea that when his father also remarried he would put Petrica in a children's home. At first, I visited my son, but it was heartbreaking because he would always beg me to take him home. I told him I couldn't because I had no money to feed or clothe him. When we moved away, it was too far to visit.

For eight years I didn't see him until one day, out of the blue, the Child Protection Agency contacted me. I have many regrets but I am so happy to see my son again. Who would have thought he would come and find me? The first time I saw him I thought, "This cannot be my little Petrica!" He looked so grown-up and handsome. I don't believe he has AIDS. He looks too healthy.

http://theforgivenessproject.org.uk/stories/page/61/

Anne A. Johnson Davis

When Anne A. Johnson Davis was just three years old, her mother and stepfather began to physically, sexually and mentally abuse her—in the name of Satan. Until she ran away from home at 17, her parents and other cult members subjected her to satanic ritual abuse, a criminally inhumane and bizarre form of devil worship. In the middle of the night, Anne would be drugged and forced to endure hours of ritualistic torture as a symbolic sacrifice.

The horrors Anne experienced, the astounding miracles that helped her to survive, and the heal-or-die choices she made as an adult to triumph over her tragic past, are revealed in her new book *Hell Minus One: My Story of Deliverance From Satanic Ritual Abuse and My Journey to Freedom.*

Hell Minus One is different from other previously published memoirs by victims of satanic ritual abuse. Instead of distressing, heart-breaking accounts without collaborative or corroborative evidence, Anne's parents confessed their atrocities – both in writing and verbally – to clergymen and to detectives from the Utah Attorney General's Office. Anne's suppressed memories, which erupted when she was in her mid-30s, were fully substantiated by her mother and stepfather.

Hell Minus One is an unforgettable and moving story that takes the reader to more than just the depths of human depravity. After Anne learned the horrible and heartbreaking truth about her childhood, she embarked on an amazing inner journey of healing – and forgiveness. She knew she had to forgive her tormentors, or they would own her – and define who she is – for the rest of her life. The steps she took to heal and forgive, and to commit herself to a new life of love and purpose, are inspirational and legendary. Her commitment to own and define her own life inspires readers to see their own challenges in a new light.

The book's foreword was written by Lt. Detective Matt Jacobson, who was the lead investigator with the Utah Attorney General's Office on Anne's case in 1995. In April 1995, Anne was interviewed by KTVX Channel 4 News and *The Deseret News* in Salt Lake City for stories regarding a then newly released three-year study by the Utah AG's Office about ritual abuse. In those news accounts, Anne's identity was concealed as she explained some of the horrors of her childhood. In *Hell Minus One*, Anne publicly blows the door open on who she is and tells her story openly for the first time.

http://hellminus1.com/

News article published 12-11-2008, the *Tooele Transcript-Bulletin*
Memoir of satanic abuse a first for Transcript-Bulletin
by Sarah Miley

Anne A. Johnson Davis stood in front of the steps leading to the Utah Attorney General's Office in the Utah State Capitol Rotunda yesterday and sketched out a harrowing childhood of satanic ritual abuse. Her story, told to the attorney general's office and subsequently reported in part under conditions of anonymity by media outlets in the mid-1990s, is now being told in full in a new memoir being published by Transcript-Bulletin Publishing.

Hell Minus One: My Story of Deliverance From Satanic Ritual Abuse and My Journey to Freedom is the tale of the atrocities Davis suffered as a child, as well as how she was able to triumph over that past.

"The project was a major undertaking for Transcript-Bulletin Publishing, and unlike any other work the company had produced in its 115-year history," according to *Hell Minus One* editor Dave Bern.

"This is the first venture we've done where we have taken a manuscript, worked with the author, provided editing, printed the book and been in charge of distribution. We've done this basically in alignment with our journalistic excellence."

Scott Dunn, president of Transcript Bulletin Publishing, added, "The uniqueness of her story caught our attention in June 2007. During our initial review of her manuscript, we knew that *Hell Minus One* was a story that must be told."

The broad outline of that story was unveiled by Davis at the press conference yesterday.

"I was tortured and terrorized physically, sexually and mentally," she said.

Davis said memories of the abuse were suppressed until she reached her mid-30s. She said she was threatened with her life if she ever told of what she'd endured. But in 1994, she came forward nonetheless.

"I came into the beautiful Utah State Capitol wearing a hot pink jacket for empowerment," she said, remembering her initial approach to the attorney general's office.

She shared her story with detectives, one of whom was Lt. Detective Matt Jacobson (now retired), the lead investigator with the Utah Attorney General's Office on Davis' case. Jacobson wrote the foreword to Davis' book.

Davis' story is unique among satanic ritual abuse crimes in that her story is substantiated with verbal and written confessions from her parents. Her parents confessed to religious leaders and to investigators from the Utah Attorney General's Office. In addition, Davis' half-siblings confirmed what had happened to her.

Davis said it felt good to tell her story under her own name and hopes the book will empower other victims of abuse.

"My hope and prayer is my story in *Hell Minus One* can also be a beacon of light for others," she said. "My gift to you is my story of conquering captivity."

Dunn said the same solid journalistic principles that underlie the Transcript-Bulletin helped give life to *Hell Minus One*.

"It's that commitment to excellence and accuracy that fueled our interest in publishing and promoting *Hell Minus One* – not as a newspaper story or even as a series of newspaper stories, but as a memoir. This is a book of substance and truth that blows the door open on satanic ritual abuse, and reveals the power of the human spirit to heal from an abusive past."

http://www.hellminusone.com/Links.html

[Note: Because Anne A, Richards Johnson recently passed away, I was unable to obtain permission to reprint the portions of her book that pertained to her forgiveness process. Anne was a devout Mormon, and after her stepfather died, she felt safe enough to go visit his grave to vent all the hatred and bitterness she had toward him. She drove about 1,000 miles to get there, and when she did, she found to her horror that at the gravesite there was a double headstone with the name of her mother etched in the stone, indicating that she would be buried beside her husband, which showed Anne that she never had any remorse. That enraged Anne and temporarily stalled her forgiveness process.

She related that God showed her at that point that she was to let go of her mother. That was very freeing for her. A significant amount of time passed, and God showed her the need to forgive so that she would be free of them. In her mind, she saw a movie of the worst of the abuse and as she began to feel revulsion, God allowed her to see the good things that her mother had done for her. He then showed her what her mother would suffer in the afterlife if she didn't repent. With that, she was able once again to release her mother.

After several more months of very hard work emotionally, she was able to forgive her mother, stepfather, and all the other members of the coven who had abused her. She realized that no reconciliation could take place, as not one of her abusers had repented (even though her parents had admitted the abuse in writing, as you read in the aforementioned articles). Anne felt free, empowered, and thrilled, as she was now able to completely move on with her life.]

Natalia Aggiano

In 1997, after 30 years of bullying and abuse, Natalia Aggiano's mother was brutally murdered by her father at his home in Scunthorpe, England. Her father later died of cancer in prison.

My dad was brought up as a Jehovah's Witness. He was the head of the house – what he said, went. My sister was a goody-goody, because even though she was ten years older than I was, she was afraid of him. But I never was: if he told me to make him a cup of tea, I'd say, "Haven't you got legs?" And I'd get a beating. Because of that, I never listened to him. My older brother was psychotic and I never got on with him, but my little brother was my support. He was always trying to look after me.

I left home at 17 and begged my mum to do the same. She used to say, "I'll leave when you are 18," and then she'd look at my little brother and say, 'I'll leave when *he's* 18'. But one day she rang up and said she was ready. She'd suddenly seen how my dad was dictating her life, and she wanted her freedom. We found her a little place near to where she was born, and I moved in with her and my brother. Dad came home one day and his wife and son were gone.

Mum and I started having the relationship we'd never had before. She was so happy and relaxed, and we'd go for coffees and just talk. She got in touch with my dad via my sister, just to let him know she was safe. She told me that she still loved him, but for who he was, not for what he had done to her.

One day he called to say he had a load of post [mail] for her to collect. She had been thinking about going back for a visit anyway, so that my brother could see his old friends. But it was as if she knew something would happen, because she told me the night before that she thought he was going to kill her. Yet somehow, she talked herself into it. I made her promise to wake me up in the morning so I could go with her. But she didn't.

I woke up the next morning to the police at my door, and I knew instantly what had happened. My first reaction was that I had to see my dad. I had to know if he had killed her deliberately, or if it was some kind of accident. I wrote him a note saying, "I know what you've done. It's OK. I love you and want to see you." I signed it, "Your daughter," hoping he would think it was my sister and agree to see me. When he saw that it was me, he burst into tears. I made up my mind there and then, that as long as he told me the truth, without a word of a lie, I would stand by him.

It was what my mum had taught me – to love him for who he was, not for what he did. I know that if I had been a mass murderer, my mum would still have visited me every day in prison. I tried my best to do what she would have done. He was the only link I still had with her.

Throughout the trial, he kept his word and never lied about what he had done, and eventually he was sentenced for manslaughter with diminished responsibility and sent to a psychiatric hospital. While he was in there we started having a proper father-daughter relationship. I'd come to him for advice on all my problems. I called him "Papa," and he would tell me he loved me. He was the dad I always wanted. But he knew that if he ever started up the old behavior, he'd never see me again.

My sister just couldn't understand what I had done. She took my little brother and brought him up, but she pretended to everyone that our parents had died naturally. I never pretend. For me, it is much easier to forgive because then you can be free. She'll have to live with her anger every day for the rest of her life. Or worse, it might turn into regret. I'd already lived most of my life with hatred for my dad. I didn't want it anymore. Forgiving him was such a big release. I'll never forget what he did – but forgiving has brought me peace inside.

When my dad got really ill with cancer and we knew he was going to die, my little brother asked to see him – just once, so that he could get some closure. The weak, bed-ridden figure he saw was nothing like the military man who used to bully us all. My dad told my brother he could die in peace now, knowing that his youngest child had forgiven him too.

We can all make mistakes – that was the best thing my mother taught me. I now automatically look for the good in people I meet. I still miss my mum everyday; but I think she would be proud of me.

http://theforgivenessproject.org.uk/stories/page/13/

Wess Stafford

"A Candle in the Darkness," Christianity Today, September, 2010

Wess Stafford is president and CEO of <u>Compassion International</u>, a Colorado Springs–based child development organization that sponsors children. This article was adapted from a talk Stafford gave at Woodmen Valley Chapel in July 2009 regarding his story of childhood abuse and deliverance in a West African boarding school.

At a turning point in my life in 2007, I realized that I needed to allow God to redeem the story of my childhood. That story was so painfully confusing that I did not speak of it for 35 years. Where did my prayers go, my cries for mercy and rescue screamed into my pillow? Did I have the laziest guardian angel in all of heaven?

I received my calling, my purpose, and my life's mission in my darkest and most painful moment, in about 90 seconds at age 10. The moment involved a pink birthday candle, one that had been trimmed with a pocketknife at the blunt end so that it could burn from both directions. The wicks were lit by the man who had authority over me, the houseparent of a boarding school for the children of missionaries in West Africa. The school had been my home for nine months of each year since I was six years old. My whole life can be divided into two parts: B.C. (before the candle) and A.D. (after the damage).

The houseparent had marched me to the school's dining hall, dragged a metal chair across the concrete floor, and slammed it down in front of my schoolmates. He threw me up on the chair and jammed the candle in my hand.

"Children," he said, "You cannot serve both God and Satan. Wesley has tried. You cannot burn a candle at both ends without getting burned. Watch what happens when you try."

Fifty children stared in silence. Nobody dared even breathe. Striking a match, the man lit both wicks. "Watch!" Standing on that chair, my knees knocking, I stared incredulously at the candle in my shaking fingers as I contemplated what this would mean. Beyond the two flames, I could see the faces of my friends – children who, like me, had been gathered up from villages and mission stations throughout West Africa.

Mission policy dictated that all MKs leave their parents at age six and travel 700 miles (a week by truck) to this isolated jungle school. They, like me, had experienced unspeakable cruelty in this place. The people in charge were missionaries who had gone to Africa to save souls but, I don't know, perhaps did not measure up linguistically or cross-culturally, so instead had been assigned to the least desirable task on the field: taking care of other missionaries' children. Unsupervised, they took out their frustration and rage on their most convenient targets: the children in their charge. I learned early that terrible things can happen when children are deemed unimportant, the lowest of priorities.

The stage for this horrendous moment had been set by four years of abuse. For all my young life at the school, I had endured beatings daily. Belt buckles and tire-tread sandals had bruised and torn my flesh since age six. There were a million ways to earn a beating here – infractions like a wrinkle in a bedspread or an open eye during naptime. At age nine, we learned in math class how to average. The most recurring event in my life I could think of was how many times I had been beaten. For a span of weeks, I kept track of my beatings, hiding the tally under my pillow. When I did the math, I discovered that I was being beaten an average of 17 times per week.

The boarding school staff abused us in every way a child can be abused—not only physically and emotionally but spiritually as well. We were terrified of their powerful and vengeful God, reminded daily that we were little sinners in the hands of their angry God.

I won't dwell on the sexual abuse we endured, but wherever evil reigns unchecked, this favorite weapon of Satan's always lurks. The people who read us Bible stories and beat us during the day prowled the dorm halls at night, preying on the defenseless. Older boys, victims themselves, learned to mimic their elders in that depraved environment to serve their own lustful desires, and they used blackmail and physical pain to silence us.

There was no one to protect us. We had no advocates, no arms to run to. The very people who should have been our defenders were, in fact, our attackers.

And now, standing on that chair with the candle gripped between my fingers, I was at my lowest, darkest moment. I cannot describe the cumulative hurt, rage, and hopelessness that welled up and wracked my 10-year-old soul. At this man's hand, I had always lost. Plain and simple, he was bigger and stronger. He was a man; I was a boy.

He spoke angrily to the assembled children. "This boy here is Satan's tool. He *told*, and the Devil used him to destroy his parents' ministry. There will be Africans in hell because of Wesley."

Hearing those words, there arose in me a rage, a passion as I had never experienced before and have not since. I had felt I could endure almost any treatment at his hands – I had for years. But the candle incident was different. Never had words cut so deeply.

Yes, I had *told*. As a desperate boy, I had cried out to my mother for help. For years, 50 of us children had courageously maintained our silence. We were repeatedly told, "If you tell what happens here, you will destroy your parents' ministry." Our abusers used our love for God, for our parents, and for Africans to secure our silence about the horrors of that place.

Oh, we wrote letters home every Sunday. But we couldn't even hint at our loneliness or the abuse. Our letters were censored, and the slightest attempt to cry out resulted in a beating, then a forced rewriting of the letter. We learned to be as silent as lambs. We had no idea that our silence perpetuated the evil against us. Even during the three months home with our parents every year, we all kept silent. We loved them so much. We knew how passionately they spread the gospel, and I loved my African village friends. If my silence could win their salvation, I would endure anything.

At school, we were not allowed to have pictures of our parents or to cry from homesickness. Each year, my mind would capture a final image of my parents saying goodbye. For the first month, I could see them every time I closed my eyes, and at the tender ages of 6, 7, and 8, I couldn't help crying myself to sleep every night, as silently as possible. But by the ninth month of school, I could no longer remember what my parents looked like. I was so afraid I would break their hearts by not recognizing them when I went home.

The crime that led to the burning candle happened at age 10, after a year on furlough in the United States. I found myself at the airport with other MKs saying goodbye to our parents. We were about to board a propeller plane that would take us back to Africa, and our parents would follow by ship.

At the gate, I took my mother's face in my hands and couldn't let go. I stared intently at her beautiful, kind face. "What are you doing, Wesley?"

"Mommy, I just don't want to forget what you look like."

She dissolved into tears, and so did I. I saw a moment of opportunity, a glimmer of hope for rescue. In 30 seconds, I blurted out my plea.

"Mommy, please don't send me back! Please don't send me back! They hate me… they beat me… I'm scared." I begged, "Please, *please!*"

I will never forget the look of horror in my mother's eyes.

"*What?*" she gasped. She held me tightly. "What… what can I do?" I could feel her sobbing in my embrace.

Not a minute later, my sister and I were whisked away with the other children. My friends, who had overheard, looked at me with dead man walking in their eyes. They didn't want to even be near me for fear of sharing in my imminent punishment. I had done the unthinkable – I had broken the code of silence.

During my parents' month-long voyage at sea, my mother, brokenhearted and confused, had an emotional and psychological breakdown. Upon arriving in Africa, she was soon sent back to the U.S. for treatment. Word of her illness and what had caused it spread like wildfire. When the news reached the boarding school, the staff was enraged.

I had resigned myself to the coming humiliation. In minutes, I would scream and throw down the candle – until I heard his last phrase: "… parents' ministry ruined… Africans in hell because of Wesley." That broke my heart more than the humiliation, more than any pain that might come my way ever could.

I loved Africans. In my heart, I *was* African. Every summer my spirit was restored by the loving-kindness of the poverty-stricken Africans in my village. I never fell down during those three months without an African woman swooping in to pick me up and wipe tears from my eyes. I used to pray every night in that village, "Lord, if You love me, let me wake up black tomorrow, like all my friends. I know You can do this!" I would check every morning to see if I had been turned black, only to be disappointed. But maybe tomorrow.

I was my dad's right-hand man. Together we opened villages to the gospel where no white person had been since the slave trade. I lobbed stones with my slingshot into the trees to keep noisy birds away so that my father's voice could be heard as he shared the gospel. I watched Africans' faces when they first heard the word *Jesu*. And I saw the hope that was built in them. I was a missionary as far as I was concerned. So, Africans in hell because of *me*?

As the flames licked closer to my skin, from deep within me a gust of strength arose that I cannot fully explain to this day. I had a desperate thought: *I could win this time*. This time, the houseparent had unwittingly put himself in a place where I could actually win, if I could endure enough pain. I knew in my heart that he was wrong. He was lying, and I felt the evil and injustice to the core of my soul. I was not Satan's tool. I was a little boy with a broken heart who had found his voice and cried out for rescue. So, *enough* – enough shame, enough abuse, enough lies. It had to stop somewhere, sometime. I made my decision: It stops now! I'm not letting go!

Nothing was going to make me cry out or drop that candle. This is where I would take my stand – this was my little Masada.

I shook violently, tears brimming in anticipation of burned flesh. He turned his back on me, his tirade growing in intensity. But I could no longer hear his voice. All I could hear was the pulsing of blood in my ears. I clenched my teeth, tightened every muscle in my body, and pinched the candle as fiercely as I could. I stared as the edges of my fingers turned red. A blister popped up. I was transported out of my body. I floated above this terrified boy, watching as if it were happening to someone else. I saw a wisp of smoke rise up on either side of my fingers. I would *not* let go.

Just then, a child in the front row couldn't stand it any longer, and he jumped up and slapped the candle out of my hand. The children scattered in all directions. The meeting was over. But standing there alone on my chair, I had received my *calling*. In an instant, I had gone from *victim* to *victor*. From that day forward, I would protect children. I would forever speak up for those who cannot speak for themselves.

The school was eventually shuttered, and many years later, the abusers were held accountable—not jailed like they would be today due to the statute of limitations, but after an official inquiry, when they were "censored" by the mission and no longer allowed to work with children. The school's MKs limped away from their childhoods, many with lifelong scars. Thankfully, for me, my story – a story that Satan intended for evil but that God redeemed for good – has a different ending.

My story finally emerged when I wrote a book, *Too Small to Ignore: Why the Least of These Matters Most*, in 2007. My idea was to present a manifesto – strategically, statistically, and scripturally sound – about the importance of championing children, one that would awaken the Church. But my publishers challenged me: "Wess, they won't care what you know until they know why you care. Are you going to write a book, or are you willing to really fight a battle for children?" At that crossroads, I realized that I must allow God to redeem even the painful parts of my story.

My story is what has fueled my passion against injustice, my crusade against abuse, my fight against poverty. It is what drove me to Compassion International. For 32 years, I have fought for little ones who have no voice and no choice. The passion that gripped me at age 10 still rages within me today.

Poverty and abuse speak the same message into the heart of a child: "Give up. Nobody cares about you. There's nothing special about you. Nothing will ever change. You always lose, so give up!" As I travel across the world, I see the fingerprints of Satan; he is using the same weapons he used on me. In children the world over, I see empty, hollow eyes where the flame of a spirit created in the image of God is reduced to a smoldering ember.

My job now is to champion the cause of these children, to help them understand the love Jesus Christ has for them. Imagine my joy when every day, hundreds of children accept Jesus as their Savior, at the knee of their pastor or with a Sunday school teacher under the mango tree. Imagine my joy that we daily vaccinate thousands of children. Imagine my joy that I get to challenge the Church about the importance of children – to explain, for example, that budgets that devote 10 percent to children's ministry make little strategic sense considering that 85 percent of people who come to Christ do so before the age of 14.

All these years later, I am still never more than 10 seconds away from tears. But not all my tears are from sorrow. Just as easily, I can be moved to tears of great joy at what I get to do. I see victories in children's lives as evil is defeated, just as it was defeated in my own life.

In finally telling my whole story, I have discovered the other side of my life's tapestry. Where I once saw only knots and tangles, I now see a beautiful picture of God's grace – His deliberate orchestration in a life lovingly entrusted to me. Sure enough, He had heard every scream, felt every blow, and wiped every tear as, through the pain, He crafted me into a tool He could use, redeemed for His glory.

http://www.christianitytoday.com/ct/2010/may/9.23.html?start=1
This article first appeared in the May 2010 issue of *Christianity Today*. Used by permission of Christianity Today International, Carol Stream, IL 60188.

Account from Wess' book on his process of forgiveness:

What an amazing irony that, after a day of hitting us, screaming at us, and humiliating us, our *tormentors would sit down at bedtime and read us Bible stories. Like little lambs, we sat at their very feet. We were so quick to forgive them (emphasis added).*

. . . .

In other words, if you dared partake of the Lord's Supper, there had better be absolutely no sin in your life, or you would condemn yourself to hell. He would then pause, look sternly at us, and intone, 'If anyone has anything to settle with anyone in the room, let him do it now.'

Instantly we children would jump to our feet and scramble to the nearest friend or adult and ask a sweeping forgiveness for "anything I might have ever done to offend or sin against you." The adults all sat in their chairs around the edges of the room, almost like Santa Claus, as a dozen children lined up in front, waiting their turn to ask forgiveness from them. From them (emphasis added)!

....

Why did God let me suffer the agonies of that boarding school? Why did He not intervene when I cried out to Him night after night for relief? I have imagined at times my guardian angel pulling on God's sleeve saying, "Don't You hear little Wesley? Don't You see his pitiful tears? Can't You do something to deliver him from this monstrous evil?"

If that ever happened, I believe God replied, "I know. I see his pain; I hear his cry. But he needs to go through this. I have plans for his life. Out of his pain, I will save others. Trust Me."

I'm not saying it was God's plan for the abuse to occur. But I do believe he can redeem anything and bring good out of evil. He was shaping me for an epic fight on behalf of abused children. When I address that issue these days, it is not just an academic topic for me, the subject of a doctoral dissertation. I've lived it. I have experience firsthand that when children are not deemed important in our world, some very ugly things can happen.

But when adults speak up for the vulnerable and the weak, working and demanding that safety and respect prevail, God's little lambs are protected and nourished.

My mind went back to a certain campfire at Woodbine Ranch, a camp in Colorado, when as a seventeen-year-old I had sat listening to a talk on forgiveness. Immediately, of course, I had thought about Bandulo. As the speaker continued that evening in the crisp Rocky Mountain air, I was saying internally, Yes, but not a single one of those people has ever asked my forgiveness. They won't even admit that what they did to us was wrong.

I stewed about that for a few minutes but then made a pivotal decision in my young life. They will never ask me to forgive them, so I will simply do it without their request, I told myself. They all but ruined my childhood. But I don't have to let them ruin my whole life! I'm going to forgive them and leave them forever behind me. I'm going to live above all this.

....

But the voices we "children" most needed to hear express regret were not there for us. Only the current mission leadership – a generation removed from the disaster – had the courage to deal with the devastation and try to make things right. Actually, there was one exception: the school nurse had made a videotape on which she admitted her guilt and requested forgiveness, and it had been mailed to our homes. We had sat in silence, listening to this now elderly lady pour out her heart, and one by one, we forgave her.

Dr. Wess Stafford with Dean Merrill, *Too Small to Ignore: Why the Least of These Matter Most* (Colorado Springs, CO: WaterBrook Press, a division of Random House, Inc., 2007).

Anita Dittman

By Kim Sampson — ksampson@sdio.com

The Holocaust saw over six million Jews killed and millions more tortured.

The survivors from that time are becoming fewer and fewer as generations change hands; one of those survivors is eighty-one-year old Anita Dittman.

Anita now lives in Northern Minnesota and recently sat down with us to tell us what it was like to live under Hitler's oppression… here is Anita's story.

Anita Dittman's childhood was filled with memories of discrimination and hatred, simply because she was Jewish. Adolph Hitler rose to power telling Germans they were the Master Race. Anita states, "And all undesirables had to be eliminated and of course the Jewish people were at the top of that list."

Soon, neighbors and friends disappeared. They were pulled from their homes and sent to so-called "work camps" never to be seen again. Anita and her family waited.

Anita recalled, "What was tough was that fear that at any moment there might be that knock at the front door."

One day the knock on the door came. First, Anita's mother was taken, seven months later, Anita… herself.

She was taken to Camp Barthold, north of her hometown of Breslau.

In her book, *Trapped in Hitler's Hell*, Anita encouraged a fellow prisoner with her opinion of Camp Barthold, "At least it's not Auschwitz," I told her, "And our heads aren't being shaved."

Now she lived with 150 women in an old cow barn. It had never been cleaned; they slept on straw beds. She described the accommodations: "We were given what they call horse blankets – just grey blankets that they would cover horses with."

For ten long hours a day, in the hot sun, Anita was ordered to dig ditches to slow the Russian tanks from advancing through the country. "We found out sort of half way through that when our work was complete we would be sent to Auschwitz to be cremated," says Dittman. "Even though I knew the ultimate would be Auschwitz, you know there is hope in the human heart somehow," said with hope in her voice.

On January 23, 1945, in advance of the Russian troops, the entire camp was ordered to start moving. Anita sates, "So that night we marched and marched and marched… I thought they would march us to death."

On the long grueling march, Anita developed a blister on her foot. But she didn't dare slow down. She had to hide the fact that she was hurt and that a massive infection was spreading up her leg and thigh. She said, "I had to cover up, you know limp, afraid the authorities would see that; you see, people who were unfit to work were either tortured to death or killed on the spot."

An opportunity came for Anita to escape... she was sent to get supplies, on the way she bribed the driver to take her to the train station with twenty deutschemarks and a pack of cigarettes, knowing that could get her and the driver killed.

In her book, Anita wondered, "What was in it for the driver except a little money, the cigarettes and probably severe punishment?"

The driver took the bribe.

Anita had escaped, only to wind up in a hospital with a Nazi nurse. The foot infection led to four surgeries on her ailing leg. Anita says the nurse knew she was Jewish and tried to kill her with an overdose of ether.

Anita remembered, "A few more drops and I would have been gone; she must have been really frustrated with me. She couldn't kill that tough little Jew girl, because you see there was a medal for every Nazi that killed a Jew."

Once out of the hospital, Anita anxiously searched for her mother. She wondered if she was alive... and... she learned her mother was at Theresienstadt in Czechoslovakia.

Dittman described Theresienstadt, "So, we came closer and closer to a site that was horrifying. The outline in the dark we could see was barracks in the center of the complex, a smokestack was in the center of it and the whole complex was surrounded by tall barbwire fences that were electronically loaded and big iron gates that swung open... and we knew what it meant."

She was relieved to find out her mother was still alive. Her camp had been liberated... or her mother it was not a moment too soon. "Twenty-four more hours in her camp... and everybody would have been dead." Anita continued, "She joked about it, she said they are making soap out of the bones and ashes of the Jews. Twenty-four more hours and you might have washed your hands with me. Anita continued, "I always said our sense of humor and our faith were the only things that carried us through."

An American organization helped Anita and her mother to begin a new life. They would eventually get on a ship and make the journey to the United States and a life of freedom. Anita said, "I arrived in New York...when we saw the Statue of Liberty, I tell you there was no dry eye when we saw that – I still get very sentimental, very weepy – it was so awesome!"

Anita went to college in Iowa and became a teacher. She married and raised two kids. She also has four grandchildren.

Anita currently lives near Brainerd and has written the book, *Trapped in Hitler's Hell,* with much more about her experiences in Nazi Germany.

http://www.wdio.com/article/stories/S450502.shtml?cat=10335

Excerpts from Anita's books on her process of forgiveness and how she trusted God during the Holocaust:

At the same time, they put unbearable pressure on Father to leave Mother, my sister, and me, for the Nazis discouraged any relations between Germans and Jews. Many intermarriages were dissolved or annulled by the state. It was considered a grave abomination to pollute the German race by marrying Jews.

Father's only real affection was for my sister, Hella, and he seldom tried to hide his luke-warm feelings for me and Mother. He often reminded me how disappointed he was that I wasn't a son. To protect my desperately hurt feelings, I pulled away from Father and cut him off emotionally. When he left our family, I shed no tears. Perhaps my inner longing for a loving father drove me to my Heavenly Father so early in life.

Perhaps to me Jesus was just a father substitute or the fantasy of a child looking for security and love in a world of hate and fear. I don't know; at the time all that mattered was that I felt safe with Him. I knew He understood me, and I was sure He heard me when I talked to him. He would become my best Friend even before He became my Lord and Savior.

Even more exciting than our Lutheran school was hearing about St. Barbara's Lutheran Church in Breslau that spring. The pastor, Ernst Hornig, and his assistant, Vicar Kathe Staritz, were especially interested in helping Jewish believers. They also desired to win Jews to Christ and then help them leave Germany…. Even Mother consented to visit the church because of the faint prospect of freedom.

Pastor Hornig because a father substitute for me. A graying man in his forties, he supported his own six children on his meager income. Whenever he talked about the Jews, tears welled up in his eyes. Of course, his insight was far beyond my understanding as a child.

….

"Don't forget to talk to Jesus about even the smallest need Anita," Pastor Hornig reminded me one morning after we left church. "He's never too busy to listen, and He cares about all our problems, not just the big ones." The noon sun was especially bright that day, and I had to squint into it as I gazed up at Pastor Hornig.

"I've talked to Jesus since I was six years old, Pastor," I replied. Mother and Hella were walking ahead, but I hung behind, hungry for even a second more of this man's warmth and attention. "Jesus is my best Friend."

———∞∞∞———

Many of those very churches had now sold out to the Führer, allowing his picture to be on their church altars. It made no sense to my aunts to worship Jesus, a phony dead man in whose name millions of Jews had been persecuted, tortured, and killed.

"But those people aren't really Christians!" I insisted, not fully grasping the accuracy of my statement. "They just give real Christians a bad name."

"Nonsense!" insisted Aunt Elsbeth. "All Gentiles are Christians."

They either couldn't or wouldn't understand. Nor would they believe Pastor Hornig when he told us that numerous Christians all over Europe were actually helping the Jews at the risk of their own lives. Ultimately, many of the believers went into concentration camps themselves just because they had aided a Jew somewhere in the Nazi world.

"You and your mother are traitors to our people!" Aunt Friede said at least once a day. "You should be ashamed of yourselves."

....

"The spiritual isolation hurts me more than the physical deprivation," Mother confessed to me that same evening. "My body has adjusted to little food or rest, but it cannot adjust to the spiritual starvation."

As I listened to the ache in Mother's voice for the believers' fellowship and inspiration, I realized that she probably never would have grown so rapidly in her faith in Christ had it not been for the war and all its absurdities. God surely comforts the afflicted, but He also afflicts the comfortable; and Mother had been comfortable years earlier in her open-ended, believe-what-you-will religion. Now God was daily testing our faith and our trust in Him, and our walk with Him was truly an adventure. Actually, He moved and worked so fast in our lives that we often wished the adventure would slow down. God had stripped us of nearly everything in life, yet we felt as if we had the wealth of a king. In fact, we did – the King of kings.

———∞∞∞———

"God is greater than all the combined evil of the Third Reich," Pastor Hornig reminded us privately that Christmas day. "He is in control of the war and in control of your lives, too. I feel He will preserve you and your mother, Anita, but you must be strong witnesses for Him everywhere."

———∞∞∞———

As I rode the streetcar to the factory that morning, I searched for an answer. Then I remembered that Mother had given me Father's phone number for just such a situation. We hadn't seen one another in years. Maybe the war had softened him and he would be responsive to my dilemma. I felt it was a risk just to call him, simply because I didn't think I could stand one more ounce of rejection. But fortified and confident of being loved by Mother, Steffi, Gerhard, Wolfgang, Rudi, and the church members, I decided to take that risk and seek Father's help.

That night after work I went to Pastor Hornig's home to make the long-distance telephone call to Father, who had remarried and moved to Sorau, about sixty-five miles away. I frankly told the pastor about my bitterness and resentment toward Father.

....

Father's genuine concern impressed me. I told him about the money mother had left me and that I had heard a prisoner's freedom could be bought. I hoped to do this for mother if I got the chance. After all, it was her money. He accepted that.

Mother's absence had put a longing in my heart for Father's love, and I knew God was at work trying to heal my huge wound of bitterness and resentment against him.

"Why does God allow this?" Steffi asked that first day. "Why does He allow our people to be slaughtered?"

We leaned back on the parched grass beneath us. "But what about those who live, Steffi? You and I will live to tell our story. I know God weeps when someone dies, especially at the hands of Satan-inspired, power-hungry men." I whispered so the guard wouldn't hear. "I think God cries real tears, as He must have done when Jesus was crucified. All the world turned black because God couldn't look at the sin on the suffering Jesus. But Steffi He does see us, and He hears the innermost longings of our hearts."

Steffi nodded skeptically.

"You'll see," I said.

"Yes, Dad, I'm at Barthold near Schmiegrode. I can't talk long now, but I can have a visitor next Saturday. Would you come and see me?

....

Our eyes met, but for an instant Father didn't recognize me. Instead, he kept moving to look for me elsewhere. Then a sad realization came over his face, and he came back to me. I saw compassion in his cold eyes as he looked at my thin body and gaunt face. When I smiled at him, Father came over and embraced me. It had taken this tragedy to bridge the enormous gap that had existed between us all those years.

....

"What about Theresienstadt? I've heard some of the camps have been liberated."

"A few in the East have, as the Russians advance, but I don't think Theresienstadt has been liberated yet."

My awful bitterness toward Father welled up again. If he had not deserted us, perhaps Mother and I wouldn't be rotting in these camps. Yet, I decided, it must be God's will for us to be in them, for we could share our faith in Jesus with other prisoners. Therefore, Father's rejection of us was also in God's plan, and I knew I should not be overly hard on him.

....

In spite of this precarious situation, we were allowed visitors one more time. I got word to Father, who had promised to come the next time visitors were allowed.

....

Father looked weary when I saw him enter the camp's main area. We met indoors in a lounge area normally used by guards. Our visit was limited to about fifteen minutes so that other visitors could then use the lounge.

"Anita, you look so much better," he said as we met.

"Jesus has helped me regain my strength."

"That's nonsense," Father replied. "Please keep such talk to yourself, Anita, because I do not want to waste our time."

For a flash, I saw the father I always knew – angry, bitter, and trying to make it through life without God, even in the hell of Germany.

The pain in my leg had intensified, and I didn't know how I would ever climb out of the clumsy Russian tank. But Waldemar and Klaus gently lifted all of us out of the hatch.

"I'm not sure I can walk on my leg," I said to the soldiers as I rolled up my pant leg. My leg was twice its normal size.

"What happened?" Waldemar asked.

"It started out as a blister and got infected from dirt. It has been getting worse for some time."

"You must get help for it," Waldemar said as he leaned down to examine the ugly blue color of my leg. "You will lose the leg if you don't get some help."

....

I could see that the hospital was run by Nazis, and something about them told me they still hadn't given up the "glorious" dream of the Third Reich.

The head nurse, Miss Grete, had to cut away my sock, which clung to my swollen leg. The infection had driven my temperature up to nearly 105 degrees.

....

Two days later emergency surgery was performed: two holes were drilled into my foot to enable the infection to drain. Since ether was at a high premium, I wasn't given enough, and I awakened in the middle of the surgery. Amid the pain, I heard Miss Grete say, "She sure talked, didn't she, Doctor?"

I was numb with fear, sensing that I'd given myself away. My fear was confirmed in the following days and weeks as the Nazi hospital staff neglected me in various subtle ways. Besides being left unattended for hours, I was never given any pain pills. Because I always refused to respond to Miss Grete's "Heil Hitler," she withheld the necessary sanitary bandages for my leg wound. She also rerouted the doctor's visits so that I would often be missed for a day or two. Due to that kind of treatment and because I developed an allergy to the medication, I had to endure six long weeks of loneliness and neglect in the hospital.

....

My leg was cut and sewn hastily and improperly in four operations. Six ugly red scars would be the result.

....

When I pulled back the covers to show Hella [fellow escapee] my ugly leg wounds, which would leave lifelong scars, she gasped.

"Don't worry, Hella," I said calmly. "Those wounds and scars will be my salvation... God has impressed that on me as I've been lying here all these weeks. He says all things work together for our good, and so will these wounds (emphasis added)."

....

About the fourth day of the battle, it grew very quiet outside. Obviously, the battle had gone one way or another, and we soon received our answer as a dozen or more Russian soldiers stormed into the air-raid shelter. Everyone stood or sat frozen with fear as the Russians surveyed our pitiful lot. Carrying huge rifles with bayonets on them, they talked among themselves and began to eye the women staff and patients. Then, one by one, they grabbed some of the women and threw them to the floor. While the rest of us looked on in horror, they raped a dozen or more women.

Two of the huge soldiers came right for me. "Oh God, help me," I pleaded out loud. Pulling me from the bed, they threw me to the floor and started to rip off my clothes. It was a scene right out of hell, as man's depraved nature was personified before my eyes.

The two soldiers gazed at my unbandaged leg, with its horrible red wounds that were only partially healed. They grimaced as they saw the leg and muttered to each other. Then they shook their heads and walked away from me in search of a more appealing victim. So this was the salvation promised by my wounds (emphasis added)!

Anita Dittman with Jan Markell, Trapped *in Hitler's Hell: A Young Jewish Girl Discovers the Messiah's Faithfulness in the Midst of the Holocaust* **(Eureka, MT: Lighthouse Publishing, 2005). Used by permission. All rights reserved.**

———— ⊶⊷⊶ ————

Waiting always made her antsy, so she jumped up and began walking along the wall, pretending to be a tightrope walker like the Russian performer she once saw in a book.

"Get down, Judenfratz." A group of six girls came toward her.

Anita remembered what Mutti had told her. With her head down and eyes averted, she continued walking the wall.

"I said, get down!" The largest girl grabbed one of her braids and yanked hard, pulling her off the wall. The rough stone scraped the side of her leg as she fell.

These girls could not be ignored. When Anita looked up, she saw six girls, including her two friends. Both of them looked away.

"Stop sniveling, Judenfratz," the same girl shouted as she grabbed Anita. One of the Dittman's neighbors turned the corner carrying a bag of groceries. When she saw Anita and her tormentors, the neighbor looked down at the street and crossed over to the other side.

The more Anita wriggled to get out of the girl's grasp, the more the bigger girl pummeled her. The others landed a few punches as well.

"There. That'll teach you to think you can play with Aryans. You need to keep to your own kind." The girl spat on the ground. "And don't think you can tell anyone. We are members of the Hitler Youth. If you tell, we'll have your mother arrested. We can do it, you know."

Anita didn't answer. She knew they could do it.

"Get up and clean yourself off. You look a mess." The girl laughed and all the others laughed with her. As they walked away, they continued to mock Anita and laugh.

She felt like staying right there, but she knew that she must not draw attention to herself.... She stood up, brushed herself off, and went inside.

———— ⊶⊷⊶ ————

Incense mixed with candle wax scented the whole church. It felt like another world to Anita.

Before they took their seats, the Menzels kneeled. Anita couldn't help but compare the quiet act of kneeling, head bowed, to the defiant "Heil Hitler" that filled every courtyard.

As the Mass began, many of the words confused Anita.

"It's Latin," whispered Gunther.

When the priest began telling about Jesus' life, Anita understood. Like Frau Menzel suggested, Anita followed the story in the stained glass windows as the priest talked. With the sun shining through the vividly colored glass, the images in the window seemed alive. Some of the glass pieces were cut like prisms and sent rainbows across the pews. The church building and Anita's friends seemed to fade as she heard the words and saw the outstretched hands of the Messiah. Just as the notes of the organ penetrated her very chest, the Jesus of the stained glass windows seemed to come right into her heart.

When the priest read a verse that said that the Heavenly Father would never leave nor forsake, Anita somehow knew that He was her Father. For the first time, she felt protected and understood. She looked at Jesus' hands in the window of the Resurrection. I know those hands better than I know Vati's [her father's] hands. Jesus will protect me. She knew it… Yes, I now have a Father who will never leave me nor forsake me.

….

Anita could attend public school, but because she was the only non-Aryan in her class, teachers took pleasure in ridiculing her before the entire class. As each year passed, school had become more and more unbearable.

….

Now Anita went into her corner with Teddy and prayed a phrase she had heard at Mass. "Cover us with the shadow of Your hand, Father." She loved the thought of curling in to her corner, covered with the hand of God.

….

"Look! Pastor Hornig brought us each a Bible."

Mutti took hers. "How can we ever thank you for all you do? The more I've come to know you, the more I realize the sacrifice you make for us and for other Jews. Not just financially, though I know these Bibles cannot have been inexpensive." Mutti opened hers. "You know the risk you take for yourself and for your family by befriending Jews, neh?"

"Of course I know. I'm already blacklisted, but the Lord continues to shield me. God does not call us to an easy faith. Too many in the church have given over and allowed Hitler to commandeer their pulpits." Pastor Hornig shook his head. "I'm not alone. There are several of us. We call ourselves the Confessing Church and are committed to following Christ no matter the cost."

….

Anita loved all her aunts even though tight quarters meant that tempers sometimes erupted. They forgave as quickly as they snipped and snapped (emphasis added). All five of them worked hard to keep despair at bay.

….

"Dittman?" The principal looked up from his desk with a question. "Ja, Anita Dittman." She stood, waiting for him to invite her to take a seat.

"Here. This came from the Gestapo." The principal shoved a letter across the desk with a swagger of his head and shoulders. "It's high time Hitler cleansed the school of riffraff." He waved his hand in a dismissive gesture.

What is he saying? Anita read the note. "Only Aryans may attend school. Because of your non-Aryan status, your enrollment at König Wilhelm Gymnasium terminates immediately."

"You are dismissed, Judenfratz. Why do you stand in my office?"

Pastor Hornig preached boldly, despite knowing that Nazi spies watched his every move. "God is greater than the combined evil of the entire Third Reich," he preached in that rich, resonant voice.

Anita believed Pastor Hornig even though Hitler's evil terrified her.

"God is in control of the war, and He's in control of your lives," he assured them. "He will preserve some of His saints."

....

After church, Pastor Hornig took Mutti's hands in his and said, "You heard what I said about God preserving some of His true saints?"

Mutti nodded. "I feel certain God will preserve you and Anita. You must be His witnesses no matter where He takes you."

[In a phone call with her father] "Mutti told me to call you if I ever needed help."

"What can I do?"

They've taken all our furniture and possessions except my bed. I can buy back some furniture and a few of my personal things, but the Gestapo inflated the price way above anything I can afford." Anita didn't wait for him to answer. She didn't know if she could handle yet another rejection.

....

"I'll get you the money tomorrow, daughter." He sounded like he wanted to say more. "I'm so glad you asked."

When Anita hung up the phone, she needed a moment to compose herself. She knew her relationship with Vati would never be whole, but today was the first time they had connected.

"Wouldn't Hilde be pleased to hear of this?" Pastor Hornig said after Anita recounted the conversation. "You know God will not allow us to harbor bitterness, no matter how much right we have to it. You've taken a hard step today, young friend. God will honor you for it."

"But I called asking him a favor."

"When we are at odds, sometimes the easiest way to reach out is to allow the person to do something for us." Pastor Hornig smiled. "And sometimes that's the hardest thing to do. It's much easier for us to keep our backs stiff and hang on to our pride."

"It's got to be Russian cannons." The sound and the percussion reminded her of the Berlin bombings. Her stomach twisted at the thought. Someone had to stop Hitler, but Anita understood

the cost. She pictured the devastation in Berlin. "Before this war is over, I fear that nothing will be left standing in Germany."

"Germany and Hitler must pay," Hella said quietly.

"You know the funny thing?" As if anything was funny. "God will call us Christians to forgive Germany." Anita put her hands over her ears, as the sound of another volley seemed to ricochet off the trees. "Besides, the German people themselves have little to do with the horrors perpetrated by Hitler – I wonder how many know what's been happening? Look at these farmers here and near Barthold and Ostlinde. As soon as they saw what the Reich did, they did everything they could to help us."

....

"I know. If I live, my hardest calling will be to follow Christ in this." Hella set the charred log she'd been moving onto the pile and sat down on top of it. With the guards preoccupied, why bother pretending to work?

Anita sat next to her and propped her swollen leg onto a stone. "I don't know how many times I read the story about when Jesus forgives those who crucified Him... but it wasn't until recently that I began to grasp the enormity of that act." Anita sighed. "Just think; it would be like walking into one of those gassing rooms at Auschwitz and stopping to ask God to forgive Hitler and all the guards – even the very ones pushing us to our deaths."

"I think it's impossible unless you are God," Hella said

"Or unless you have the Spirit of God inside you."

Wendy Lawton, *Shadow of His Hand: A Story Based on the Life of Holocaust Survivor Anita Dittman* (Chicago, IL: Moody Publishers, 2004). Used by permission. All rights reserved.

J. E. Norris-Bernal
My process of healing and forgiveness:

You became acquainted with my story in the Introduction to this book. Now for the rest of the story....

When I could no longer suppress the pain of the abuse, I decided to attend a class at my church, "Recovering from Child Abuse." You would have thought we were gathering to discuss some kind of shameful addiction. Here we were, gathering in a side room off the sanctuary, feeling like a bunch of criminals who are in mandated group therapy for the crimes they've committed. What's wrong with this picture? We were victims of crime, not perpetrators!

There is a lot of irony in that, and I am gratified that we have come such a long way since the days of that church class. Why gratified? For two reasons: (1) Because I've had the tremendous privilege of working with other survivors of abuse to become whole; and (2) We can now be far more open about having been abused and receive the treatment and support necessary.

During the times I was utterly miserable and felt hopeless about my life being any different, I just wanted to go to sleep, wake up with Jesus, and not have to deal with all the emotional pain anymore. In retrospect, I see how much suicidal thinking I had at that time.

My father's verbal and emotional abuse of my brothers and me often took place when my mother was not around to defend or protect us. Looking back, it seems as though he waited for those times. When my mother was there, she did her best to silence him and "undo" the damaging messages with love and nurture. I again state unequivocally that without God's grace and my mother telling me the truth about myself, rather than the lies my father perpetually planted, I would surely have died at a young age. I am convinced I wouldn't have made it beyond my 30th birthday.

It is often stated in abuse recovery literature that children who have been abused cannot really envision a future with themselves in it. That was definitely true of me... I never visualized my own wedding, having children, or pursuing a career. If someone asked at the time what my "five-year plan" looked like, I would have stared uncomprehendingly at that person and had no ready reply.

Because my mother insisted that my father not use corporal punishment on us kids, he had made a conscious decision to abuse us emotionally in every way possible. At times, I wondered whether the physical beatings he would have given us would have been better than the alternative, and that was a theoretical question that I thought could never be answered. Actually, after my husband and I had moved to Arizona, I got my answer – at the expense of a four-year-old child.

I had a friend, a single mother of three young children, visiting me as a part of her move to the Midwest. My father, in his sneaky way, took advantage of the time that my friend and I were indoors, "catching up" as the children played outside. My father casually strolled out to the backyard, ostensibly to smoke his pipe, and on two separate occasions ended up hitting my friend's son, while yelling at him, "Never hit your sister! She's a girl, and you must never hit girls'" and "Watch what you're doing, you little idiot, you're going to break something!"

As her son ran into the house and flung himself in his mother's arms, he was sobbing and deeply hurt and afraid. My friend was appalled and furious. Not simply over my father abusing her child, but with his utter arrogance – his feeling of entitlement to punish someone else's child! What had been a pleasant visit between friends ended prematurely, because my father just <u>had</u> to set this little boy straight. I got to see up close and personal that he abused the child both physically and emotionally, which proved my mother's fears to be valid some 45 years later.

———— ✇ ————

So there I was in my late twenties, beginning to cope with the emotional damage and subsequent scars of my father's abuse. I had the theoretical question of whether I would have been better off if my father had beaten me instead of emotionally abusing me and a pressing need to know the answer, which I eventually saw played out with my friend's child. In all the reading I had done on child abuse, clinicians agreed that while the scars of physical abuse fade and can disappear at times, the scars of emotional abuse <u>never go away</u>. The beatings can fade from memory; the toxic messages will always affect the survivor's life in numerous ways.

I was the recipient of the following verbal and non-verbal messages on a consistent basis:

1. *You're worthless.*
2. *You'll never amount to anything.*
3. *You're ugly, and I'm embarrassed by your appearance.*
4. *You'll never have a figure like your mother's.*
5. *You're so stupid in math! A related abusive statement was, "Buy her books, send her to college, and look how she turned out!" announced in a derogatory way.*
6. *Can't you do any better than that?*
7. *I can't believe a daughter I raised could believe such nonsense (not the word he used) referring to the truth of God's Word, the necessity of being born again, the attempts to be more like Jesus, etc.*
8. *Sometimes you're just a pain in the rear end (although he always used the vulgar word instead).*
9. *You cost too much.*
10. *I don't love you.*
11. *I should never have had children.*

As you can see, these statements pretty well cover the territory. They range from his being contemptuous of my physical, intellectual, and spiritual attributes to utterly shaming me for my very existence. Shame is different from guilt, and I have not yet questioned a client who knew the distinction. You feel guilt when you've violated God's Word, man's law, and/or your own moral code. You feel shame when you feel completely broken and defective as a person. Guilt says, "I did something bad." Shame says, "I am bad." Big difference! As Joel Covitz states in <u>Emotional Child Abuse: The Family Curse</u>, this constitutes <u>rejection and abandonment</u>:

Whenever Elizabeth's mother was frustrated, she would tell her daughter, 'If I had it to do all over again, I would never have children. I would travel and spend my time on myself.' This is an honest confession of the wish to abandon, and it is correctly interpreted by the child as an outright rejection, even when the mother does not desert

the child.... Parents who are so tied up in their work that they have no time for their children are abandoning them, in effect.[1]

In spite of my mother's attempts to reform him (which she ruefully admits now was a hopeless endeavor), my father was a workaholic, as well as an alcoholic. I always knew that he didn't have time for me, and that I was just a bother. When I was an adult, he would say philosophically, "I should never have had children... but it was just what you did back then, you got married and had children. No one thought much about the alternatives." There was no question of the total rejection by that time, but I had already internalized the statement years before.

My father could be a very scary guy when he yelled at my mother or us kids. I could tell he wanted to hit us but was really restraining himself. The rage he displayed was palpable – something else I was to internalize.

Whenever we showed fear, anger, or sadness, my dad would either ignore or laugh at us. Covitz comments on the results of this treatment:

Sadistic parents who laugh at their children's fear or anger make their children feel stupid, unworthy or inadequate. Molly suffered from a phobia of loud noises. She would startle easily at the popping of balloons, drilling on construction sites, fireworks on the Fourth of July. Her parents, instead of helping her to relax and overcome her fear, reinforced it by making fun of it.[2]

My father said many devastating, demeaning, and belittling things while he was supposedly "teasing" us. To this day, whenever I find myself starting to tease others, I stop as quickly as I can and say something positive to them. I know firsthand how much hostility is cloaked by just "plain, old, (supposedly) harmless kidding." He teased us privately and publicly and said many cruel and shaming things in the name of teasing that were particularly devastating to us when stated in front of others. He abused my Mom in a similar way, making critical or lewd comments about her in front of work associates and family friends.

As his drinking worsened, so did my dad's language. He was so coarse, foul, vulgar, and profane that it's difficult for me to hear any streams cursing without cringing and wanting to hide somewhere. If God's or Jesus' name is being taken in vain, I have an actual physical sensation of pain in my chest cavity (the bodily manifestation of feeling stabbed in the heart).

Whenever any of us kids tried to express an independent thought or opinion, my dad would either directly contradict it or say something to the effect that, "You don't have anything to say, really, because you're not even worth listening to until you reach the age of 21. That's when you become a person." If he said that once, he said it a hundred times while we were growing up. He thought he was being funny, but the message was clear – as children we did not deserve or receive any respect from him:

Numerous men and women tell of the frustration they felt when young at having their opinions and ideas treated as worthless just because the holders of these opinions were children. The parent who consistently takes the attitude 'I know better than you because I'm older and I'm your parent' may give his children the lasting feeling that their views are absolutely worthless. The damage done… in the early years of the child's development is hard to undo. [3]

Bingo! Covitz put his finger right on how I felt whenever I ventured forth with an idea at the dinner table. Ah, Joel Covitz said that, did he? A Jew? One of my father's worst characteristics, if not the worst, was that he was an unmitigated racist and proud of it! He used every racial epithet in the book, and some that he simply made up. He despised people who were of different racial, ethnic, or religious origin than he – woe be unto them if they were Jewish or Catholic – and the only truly acceptable people had to purebred WASPs.

I have a very strong love for Israel and Jewish people, and when informed of my father's feelings about them, while I shouldn't have been surprised, I was completely unprepared for what he was about to say. Years ago, I asked him whether he and my stepmother had ever seen the movie "Schindler's List." He looked at me and disgustedly muttered that "Everything is always about the Jews… maybe Hitler had the right idea after all." I was shocked and sickened beyond words. Who was this man I continued to love despite everything? I always felt sick inside and utterly humiliated whenever my dad would hurl out one of his racial epithets. His racism seriously affected all his kids, who, perhaps predictably, went on to have mates who were African-American and Hispanic.

My dad loved to shock people with his coarse, vulgar expressions. He had very poor sexual boundaries, resulting in my covert sexual abuse at his hands. To quote from the Introduction of this book (where I began this autobiographical account):

I suffered from what is called 'covert sexual abuse' at the hands of my father. This entailed (1) his detailed probing of my nonexistent sex life, (2) his continuing evaluation of my developing body, and (3) his none-too-welcome, comprehensive accounts of his and my mother's sexual relationship. His coarse and vulgar language, meant to shock, never failed to "gross me out" (the term we used back then for being repulsed by someone or something). The crude labels he had for women and their body parts would invariably make me cringe and feel queasy.

All my father's communication about sexuality was crude, filthy, and disgusting. Yet I had no way of stopping him. If I tried to change the flow of the conversation, he'd just go right back to it, relentlessly returning to his favorite subject. I have a distinct memory of a time when he was driving me somewhere (a rare occurrence) and how trapped I felt at his questions, yet simultaneously compelled to answer him.

I would invariably laugh (not because the way he was talking or what he was saying was funny, but because it was simply a nervous habit I had when I felt helpless). My father never could see the laughter for what it was, so it just served to encourage him. I felt completely powerless at setting any kind of boundaries with him when he abused me this way, for he and others had already broken down my "fences." When I told my mother about all this years later, she was devastated, stating that she would have left him without a second thought had she known what all he was saying to me.

Some would question why my mother didn't leave my father until we children were grown, but I always understood. With the generation she was from and the family in which she was raised, divorce was simply not an option. It would have constituted more than a scandal, more of a moral disaster. As it was, in her mind she had to stick it out until her own mother died because it would have seriously affected my grandmother's rather precarious health and would have hurt her deeply... she simply wouldn't have been able to handle the "shame" of having a divorced daughter.

My dad was far from being affectionate, but whenever he tried to hug me during my adolescence and early adulthood, I pulled away as quickly as possible. He would only show this affection when he was dead drunk, and I hated the sloppy sentimentality and stench of the booze on his breath. I started forgiving him in my early twenties.

Sometime when I was in elementary school, perhaps in the third or fourth grade, the son of a couple who were friends of the family molested me. We were at a mountain cabin on a family vacation, and the adults had left us children in the care of this teenage boy. I was sleeping peacefully but awakened to this young man's having his hand down my pajamas fondling me. I was utterly terrified – here I was, a small, skinny kid, and this teenager, who was maybe 17 or 18 at the time, was huge by comparison. I froze. What to do? I finally turned onto my side, which worked, because when I did, he took his hand out of my pajamas and left. He never said a word afterward, and it never happened again, but there was just no way I could tell my parents – I felt ashamed and had no idea how to even begin this kind of dialog.

Because of this incident and my father's ongoing covert abuse, I became vulnerable to further sexual abuse. Once a person's boundaries have been violated, s/he feels unable to reset them. It seemed as though I were wearing a sign around my neck that said, "Go ahead – molest me – I'll never tell!"

Enter the youth pastor of our church. He was 15 years older than I, charismatic, and good-looking, even though somewhat handicapped by his size... 5'4" at the most. That wasn't a signif-

icant problem, however, as he had a petite, gorgeous wife whom everyone at the church adored. The pastor was young enough, and in touch with where we were coming from as teenagers, that he became a revolutionary of sorts. He introduced dancing to the music of the Beatles, Monkees, and Simon and Garfunkel as an acceptable activity for the junior high and high school youth groups. While he was unorthodox and liberal, he "toed the line" enough not to cause waves in our rather conservative church. [Note: **The reason for mentioning this is that when the Internet came along and I looked him up, he had given himself completely over to New Age spirituality and was engaging in some very strange, downright occult activities.**]

When his wife became pregnant and delivered a sweet baby boy, our congregation was elated. They were the "perfect" little family and universally liked. Intense competition sprang up among the junior high and high school girls as they were vying for his attention at all times. There was, however, a limitation in the competition that gave me a real advantage. The girl in question had to be 5'4" or shorter or he wouldn't dance with them at the dances held both at church and summer youth camps. There I was, all 5'3" of me. I was the perfect candidate for abuse because of my height, neediness, and vulnerability to predators. What gave me one more "advantage" was that I had gone in to counsel with him, and he was thoroughly informed about my family problems. And so the abuse began.

I was initially very honored and excited at the frequent invitation to be his and his wife's babysitter. Someone from home would take me to his house, drop me off, and then the youth pastor would drive me home. Like my father, this man wanted to talk about sexual matters. I was a late-bloomer and quite self-conscious about my body. He gave me many compliments, especially about how I looked in a bathing suit at the summer camps, where the abuse actually began. He would ask to "slow dance" and hold me uncomfortably close to his body so I would feel his arousal.

I both loved the attention and hated the sexual part, primarily because I so adored his wife I felt as though I were an adulteress – not a good feeling for a little church girl to have! At one of these summer camps, I once spoke long into the night with his wife. She confided that he just wanted to have sex all the time and that she didn't want him as often as he did her. There I was, walking around with intimate knowledge about this couple's problems yet feeling like I couldn't tell anyone about the abuse.

When the pastor would take me home from babysitting his son, he would park the car on a dark street about halfway between his home and mine. I felt helpless to stop what he was doing. He would engage in open-mouthed kissing with me, embrace me tightly, and move my hand to his crotch. After a while, he would stop and gaze soulfully at me. He never discussed what he was doing to me – it was simply a frequent ritual. That strange combination of feeling flattered and wanted vs. scared and repulsed left me in a world of confusion. One night when he and his wife were going out, he slipped me a pornographic book and told me to read it and return it to him whenever I was finished.

We reached a point of crisis the last summer the couple was with working with the youth of the church. At the youth camp, he did the most daring thing yet. As he was teaching me how to snorkel in the ocean waters and be able to stand the feeling of the kelp beds, he reached underwater and fondled me inside my bathing suit. The episode was brief, but it really scared me as to where all this was going. I finally confided in my camp counselor who was just a college kid herself, but she had the right reaction. As I related the sequence of events to her, she became outraged. She asked me if I had told my parents, and I told her that I hadn't. At that point, she brought two other counselors with her and, as a group, they strongly urged me to expose him by telling my parents. One of the three was always by my side the rest of the week of camp, and the pastor was thwarted in any further attempts to molest me.

I told my Mom when I came home. The reader must bear in mind that these things were just not talked about at the time (late sixties and early seventies). I glossed over many of the details and was actually relieved when she replied that we wouldn't do anything formal at this point, because he and his wife were moving away and he would no longer be a threat. What I had no way of knowing at the time but found out some years later was that he had attempted to molest two other petite girls in our group, but they "turned him down" without a second thought, as one had a boyfriend and the other just had a great deal of self-confidence. What I discovered later was that he had been successful at molesting yet another girl in our fellowship group, and the secondhand information I got was that they had "gone all the way." It is easy to see in hindsight that we girls saw ourselves as complicit in the abuse, certainly not as victims.

I knew there were never any consequences for him – he seemed to have gotten away with it! I now realize this is a fallacy, as the Lord saw everything and will hold him accountable for what he did to very vulnerable young girls. Many years later as I trained to become a therapist and began reporting child abuse myself, I started getting irate whenever I would think of his perpetrating crimes actually punishable in our state. A requirement for all therapist trainees in our graduate program was that we all get some kind of personal therapy. It was at this point that I began dealing with the issues stemming from my abuse with the encouragement of an excellent university staff psychologist.

As part of my healing process, I reported my abuse at the hands of the youth pastor to Child Protective Services, mostly as a symbolic act of taking back the power he had stolen from me. As far as possible prosecution, the abuse was way past the statute of limitations. However, the CPS worker who took my call, sensing my frustration, told me that he would enter the pastor's name in the database. This was so that if anyone else reported abuse at his hands his name would come up flagged because of my report. With the help of my classmates, I began to gain the courage to go "public" with what had happened to me. I no longer needed to feel ashamed – the pastor had been the abuser and I the victim. I was not an adulteress or anything close to it!

The process of forgiving the youth pastor took a long time because the damage was so deep, going to the core of my identity. I was to peel that onion on and off for many years.

————— ⚬⚬⚬ —————

I worked very hard during my ongoing counseling to heal from the emotional and sexual abuse I had endured. During my teens, I became very self-destructive. I started out shoplifting – a little lipstick here, a little mascara there, and so on. I was never caught at either of the drugstores, but the day came when I was in a large department store, and a very merciful salesperson approached me and whispered, "You'd better put that down and walk out of here right now." With heart pounding violently and difficulty catching my breath, I didn't walk, I virtually ran out of that store.

Years afterward, when I learned about the restitution required of thieves in the Bible, I saved up a substantial amount of cash and sent it via anonymous cashiers' checks to the two drugstores, with an accompanying note confessing what I had done and how I was trying to pay them back. I felt horrendously ashamed about the shoplifting, until during my training as a therapist I read that when girls are sexually abused they often begin shoplifting as one way of acting out. When I saw how common it was among my clients, I decided to accept God's forgiveness and move on.

During my adolescence and early twenties, I wasn't tempted to drink or use drugs, in reaction to my father and brothers' substance abuse. I was still the good little church girl, after all! However, when the dating years began, I never could get my fill of being held. Therefore, when the sexual expectations/demands started coming my way, I couldn't refuse because that need to just be held and loved was so overwhelming. I had so wanted to stay pure and be a virgin when I got married that I wept bitterly after my first sexual experience.

Once again, I was quite relieved to find out that this was a very normal result of being sexually abused (survivors confuse love and sex), but it took many years for my shame about my sexual behavior to lessen and finally disappear. The expression that I now use for clients I had to repeat many, many times to myself before I actually believed it: you are acting completely normally for growing up with abnormal things happening to you.

As I acted out sexually, I was terrified I would get pregnant… the Lord was merciful – I never did and didn't have to face what would have been an excruciating dilemma for me as to whether or not to have an abortion. I know I would have wanted to do the right thing, but I wouldn't have had the courage to either have a baby and give her/him up for adoption or keep the baby and care for him/her myself. An additional factor would have been my self-focus – I honestly believed that I wouldn't survive the shame and stigma of being pregnant and unmarried (still in my mind, I was the good, Christian college girl!). This experienced humbled me early on, for I learned never to look down in judgment on a woman who had had an abortion.

———— ∞∞∞ ————

The other profoundly important effect my father's abuse had on me was that I picked up his rage. No one would have ever dreamed from looking at me just how angry I was – and I wasn't even aware of it. It manifested one night when I was babysitting for a couple who lived at few houses down our street. The little boy was very cute to look at, but as soon as they closed the door to embark on their couple's night out, this child became a little monster. As we played with his set of blocks, he got upset with me for something I did or didn't do in our game, picked up a large wooden block and began hitting me with it. He was only four or five years old, but he packed a wallop with that block and it hurt.

Using the excuse of self-defense (as I tried explaining to his parents later), I grabbed the boy, turned him over my knee, and gave him a spanking. I began to feel out of control – ironically enough like I would beat him if I kept going (shades of my father) – and stopped by going into another room. Naturally, he cried and told his parents all about the incident the next morning, thus they called and "uninvited" me from every babysitting their child again (understandably so).

That incident stayed with me, and I began to become afraid of my own anger and lack of control. It was such a shameful feeling that I quickly stuffed it down in a place where I repressed ugly things and didn't consider it until many years later. The upshot of all this was that while I said with my mouth that of course I "wanted children," in my heart of hearts I was terrified of having any. With the spanking incident in mind and the fact that I just could not stand it when babies cried incessantly and couldn't be comforted (another terrible babysitting experience), I somehow subconsciously came to the conclusion that I would make a terrible mother, would damage any child I had, and the cycle of abuse would continue.

Therefore, while I watched my friends all having beautiful babies and enjoying motherhood, I did not follow suit. I loved to play with my nieces and nephews, and they responded very positively to me and always wanted to be around me. This was not, however, enough to convince me that I wouldn't be an abusive mother… so I never had children of my own. I "inherited" three wonderful junior high school-aged kids when I married my husband, and they were so great that our little family was enough for me (amazingly enough, I experienced <u>none</u> of the usual step-family issues). It used to bother me when people would ask why I hadn't had children, because I still had a great deal of shame inside me and was sensitive to the slightest hint that I might not like children or didn't want to deal with them. Nothing could have been further from the truth.

The ultimate heaping of insult upon injury happened one time when my father and I were talking. He made a very emphatic statement: "It's a good thing you never had kids; you're just too selfish to have ever been a good mother." Although I was livid at the time, it took me a while to fall back and regroup. When he repeated the accusation, I finally told him off. After working up the nerve and rehearsing it with my therapist, I informed him that the reason I didn't ever have children was that I was afraid I would be as abusive to them as he had been to me. That's one of the very few times I can remember my father being so shocked that he was rendered speechless! I imagine he was stunned that his little girl actually had the nerve to stand up and inform him of a painful truth.

You might wonder why I am baring my soul this way. I need to reinforce that no matter what you've done as a part of acting out (which is often the result of the abuse you experienced), the Lord can and wants to forgive, heal, and set you free!

Now we'll fast forward to the rest of the saga of the continuing abuse at the hands of my father. In my counseling at that time, I felt discouraged about dealing with my childhood abuse, never dreaming that the healing would be taking that long. One day I just had it and didn't want to talk about it anymore. As far as I was concerned, I was done dealing with the past and wanted to stay in the "here and now" during my counseling sessions. I was actually getting along reasonably well with my father at the time, and I so longed for a close relationship with him. After my mother divorced him, his alcoholism had escalated to the point that he was confronted on his job and told if he didn't seek help, they would fire him. The job was all he had left, so he entered treatment – albeit unwillingly – he was just going in to dry out a little and then he would simply have more control over his drinking – or so he thought. However, while in treatment, he came out of denial and began working the A.A. program.

While I do not agree with everything that is espoused by Twelve-Step groups, my father's work with A.A. literally saved his life. He was angry with me during his hospitalization, as a few months before he went into treatment, I did something very bold (considering my emotional fragility at the time). I firmly informed him I couldn't see him anymore, because I couldn't stand watching him kill himself. Whoopee – I actually set a boundary! He got over it before the end of his hospitalization, made his amends to me, I happily forgave him, and things went quite well between us for a couple of years. He was a changed man, so I thought, and I was happy with that.

When I announced to my father, however, that I was marrying my boyfriend, a Hispanic man who was Catholic, he flipped! We were at a restaurant at the time, and he just shut down and stopped talking. In answer to my question about what was wrong, he said something to the effect that what I wanted from him he couldn't and wouldn't give, i.e., congratulations. Did I really expect him to be happy that I was marrying out of my race and religion? he wondered aloud. I was shocked, because I had been seeing my husband for over a year at that point, and my dad hadn't said a word about his disapproval until our ill-fated luncheon. He ultimately ended up capitulating and walking me down the aisle, which was more than he did for my older brother.

When Jim announced his engagement, my dad became furious. The "deal" that he had with my brother was that in exchange for my father paying his tuition, books, room and board, he would graduate from the university he was attending before getting married. Because my brother didn't want to wait, <u>my father actually did not attend his wedding</u> in protest. That rocked everyone to the core, and if people didn't know by then how selfish and unloving he was, he revealed himself in a big way then! My parents' marriage unofficially ended that day, because my Mom, in her wildest imaginings, could not conceive that my father would actually carry out his threat and break my brother's and the rest of the family's heart. To this day, whenever I think of that part of my brother's life, I feel great sorrow over my brother being crushed like that. And to think his bride was actually a WASP…. and that his next partner would be an African-American gay man!

Now we'll really fast forward. For almost 25 years of my marriage, I thought that things were all right between my husband and my father. Unbeknown to me, my father had been verbally abusing my husband intermittently. My husband chose not to tell me about these episodes; instead, he simply announced one day that he didn't want to see my dad anymore. He knew how hard Dad and I had worked on our relationship, so my husband wanted me to continue seeing him. Although I was utterly baffled, I miserably accepted the fact, went on with my relationship with my dad, and just prayed that somehow things would change.

I saw my father socially for a while longer, but as I became progressively more upset about this estrangement I came to a point of demanding an explanation from my husband as to why he refused to see my dad. He finally revealed what my father had been saying to him from time to time all those years. The suggestions that my father was making were unbelievably vile and disgusting and upon hearing them, I immediately confronted him. He didn't deny making any of the statements, but once again brought up my husband being Hispanic and Catholic. I almost fell out of my chair… how could my dad have not changed one iota in all those years? At one time during our marriage, he had actually told me that he felt my husband was a good man – that he didn't have to worry about me as a father might, because he knew that my husband would always take care of me. Now he had regressed some 25 years.

More details might flesh out the story, but the upshot of this was that my father, after two strokes, having a pacemaker implanted, and going through triple-bypass surgery, informed me that my husband would not be "allowed" to come to his home. He was in an extremely debili-

tated state but continually refused to let my husband help in any way. Sheer pride and stubbornness won out, even with my husband's gracious offer to help with my dad's impending move. My father coldly informed me over the phone that my husband was no longer welcome in his home. What???

Earlier that year, my dad had become suicidal, and at his request, I was able to help find him a good program in a mental health facility. While there, he was diagnosed as having Bipolar Disorder. Aha! At last, the pieces of a family genetic puzzle started falling into place. My father's mother was an <u>extremely</u> dysfunctional person, and with that information, I now know that she suffered from bipolar disorder as well.

One time my husband and I had visited her and my grandfather shortly after we were married. It hadn't even occurred to me at that point in time to change fields – I was an editor and reasonably satisfied with my work. In other words, becoming a counselor hadn't even entered my mind at the time. I was looking at some old photos and innocently asked, "What was my dad like when he was a little boy?" She paused and then, to my utter shock and horror, began sobbing and said "I a-a-abused him." So there it was, albeit in a different forum than I ever thought I would hear it... the admission that she abused him, he abused us, etc. The poignant saying had played itself out in our family: "Abuse is the gift that just keeps on giving."

There is substantial evidence of genetic predisposition with respect to mood disorders. Unfortunately, I inherited the chemical imbalance in the brain that manifests as major depression. While I have been through many rough times due to this disorder, I do thank the Lord that there is quite a body of knowledge about depression, as well as doctors and medication that can now treat it. I have availed myself of every kind of treatment over the years, and it is my firm belief that the Lord works through doctors and medicine so that I can be the person He created me to be.

Ignorance about depression abounds in Christian circles, which I have fought relentlessly, but feel in many ways is a losing battle. If one has a brain injury, that's all right, you poor thing, you can't help what you're doing as a result. If you suffer from depression, you're told to pull yourself up by your bootstraps, stop feeling sorry for yourself, start praying, read the Bible more, and everything will be just fine! My complaint is that we Christians don't give other believers, with thyroid imbalances, for instance, the same "get over it" kind of message. When believers suffer from hypo- or hyper-thyroidism, it's perfectly all right with us for them to go to their doctors and be put on a medication that, more than likely, they will be on the rest of their lives.

An even more obvious disparity in Christian circles is that we don't shame diabetics when they become insulin-dependent – or people who have to take medication to regulate their blood pressure. The fact that certain well-known Christian women including Sheila Walsh, Mary Beth Chapman, Jan Dravecky, Sandi Patti, and Cherry Boone O'Neill have all taken antidepressants has helped a bit with the stigma associated with them. I've just seen way too many clients who are ignorant or misinformed at their churches about the nature and treatment of depression. I'll step down from my soapbox now and return to the conclusion of this account.

When my dad issued the ultimatum that my husband was no longer welcome in his home, I was devastated. As I had somehow sensed this "choice" would one day be thrust upon me, I pleaded with my dad several times never to make me choose between him and my husband… that I would choose my husband over him every time based on Genesis 2:24: Therefore a man shall leave his father and mother and be joined to his wife, and they shall become one flesh. After he had rendered his judgment and issued his ultimatum (although he still wanted me around), I hung up crying and immediately called my brother. He didn't even hesitate but came riding in on his white horse and offered to talk with our dad about it. I gratefully accepted his proposal and waited expectantly to hear what I thought would be the positive results of their phone call. Alas, it was not to be. Apparently the conversation was brief, to the point, and went something like this:

John: Do you realize that with what you are doing now you might never see your daughter again?

Dad: So be it.

My dad had finally forced my hand, and the estrangement has continued. Prior to that historic day, my brother married a Hispanic woman from Nicaragua. During a visit with my father, he tried to show him a picture of their beautiful daughter. My dad actually pushed the photo away, having previously refused to even acknowledge their wedding invitation (my father is an equal opportunity racist). Afterward, my father told me privately that he just couldn't understand why my brother would marry that "vermin," and how disappointed he was in him.

On what would be my brother's final visit with my dad, John had decided to confront him about the abusive treatment he received as a child. <u>All my dad would have had to say was, "Yes. I did that. I'm sorry."</u> Instead, he talked about himself, going on and on about how his father had done the same things to him. This reaction is well-explained in the following excerpt from Covitz' book:

Norma's mother had been a narcissistically abused child, and she abused Norma as well. She was a cold, angular (stiff) person, rarely showing affection to Norma and spending most of her time, as Norma recalls, either in a depression or a frus-

trated rage. Her mother had little respect for herself, and she took out her emotions on Norma. When Norma did something well, she became her mother's narcissistic showpiece; the mother used her daughter's successes to boost her own self-esteem. Although Norma instinctively knew that her mother's praise and rage both had little to do with her, she was never respected as a person with her own needs. Her mother's needs always came first.[4]

I picked this excerpt for two reasons. One, it very much reflects my father's relationships with his children. When we did well, he would boast to others about us (never to us directly), and when we weren't doing so well that was all we heard about.

One other thought on this last excerpt from Covitz' book. My brother John is an incredible person: a committed Christian, brilliant, accomplished (a well-respected expert in the field of environmental protection), kind and generous to a fault, an extremely loving husband and father, a gifted musician, a licensed pilot, etc., etc., etc. (I could go on for quite awhile listing his attributes and accomplishments). Following is a brief description of his professional life alone:

Mr. Norris is Vice President and Principal Environmental Scientist of Kennedy/Jenks Consultants, Inc. He is a licensed Professional Geologist with over 30 years of experience in the assessment and remediation of contaminated sites and waste disposal facilities. His experience includes managing large site investigations and cleanup programs for private industrial and military clients. He has developed facility-wide remedial action strategies at large industrial complexes and directed the development of computer databases used for monitoring reporting and integration with numerical models, graphical displays, and geographic information systems. He has managed comprehensive environmental assessments of large military installations and prepared closure/post-closure plans, including implementation cost estimates for chemical weapons manufacturing waste disposal sites under contract to the U.S. Army Corps of Engineers. Mr. Norris has been designated as an expert witness in a number of cases involving hazardous waste site litigation. Mr. Norris served on the U.S. Air Force Center for Environmental Excellence Committee for development of the USAF Remedial Design/Remedial Action Guidance Document for Installation Restoration Program sites.

Despite all that he has accomplished and the wonderful person he is, John says when he is alone and everything is quiet, the tape of my father's voice is the only one playing in his head: "You're a worthless piece of s- -t!" I can think of no better example of the scars of emotional child abuse than this.

I have worked many years in and out of therapy to deal with the issues surrounding my childhood abuse, and the Lord has graciously healed me in profound ways. There are still areas to work on, as the sanctification process continues over the entire lifetime, but I feel whole and free as far as what happened to me as a child. What about my process of forgiveness? It took going through an incredible number of layers to get to the core of that onion. I was greatly helped by Neil Anderson's book <u>The Steps to Freedom</u> (discussed in Chapter Nine). It gave me steps and structure, and I have used it for not only past offenses but current ones, as well. Forgiveness must become a lifestyle for all Christians if they are ever to be conformed to the image of the Lord Jesus Christ.

If the tone of this account still seems to you to be one of anger toward my father, family "friend," and youth pastor, I need to clarify something. I have always been and will always be angry when I speak of anyone's abuse, particularly a child's. That is what you might be discerning, for I have long ago forgiven my abusers and pray only for their salvation and that blessings are poured out upon them. You can "let go," as we learned is one of the definitions of forgiveness, without having warm feelings toward your abusers or re-establishing relationships with them. I am convinced that when Jesus told us to love our enemies, He was referring to treating them lovingly… sometimes loving feelings might be present, sometimes not.

Love is a decision, a commitment – certainly not an emotion that varies from one day to the next. When my old, human kind of love is completely worn out, I simply pray and ask Abba for His eyes through which to view them and His love to pass on to them. Although reconciliation between my father and me has not happened at this time, I would be open to it if he were to approach my husband and me in a humble manner. I will always love and pray for him. It is nearly impossible to kill a child's love for a parent, no matter what kind of abuse has occurred. I was examining some material about girls and their fathers, and one of the questions asked was "What would be the first thing you would say to your father if you saw him today?" The question pertained to women whose dads weren't in their lives. Without hesitating, I answered, "Papa, I surely do love you!"

I had two spiritual fathers, Herb Ezell and Jack Hayford, who brought real fatherly love into my life and helped me in significant ways to internalize an accurate view of Father God. How blessed I feel to have had these two wonderful men in my life!

Over the decades of my life, continuously forgiving others has opened the door for me to begin trusting the Lord. When traumatic things happen in my life, sometimes washing over me

in wave after wave of excruciating, agonizing pain, I have learned to lean hard on my Father as He has the only answers for my bruised and broken heart. With each wave of pain, I realize that I must come before Him on my face and He has been faithful to heal me every time. What makes this so amazing is that when these excruciating things happen, I cannot even begin to fathom ever feeling whole again – but nothing is too hard for the Lord.

Since we moved from California to Arizona, events have occurred in my life that I would never have anticipated, much less believed, that I would not only survive and one day even thrive. The best part of all is that because of his healing grace, I emerge from these events having even gained more spiritual If you had told me before that move that such crushing things would ever happen to me, I simply would not have believed you, so surreal and heartbreaking have they been. Even as the words of the old hymn echo in my heart, I can say, "It is well with my soul."

The backgrounds of so many of these classic hymns are fascinating and well worth the time you might spend in researching them. You will be amazed what the man who wrote the lyrics went through in his life. His story is quite inspiring:

"It Is Well with My Soul" is a very influential <u>hymn</u> penned by hymnist <u>Horatio Spafford</u> and composed by <u>Philip Bliss</u>. This hymn was written after several traumatic events in Spafford's life. The first was the death of his only son in 1871 at the age of four; shortly followed by <u>the great Chicago Fire</u> that ruined him financially (he had been a successful <u>lawyer</u>). Then in 1873, he had planned to travel to Europe with his family on the *SS Ville du Havre*, but sent the family ahead while he was delayed on business concerning zoning problems following the Great Chicago Fire. While crossing the <u>Atlantic</u>, the ship sank rapidly after a collision with a sailing ship, the <u>Loch Earn</u>, and all four of Spafford's daughters died. His wife Anna survived and sent him the now famous telegram, "Saved alone." Shortly afterwards, as Spafford traveled to meet his grieving wife, he was inspired to write these words as his ship passed near where his daughters had died. Bliss called his tune *Ville du Havre*, from the name of the stricken vessel. The Spaffords later had three more children, one of whom (a son) died in <u>infancy</u>. In 1881, the Spaffords, including baby Bertha and newborn Grace, set sail for <u>Israel</u>. The Spaffords moved to <u>Jerusalem</u> and helped found a group called the <u>American Colony</u>; its mission was to serve the poor.[5]

There is so much spiritual "meat" in this hymn. Please read and/or sing through all the verses and see for yourself how the Lord brings us through trials and tragedies while imparting His peace which passes all understanding to us:

It Is Well With My Soul

By *Horatio Spafford*

When peace like a river, attendeth my way,
When sorrows like sea billows roll;
Whatever my lot, Thou hast taught me to say,
It is well, it is well, with my soul.

Refrain:
It is well, with my soul,
It is well, with my soul,

It is well, it is well, with my soul.
Though Satan should buffet, though trials should come,
Let this blest assurance control,
That Christ has regarded my helpless estate,
And hath shed His own blood for my soul.

My sin, oh, the bliss of this glorious thought!
My sin, not in part but the whole,
Is nailed to the cross, and I bear it no more,
Praise the Lord, praise the Lord, O my soul!

For me, be it Christ, be it Christ hence to live,
If Jordan above me shall roll,
No pang shall be mine, for in death as in life,
Thou wilt whisper Thy peace to my soul.

But Lord, 'tis for Thee, for Thy coming we wait,
The sky, not the grave, is our goal;
Oh, trump of the angel! Oh, voice of the Lord!
Blessed hope, blessed rest of my soul.

And Lord, haste the day when my faith shall be sight,
The clouds be rolled back as a scroll;
The trump shall resound, and the Lord shall descend,
Even so, it is well with my soul.

———⠿⠿⠿———

Through all the events of my life, I have come to experience God as my REAL Father – He never abuses me and is always there for me. He is the final Agent of healing, and He does all things well. It has been said that every person's life is a novel – You just got the Reader's Digest version of mine. It is my deepest hope and prayer that my story might provide assistance in your quest of healing from child abuse and becoming intimate with the Father.

Appendix C

The Abuse Jesus Suffered and His Choice to Forgive

Our model for forgiveness is, of course, the Lord Jesus Christ. We will find that (though not a child), He did suffer every type of abuse specified in Chapter One during His ministry, trial, and execution. However, you still might be thinking, *Yes, but He was an adult and therefore had more coping mechanisms to endure the abuse. He can't possibly understand what I went through as a child….*

That would be true if we were considering the life and death of an ordinary person. Yet when the sins of the whole world and for all time were placed upon Him, He then experienced all the trauma that has ever been perpetrated against children. He also took on all our diseases, so during those three hours, He experienced all the after-effects that any child, past, present, or future, would suffer because of being abused. This was a profound discovery for me, as the thought never crossed my mind that Jesus suffered abuse two different ways… first during His adult life and ministry, and secondly, on the cross. Therefore, **He does understand every kind of pain you have ever suffered**, and we have scriptural proof that He made the choice to forgive His abusers.

The idea of this appendix all began with my reading the book *Died He for Me: A Physician's View of the Crucifixion of Jesus Christ*. In addition, as was the case with many other believers, I was touched and deeply affected by the movie *The Passion of the Christ*. Whatever else one may say about Mel Gibson, his desire was to accurately depict what he believed Jesus actually endured.

Reading a book about the torture Jesus experienced was an altogether different experience from seeing the movie. While I suppose it would be possible to remove oneself emotionally while reading the book and simply concentrate on all the medical facts in a sort of detached manner, I just couldn't do it! *Died He for Me*, in its graphic, detailed account of the horrific abuse of Jesus, made me cry about ever other sentence. **I will never again wonder if Jesus really knows how I felt when I was being abused.**

There is a powerful theological explanation for Jesus' up close and personal knowledge of what it is like to be abused. Dr. David Ball, in *The Crucifixion and Death of a Man Called Jesus: From the Eyes of a Physician*, makes a crucial distinction between God coming to earth in human form and being made in the flesh:

If God, sometime in the past, had chosen to come to visit earth, in recognizable form, it would have been incredible. But that is not exactly what happened... God chose not simply to come to earth for a visit, but rather, God chose to be made in the flesh. And these facts get to the very heart of who Jesus was – and is. To appear as a human being is not the same as to be made in the flesh. The flesh is that part of our humanness that is vulnerable. It is vulnerable to pain and suffering: sickness and death; hunger and thirst; temptation and sin; and yes, even the consequences of sin. The omnipotent and omniscient Creator of this universe chose, for some reason, to subject Himself to the frailties of human flesh! <u>*At the least, one would have to conclude that the God of this universe suffered just like you and me. But the most significant realization for the serious inquisitor (whether he accepts the deity of Jesus or not) is that Jesus suffered not simply like you and me but for you and me*</u> *(emphasis added)![1]*

Only as I have been writing this book have I started to see how Jesus' suffering – His own family's and the town of Nazareth's wholesale rejection of His divinity; the constant mockery that He contended with during his ministry; and His trial, scourging, and crucifixion – related to the horrors of child abuse. **The following Bible verses demonstrate Jesus' complete identification with us when we suffer:**

Therefore, in all things He had to be made like His brethren, that He might be a merciful and faithful High Priest in things pertaining to God, to make propitiation for the sins of the people. For in that He Himself has suffered, being tempted, He is able to aid those who are tempted.... Seeing then that we have a great High Priest who has passed through the heavens, Jesus the Son of God, let us hold fast our confession. For we do not have a High Priest who cannot sympathize with our weaknesses, but was in all points tempted as we are, yet without sin (Hebrews 2:17-18; 4:14-16).

For Christ also suffered once for sins, the just for the unjust, that He might bring us to God, being put to death in the flesh but made alive by the Spirit (Hebrews 5:18).

From that time Jesus began to show to His disciples that He must go to Jerusalem, and suffer many things from the elders and chief priests and scribes, and be killed, and be raised the third day.... Now while they were staying in Galilee, Jesus said to them, 'The Son of Man is about to be betrayed into the hands of men, and they will kill Him and the third day He will be raised up'. . . Now Jesus, going up to Jerusalem, took the twelve disciples aside on the road and said to them, 'Behold, we are going up to Jerusalem, and the Son of Man will be betrayed to the chief priests and to the scribes; and they will condemn Him to death, and deliver Him to the Gentiles to mock and to scourge and to crucify. And the third day He will rise again' (Matthew 16:21; 17:22-23; 20:17-19).

Then He took the twelve aside again and began to tell them the things that would happen to Him: 'Behold, we are going up to Jerusalem, and the Son of Man will be betrayed to the chief priests and to the scribes; and they will condemn Him to death and deliver Him to the Gentiles; and they will mock Him, and scourge Him, and spit on Him, and kill Him.' And the third day He will rise again (Mark 10:32-34).

Now as they came down from the mountain, He commanded them that they should tell no one the things they had seen, till the Son of Man had arisen from the dead. So they kept this word to themselves, questioning what the rising from the dead meant. And they asked Him, saying, 'Why do the scribes say that Elijah must come first?' Then He answered and told them, 'Indeed, Elijah is coming first and restores all things. And how is it written concerning the Son of Man, that He must suffer many things and be treated with contempt? But I say to you that Elijah has also come, and they did to him whatever they wished as it is written of him' (Mark 9:9-13).

No description of the sufferings of Jesus should ever be considered without first including the prophecies of the Suffering Servant given through Isaiah and King David:

Isaiah 53

¹ Who has believed our report?
And to whom has the arm of the LORD been revealed?
² For He shall grow up before Him as a tender plant,
And as a root out of dry ground.
He has no form or comeliness;
And when we see Him,
There is no beauty that we should desire Him.
³ He is despised and rejected by men,
A Man of sorrows and acquainted with grief.
And we hid, as it were, our faces from Him;
He was despised, and we did not esteem Him.
⁴ Surely He has borne our griefs
And carried our sorrows;

Yet we esteemed Him stricken,
Smitten by God, and afflicted.
[5] *But He was wounded for our transgressions,*
He was bruised for our iniquities;
The chastisement for our peace was upon Him,
And by His stripes we are healed.
[6] *All we like sheep have gone astray;*
We have turned, every one, to his own way;
And the LORD has laid on Him the iniquity of us all.
[7] *He was oppressed and He was afflicted,*
Yet He opened not His mouth;
He was led as a lamb to the slaughter,
And as a sheep before its shearers is silent,
So He opened not His mouth.
[8] *He was taken from prison and from judgment,*
And who will declare His generation?
For He was cut off from the land of the living;
For the transgressions of My people, He was stricken.
[9] *And they made His grave with the wicked –*
But with the rich at His death,
Because He had done no violence,
Nor was any deceit in His mouth.
[10] *Yet it pleased the LORD to bruise Him;*
He has put Him to grief.
When You make His soul an offering for sin,
He shall see His seed, He shall prolong His days,
And the pleasure of the LORD shall prosper in His hand.
[11] *He shall see the labor of His soul, and be satisfied.*
By His knowledge, My righteous Servant shall justify many,
For He shall bear their iniquities.
[12] *Therefore I will divide Him a portion with the great,*
And He shall divide the spoil with the strong,
Because He poured out His soul unto death,
And He was numbered with the transgressors,
And He bore the sin of many,
And made intercession for the transgressors.

Psalm 22

To the Chief Musician. Set to "The Deer of the Dawn." A Psalm of David.

[1] My God, My God, why have You forsaken Me?
Why are You so far from helping Me,
And from the words of My groaning?
[2] O My God, I cry in the daytime, but You do not hear;
And in the night season, and am not silent.
[3] But You are holy,
Enthroned in the praises of Israel.
[4] Our fathers trusted in You;
They trusted, and You delivered them.
[5] They cried to You, and were delivered;
They trusted in You, and were not ashamed.
[6] But I am a worm, and no man;
A reproach of men, and despised by the people.
[7] All those who see Me ridicule Me;
They shoot out the lip, they shake the head, saying,
[8] "He trusted in the LORD, let Him rescue Him;
Let Him deliver Him, since He delights in Him!"
[9] But You are He who took Me out of the womb;
You made Me trust while on My mother's breasts.
[10] I was cast upon You from birth.
From My mother's womb,
You have been My God.
[11] Be not far from Me,
For trouble is near;
For there is none to help.
[12] Many bulls have surrounded Me;
Strong bulls of Bashan have encircled Me.
[13] They gape at Me with their mouths,
Like a raging and roaring lion.
[14] I am poured out like water,
And all My bones are out of joint;
My heart is like wax;
It has melted within Me.
[15] My strength is dried up like a potsherd,
And My tongue clings to My jaws;

You have brought Me to the dust of death.
[16] For dogs have surrounded Me;
The congregation of the wicked has enclosed Me.
They pierced My hands and My feet;
[17] I can count all My bones.
They look and stare at Me.
[18] They divide My garments among them,
And for My clothing they cast lots.
[19] But You, O LORD, do not be far from Me;
O My Strength, hasten to help Me!
[20] Deliver Me from the sword,
My precious life from the power of the dog.
[21] Save Me from the lion's mouth
And from the horns of the wild oxen!
You have answered Me.
[22] I will declare Your name to My brethren;
In the midst of the assembly I will praise You.
[23] You who fear the LORD, praise Him!
All you descendants of Jacob, glorify Him,
And fear Him, all you offspring of Israel!
[24] For He has not despised nor abhorred the affliction of the afflicted;
Nor has He hidden His face from Him;
But when He cried to Him, He heard.
[25] My praise shall be of You in the great assembly;
I will pay My vows before those who fear Him.
[26] The poor shall eat and be satisfied;
Those who seek Him will praise the LORD.
Let your heart live forever!
[27] All the ends of the world
Shall remember and turn to the LORD,
And all the families of the nations
Shall worship before You.
[28] For the kingdom is the LORD's,
And He rules over the nations.
[29] All the prosperous of the earth
Shall eat and worship;
All those who go down to the dust
Shall bow before Him,
Even he who cannot keep himself alive.

³⁰ A posterity shall serve Him.
It will be recounted of the Lord to the next generation,
³¹ They will come and declare His righteousness to a people who will be born,
That He has done this.

———— ✇ ————

The Sexual Abuse Jesus Suffered

Although we don't know of any specific instances of Jesus being sexually assaulted, there is an overwhelming preponderance of information that indicates that Jesus was naked during His scourging, on His way to the cross, and during His crucifixion. David Reagan, on the website called "Learn the Bible" has written a concise exposition of what is said about nakedness (other than with one's spouse) in the Bible.

... I will use the Bible word nakedness. It is true that Adam and Eve went without clothes when they were created. However, they were... in a state of innocence. Though they were intelligent creatures, they had no more sense of right and wrong than a baby does today. However, as soon as sin entered the world, they were ashamed of their nakedness and sought to cover themselves. From that time until now, God has treated nakedness outside of marriage as a shameful thing. Several actions concerning nakedness are condemned in the Bible:

It is a shame and wrong to uncover your nakedness to others. The priests were warned to wear undergarments so that their nakedness would not be discovered when they went up the steps to the altar in their robes. Their undergarments (linen breeches) were to cover from their loins (waist) to their thighs (Exodus 28:42). When the children of Israel made and worshipped the golden calf, Aaron 'made them naked unto their shame' (Exodus 32:25). Isaiah 47:3 speaks of the shame of having your nakedness uncovered.

It is a sin to uncover the nakedness of another. This is seen as leading to other sins (see Leviticus 18:6-18). It is wrong to look on the nakedness of others. Ham's son was cursed because Ham saw the nakedness of his father and went and talked about it (Genesis 9:22-23). Habakkuk 2:15 speaks of the wickedness of those who get someone drunk in order to 'look on their nakedness.'²

In a movie I recently saw about World War II, there was a scene in which the Nazi guards were "escorting" the women (who were all Jewish – fresh off the cattle car) to the so-called showers in which they were to be gassed. The director depicted all the women wailing and running to the showers because of the shame of their nakedness. I had never seen that interpretation of the enforced nakedness portrayed in any other Holocaust film. In exploring the question as to whether Jesus was naked on the cross, Dr. Ralph Wilson shows us the scope of the historical debate about its answer:

> *Was Jesus naked and exposed on the cross? Men were ordinarily crucified naked. Schneider tells us, 'Sometimes [the condemned person] was stripped and his clothes were divided among the executioners, though this was not the common rule. The very purpose of crucifixion was utter humiliation for the condemned. What would be more humiliating than to strip a person naked? But among the Jews, nakedness, particularly nakedness in public, was considered exceedingly shameful.' Edersheim cites Sanhedrin vi.3.4 that in Jewish executions by stoning, 'The criminal was undressed, only the covering absolutely necessary for decency being left.' While he concedes that Jesus was executed by Romans, not Jews, he feels that 'every concession would be made to Jewish custom' and thus Jesus would have been spared the indignity of exposure as being 'truly un-Jewish.' Green, on the other hand, assumes Jesus' nakedness at the crucifixion. Was Jesus naked on the cross? We just can't be sure.[3]*

On another website, www.answerbag.com, the question, "Was Jesus naked on the cross?" was answered as follows:

> *Yes, he was fully naked, and so were the other two convicts. Though all forms of public nudity is against Hebrew custom, the perverted Romans seemed to have delighted in it, especially when executing condemned prisoners. Most historians say flogging and beating a convict, then stripping him naked is part of the Roman's procedure before and during crucifixion.[4]*

Noted Christian author Rick Renner gives this account of crucifixion in the debate as to Jesus' nakedness on the cross:

> *Although the Romans did not invent crucifixion, they perfected it as a form of torture and capital punishment that was designed to produce a slow death with maximum pain and suffering. It was one of the most disgraceful and cruel methods of execution and usually was reserved only for slaves, foreigners, revolutionaries, and the vilest of criminals. It was customary for the condemned man to carry his own cross from the flogging post to the site of crucifixion outside the city walls. He was usually naked, unless this was prohibited by local customs.... In the Jewish world, nakedness was a particularly profound shame. Because the body was made in the image of God, the Jewish people believed it was a great dishonor to display a naked body. So as if Jesus' suffering had*

not already been enough, He experienced the ultimate act of degradation and shame as He hung on the Cross, naked and exposed before all those who watched the unfolding drama.[5]

Mark Huppert made this statement on his website about Jesus' nakedness and our culture today:

He is stripped.... All of the crucifixes that show Jesus still on the cross lie in one very important respect. They all give Jesus a loincloth, which Jesus never had. Jesus, as He hung on that cross, was absolutely completely... naked. That's the only way that the Romans crucified people. But we are so hung up on our stupid childishness, that we cannot even portray the highest holiest icon of Western civilization, Christ upon the cross. We cannot portray that as it was. We must constantly lie to ourselves and give Him these stupid little loin cloths to protect our modesty. We cannot look upon the face of truth.[6]

In Dr. Bell's *The Crucifixion and Death of a Man Called Jesus: From the Eyes of a Physician,* he makes the following observations concerning Jesus' nakedness during his scourging and carrying his own instrument of death along the Via Dolorosa:

Jesus was completely stripped of His clothes. Absolutely humiliated. He probably didn't even have on a loincloth, which would have protected His buttocks from the lashes of the Roman flagrum. [The image on the Shroud of Turin clearly has marks on the buttocks.]... The trip was difficult for a healthy man, but remember, Jesus had been stripped of His clothes and nearly beaten to death.[7]

In Dr. Mark Marinella's recent work, *Died He for Me: A Physician's View of the Crucifixion of Jesus Christ,* the following point is made with regard to the nakedness of Jesus on the procession to Golgotha:

After the victim was found guilty and sentenced to death by crucifixion, a team of Roman soldiers led him in a humiliating procession to the death site.... The victim was usually stripped at the time of the pre-crucifixion scourging and forced to carry the patibulum [crosspiece] naked, a tactic aimed at causing further humiliation.[8]

A Christian psychologist, Dr. Deborah Newman, weighs in next. She is transparent and articulate concerning her personal discomfort with perceiving Jesus naked on the cross:

I really don't like to picture Jesus on the cross. I know He has conquered death and the cross has now become a thing of beauty, but I can't fully accept the beauty of the empty cross without first wholly embracing the ugliness of it. Mel Gibson gave me a vision in his movie **The Passion of the Christ.** *My mind took in another aspect after reading an article in my alumni magazine. My alma mater has a painting on display of the crucifixion. The artist, a Bryan College alumnus, painted this scene to depict the reality of the Bible's descriptions, rather than the beautiful museum renderings. The artist felt it was vital to paint Jesus without clothing since the Bible says that they took His clothes from Him. I can understand why other artists would rather give at least an ounce of dignity to the blood-smeared, unbecoming, dying Christ. Just a little loincloth to cover His nakedness makes sense. As I pondered Jesus naked on the cross, I realized that I wanted Jesus to be clothed for me, for my sake. I want to make the cross less humiliating for me to look at. I don't want to think of Jesus hanging naked.[9]*

Dr. Pierre Barbet's account in the first book of its kind, which resulted in people with no background in medicine getting a detailed picture of what Jesus actually suffered to redeem us, weighs in on Jesus being naked through the ordeal of the scourging, at the very least. He wrote *A Doctor at Calvary: The Passion of Our Lord Jesus Christ as Described by a Surgeon* in 1953, and it became the textbook against which other books about the sufferings of Jesus are measured. Dr. Barbet was a firm believer in the authenticity of the Shroud of Turin, so nearly all his medical observations are coupled with corresponding marks on the Shroud. He observes that:

We may assume that during the scourging our Lord was completely naked, for the halter-like wounds are to be seen all over the pelvic region, which would otherwise have been protected by the subligaculum, and they are as deep as on the rest of the body.[10]

Although Jesus was not a child when He suffered this abuse, He was innocent. He took the physical pain of your sexual abuse into His body as He was being beaten and crucified, but the humiliation and the shame that is mentioned repeatedly in these sources indicates that He knows the feelings provoked by being stripped and paraded around naked. Could anyone be more vulnerable than being unable even to cover His genitals because His hands were nailed to the cross? The same demonic spirit that gives pedophiles their enjoyment and the Nazi guards their perverse pleasure at seeing all their prisoners naked was the one working that day through the Roman soldiers.

The first inkling I had that Jesus was naked on the cross resonated as truth within my spirit and has been there ever since. I quote now from *The Hiding Place* by Corrie Ten Boom. As she and her family (Gentiles) were placed in the concentration camp Ravensbruck because of their work with the Dutch underground in hiding Jews, the following exchange occurs between Corrie and her sister, Betsie:

Fridays – the recurrent humiliation of medical inspection. The hospital corridor in which we waited was unheated, and a fall chill had settled into the walls. Still we were forbidden even to wrap ourselves in our own arms, but had to maintain our erect, hands-at-sides position as we filed slowly past a phalanx of grinning guards. How there could have been any pleasure in the sight of these stick thin legs and hunger-bloated stomachs I could not imagine. Surely there is no more wretched sight than the human body unloved and uncared for. Nor could I see the necessity for the complete undressing: when we finally reached the examining room a doctor looked down each throat, another – a dentist presumably – at our teeth, a third in between each finger. And that was all. We trooped again down the long, cold corridor and picked up our X-marked dresses at the door. But it was one of these mornings while we were waiting, shivering in the corridor, that yet another page in the Bible leapt into life for me. He hung naked on the cross. I had not known – I had not thought.... The paintings, the carved crucifixes showed at the least a scrap of cloth. But this, I suddenly knew, was the respect and reverence of the artist. But oh – at the time itself, on that other Friday morning – there had been no reverence. No more than I saw in the faces around us now. I leaned toward Betsie, ahead of me in line. Her shoulder blades stood out sharp and thin beneath her blue-mottled skin, 'Betsie, they took His clothes too.' Ahead of me, I heard a little gasp. 'Oh, Corrie. And I never thanked Him....' [11]

Doing this research on the subject made it quite clear to me that Jesus, indeed, was naked during the majority of His trial, punishment, and execution. He knows all our feelings, because He felt them too. People being what they are, I imagine that He was mocked verbally by someone, if not many people, for the appearance of His genitals. As Romans weren't circumcised, one can only imagine the insults being hurled about. Whatever word you choose for His nakedness during the scourging, procession, and crucifixion – humiliating, degrading, shameful, dehumanizing, embarrassing, mortifying, crushing, debasing, humbling, disgraceful, etc. – they all describe what He suffered for you and me. If that doesn't show His love for and identification with us, I don't know what would!

The Physical Abuse and Neglect Jesus Suffered

We will examine the physical abuse and neglect Jesus suffered in the order of its occurrence. In *Died He for Me*, Dr. Mark Marinella, begins at what is commonly known as the Last Supper or Jesus celebrating Passover early with His disciples. I haven't ever thought of the Passover meal as a stressful time for Jesus, but of course it was! With His foreknowledge of what He was about to experience, combined with eating with His betrayer, Marinella's first observation makes sense. He probably ate very little due to the above-mentioned factors. [12]

We move to the garden of Gethsemane where Jesus suffered great mental anguish and torment (see "The Verbal/Emotional Abuse Jesus Suffered" below). As we return to His physical condition, Marinella continues his description of Jesus' bodily state:

Another physical problem that may have affected Jesus while in Gethsemane was weak-ness due to poor food and water intake…. As a result, by the time Jesus reached the garden of Gethsemane, He may have already been mildly dehydrated; and if so, we know that this would have been compounded by fluid loss from His sweating, which in medical terms is called insensible fluid loss. Most of us have missed meals for a day or two when ill with a virus. Due to low caloric and fluid intake, low blood pressure (hypo-tension), physical weakness, dizziness, and shakiness can occur, and possibly Jesus was experiencing these that last night. Also, if one goes without sufficient food for more than twenty-four hours, the sugar-supplying glycogen stores in the liver become depleted and the body burns other fuels called ketones, which are formed in the muscles and liver… by the time Jesus reached the garden, He may have already been weak…. Another factor to consider… is sleep deprivation. Jesus may not have experienced restful sleep during the entire Passover week, and certainly not on the night before the crucifixion, since He was kept awake in all-night trials that started with appearing before the Sanhedrin…. When one goes without restful sleep for a few days, weakness, fatigue, nausea, loss of appetite, muscle aches, and headaches may occur.[13]

One of the more well-known physiological effects of the extreme stress, sorrow, and dread that Jesus was suffering in the Garden of Gethsemane was when He sweat great drops of blood. Here is how this phenomenon is explained medically:

As Jesus prayed, His mental anguish was unbearable: My soul is overwhelmed with sorrow to the point of death (Mark 14:34). His deep anguish of soul was no doubt aug-mented when several times He returned to His 'inner circle' of Peter, James, and John and found them sleeping. He had been betrayed by Judas, and His disciples, who claimed to be followers, had abandoned their watch. Jesus was left to pray alone and wrestle with the enormity of what His Father's will asked of Him. Luke, a physician known for attention to detail, makes a fascinating statement of Jesus' situation in Gethsemane: And being in anguish, He prayed more earnestly, and His sweat was like drops of blood falling to the ground (Luke 22:44). This phenomenon is known as hematidrosis and has been reported to occur in situations of intense stress. The capillaries supplying blood to the sweat glands actually break and leak blood into the sweat ducts, which results in blood being mixed with sweat. This could well have caused severe skin pain due to the underlying inflammation and swelling within the sweat glands.[14]

In His trial before the Sanhedrin, we are told in Mark 14:65 "…. And the guards took Him and beat Him." Marinella describes what probably happened because of this first beating: "This beating should not be confused with the scourging…. No doubt, the guards were strong and able to inflict very hard blows with their fists, likely causing facial trauma such as lacerations, bruises, black eyes, or even tooth injury; a mild concussion is certainly feasible as well. Indeed, Jesus' face was probably swollen and painful."[15]

Rick Renner wrote about this beating adding Matthew's depiction. "Then they did spit in his face, and buffeted him; and others smote him with the palms of their hands, saying, Prophesy unto us, thou Christ. Who is he that smote thee?" The mockery of the spitting will be described in the verbal/emotional abuse later in this appendix. Renner concludes:

> *The word 'they' refers to all the scribes and elders who were assembled for the meeting that night. One scholar notes that there could have been 100 or more men in this crowd.... The word 'buffet' is the Greek word kolaphidzo, which means to strike with the fist. It is normally used to picture a person who is violently beaten.... Humiliating Jesus with their spit and curses didn't satisfy the hatred of these men; they wouldn't be satisfied until they knew He had been physically maltreated. To ensure that this goal was accomplished, their own fists became their weapons of abuse... they voted to murder Him. But first they wanted to take some time to personally make sure He suffered before He died.*[16]

After Jesus admitted that He was the Messiah and equal to God, the charge of blasphemy was made and the Sanhedrin's consensus was that He deserved death. He had already walked from the Garden of Gethsemane to the residence of Caiaphas, from there to the judgment seat of Pilate (the Praetorium), from there to Herod's temporary quarters in Jerusalem for Passover (the Citadel), and from there back to Pilate's location. Dr. Zugibe, the physician/forensic investigator, mapped (using historical sources) the entire area Jesus had to have walked from the Gethsemane to Golgotha... the total distance was calculated to be approximately five miles.[16] The idea that he was weakened due to hunger, sleep deprivation, and an initial beating and then walked a majority of that five-mile distance gives us insight into the torment He suffered simply getting from one place to another.

The next scene of brutal physical abuse that Jesus endured was just prior to the scourging depicted in the gospel of Mark. "The soldiers led Jesus away into the palace (that is, the Praetorium) and called together the whole company of soldiers. They put a purple robe on Him, then twisted together a crown of thorns and set it on Him. And they began to call out to Him, 'Hail, king of the Jews!' Again and again, they struck Him on the head with a staff and spit on Him. Falling on their knees, they paid homage to Him" (Mark 15:16-19). The order of these two events is reversed in Matthew. However, both events did occur and the abuse was heinous on many levels. Once again, I will separate the mockery portion of the abuse from the physical torture and discuss it in the verbal/emotional abuse section.

First, the crown of thorns. Once again, what is depicted in artwork concerning the crown of thorns is far different from its reality. Matthew 27:27-29 describes the ordeal, but my research on the subject is overwhelming as the horror of each phase of the "passion of the Christ" is described in its true, historical context:

Then the soldiers of the governor took Jesus into the common hall, and gathered unto him the whole band of soldiers. And they stripped him, and put on him a scarlet robe. And when they had platted a crown of thorns, they put it upon His head, and a reed in His right hand: and they bowed the knee before Him, and mocked Him saying, Hail, King of the Jews (Matt. 27:27-29)!

I highly recommend reading this book: Rick Renner's, *Paid in Full: An In-Depth Look at the Defining Moments of Christ's Passion.* His extensive knowledge of the Greek terminology, as well as his grasp of the Roman culture at the time of Jesus, supply us with details that we would never otherwise even consider (and I have not found in any source material prior to this). This is his description of the so-called "crown" of thorns:

Verse 27 says the soldiers '... took Jesus into the common hall, and gathered unto him the whole band of soldiers.' The 'common hall' was the open courtyard in Pilate's palace.... All we know for sure is that the courtyard was so large, it was able to hold 'the whole band of soldiers.' This phrase comes from the Greek word **spira,** *referring to a cohort or a group of* <u>300 to 600 Roman soldiers</u> *(emphasis added).... After the soldiers '... had platted a crown of thorns, they put it upon his head....' The word 'platted' is the Greek word empleko. Thorns grew everywhere, including the imperial grounds of Pilate. These thorns were long and sharp like nails. The soldiers took vines that were loaded with sharp and dangerous thorns; then they carefully wove together the razor-sharp, prickly, jagged vines until they formed a tightly woven dangerous circle that resembled the shape of a crown. Afterward, the soldiers, '... put it upon His head.... 'Matthew uses the Greek word epitithimi, a word that implies they violently pushed and forcefully shoved this crown of thorns onto Jesus' head. These thorns would have been extremely painful and caused blood to flow profusely from His brow. Because the thorns were so jagged, they would have created terrible wounds as they scraped across Jesus' scalp and literally tore the flesh from His skull.*[18]

Dr. Marinella, in *Died He for Me*, goes into a lengthy explanation of the medical results of what he alternatively identifies as a "cap" of thorns being pounded into Jesus' scalp:

If you have spent time in a garden, you may have experienced being punctured by a rose thorn.... Imagine then, a cap with thorns one to two inches long being pressed into your scalp by a firm hand. The thorns became embedded within Jesus' scalp and likely were abutting the skull bone (calvarium). There were probably upwards of one hundred thorns on this cap.... Some of the thorns likely broke off within the nerve-laden flesh of the scalp – invoking severe pain.... In Christ's situation, numerous sharp, long thorns would have easily pierced down to the skull, through the galea aponeurotica. While cut-

ting through skin and flesh, small arteries and veins would have been pierced and significant bleeding would have ensued. The blood likely dripped into His eyes, which may have already been quite irritated from weeping and sweat dripping into them. As a result, it would have been difficult for Jesus to see…. In addition, as the thorns passed through the flesh, sensory nerves would have been damaged resulting in unbearable scalp and head pain. It is also quite feasible that Jesus' top eyelids could have been torn by a stray thorn depending on how far the cap or crown was pushed by His persecutor.[19]

Rick Renner describes the significance of the "cohort" of Roman soldiers who tormented Jesus. Evidently after the scarlet or purple "robe" was draped across His naked body, the crown pounded into his head, and the reed, signifying a scepter, given to Him to hold, **each soldier** came and bowed, spit on Him, mocked him verbally (described later), and took the reed and used it as a bat to hit Him over the head:

So as each soldier passed by Jesus, he would first mockingly bow before Him; then he'd lean forward to spit right in Jesus' blood-drenched face. Next, the soldier would grab the reed from Jesus' hand and strike Him hard on His already wounded head. Finally, he would stick the reed back in Jesus' hand to make Him ready for the next soldier to repeat the whole process. The Greek clearly means that the soldiers repeatedly struck Jesus again and again on the head. Here was another beating that Jesus endured, but this time it was with the slapping action of a hard reed. This must have been excruciatingly painful for Jesus, since His head was deeply gashed by the cruel crown of thorns.[20]

Dr. Zugibe, the forensic investigator, agrees that it was a "cap" of thorns, which covered the entire scull going down onto Jesus' forehead (in agreement with Marinella). He describes a disorder called "major trigeminal neuralgia," which would have been a result of having the cap of thorns pounded down into Jesus' head. The description of this disorder and what Jesus experienced follows:

This condition, first described by Fothergill in 1776, causes paroxysmal bouts of stabbing, lancinating, and explosive pain to the right or left half of the face, lasting from seconds to minutes with intermittent refractory periods…. Patients describe their pains as 'knifelike stabs,' 'electric shocks,' or 'jabs with a red-hot poker.' During the attack, tics or distortion of the face may occur and the patients may hold on to a bedpost in absolute agony. Light touches, facial movements, chewing, talking, or drafts of air across the face can precipitate an attack…. Trigeminal neuralgia is said to be the worst pain that man is heir to. It is a devastating pain that is just unbearable in its several forms.'[21]

As we move on to Jesus' scourging, every author whose work I read on the subject could not stress highly enough how horrifying this event was. According to Renner, "This was considered to be one of the most feared and deadly weapons of the Roman world. It was so ghastly that the mere threat of scourging could clam a crowd or bend the will of the strongest rebel. Even the most hardened criminal recoiled from the prospect of being submitted to the vicious beating of a Roman scourge." He then emphasizes the humiliation of the nakedness once again:

When a decision was made to scourge an individual, the victim was first stripped completely naked so his entire flesh would be open and uncovered to the beating action of the torturer's whip. Then the victim was bound to a two-foot-high scourging post…. When in this locked position, the victim couldn't wiggle or move, trying to dodge the lashes that were being laid across his back. Romans were professionals at scourging…. Once the victim was harnessed to the post and stretched over it, the Roman soldier began to put him through unimaginable torture. One writer notes that the mere anticipation of the whipping caused the victim's body to grow rigid, the muscles to knot in his stomach, the color to drain from his cheeks, and his lips to draw tight against his teeth as he waited for the first sadistic blow that would begin tearing his body open. The scourge itself consisted of a short, wooden handle with several 18- to 24-inch-long straps of leather protruding from it. The ends of these pieces of leather were equipped with sharp pieces of metal, wire, glass, and jagged fragments of bone….

Most often, two torturers were utilized to carry out this punishment, simultaneously lashing the victim from both sides. As these dual whips struck the victim, the leather straps with their sharp, jagged objects descended and extended over his entire back. Each piece of metal, wire, bone, or glass cut deeply through the victim's skin and into his flesh, shredding his muscles and sinews. Every time the whip pounded across the victim, those straps of leather curled tortuously around his torso, biting painfully and deeply into the skin of his abdomen and upper chest…. Every time the torturers struck a victim, the straps of leather… would cause multiple lashes as the sharp objects at the end of each strap sank into the flesh and then raked across the victim's belly. Then the torturer would jerk back, pulling hard in order to tear whole pieces of human flesh from the body. The victim's back, buttocks, back of the legs, stomach, upper chest, and face would soon be disfigured by the slashing blows of the whips.

Historical records describe a victim's back as being so mutilated after a Roman scourging that his spine would actually be exposed. Others recorded how the bowels of a victim would actually spill out through the open wounds created by the whip. The Early Church historian Eusebius wrote: 'The veins were laid bare, and the very muscles, sinews, and bowels of the victim were open to exposure.' The Roman torturer would so aggressively strike his victim that he wouldn't even take the time to untangle the bloody, flesh-filled straps as he lashed the whip across the victim's mangled body over and over again. If the scourging wasn't stopped, the slicing of the whip would eventually flay the victim's flesh off his body.[22]

Simply reading this account can cause us to feel slightly sick to our stomachs. Some people will even refuse to read it, as they "don't need to dwell on every gory detail of Jesus' suffering." Maybe that's the rationalization of many believers, but knowing a lot more about it makes me appreciate and love Him even more. I can be guilty of just glossing over all the agony that Jesus went through to just get to the other side – the glory of the empty tomb and its implications for us. However, forcing myself to read these books has added another dimension of intensity to my love for Jesus that I could never have foreseen. Returning to the horror of Jesus' abuse:

With so many blood vessels sliced open by the whip, the victim would begin to experience a profuse loss of blood and bodily fluids. The heart would pump harder and harder, struggling to get blood to the parts of the body that were bleeding profusely. But it was like pumping water through an open water hydrant; there was nothing to stop the blood from pouring through the victim's open wounds. This loss of blood caused the victim's blood pressure to drop drastically. Because of the massive loss of bodily fluids, he would experience excruciating thirst, often fainting from the pain and eventually going into shock. Frequently the victim's heartbeat would become so irregular that he would go into cardiac arrest.

According to Jewish law in Deuteronomy 25:3, the Jews were permitted to give 40 lashes to a victim, but because the fortieth lash usually proved fatal, the number of lashes was reduced to 39, as Paul noted in 2 Corinthians 11:24. But the Romans had no limit to the number of lashes they could give a victim, and the scourging Jesus experienced was at the hands of Romans, not Jews. Therefore, it is entirely possible that after the torturer pulled out his whip to beat Jesus, he may have laid more than 40 lashes across Jesus' body

So when the Bible tells us that Jesus was scourged, we now know exactly what type of beating Jesus received that night. What toll did the cruel Roman whip exact on Jesus' body? The New Testament doesn't tell us exactly what Jesus looked like after He was scourged, but Isaiah 52:14 says, 'As many were astonished at thee; His visage was so marred more than any man, and His form more than the sons of men.' If we take this scripture literally... we can conclude that Jesus' physical body was marred nearly beyond recognition. As appalling as this sounds, it was only the overture to what was to follow. Matthew 27:26 continues to tell us, '... and when he had scourged Jesus, he delivered Him to be crucified' (KJV). The scourging was only the preparation for Jesus' crucifixion![23]

Dr. Marinella has the following medical analysis to add to our knowledge of what happened to the human body during scourging:

Coursing through these muscles of the back are numerous sensory nerves, most of which originate from the spinal nerves of the spinal cord. It is probable the bone and metal directly tore many of these small sensory nerves resulting in severe, lancinating pain. When a nerve is torn, it produces a sharp, searing, and ripping, unbearable sensation – a type of pain referred to as neuropathic pain. Imagine hundreds of deep wounds inflicted over the period of a few minutes. The amount of pain associated with this is indescribable and impossible to adequately put into words.[24]

Many years ago, my husband was cleaning out our garage, and unbeknown to him, a wall-length mirror had gotten broken and there were many jagged pieces of glass sticking up at odd angles on the cement floor. I can't describe how it happened, I only know that I was inside, and he came to our front door telling me in a hoarse voice to please come out there right now and bring him a towel. I had no idea what had happened, so I brought out the requested towel and saw the blood gushing from a wound he sustained from somehow falling onto one of the jagged pieces of the glass. We wrapped the towel around his bleeding calf, and I drove like a maniac to an Urgent Care. They took him on back to the treatment area immediately, and I was not permitted to accompany him. That upset me, but I did not intend to antagonize the medical staff, so I obediently sat down in the waiting room.

Not more than a minute later, I heard my husband let out a blood-curdling scream and my heart almost stopped! Apparently, the physician had to perform internal, as well as external, suturing. When she was working on the internal sutures, she inadvertently hit one of the nerves in his leg with the needle and that's how the scream was induced. Therefore, I have a very graphic image of what Marinella is describing here, and to think of that pain multiplied many times over is inconceivable. My husband is quite strong physically, so if he screamed when that one nerve was touched, how could Jesus endure that hundreds of times? We'll never know.

Dr. Marinella speculates on other injuries Jesus might have sustained during the scourging:

Multiple rib fractures sometimes occurred due to the severe force inflicted by the flagellum. The bone and metal pieces could also tear through the small muscles between the ribs, the intercostal muscles, and enter the thoracic cavity, causing bleeding into the chest (hemothorax) or even causing collapse of the lung (pneumothorax). Scripture is definite that none of Jesus' bones was broken, but there is no Scripture to prove it wasn't possible that Christ suffered some of these other complications. It is doubtful His lungs fully collapsed, as this would have resulted in rapid death due to inability of the lungs to oxygenate the blood. Contusion or bruising of the lungs was possible, as sometimes complicates blunt trauma... it might have been very difficult for Jesus to breathe due to the severe pain, blood loss, and trauma to the back and intercostal muscles. A small pulmonary contusion, hemothorax, or pneumothorax cannot be ruled out, and would have added to Jesus' shortness of breath, a sensation known as dyspnea. One last injury that could potentially complicate scourging would be damage to the kidneys... the top portion of the kidneys has some protection provided by the rib cage, but the lower part is not afforded such protection and lies basically underneath the layers of back muscles. In fact, it is plausible that during a severe scourging the metal or bone fragments on the flagrum could tear through the muscle and dig into the kidney causing significant damage. I suspect Jesus suffered contusion to His kidneys which could have resulted in bleeding into the urinary tract, a condition known as hematuria. If the bleeding was significant, a clot could have formed within the ureter (the tube that connects the kidneys to the bladder) and caused obstruction and spasm of the ureter resulting in pain similar to passing a kidney stone.[25]

I have suffered as a result of passing two kidney stones, and the pain feels quite unbearable. Now I know that my Lord suffered from such pain and can understand those feelings of agony. What He went through because of His scourging alone killed many men. What I don't like to think about (and would prefer to just zoom on to the Resurrection) was real, agonizing, bodily suffering, the likes of which we cannot begin to fathom. What I can't imagine would be the pain coming from everywhere inside His body and on His skin. However, these graphic descriptions have given me an idea of what it might have been like for Jesus during His scourging.

Mel Gibson was criticized for making *The Passion of the Christ* so graphic and violent. When interviewed, his comment on that evaluation was that he only got somewhat close to depicting Jesus' true suffering and that if he showed what actually happened, no one would be able to tolerate seeing the film. Now that I have read medical accounts by physicians who have studied the scourging for years, Gibson's statement is completely credible.

———— ⟨∞⟩ ————

What did Jesus suffer while carrying the cross to Golgotha? Dr. Zugibe gives the most compelling description that I found during my research:

Most scholars support the theory that usually only the crosspiece or patibulum, weighing about 50 to 60 pounds, was carried by the crucarius to the place of crucifixion. The fact that the entire cross has been estimated to weigh well over 175 to 200 pounds and that scourging as a prelude to crucifixion causes extreme weakness further support the theory. While Mel Gibson's movie The Passion of the Christ depicts Jesus carrying the entire cross, it is unlikely that the victims [He] would have been physically able to do so.... When Jesus arrived at the crucifixion site, He was almost numb with severe exhaustion resulting from the severe mental and physical sufferings endured at the Garden of Gethsemane, the brutal flogging at the Praetorium, and the nerve-racking, lancinating pains from the crown of thorns. The exhaustion was accompanied by marked shortness of breath, the pleural fluid that was slowly accumulating around and within His lungs, and possible pneumothorax due to the brutal scourging, as well as the effects of the trek to Calvary. The noon sun was high, and the sweat poured all over Jesus' face and body. The intense heat of the sun and the weight of the crosspiece on His abraded shoulders considering the condition He was in would have induced intense weakness.... It was the exactor mortis's responsibility to make certain the crucarius did not die on the way to his crucifixion. The severity of Jesus' condition was obviously known by the exactor mortis. He was fearful that Jesus might not get up again and that he would not be able to execute his orders.... During the time that Jesus carried the cross, the extreme pains from trigeminal neuralgia radiated across His face and scalp every time He tripped and fell, and He suffered severe pains in all of His muscles and joints. He had more and more difficulty getting up each time He fell while bearing the weight of the cross.[26]

Other aspects of Jesus' suffering while carrying the cross are carefully set forth by Marinella:

Jesus began the approximately half-mile walk to Golgotha in an exhausted and near-shock-like condition. His legs were very weak due to the lack of food and from standing during the night trials, walking from place to place, and wounds inflicted during the scourging. Painful wounds on His back and on the back of Jesus' thighs from the scourging made it difficult to walk, let alone carry a large log upon His shoulders.... The pain of a heavy, rough, splinter-laden piece of wood must have been severe as it rubbed against the gaping wounds. For all the reasons noted in above sections, from a medical perspective it is surprising Christ could walk, even without carrying the wooden beam. Jesus likely had a significant drop in blood pressure shortly after embarking on the journey to Calvary. Dehydration, blood loss, severe pain, and stress can result in hypoten-sion, especially if one remains in the upright position…. Jesus' injuries could certainly have so weakened His body that He fell to the ground under the great weight of the pati-bulum. It likely was impossible for Him to rise from the ground without having the pati-bulum taken off of His shoulders. Also, as Jesus fell forward, His arms could not brace His fall since they were tied with ropes to the beam. This likely resulted in a full-force fall upon His chest, probably knocking the wind out of Him. A significant blunt force trauma to the breastbone can result in bruising of the heart muscle. This could result in a fluid collection around Jesus' heart which could lead to shock and low blood pressure, if not to death, making it impossible to finish this otherwise relatively short walk.[27]

Marinella then goes on to give a succinct description of crucifixion as a form of capital punish-ment in Jesus' time:

Capital punishment in the ancient world could be very brutal. In fact, the three most bar-baric forms of execution are said to be crux (Latin: cross, torture; crucifixion), cremate (burning alive with fire) and decollation (decapitation) of these crucifixion was consid-ered the most brutal. Cicero, a Roman politician and orator, stated that crucifixion was 'the most cruel and horrifying death'…. Some have stated that Titus crucified so many people during the A.D. 70 Jerusalem massacre that there was not enough room for all the crosses and not enough crosses for all of the bodies.[28]

In an article entitled "On the Physical Death of Jesus Christ" by William D. Edwards, M.D.; Wesley J. Gabel, M.Div.; and Floyd E Hosmer, M.S., AMI from *JAMA - The Journal of the American Medical Association,* there is a comprehensive description of the physical and medical aspects of the crucifixion. You can find a list of Edwards', Gabel's, and Hosmer's footnotes in my endnotes for Appendix C, number 29. The article has been quoted verbatim with permission.

It was customary for the condemned man to carry his own cross from the flogging post to the site of crucifixion outside the city walls.[8,11,30] He was usually naked, unless this was prohibited by local customs.[11] Since the weight of the entire cross was probably well over 300 lb. (136 kg), only the crossbar was carried.[11] The patibulum, weighing 75 to 125 lb. (34 to 57 kg),[11,30] was placed across the nape of the victim's neck and balanced along both shoulders. Usually, the outstretched arms then were tied to the crossbar.[7,11] The processional to the site of crucifixion was led by a complete Roman military guard, headed by a centurion.[3,11] One of the soldiers carried a sign (titulus) on which the con-demned man's name and crime were displayed.[3,11] Later, the titulus would be attached to the top of the cross.[11] The Roman guard would not leave the victim until they were sure of his death.[9,11]

Outside the city walls were permanently located the heavy upright wooden stipes, on which the patibulum would be secured. In the case of the Tau cross, this was accomplished by means of a mortise and tendon joint, with or without reinforcement by ropes. [10],[11],[30] To prolong the crucifixion process, a horizontal wooden block or plank, serving as a crude seat (sedile or sedulum), often was attached midway down the stipes.[3],[11],[16] Only very rarely, and probably later than the time of Christ, was an additional block (suppedaneum) employed for transfixion of the feet.[9],[11]

At the site of execution, by law, the victim was given a bitter drink of wine mixed with myrrh (gall) as a mild analgesic.[7],[17] The criminal was then thrown to the ground on his back, with his arms outstretched along the patibulum.[11] The hands could be nailed or tied to the crossbar, but nailing apparently was preferred by the Romans.[8],[11] The archaeological remains of a crucified body, found in an ossuary near Jerusalem and dating from the time of Christ, indicate that the nails were tapered iron spikes approximately 5 to 7 in. (13 to 18 cm) long with a square shaft 3/8 in. (1 cm) across. [23], [24], [30] Furthermore, ossuary findings and the Shroud of Turin have documented that the nails commonly were driven through the wrists rather than the palms. [22-24], [30]

After both arms were fixed to the crossbar, the patibulum and the victim, together, were lifted onto the stipes.[11] On the low cross, four soldiers could accomplish this relatively easily. However, on the tall cross, the soldiers used either wooden forks or ladders.[11]

Next, the feet were fixed to the cross, either by nails or ropes. Ossuary findings and the Shroud of Turin suggest that nailing was the preferred Roman practice.[23], [24], [30] Although the feet could be fixed to the sides of the stipes or to a wooden footrest (suppedaneum), they usually were nailed directly to the front of the stipes.[11] To accomplish this, flexion of the knees may have been quite prominent, and the bent legs may have been rotated laterally.[23-25],[30]

When the nailing was completed, the titulus was attached to the cross, by nails or cords, just above the victim's head.[11] The soldiers and the civilian crowd often taunted and jeered the condemned man, and the soldiers customarily divided his clothes among themselves. [11],[25] The length of survival generally ranged from three or four hours to three or four days and appears to have been inversely related to the severity of the scourging.[8],[11] However, even if the scourging had been relatively mild, the Roman soldiers could hasten death by breaking the legs below the knees (erurifragium or skelokopia).[8], [11]

Not uncommonly, insects would light upon or burrow into the open wounds or the eyes, ears, and nose of the dying and helpless victim, and birds of prey would tear at these sites.[16] Moreover, it was customary to leave the corpse on the cross to be devoured by predatory animals.[8, 11, 12, 28] However, by Roman law, the family of the condemned could take the body for burial, after obtaining permission from the Roman judge.[11]

Since no one was intended to survive crucifixions, the body was not released to the family until the soldiers were sure that the victim was dead. By custom, one of the Roman guards would pierce the body with a sword or lance.[8, 11] Traditionally, this had been considered a spear wound to the heart through the right side of the chest — a fatal wound probably taught to most Roman soldiers.[11] The Shroud of Turin documents this form of injury.[5, 11, 22] Moreover, the standard infantry spear, which was 5 to 6 ft (1.5 to 1.8 m) long, could easily have reached the chest of a man crucified on the customary low cross.

Medical Aspects of Crucifixion

With knowledge of both anatomy and ancient crucifixion practices, one may reconstruct the probable medical aspects of this form of slow execution. Each wound apparently was intended to produce intense agony, and the contributing causes of death were numerous.

The scourging prior to crucifixion served to weaken the condemned man and, if blood loss was considerable, to produce orthostatic hypotension and even hypovolemic shock.[8, 12] When the victim was thrown to the ground on his back, in preparation for transfixion of the hands, his scourging wounds most likely would become torn open again and contaminated with dirt.[2, 16] Furthermore, with each respiration, the painful scourging wounds would be scraped against the rough wood of the stipes.[7] As a result, blood loss from the back probably would continue throughout the crucifixion ordeal.

With arms outstretched but not taut, the wrists were nailed to the patibulum.[7, 11] It has been shown that the ligaments and bones of the wrist can support the weight of a body hanging from them, but the palms cannot.[11] Accordingly, the iron spikes probably were driven between the radius and the carpals or between the two rows of carpal bones, [2, 10, 11, 30] either proximal to or through the strong band like flexor retinaeulum and the various interearpal ligaments. Although a nail in either location in the wrist might pass between the bony elements and thereby produce no fractures, the likelihood of painful periosteal injury would seem great. Furthermore, the driven nail would crush or sever the rather large sensorimotor median nerve.[2, 7, 11] The stimulated nerve would produce excruciating bolts of fiery pain in both arms.[7, 9] Although the severed median nerve would result in paralysis of a portion of the hand, isehemie eontraetures and impalement of various ligaments by the iron spike might produce a claw-like grasp.

Most commonly, the feet were fixed to the front of the stipes by means of an iron spike driven through the first or second inter metatarsal space, just distal to the tarsometa-tarsal joint.[2], [5], [8], [11], [30] It is likely that the deep peroneal nerve and branches of the medial and lateral plantar nerves would have been injured by the nails. Although scourging may have resulted in considerable blood loss, crucifixion per se was a relatively blood-less procedure, since no major arteries, other than perhaps the deep plantar arch, pass through the favored anatomic sites of transfixion. [2], [10], [11]

The major pathophysiologic effect of crucifixion, beyond the excruciating pain, was a marked interference with normal respiration, particularly exhalation. The weight of the body, pulling down on the outstretched arms and shoulders, would tend to fix the intercostal muscles in an inhalation state and thereby hinder passive exhalation. [2], [10], [11] Accordingly, exhalation was primarily diaphragmatic, and breathing was shallow. It is likely that this form of respiration would not suffice and that hypercarbia would soon result. The onset of muscle cramps or tetanic contractions, due to fatigue and hyper-carbia, would hinder respiration even further.[11]

Adequate exhalation required lifting the body by pushing up on the feet and by flexing the elbows and adducting the shoulders. [2] However, this maneuver would place the entire weight of the body on the tarsals and would produce searing pain.[7] Furthermore, flexion of the elbows would cause rotation of the wrists about the iron nails and cause fiery pain along the damaged median nerves.[7] Lifting of the body would also painfully scrape the scourged back against the rough wooden stipes. [2], [7] Muscle cramps and paresthesias of the outstretched and uplifted arms would add to the discomfort. [7] As a result, each respiratory effort would become agonizing and tiring and lead eventually to asphyxia. [2], [3], [7], [10], [11]

The actual cause of death by crucifixion was multifactorial and varied somewhat with each ease, but the two most prominent causes probably were hypovolemic shock and exhaustion asphyxia.[2], [3], [7], [10] Other possible contributing factors included dehydration, [7], [16] stress-induced arrhythmias,[3] and congestive heart failure with the rapid accumulation of pericardial and perhaps pleural effusions. [2], [7], [11] Crucifracture (breaking the legs below the knees), if performed, led to an asphyxic death within minutes.[11] Death by crucifixion was, in every sense of the word, excruciating (Latin, excruciatus, or "out of the cross").[29]

After studying all the medical accounts of the crucifixion, I have come to believe what the forensic investigator, Dr. Frederick Zugibe, concluded about the cause of Jesus' death:

If I were to certify the cause of Jesus' death in my official capacity as Medical Examiner, the death certificate would read as follows. Cause of Death: Cardiac and respiratory arrest, due to hypovolemic and traumatic shock, due to crucifixion[30]

It also became obvious from my studies that Jesus decided Himself when He was going to die, not anyone else. This only confirms His statement, "Father, into Your hands I commit My spirit." In addition, the fact that He died after yelling, "It is finished," leads me to that conclusion, because His other six statements from the cross came with much effort amidst all the trouble He was having breathing. Jesus was letting us know, by that loud voice, that He was laying His life down... no one was taking it from Him.

The Verbal, Emotional, and Spiritual Abuse Jesus Suffered

That Jesus suffered verbal, emotional, and spiritual abuse during His ministry, trial, and cruci-fixion is definitely backed up by Scripture (when He was 30-33 years of age). I can only speculate that even during His childhood, people might have ridiculed His status as a child conceived out of wedlock.

However, once He started His ministry, the abuse never stopped! He was accused, condemned, scorned, ridiculed, mocked, and overall rejected. The following Bible verses illustrate how Jesus was verbally, emotionally, and spiritually abused. The verses quoted below are all from the Amplified Bible:

And the tempter came and said to Him, If You are God's Son, command these stones to be made (loaves of) bread. But He replied, It has been written, Man shall not live and be upheld and sustained by bread alone, but by every word that comes forth from the mouth of God. Then the devil took Him into the holy city and placed Him on a turret (pinnacle, gable) of the temple sanctuary. And he said to Him, If You are the Son of God, throw Yourself down; for it is written, He will give His angels charge over you, and they will bear you up on their hands, lest you strike your foot against a stone. Jesus said to him, On the other hand, it is written also, You shall not tempt, test thoroughly, or try exceed-ingly the Lord your God (Matthew 4:3-8).

And behold, the whole town went out to meet Jesus; and as soon as they saw Him, they begged Him to depart from their locality (Matthew 8:34).

And behold, some of the scribes said to themselves, This man blasphemes [He claims the rights and prerogatives of God]! (Matthew 9:3).

He said, Go away; for the girl is not dead but sleeping. And they laughed and jeered at Him (Matthew 9:24).

The Son of Man came eating and drinking [with others], and they say, Behold, a glutton and a wine drinker, a friend of tax collectors and [especially wicked] sinners! (Matthew 11:19).

And when the Pharisees saw it, they said to Him, See there! Your disciples are doing what is unlawful and not permitted on the Sabbath. And behold, a man was there with one withered hand. And they said to Him, Is it lawful or allowable to cure people on the Sabbath days? that they might accuse Him. But the Pharisees, hearing it, said, This Man drives out demons only by and with the help of Beelzebub, the prince of demons. Then some of the scribes and Pharisees said to Him, Teacher, we desire to see a sign or miracle from You [proving that You are what You claim to be] (Matthew 12:2, 10, 24, 38).

And coming to His own country [Nazareth], He taught in their synagogue so that they were amazed with bewildered wonder, and said, Where did this Man get this wisdom and these miraculous powers? Is not this the carpenter's Son? Is not His mother called Mary? And are not His brothers James and Joseph and Simon and Judas? And do not all His sisters live here among us? Where then did this Man get all this? And they took offense at Him [they were repelled and hindered from acknowledging His authority, and caused to stumble]. But Jesus said to them, A prophet is not without honor except in his own country and in his own house. And He did not do many works of power there, because of their unbelief (their lack of faith in the divine mission of Jesus) (Matthew 13:54-59).

Then from Jerusalem came scribes and Pharisees and said, Why do Your disciples transgress and violate the rules handed down by the elders of the past? For they do not practice [ceremonially] washing their hands before they eat (Matthew 15:1-2).

Now the Pharisees and Sadducees came up to Jesus, and they asked Him to show them a sign (spectacular miracle) from heaven [attesting His divine authority] (Matthew 16:1).

When they arrived in Capernaum, the collectors of the half-shekel [the temple tax] went up to Peter and said, Does not your Teacher pay the half shekel? (Matthew 17:24).

And Pharisees came to Him and put Him to the test by asking, Is it lawful and right to dismiss and repudiate and divorce one's wife for any and every cause? (Matthew 19:3).

But when the chief priests and the scribes saw the wonderful things that He did and the boys and the girls and the youths and the maidens crying out in the porches and courts of the temple, Hosanna (O be propitious, graciously inclined) to the Son of David! they were indignant. And they said to Him, Do You hear what these are saying? And Jesus replied to them, Yes; have you never read, Out of the mouths of babes and unweaned infants You have made (provided) perfect praise? And when He entered the sacred enclosure of the temple, the chief priests and elders of the people came up to Him as He was teaching and said, By what power of authority are You doing these things, and who gave You this power of authority? (Matthew 21:15-16, 23).

Then the Pharisees went and consulted and plotted together how they might entangle Jesus in His talk. And they sent their disciples to Him along with the Herodians, saying, Teacher, we know that You are sincere and what You profess to be and that You teach the way of God truthfully, regardless of consequences and being afraid of no man; for You are impartial and do not regard either the person or the position of anyone. Tell us then what You think about this: Is it lawful to pay tribute [levied on individuals and to be paid yearly] to Caesar or not? But Jesus, aware of their malicious plot, asked, Why do you put Me to the test and try to entrap Me, you pretenders (hypocrites)? (Matthew 22:15-18).

Then the high priest tore his clothes and exclaimed, He has uttered blasphemy! What need have we of further evidence? You have now heard His blasphemy. Then they spat in His face and struck Him with their fists; and some [y]slapped Him in the face, Saying, Prophesy to us, You Christ (the Messiah)! Who was it that struck You? (Matthew 26:65-68).

And, weaving a crown of thorns, they put it on His head and put a reed (staff) in His right hand. And kneeling before Him, they made sport of Him, saying, Hail (greetings, good health to You, long life to You), King of the Jews! And they spat on Him, and took the reed (staff) and struck Him on the head. And when they finished making sport of Him, they stripped Him of the robe and put His own garments on Him and led Him away to be crucified (Matthew 27:29-31).

And those who passed by spoke reproachfully and abusively and jeered at Him, wagging their heads, And they said, You Who would tear down the sanctuary of the temple and rebuild it in three days, rescue Yourself from death. If You are the Son of God, come down from the cross. In the same way, the chief priests, with the scribes and elders, made sport of Him, saying, He rescued others from death; Himself He cannot rescue from death. He is the King of Israel? Let Him come down from the cross now, and we will believe in and acknowledge and cleave to Him. He trusts in God; let God deliver Him now if He cares for Him and will have Him, for He said, I am the Son of God. And the robbers who were crucified with Him also abused and reproached and made sport of Him in the same way (Matthew 27:39-43).

After these things Jesus walked in Galilee; for He did not want to walk in Judea, because the Jews sought to kill Him. Now the Jews' Feast of Tabernacles was at hand. His brothers therefore said to Him, Depart from here and go into Judea, that Your disciples also may see the works that You are doing. For no one does anything in secret while he himself seeks to be known openly. If You do these things, show Yourself to the world. For even His brothers did not believe in Him. Then Jesus said to them, My time has not yet come, but your time is always ready. The world cannot hate you, but it hates Me because I testify of it that its works are evil. You go up to this feast. I am not yet going up to this feast, for My time has not yet fully come. When He had said these things to them, He remained in Galilee (John 7:1-9).

Then He went out from there and came to His own country, and His disciples followed Him. And when the Sabbath had come, He began to teach in the synagogue. And many hearing Him were astonished, saying, Where did this Man get these things? And what wisdom is this that is given to Him, that such mighty works are performed by His hands! Is this not the carpenter, the Son of Mary, and brother of James, Joses, Judas, and Simon? And are not His sisters here with us? So they were offended at Him. But Jesus said to them, A prophet is not without honor except in his own country, among his own relatives, and in his own house. Now He could do no mighty work there, except that He laid His hands on a few sick people and healed them. And He marveled because of their unbelief. Then He went about the villages in a circuit, teaching (Mark 6:1-6).

So He came to Nazareth, where He had been brought up. And as His custom was, He went into the synagogue on the Sabbath day, and stood up to read. And He was handed the book of the prophet Isaiah. And when He had opened the book, He found the place where it was written:

> *The Spirit of the LORD is upon Me,*
> *Because He has anointed Me*
> *To preach the gospel to the poor;*
> *He has sent Me to heal the brokenhearted,*
> *To proclaim liberty to the captives*
> *And recovery of sight to the blind,*
> *To set at liberty those who are oppressed;*
> *To proclaim the acceptable year of the LORD.*

Then He closed the book, and gave it back to the attendant and sat down. And the eyes of all who were in the synagogue were fixed on Him. And He began to say to them, Today this Scripture is fulfilled in your hearing. So all bore witness to Him, and marveled at the gracious words that proceeded out of His mouth. And they said, Is this not Joseph's son? He said to them, You will surely say this proverb to Me, Physician, heal yourself! Whatever we have heard done in Capernaum do also here in Your country. Then He said, Assuredly, I say to you, no prophet is accepted in his own country. But I tell you truly, many widows were in Israel in the days of Elijah, when the heaven was shut up three years and six months, and there was a great famine throughout all the land; but to none of them was Elijah sent except to Zarephath, in the region of Sidon, to a woman who was a widow. And many lepers were in Israel in the time of Elisha the prophet, and none of them was cleansed except Naaman the Syrian. So all those in the synagogue, when they heard these things, were filled with wrath, and rose up and thrust Him out of the city; and they led Him to the brow of the hill on which their city was built, that they might throw Him down over the cliff. Then passing through the midst of them, He went His way (Luke 4:16-30).

※

Jesus suffered complete and total abandonment through the majority of His passion. When He needed His disciples to intercede for Him, they were asleep at the switch:

Rarely, if ever, did Jesus need His friends' assistance. More of the time, they needed His! But in this intense moment, Jesus really felt a need to have the three disciples who were closest to Him pray with Him. Jesus asked these disciples to pray for just one hour. But instead of faithfully praying when Jesus desperately needed their support, the three disciples kept falling asleep! The mental and spiritual battle Jesus experienced that night in the Garden of Gethsemane was intense. In fact, Luke 22:44 says, 'And being in an agony….' I want you to especially notice the word 'agony' in this verse. It comes from the Greek word agonidzo, a word that refers to a struggle, a fight, great exertion, or effort. It is a word often used in the New Testament to convey the ideas of anguish, pain, distress, and conflict. The word agonidzo itself comes from the word agaon, which is the word that depicted the athletic conflicts and competitions that were so famous in the ancient world. The Holy Spirit used this word to picture Jesus in the Garden of Gethsemane on the night of His betrayal…. The spiritual pressure that bore down upon Jesus' soul was so overwhelming that the Bible says it was agonidzo… It was so strenuous that it involved all of Jesus' spirit, soul, and body. He was in the greatest fight He had ever known up to that moment…. This was the worst spiritual combat Jesus had ever endured up to this time. And where were His disciples when He needed them? They were sleeping! Jesus needed His closest friends – yet they couldn't even pray for one hour! [31]

The next abandonment consisted of the Jesus' betrayal by Judas:

Betraying Jesus with a kiss was about as low as a person could go. It was like saying, 'You and I are friends forever. Now please turn around so I can sink my dagger into your back! You see, the kiss Judas gave was a false kiss that revealed insincerity, bogus love, and a phony commitment. The fact that it was premeditated made it even worse. This was no last minute, accidental betrayal; it was well planned and very deliberate…. Judas played the game all the way to the end, working closely with Jesus and remaining a part of His inner circle. Then at the preappointed time, Judas drove in the dagger as deeply as he could.[32]

The worst abandonment came for Jesus when He was on the cross. When He uttered, "My God, My God, why has Thou forsaken me," He wasn't just quoting Scripture. John Macarthur sums up those moments on the cross:

Some commentators have gone to great lengths to explain why Jesus would utter such words. To them, it seems unthinkable that Jesus would actually feel abandoned on the cross – and even more unthinkable to surmise that God in any sense abandoned His beloved Son. And so they insist that Jesus was merely reciting Scripture, not expressing what He truly felt in His heart. But that betrays a serious misunderstanding of what was taking place on the cross As Christ hung there, He was bearing the sins of the world. He was dying as a substitute for others. To Him was imputed the guilt of their sins, and He was suffering the punishment for those sins on their behalf. And the very essence of that punishment was the outpouring of God's wrath against sinners. In some mysterious way during those awful hours on the cross, the Father poured out the full measure of His wrath against sin, and the recipient of that wrath was God's own beloved Son! In this lies the true meaning of the cross…. Here's what was happening on the cross: God was punishing His own Son as if He had committed every wicked deed done by ever sinner who would ever believe. And He did it so that He could forgive and treat those redeemed ones as if they had lived Christ's perfect life of righteousness.[33]

———— ⬿⬿ ————

Sometimes, when one is very familiar with a story, when they recite it or teach about it they have lost the depth of meaning represented by the account. This can certainly be true about Jesus' choice to forgive those who mocked, scourged, and crucified Him. He made a conscious, volitional choice to forgive what those who abused Him. We can certainly see Him as the ultimate role model when it comes to forgiving abuse and trusting His Father to work everything out for His good.

> *The first [saying of the seven last sayings of Christ] was a plea for mercy on behalf of His tormentors. Luke records that shortly after the cross was raised on Calvary – while the soldiers were still gambling for His clothing, He prayed to God for forgiveness on their behalf: 'And when they had come to the place called Calvary, there they crucified Him, and the criminals, one on the right hand and the other on the left. Then Jesus said, 'Father, forgive them, for they do not know what they do.' While others were mocking Him – just as the taunting and jeering reached a fever pitch – Christ responded in precisely the opposite way most men would have. Instead of threatening, lashing back, or cursing His enemies, He prayed to God on their behalf…. Certainly, any mortal man would have desired only to curse or revile his killers under these circumstances…. But Christ was on a mission of mercy. He was dying to purchase forgiveness for sins. And even at the very height of His agony, compassion was what filled His heart.*[34]

I've had a certain gripe that has permeated my process of forgiveness. It was almost impossible to believe that those who abused me really had no idea what they were doing. I simply couldn't make this statement as I prayed for them. MacArthur addresses this question with his unique take on the seven last sayings of Jesus:

> *The phrase 'for they do not know what they do' does not suggest that they were unaware that they were sinning. Ignorance does not absolve anyone from sin. These people were behaving wickedly, and they knew it. Most were fully aware of the fact of their wrongdoing. Pilate himself had testified of Jesus' innocence. The Sanhedrin was fully aware that no legitimate charges could be brought against Him. The soldiers and the crowd could easily see that a great injustice was being done, and yet they all gleefully participated. Many of the taunting spectators at Calvary had heard Christ teach and seen Him do miracles. They could not have really believed in their hearts that He deserved to die this way. Their ignorance itself was inexcusable, and it certainly did not absolve them of guilt for what they were doing. But they were ignorant of the enormity of their crime. They were blinded to the full reality that they were crucifying God the Son. They were spiritually insensitive, because they loved darkness rather than light. Therefore, they did not recognize that the One they were putting to death was the Light of the World. 'Had they known they would not have crucified the Lord of glory' (1 Corinthians 2:8).*[35]

MacArthur continues to relate the fruit of this High Priestly prayer. The thief on the cross was converted. The next one converted was the centurion. Untold numbers of people were saved at Pentecost. "No doubt many of them were the same people who had clamored for Jesus' death and railed at Him from the foot of the cross. We're told in Acts 6:7, for example, that a great number of the temple priests later confessed Jesus as Lord."[36] But he then makes a crucial distinction:

> *It is important to understand that Jesus' plea for his killers' forgiveness did not guarantee the immediate and unconditional forgiveness of everyone who participated in the crucifixion. He was interceding on behalf of all who would repent and turn to Him as Lord and Savior. His prayer was that when they finally realized the enormity of what they had done and sought the heavenly Father's forgiveness for their sin, He would not hold the murder of His beloved Son against them. <u>Divine forgiveness is never granted to people who remain in unbelief and sin</u> (emphasis added).* [37]

How did Jesus demonstrate His utter trust in the Father? There are verses that can pass by largely unnoticed that explains everything:

> *Therefore we also, since we are surrounded by so great a cloud of witnesses, let us lay aside every weight, and the sin which so easily ensnares us, and let us run with endurance the race that is set before us, looking unto Jesus, the author and finisher of our faith, who for the joy that was set before Him endured the cross, despising the shame, and has sat down at the right hand of the throne of God. For consider Him who endured such hostility from sinners against Himself, lest you become weary and discouraged in your souls (Hebrews 12:1-3).*

Please know that I have barely scratched the surface of all the material that has been written and disseminated concerning the abuse Jesus suffered. If you ever begin to fall into the trap of thinking that Jesus doesn't know what you feel because of your abuse, or you begin to take for granted what He did for you, please refer to the endnotes and bibliography for excellent resources that thoroughly address this question.

Appendix D

Who You Are in Christ (Developing Christ-Esteem)

I am accepted.

John 1:12	I am God's child.
John 15:15	I am Christ's friend.
Romans 5:1	I have been justified.
1 Corinthians 6:17	I am united with the Lord, and I am one spirit with Him.
1 Corinthians 6:19-20	I have been bought with a price. I belong to God.
1 Corinthians 12:27	I am a member of Christ's Body.
Ephesians 1:1	I am a saint.
Ephesians 1:5	I have been adopted as God's child.
Ephesians 2:18	I have direct access to God though the Holy Spirit.
Colossians 1:14	I have been redeemed and forgiven of all my sins.
Colossians 2:10	I am complete in Christ.

I am secure.

Romans 8:1-2	I am free from condemnation.
Romans 8:28	I am assured that all things work together for good.
Romans 8:31-34	I am free from any condemning charges against me.
Romans 8:35-39	I cannot be separated from the love of God.
2 Corinthians 1:21-22	I have been established, anointed and sealed by God.
Philippians 1:6	I am confident that the good work God has begun in me will be perfected.
Philippians 3:20	I am a citizen of heaven.
Colossians 3:3	I am hidden with Christ in God.
2 Timothy 1:7	I have not been given a spirit of fear but of power, love, and a sound mind.
Hebrews 4:16	I can find grace and mercy to help in time of need.
1 John 5:18	I am born of God and the evil one cannot touch me.

I am significant.

Matthew 5:13-14	I am the salt and light of the earth.
John 15: 1, 5	I am a branch of the true vine, a channel of His life.
John 15:16	I have been chosen and appointed to bear fruit.
Acts 1:8	I am a personal witness of Christ.
1 Corinthians 3:16	I am God's temple.

2 Corinthians 5:17-21	I am a minister of reconciliation for God.
2 Corinthians 6:1	I am God's coworker (see 1 Corinthians 3:9).
Ephesians 2:6	I am seated with Christ in the heavenly realm.
Ephesians 2:10	I am God's workmanship.
Ephesians 3:12	I may approach God with freedom and confidence.
Philippians 4:13	I can do all things through Christ who strengthens me.

In Christ

Since I am in Christ:

Matthew 5:13	I am the salt of the earth.
Matthew 5:14	I am the light of the world.
John 1:12	I am God's child.
John 15:1,5	I am a branch of the true vine, a channel of Christ's life.
John 15:15	I am Christ's friend.
John 15:16	I have been chosen and appointed to bear fruit.
Romans 6:18	I am a slave of righteousness.
Romans 6:22	I am enslaved to God.
Romans 8:14-15	I am a son or daughter of God.
Romans 8:17	I am a joint heir with Christ, sharing His inheritance with Him.
1 Corinthians 3:16	I am God's temple.
1 Corinthians 6:17	I am united with the Lord, and I am one spirit with Him.
1 Corinthians 12:27	I am a member of Christ's Body.

2 Corinthians 5:17	I am a new creation.
2 Corinthians 5:18-19	I am reconciled to God and am a minister of reconciliation.
Galatians 3:26-28	I am a son or daughter of God and one in Christ.
Galatians 4:6-7	I am an heir of God since I am a son or daughter of God.
Ephesians 1:1	I am a saint.
Ephesians 2:10	I am God's workmanship.
Ephesians 2:19	I am a fellow citizen with the rest of God's people in His family.
Ephesians 3:1; 4:1	I am a prisoner of Christ.
Ephesians 4:24	I am righteous and holy.
Philippians 3:20	I am a citizen of heaven.
Colossians 3:3	I am hidden with Christ in God.
Colossians 3:4	I am an expression of the life of Christ because He is my life.
Colossians 3:12	I am chosen of God, holy and dearly loved.
1 Thessalonians 1:4	I am beloved and elected by God.
1 Thessalonians 5:5	I am a son or daughter of light and not of darkness.
Hebrews 3:1	I am a holy brother or sister, partaker of a heavenly calling.
Hebrew 3:14	I am a partaker of Christ...I share in His life.
1 Peter 2:5	I am one of God's living stones and am being built up as a spiritual house.
1 Peter 2:9	I am a chosen race, a royal priesthood, a holy nation, a people for God's own possession to proclaim the excellencies of Him.

1 Peter 2:11	I am an alien and a stranger to this world in which I temporarily live.
1 Peter 5:8	I am an enemy of the devil.
1 John 3:1-2	I am now a child of God. I will resemble Christ when He returns.
1 John 5:18	I am born of God and the evil one cannot touch me.
Exodus 3:14; John 8:58; 1 Corinthians 15:10	I am not the great I AM, but by the grace of God, I am who I am.

Twenty Cans of Success

1. Why should I say I can't when the Bible says I can do all things through Christ who gives me strength? (See Philippians 4:13.)

2. Why should I worry about my needs when I know that God will take care of all my needs according to His riches in glory in Christ Jesus? (See Philippians 4:19.)

3. Why should I fear when the Bible says God has not given me a spirit of fear, but of power, love and a sound mind? (See Timothy 1:7.)

4. Why should I lack faith to live for Christ when God has given me a measure of faith? (See Romans 12:3.)

5. Why should I be weak when the Bible says the Lord is the strength of my life and that I will display strength and tack action because I know God? (See Psalm 27:1; Daniel 11:32.)

6. Why should I allow Satan control over my life when He that is in me is greater than he that is in the world? (See 1 John 4:4.)

7. Why should I accept defeat when the Bible says that God always leads me in victory? (See 2 Corinthians 2:14.)

8. Why should I lack wisdom when I know that Christ became wisdom to me from God and that God gives wisdom to me generously when I ask Him for it? (See 1 Corinthians 1:30; James 1:5.)

9. Why should I be depressed when I can recall to mind God's loving-kindness, compassion, faithfulness and have hope: (See Lamentations 3:21-23.)

10. Why should I worry and be upset when I can cast all my anxieties on Christ who cares for me? (See 1 Peter 5:7.)

11. Why should I ever be in bondage knowing that there is freedom where the Spirit of the Lord is? (See 1 Corinthians 3:17; Galatians 5:1.)

12. Why should I feel condemned when the Bible says there is no condemnation for those who are in Christ Jesus? (See Romans 8:1.)

13. Why should I feel alone when Jesus said He is with me always and He will never leave nor forsake me? (See Matthew 28:20; Hebrews 13:5.)

14. Why should I feel like I'm cursed or have bad luck when the Bible says that Christ rescued me from the curse of the law that I might receive His Spirit by faith? (See Galatians 3:13-14.)

15. Why should I be unhappy when I, like Paul, can learn to be content whatever the circumstances? (See Philippians 4:11.)

16. Why should I feel worthless when Christ became sin for me so that I might become the righteousness of God? (See 2 Corinthians 5:21.)

17. Why should I feel helpless in the presence of others when I know that if God is for me, who can be against me? (See Romans 8:31.)

18. Why should I be confused when God is the author of peace and He gives me knowledge through His Spirit who lives in me? (See 1 Corinthians 2:12; 14:33.)

19. Why should I feel like a failure when I am more than a conqueror through Christ who loved me? (See Romans 8:37.)

20. Why should I let the pressures of life bother me when I can take courage knowing that Jesus has overcome the world and its problems? (See John 16:33.)

Scriptures Pertaining to Forgiving Others and Trusting God

Forgiving Others

1. <u>Genesis 50:17</u>. Thus you shall say to Joseph: I beg you, please forgive the trespass of your brothers and their sin; for they did evil to you. Now, please, forgive the trespass of the servants of the God of your father. And Joseph wept when they spoke to him.
2. <u>Exodus 10:17</u>. Now therefore, please forgive my sin only this once, and entreat the LORD your God, that He may take away from me this death only.
3. <u>1 Samuel 25:28</u>. Please forgive the trespass of your maidservant. For the LORD will certainly make for my lord an enduring house, because my lord fights the battles of the LORD, and evil is not found in you throughout your days.
4. <u>Matthew 6:12</u>. And forgive us our debts, as we forgive our debtors.
5. <u>Matthew 6:14</u>. For if you forgive men their trespasses, your heavenly Father will also forgive you.
6. <u>Matthew 6:15</u>. But if you do not forgive men their trespasses, neither will your Father forgive your trespasses.
7. <u>Matthew 18:21</u>. Then Peter came to Him and said, Lord, how often shall my brother sin against me, and I forgive him? Up to seven times?
8. <u>Matthew 18:35</u>. So My heavenly Father also will do to you if each of you, from his heart, does not forgive his brother his trespasses.
9. <u>Mark 11:25</u>. And whenever you stand praying, if you have anything against anyone, forgive him, that your Father in heaven may also forgive you your trespasses.
10. <u>Mark 11:26</u>. But if you do not forgive, neither will your Father in heaven forgive your trespasses.

11. Luke 6:37. Judge not, and you shall not be judged. Condemn not, and you shall not be condemned. Forgive, and you will be forgiven.
12. Luke 11:4. And forgive us our sins, for we also forgive everyone who is indebted to us. And do not lead us into temptation, but deliver us from the evil one.
13. Luke 17:3. Take heed to yourselves. If your brother sins against you, rebuke him; and if he repents, forgive him.
14. Luke 17:4. And if he sins against you seven times in a day, and seven times in a day returns to you, saying, I repent, you shall forgive him.
15. Luke 23:34. Then Jesus said, Father, forgive them, for they do not know what they do. And they divided His garments and cast lots.
16. John 20:23. If you forgive the sins of any, they are forgiven them; if you retain the sins of any, they are retained.
17. 2 Corinthians 2:7.... so that, on the contrary, you ought rather to forgive and comfort him, lest perhaps such a one be swallowed up with too much sorrow.
18. 2 Corinthians 2:10. Now whom you forgive anything, I also forgive. For if indeed I have forgiven anything, I have forgiven that one for your sakes in the presence of Christ,
19. Ephesians 4:32. And be kind to one another, tenderhearted, forgiving one another, even as God in Christ forgave you.
20. Colossians 3:13. ...bearing with one another, and forgiving one another, if anyone has a complaint against another; even as Christ forgave you, so you also must do.

Trusting God

1. 2 Samuel 22:3. The God of my strength, in whom I will trust; my shield and the horn of my salvation, my stronghold and my refuge; my Savior, You save me from violence.
2. 2 Samuel 22:31. As for God, His way is perfect; the word of the LORD is proven; He is a shield to all who trust in Him.
3. 2 Kings 18:5. He trusted in the LORD God of Israel, so that after him was none like him among all the kings of Judah, nor who were before him.
4. 2 Kings 18:22. But if you say to me, We trust in the LORD our God, is it not He whose high places and whose altars Hezekiah has taken away, and said to Judah and Jerusalem, You shall worship before this altar in Jerusalem?
5. 2 Kings 18:30. Nor let Hezekiah make you trust in the LORD, saying, The LORD will surely deliver us; this city shall not be given into the hand of the king of Assyria.
6. 2 Kings 19:10. Thus you shall speak to Hezekiah, king of Judah, saying: Do not let your God in whom you trust deceive you, saying, Jerusalem shall not be given into the hand of the king of Assyria.

7. <u>1 Chronicles 5:20</u>. And they were helped against them, and the Hagrites were delivered into their hand, and all who were with them, for they cried out to God in the battle. He heeded their prayer, because they put their trust in Him.
8. <u>Job 13:15</u>. Though He slay me, yet will I trust Him. Even so, I will defend my own ways before Him.
9. <u>Psalm 2:12</u>. Kiss the Son, lest He be angry, and you perish in the way, When His wrath is kindled but a little. Blessed are all those who put their trust in Him.
10. <u>Psalm 4:5</u>. Offer the sacrifices of righteousness, and put your trust in the LORD.
11. <u>Psalm 5:11</u>. But let all those rejoice who put their trust in You; let them ever shout for joy, because You defend them; let those also who love Your name be joyful in You.
12. <u>Psalm 7:1</u>. O LORD my God, in You I put my trust; save me from all those who persecute me, and deliver me,
13. <u>Psalm 9:10</u>. And those who know Your name will put their trust in You; for You, LORD, have not forsaken those who seek You.
14. <u>Psalm 11:1</u>. In the LORD I put my trust; how can you say to my soul, flee as a bird to your mountain?
15. <u>Psalm 13:5</u>. But I have trusted in Your mercy; my heart shall rejoice in Your salvation.
16. <u>Psalm 16:1</u>. Preserve me, O God, for in You I put my trust.
17. <u>Psalm 17:7</u>. Show Your marvelous lovingkindness by Your right hand, O You who save those who trust in You from those who rise up against them.
18. <u>Psalm 18:2</u>. The LORD is my rock and my fortress and my deliverer; my God, my strength, in whom I will trust; my shield and the horn of my salvation, my stronghold.
19. <u>Psalm 18:30</u>. As for God, His way is perfect; the word of the LORD is proven; He is a shield to all who trust in Him.
20. <u>Psalm 20:7.</u> Some trust in chariots, and some in horses; but we will remember the name of the LORD our God.
21. <u>Psalm 21:7</u>. For the king trusts in the LORD, and through the mercy of the Most High he shall not be moved.
22. <u>Psalm 22:4</u>. Our fathers trusted in You; they trusted, and You delivered them.
23. <u>Psalm 22:5</u>. They cried to You and were delivered; they trusted in You and were not ashamed.
24. <u>Psalm 22:8</u>. He trusted in the LORD, let Him rescue Him; let Him deliver Him, since He delights in Him!
25. <u>Psalm 22:9</u>. But You are He who took Me out of the womb; You made Me trust while on My mother's breasts.
26. <u>Psalm 25:2</u>. O my God, I trust in You; let me not be ashamed; let not my enemies triumph over me.
27. <u>Psalm 25:20</u>. Keep my soul, and deliver me; let me not be ashamed, for I put my trust in You.
28. <u>Psalm 26:1</u>. Vindicate me, O LORD, For I have walked in my integrity. I have also trusted in the LORD; I shall not slip.

29. Psalm 28:7. The LORD is my strength and my shield; my heart trusted in Him, and I am helped; therefore my heart greatly rejoices, and with my song I will praise Him.
30. Psalm 31:1. In You, O LORD, I put my trust; let me never be ashamed; deliver me in Your righteousness.
31. Psalm 31:6. I have hated those who regard useless idols; but I trust in the LORD.
32. Psalm 31:14. But as for me, I trust in You, O LORD; I say, You are my God.
33. Psalm 31:19. Oh, how great is Your goodness, which You have laid up for those who fear You, which You have prepared for those who trust in You in the presence of the sons of men!
34. Psalm 32:10. Many sorrows shall be to the wicked; but he who trusts in the LORD, mercy shall surround him.
35. Psalm 33:21. For our heart shall rejoice in Him, because we have trusted in His holy name.
36. Psalm 34:8. Oh, taste and see that the LORD is good; blessed is the man who trusts in Him!
37. Psalm 34:22. The LORD redeems the soul of His servants, and none of those who trust in Him shall be condemned.
38. Psalm 36:7. How precious is Your lovingkindness, O God! Therefore, the children of men put their trust under the shadow of Your wings.
39. Psalm 37:3. Trust in the LORD, and do good; dwell in the land, and feed on His faithfulness.
40. Psalm 37:5. Commit your way to the LORD, trust also in Him, and He shall bring it to pass.
41. Psalm 37:40. And the LORD shall help them and deliver them; He shall deliver them from the wicked, and save them, because they trust in Him.
42. Psalm 40:3. He has put a new song in my mouth – praise to our God; many will see it and fear, and will trust in the LORD.
43. Psalm 40:4. Blessed is that man who makes the LORD his trust, and does not respect the proud, or such as turn aside to lies.
44. Psalm 52:8. But I am like a green olive tree in the house of God; I trust in the mercy of God forever and ever.
45. Psalm 55:23. But You, O God, shall bring them down to the pit of destruction; bloodthirsty and deceitful men shall not live out half their days; but I will trust in You.
46. Psalm 56:3. Whenever I am afraid, I will trust in You.
47. Psalm 56:4. In God (I will praise His word), in God I have put my trust; I will not fear. What can flesh do to me?
48. Psalm 56:11. In God, I have put my trust; I will not be afraid. What can man do to me?
49. Psalm 57:1. Be merciful to me; O God, be merciful to me! For my soul trusts in You, and in the shadow of Your wings I will make my refuge, until these calamities have passed by.
50. Psalm 61:4. I will abide in Your tabernacle forever; I will trust in the shelter of Your wings. Selah.
51. Psalm 62:8. Trust in Him at all times, you people; pour out your heart before Him; God is a refuge for us. Selah.

52. Psalm 64:10. The righteous shall be glad in the LORD, and trust in Him. And all the upright in heart shall glory.
53. Psalm 71:1. In You, O LORD, I put my trust; Let me never be put to shame.
54. Psalm 71:5. For You are my hope, O Lord GOD; You are my trust from my youth.
55. Psalm 73:28. But it is good for me to draw near to God; I have put my trust in the Lord GOD, that I may declare all Your works.
56. Psalm 84:12. O LORD of hosts, blessed is the man who trusts in You!
57. Psalm 86:2. Preserve my life, for I am holy; You are my God; save Your servant who trusts in You!
58. Psalm 91:2. I will say of the LORD, He is my refuge and my fortress; my God, in Him I will trust.
59. Psalm 112:7. He will not be afraid of evil tidings; his heart is steadfast, trusting in the LORD.
60. Psalm 115:10. O house of Aaron, trust in the LORD; He is their help and their shield.
61. Psalm 115:11. You who fear the LORD, trust in the LORD; He is their help and their shield.
62. Psalm 118:8. It is better to trust in the LORD than to put confidence in man.
63. Psalm 118:9. It is better to trust in the LORD than to put confidence in princes.
64. Psalm 119:42. So shall I have an answer for him who reproaches me, for I trust in Your word.
65. Psalm 125:1. Those who trust in the LORD are like Mount Zion, which cannot be moved, but abides forever.
66. Psalm 135:18. Those who make them are like them; so is everyone who trusts in them.
67. Psalm 143:8. Cause me to hear Your lovingkindness in the morning, for in You do I trust; cause me to know the way in which I should walk, for I lift up my soul to You.
68. Proverbs 3:5. Trust in the LORD with all your heart, and lean not on your own understanding;
69. Proverbs 16:20. He who heeds the word wisely will find good, and whoever trusts in the LORD, happy is he.
70. Proverbs 22:19. So that your trust may be in the LORD, I have instructed you today, even you.
71. Proverbs 28:25. He who is of a proud heart stirs up strife, but he who trusts in the LORD will be prospered.
72. Proverbs 29:25. The fear of man brings a snare, but whoever trusts in the LORD shall be safe.
73. Proverbs 30:5. Every word of God is pure; He is a shield to those who put their trust in Him.
74. Isaiah 26:3. You will keep him in perfect peace, whose mind is stayed on You, because he trusts in You.
75. Isaiah 26:4. Trust in the LORD forever, For in YAH, the LORD, is everlasting strength.
76. Isaiah 36:7. But if you say to me, We trust in the LORD our God, is it not He whose high places and whose altars Hezekiah has taken away, and said to Judah and Jerusalem, you shall worship before this altar?

77. <u>Isaiah 36:15</u>. Nor let Hezekiah make you trust in the LORD, saying, The LORD will surely deliver us; this city will not be given into the hand of the king of Assyria.

78. <u>Isaiah 37:10</u>. Thus you shall speak to Hezekiah, king of Judah, saying: Do not let your God in whom you trust deceive you, saying, Jerusalem shall not be given into the hand of the king of Assyria.

79. <u>Isaiah 50:10</u>. Who among you fears the LORD? Who obeys the voice of His Servant? Who walks in darkness and has no light? Let him trust in the name of the LORD and rely upon his God.

80. <u>Isaiah 51:5</u>. My righteousness is near, My salvation has gone forth, and My arms will judge the peoples; the coastlands will wait upon Me, and on My arm they will trust.

81. <u>Isaiah 57:13</u>. When you cry out, let your collection of idols deliver you. But the wind will carry them all away, a breath will take them. But he who puts his trust in Me shall possess the land, and shall inherit My holy mountain.

82. <u>Jeremiah 7:14</u>. Therefore, I will do to the house that is called by My name, in which you trust, and to this place that I gave to you and your fathers, as I have done to Shiloh.

83. <u>Jeremiah 17:7</u>. Blessed is the man who trusts in the LORD, and whose hope is the LORD.

84. <u>Jeremiah 39:18</u>. For I will surely deliver you, and you shall not fall by the sword; but your life shall be as a prize to you, because you have put your trust in Me, says the LORD.

85. <u>Jeremiah 49:11.</u> Leave your fatherless children, I will preserve them alive; and let your widows trust in Me.

86. <u>Daniel 3:28</u>. Nebuchadnezzar spoke, saying, Blessed be the God of Shadrach, Meshach, and Abed-Nego, who sent His Angel and delivered His servants who trusted in Him, and they have frustrated the king's word, and yielded their bodies, that they should not serve nor worship any god except their own God!

87. <u>Nahum 1:7</u>. The LORD is good, a stronghold in the day of trouble; and He knows those who trust in Him.

88. <u>Zephaniah 3:12</u>. I will leave in your midst a meek and humble people, and they shall trust in the name of the LORD.

89. <u>Matthew 12:21</u>. And in His name, Gentiles will trust.

90. <u>2 Corinthians 1:10</u>.... who delivered us from so great a death, and does deliver us; in whom we trust that He will still deliver us,

91. <u>2 Corinthians 3:4</u>. And we have such trust through Christ toward God.

92. <u>Ephesians 1:12</u>.... that we who first trusted in Christ should be to the praise of His glory.

93. <u>Ephesians 1:13</u>. In Him you also trusted, after you heard the word of truth, the gospel of your salvation; in whom also, having believed, you were sealed with the Holy Spirit of promise,

94. <u>Philippians 2:19</u>. But I trust in the Lord Jesus to send Timothy to you shortly, that I also may be encouraged when I know your state.

95. <u>Philippians 2:24</u>. But I trust in the Lord that I myself shall also come shortly.

96. <u>1 Timothy 1:11</u>.... according to the glorious gospel of the blessed God that was committed to my trust.
97. <u>1 Timothy 4:10</u>. For to this end we both labor and suffer reproach, because we trust in the living God, who is the Savior of all men, especially of those who believe.
98. <u>1 Timothy 5:5</u>. Now she who is really a widow, and left alone, trusts in God and continues in supplications and prayers night and day.
99. <u>Hebrews 2:13</u>. And again, I will put My trust in Him. And again, Here am I and the children whom God has given Me.
100. <u>1 Peter 3:5</u>. For in this manner, in former times, the holy women who trusted in God also adorned themselves, being submissive to their own husbands...

Appendix F

Words to Me from the Father

I originally did not intend to publish the Father's words to me in this book. However, when we listen to Abba's voice, He often changes our plans. Apparently, I am supposed to share them. They were spoken to me over about a span of many years, and while I certainly won't include them all, I have tried to select ones that relate to forgiving others, trusting God, and yielding to His process of conforming His children to the image of Christ. I pray that they would encourage and inspire you on your journey with the Lord. There will also be words of encouragement about seeking intimacy with the Father. Bear in mind that these are excerpts from much longer journal entries… the Lord has plenty to say to us if we'll only listen to Him.

Many times the words He speaks to me are relevant to the Body of Christ at-large. We believers have so much in common when it comes to walking out our faith! You will see how slow I am at putting into practice what I know to be truth. Our growth in the Lord most often comes in fits and starts. Would that it were just a nice, steady ascent, but for most of us, it will be two steps forward and one back, as we are slow, sometimes stubborn, sheep.

As I read back over these selections, I can readily see how many times I bounced back and forth between trusting God and taking things into my own hands; feeling accepted and condemned by the Father; being obedient and disobedient; having faith and doubt; and learning/applying a spiritual principle only to revert back to old mindsets and behaviors. What a humbling realization that my walk with the Lord has been just like the Israelites going through the Wilderness to get to the Promised Land. In her article, "Are You Tired of Going Around the Same Mountain? Reasons Why You Haven't Made Progress," Nevada York makes some salient and incisive points that caused me to exclaim, "Ouch!" when I read it.

It took the Israelites forty years to make an eleven-day trip from Egypt to the Promised Land. Have you ever wondered why it took them so long? After all, the God of Israel performed miraculous signs – the 10 plagues of Egypt, parting of the Red Sea, and pillars of fire [and cloud] to free them from slavery only to have them wander around in the wilderness for 40 years? Do you feel as though you are currently in the wilderness? Have you been going around the 'same mountain' over and over, unable to make it to the Promised Land that the Lord has waiting for you? Let's take a moment to look at the mindset of the newly freed Israelites to see what took them so long. The Lord declared to the Children of Israel: 'Because the men who explored the land were there for forty days, you must wander in the wilderness for forty years – a year for each day, suffering the consequences of your sins... (Numbers14:34).' From the moment the Lord brought them out Egypt, the children of Israel tested His patience by murmuring and complaining about the food (manna from Heaven) and constantly speaking unbelief in God's promise of the Promised Land. Numbers chapter 14 records the most impressive and important... lesson learned when one is going through a testing period (wilderness) – our attitude toward God. Are we complaining over and over about our situation, and from the complaining do we allow the seed of unbelief to sprout in our life causing our never-ending existence in the wilderness?[1]

Ouch again! I have definitely been guilty of judging the Israelites and their lack of faith. Why did they spend 40 years out there, going around that same old mountain repeatedly? Even though the Lord makes the reason for their continuing struggle quite clear, it didn't occur to me that it just might apply to my own walk with Him! The longer I walk with the Lord, the more I see how capable I am of committing any sin under certain circumstances. This realization didn't make me humble – it broke me in a way that I needed to be re-broken while considering the Israelites now. I have repented and will never again look down on the Israelites!

Yet a funny thing happened as I was being broken while reviewing these words. Through reading all that back and forth motion in my own journey, I also saw the Lord's patience, faithfulness, gentleness, tenderness, as well as His even being stern when the situation warranted it (but never harsh or condemning). During the period that these words were given me, I grew from being a hypersensitive, fearful, mistrustful, insecure child of God to a reasonably secure, confident, even sometimes bold, warrior in His army.

Another noteworthy observation and conclusion: I feel great sorrow when I see how the Lord had to virtually beg me repeatedly to come into His presence. Sheer busyness can crowd Him out of our lives, even when we want that intimacy with Him! What I also noted was that the purification and refining process was constant, and I now conclude, is lifelong. That's what I have said elsewhere in this book regarding sanctification – that it takes your entire life. It is my belief that we never "arrive" spiritually while living in these mortal bodies.

If these words don't touch you or ring true to your spirit, that's fine, but at least you can get the sense of how the Father's voice differs from Satan's or your own self-talk (see Chapter Fourteen). **You will also notice that they never contradict Scripture and contain many quotes and paraphrases of Bible verses that I had never memorized.** May the Lord bless you through these His words to His loving, but sometimes slow and/or stubborn, daughter.

Come to Me, My Child, and rest. You become so tired and exhausted and can only be refreshed at My table. I would pour out on you rest and peace, you need only come to My feet and worship. Struggle not with the snares of people liking and approving of you; My approval needs to be your number one desire. I love you, My dear little Daughter, and that is the most important thing. Nothing you can or ever will do can take that away. My mercies are from everlasting to everlasting; My ways are truth and grace. Walk ye in them and henceforth you shall know a sweet, satisfying peace that is a balm to the torn places in your soul. I want to bandage and heal those ripped places that you might comfort others even as I have comforted you, My little one. Come to Me, and all will be well within.

Beloved one, you are mine and I AM yours. How can you ever give in to loneliness in a human sense when you have only to turn to Me and I AM with you – holding you in My firm but gentle embrace. I AM never rejects you, never compares you, never condemns you. You will find that nurture, that building up, that tenderness, that security that you have longed for all your life. Daughter, <u>know</u> that I AM pleased with you. You don't have to dance for Me, earn My love, perform, perform, perform. I love you because you are Mine – My very own dearly loved and cherished child. Bask in the warmth and the security of that love even as you bask in rays of sunshine.

I love you, My Child. Come to the foot of the cross with your burdens and cares, and I Myself shall lighten your load. Know and understand My might and power, and that all you need to do is kneel in My presence and I will work on thy behalf. My Spirit shall work; you shall rest. You are a lovely flower to Me, blossoming and blooming in My presence. The enemy would seek to squash you, to burden you with cares too great to bear. Let Me always be your burden-bearer. Rest in Me, My Child and your peace will be great. Lose yourself in My presence, for I seek to do great things through you as you yield all to Me, and I will bless you greatly. Die to yourself and I will lift you up - resurrect you to a new plane of thought and emotion. React not to the circumstances all around; give them no power in your life. They are fleeting, but I AM your anchor – steady for life. You can never trust Me too much, nor lean on Me too hard. Focus on Me and look not around you, for lo, I do a marvelous work in those who lean on Me, who trust Me with <u>every</u> aspect of their lives. I AM your safe place, My Daughter… run to Me.

Keep your eyes more on Me. You continue to become distracted with even well-meaning pursuits. Keep your eyes fixed on Me, and you will <u>never</u> regret it. Up 'til now, your life has been filled with hurts and regrets. No <u>more</u>, My Child. Instead, we will walk together on a path of blessing. Seek Me out as meaning EVERYTHING to you and you shall never be disappointed. Precious one, <u>abide</u> in Me. That's right, live in Me... drawing your nourishment from <u>Me</u> alone. Don't eat the leftovers the world has to offer. Rejoice in Me, Daughter, for the time is short on earth as you know it. Dig into my Word and let Me cultivate your ground, for I want My seedlings in you to become bountiful trees that produce much fruit.

Good morning, My Daughter. I would send you peace and courage this day. Courage to hold on, to have stamina and endurance during this time of testing and trial. Give all your cares to Me, for I, the Lord of the Universe, care deeply about everything that concerns you. Nothing is too small or minor for My attentive eye. Go out and deliver this message to those I send to you. I desire to heal their hurts and make them whole. All I need to do My work is a willing heart on the part of My Child. Unbeknown to you, I have been fashioning and shaping and molding and tailoring these circumstances in your life to aid in your development, your growth, and your walk with Me. It is natural for man to shrink away from pain... I ask you to do the supernatural, with My help. Face the pain and plunge into the center of it, for there You will find Me where I have been all along. I will never, ever, ever leave you in the midst of the storm even as I did not leave My disciples but came walking on the water to them. Fear not, My dear one, for truly I have already overcome the world. Call and I will answer you... I will meet you in the middle of the storm. Cling to Me, My fair one, and you will never be abandoned.

My Child, <u>know</u> that I love you. And as you internalize that fact, you will walk in confidence and boldness. You will not continue to feel needy in man's presence, seeking their approbation. That need is left out of your wounded child-heart. Come to Me more often, and I will flood you with My approval and encouragement. It will be <u>more</u> than enough for you.

My Child, I AM doing a beautiful work in you. My temple in you is being rebuilt. Continue to cast <u>all</u> your cares on Me, for I care so deeply for you. Be not dismayed by worldly events or the vicissitudes of life. Give every up and down cycle to Me, and I will make straight your paths. Nothing is too great for Me to overcome, but I need your trust to fully work in your life the way I long to do. Open wide the gates of your heart, and your healing will continue.

My Daughter, know My great love for you. Truly, it is unfathomable – it has no limits. You are a delight to Me, as I watch you grow and develop. You are truly becoming Mine in every way. Disregard the enemy's shouts to you; shout back with joy and praise. He is defeated and knows it, and his time is extremely short. Laugh at him and dismiss him, for you are pressing on in My Kingdom and I AM well pleased with that. Continue to come to our secret place of communion and fellowship, and you will never be disappointed. Our bond grows stronger daily as you put more and more of your trust in Me. I delight in that, Daughter – when you trust yourself to Me wholly, completely. Then I can work mighty wonders in your life and others, and there are no limitations. Trust in Me completely, My little one, and see the great and mighty things begin to happen which you have known not before.

My little one, know truly that I have dispensed My angels over you, to guard, guide, and protect you. You are safe in My keeping, Child, and you need never be afraid or carry that torment. Would that you knew exactly how safe you are, My lovely little one. For you are still anxious over thy loved ones, Child, and their power to hurt you with their words and actions. I want you to roll that heavy load over onto Me, My Child, the Rock of their offense. It is I they stumble over, and it is I whom they reject. Please see that clearly… it is I whom they reject. Know with certainty that any loss of people (family) that you sustain I will more than make up for. You will have more family than you know what to do with. So look not to these frail ones, these ones of clay and dust to fulfill you, satisfy you, and meet your needs. They never have and they never will. Only I will feed you and fill your every need. Just keep your eyes <u>fixed</u> on Me, your Abba.

Daughter, you have drifted away in your pain and frustration, and I AM drawing you back with cords of love. Fear not and fret not as the turmoil and chaos increase. Increase they will and must, but I, the Sovereign One, am working everything out perfectly according to My timetable. Do keep your eyes fixed on Me, for so many distractions will arise that you will lose sight of what I AM doing. Everything in your life lies in My hands, and I AM utterly trustworthy, utterly true. Do not dwell on the flaws and failures of your brothers and sisters in Christ, because I AM the author and finisher of their faith as well [my counseling clients]. Yield them to Me, surrender them as your spiritual children to Me. Their progress is My responsibility, not yours. Trust Me with them and do not agonize over their trials, for I AM working all things together for their good. Just continue to lift Me up, exalt Me and always turn their focus back to Me, whatever happens.

Your passion for justice and hatred for evil mirrors My heart. I gave you those feelings – just be sure not to confuse the sin and sinner. Continue to see in the spirit realm that you are wrestling with your archrival, Satan, and the principalities and powers of the nether world. Be not dismayed that the warfare intensifies – that just shows how quickly I AM returning and how near the enemy's doom is. Continue to teach your clients how to wage warfare, demonstrating all the principles I have taught you.

Love Me, My Daughter. When you feel overwhelmed and agitated, just love Me and My peace and calm will return to you. For as you love Me, I, the Lover of your soul, will flood and fill your being with light so bright it will eradicate the shadows of gloom that threaten to envelop you. I love you deeply and unreservedly, My Child.

My little Daughter, take heart! I AM your Sustainer, your Healer, and your Holy One. I will never fail nor forsake you. Look not to the arm of flesh to save you, only I can do that. I want to be your all in all, your sole support. People can comfort, people can give and encourage, but I alone provide life to your body and health to your marrow and bones. Let your love for Me grow and grow until you are saturated with it through and through. You can never love Me too much, nor overwhelm Me with your needs. I take care of everything that concerns you; I AM your Source. If there were no one else on this earth, I would take care of you fully and beautifully. I am weaning you from your dependence on man, for I AM your Rock, your High Tower, your Fortress, and your Refuge. Run into Me and you will find that rest for your soul. I love you deeply and tenderly, My beloved Daughter, and you need seek no other for that kind of love. It will never falter, change, waver, or be dependent on how well you perform or whether you are perfect. I came to save and seek the lost, the sinner. Amazing grace! Lean on that, not on performance. I, the Lord your God, love you with an everlasting love. I change not, nor fail not. Abide in Me, My lovely one.

I AM the Lord that healeth thee. Know with certainty that I see your need and your pain and have compassion for you, My wounded little lamb. I won't leave you; I will provide for you; I won't let you down. Keep hanging on and listening for My still, small voice. I will restore all that the enemy has stolen from you. Do not give in to despair, despondency, and futility. That's what Satan wants. He fights against you in a strong way, because you walk closely with Me and love Me. This feels like a gigantic setback, My Child, but I am using every day, every painful moment in My developing your endurance, your resistance against the enemy, and your trust in Me that cannot be shaken, no matter what comes. See to it that you do not give up; just lean fully on Me, and I will undertake your cause. Be obedient to my revelations about the condition of your heart and pursue forgiveness heartily.

O My little one, guard your heart. These are dark and dangerous days, filled with strife, contention and controversy. Be wise as a serpent and gentle as a dove. Speak blessing, not cursing, over those who do evil to you and others. Ask for My love when your own human love is finished, and you are repulsed or sickened at heart by what you hear. Again, I say to you, bless your enemies, and I will reward you with a peace so satisfying that nothing this world has to offer will compare with it. Know with certainty that I, the Master of the Universe, have all things under control and am working out My divine purposes in every area of your life. The struggle you are engaged in will produce the peaceable fruit of righteousness. Hang on, cling to Me, and I will bring it to pass.

My lovely Daughter, you bring joy to <u>My</u> heart. I AM with you always, undergirding and supporting you. Never go out alone, <u>always</u> acknowledge My presence within you and

surrounding you. That is your protection and your power, and you need <u>not</u> be defeated. Satan is viciously attacking My holy ones in this hour, and he is a cunning, sly opponent. But you need not be defeated by his antics, his strategy. Cover yourself and your loved ones with My blood, and he <u>shall</u> be conquered forever.

———— ✕✕✕ ————

O, My tender one, I long to shower you with My love. But you do not keep still for long enough periods of time to fully receive all that I have for you. Keep your eyes fixed firmly on Me and do not be distracted by the tumult in the land. For the waves are roaring loudly and there is much commotion. But I long to give you an inner peace that defies all human attempts at description.

———— ✕✕✕ ————

My little lamb, I AM your Wonderful, all-powerful Shepherd who cares for your needs and you need not turn to another. For we are linked, so bonded that our hearts can beat together. Just please keep focused on Me, for the enemy would distract you in subtler and subtler ways. He hates the communion we already share, and he wants to diminish your opportunities to spend time with your Beloved. Stand firm against these attacks, as subtle as they may be. I love you with all My heart, My precious, precious Daughter.

———— ✕✕✕ ————

I AM more than able to deliver those who walk closely with Me and seek My face above all else. Cling to Me closely as a toddler clings to her mother, for I will protect you, My little one. Give Me your unqualified trust, for I AM the utterly trustworthy One. Commit everything into My hand, especially things that perplex you – which you don't understand. For My ways and thoughts are higher than yours, but I AM always working everything together for your good.

———— ✕✕✕ ————

My little one, know that My love for you has no beginning and no end. It is not contingent on your actions but is unconditional in every sense. Do not walk in condemnation. Confess, repent, and get back up again and into the battle; do not be derailed by your failures. Satan likes you to stop fighting and slip down into the doldrums. But I say to you, "Stand up and keep on fighting… don't sit down and mope and brood for then the enemy exults over you for a longer period of time." I AM a God of continuous, progres-

sive action who cannot be stopped by any obstacle. Live in Me and you will not stop either, even as did Elijah under the tree after his great victory. Yes, you need to stop sometimes to recover, relax, and regroup, but don't let that become a long period of time, for the enemy can win many battles if you are AWOL.

My Child, you are learning the key to everything: forgiveness. For My people are weighted down with their burdens of offense, unresolved conflict, and bitterness. Truly, it is in My heart to free My people, but many will not be freed. Be not a part of that multitude, come out from among them and be separate. Be known for your forgiving spirit, kindness, graciousness, gentleness, and forbearing spirit. For these qualities in you bring joy to My heart and glory to My Name.

Lovely one, you bring joy to My heart as I watch your spiritual progress. You are beginning to see what death to self and sacrifice are all about. You need not struggle and strive; simply keep letting go and trusting Me with the things that frustrate you and the problems that bring you pain. Bring them to the foot of My Son's cross and lay them down. Watch what I, the Master Planner, do with them, as I tailor them to fit into the fashioning and molding of your soul. You have been allowing yourself lately to stay on the Potter's wheel and let Me shape you into a vessel I can use. For I alone determine a vessel's shape and function on the earth. If that vessel is quiescent in My hands, it will fulfill the magnificent plans and purposes I have for it. I saw your destiny before the foundations of the world were formed, just as I knew you before you drew your first breath. Truly, My Daughter, you bring Me pleasure when you yield to Me and allow My purposes to be fulfilled in you. It has been a long and arduous journey, I know, but it's starting to feel worth it, isn't it? Every agonizing situation of your childhood, teenage, and young adult years were grist for the mill, so to speak. No event, no matter how painful, has been wasted in your life. Especially as you deal with My broken ones, you minister out of a heart that has been tenderized like a piece of meat that has been pounded repeatedly. That pounding can be exquisitely painful, but, oh, is that piece of meat splendid and flavorful when it is cooked. This analogy extends further to the fires of consecration and purification that you are undergoing even now. They also bring out that flavor in you, My little one. Continue to entrust yourself into My care daily as you go forth, and I will continue to make all these things work together for your good.

My chosen one: Rise up and be not prostrated by the warfare you have been experiencing. Don't you know that I, King of the Universe, have been with you each step of the way? You are learning how much of the battle takes place in your mind in the war the enemy wages against you. The attack comes and your need to process it is necessarily bound to thinking My thoughts about that person or that situation. You really can choose whether to take offense or whether to cling more closely to Me and thus to be more intimate with Me than with anyone else.

Bless those who curse you and pray for those by whom you feel used and betrayed. That is a sure way to be more like Jesus. You are continually being molded into His image. Continue to remember that My approval is all you will truly ever need and that much of the time that will run counter to the opinions of men. Endure suffering, misunderstanding, and persecution as a good soldier and I will reward you richly for it. Rejoice and be glad in that suffering! Climb into My arms, My embrace, and you will never feel truly lonely again, My precious one.

Satan would seek to destroy you, but he cannot touch your spirit, for it is completely Mine. But he can bombard your thoughts, feelings, and body, so continue to consecrate everything unto Me, so there will be no opportunity for him to gain a foothold. Keep casting down vain imaginations and bringing every thought captive to the obedience of Christ, for this is My will for you, Daughter. Then you will walk in peace and rest, for the battleground is in the mind. When you trust Me completely for your past, present, and future, nothing will cause you alarm. This is the peace that passes all understanding that I promised to My followers. Don't be distracted by the turmoil in your land now, because I told you these things would happen, must happen before My return.

Daughter, I love you dearly. I see your sorrow over your sins, your repentance. This pleases Me, little one. It is all I ask of you – surrender of those things that are not My highest good for you. Let them slip from your fingers – as they are solely temporal and I will give you eternal rewards in place of them.

It is out of your brokenness that I fashion a true warrior in the Spirit. If you are not broken, you cannot serve Me with complete obedience. Brokenness engenders true submission, true humility. You took control over your life almost from the very beginning and notice how wonderful it feels to surrender and fall into My comforting, nurturing embrace. It is so restful, so calm, so peaceful, and so free from agitation and conflict. Your trust in Me is developing beautifully as you marvel at My power, My sovereignty, My exquisite timing. Rest in My arms, beloved, and there you will find perfect peace and tranquility. Notice that you are not passive, spiritually, in this state. It is that you are at peace and so calm inwardly that you can engage in fierce spiritual combat in the power of My strength in you, because you are unified, undivided. That is what is meant by being holy – becoming whole, unified, all parts operating in complete harmony. O My precious Daughter, continue drinking from My fountain of love and you will <u>never</u> thirst after the things of the world again.

My little one, you are so very precious in My sight. I long to gather you in My arms and hold you until everything of the earth life fades away to obscurity and our holy bond is sealed. I put your love for Me in your heart, but you have nourished and sustained it by continuing to seek My face with all your heart. Do that daily and be not content until you have established that conscious contact with Me, the Lover of your soul, as you go back into the fray. I AM always at your side, battling with you, and you never need to feel any fear again. Place any remaining fears of the future into My hand and leave them there. Didn't I tell you long ago that I would keep you? Haven't I kept My word up until now? So what prevents Me, the King of the Universe, from continuing to keep, shelter, abide in, and shower My grace upon you daily as you go forth? Just turn to Me whenever you feel uneasy or disquieted, and I will calm you, soothe you, fortify you, and build you up.

I continue to give you a tender heart for the broken ones, the crushed ones, and the hearts that truly want to know Me. Keep on pointing them to me, the Wonderful One, Counselor, and Great Physician. I will heal them, for that is My will for all who come to Me in humility and brokenness. Be a vessel through which I can flow, unhindered by human ego and unaware of the approbation or disdain of men, concentrating solely on being a conduit of grace, of the Holy Spirit's divine touch on their lives. Love them, Child, as I have loved you.

———∞∞———

Leave your schedule to Me and I will fill it as I see fit. Continue in your forgiveness work until it becomes a way of life and as natural as inhaling and exhaling. Then there will not be gaps in the wall of My protection surrounding you. Give me every care, and do <u>not</u> become overwhelmed. I will redeem your time and you will come to prioritize in such a way that anything extraneous will be quickly discarded. The steps of the righteous are ordered… commit your steps to your Me as I delight in leading and guiding My children. Spend more time in praise and worship and you will <u>never</u> regret or begrudge it.

———∞∞———

My precious, precious one, you fill My heart with delight when you come and love Me. You have found the secret to abundant life – not looking to anything or anyone else but Me, the Author and Finisher of your faith. I AM your all in all and will sustain and uphold you in the worst of times – whether they consist of your internal struggles or external circumstances. I AM that I AM. You really do not need to lean on any other for they are, after all, but dust. Come to Me, My fair one, and you will find what you so deeply long for, yes crave. I <u>never</u> leave you alone or forsake you, so come to Me when these pangs of spiritual loneliness are so acute, and I will leave you refreshed, full and satisfied. You have become scattered, and your time with Me will bring an inner unity and solidity that is so lacking now. <u>I have brought you to this place to strip you of all you have leaned on in order to encourage you to look to Me, your El Shaddai, for every-thing.</u> Anything else in the universe can be destroyed or taken from you, but My presence cannot (Psalm 139). O My Child, deprive yourself not of My sweet, satisfying presence even one day longer.

———∞∞———

Continue on each day holding My hand. I will lead and guide you as the faithful Shepherd that I AM. Nothing will be able to intimidate or harass you, for you know who you are in Me and can boldly and confidently command your enemy to "GO!" Think not that things will be easier, for they will not; however, you will be moving in such power that obstacles will tumble down in front of your eyes. Hesitate not; move out in boldness, knowing you are walking in the perfect will of God for your life. That creates a confidence that the world cannot begin to match. Continue walking in My grace and forgiveness for others, for truly they know not what they do. Commit them to Me and <u>keep moving</u>, do not linger at the places of trouble or you will come to an impasse. Keep moving, My little soldier, keep walking.

Ah, My dear little one, you have heard Me speaking to your spirit. The joy of the Lord is your strength. You do need to encourage yourself in Me when all seems bleak and dreary around you. For my gift of salvation is a wellspring of joy in you – constantly reviving and refreshing you... also, the hope (hatikvah) that I have given you. Hope never disappoints, because My words to you are true and I cannot lie. The great and precious promises in My Word are for you, and you must cling to them as the stormy tempest rages all around you. Know that you can have inner calm and rest no matter what is happening outside of you.

Daughter, keep on seeking My face – intimacy with Me – the Lord of glory, and I will lift you up. Your desire is to serve Me and I see that, Daughter. Just keep your focus on Me and let Me do the work, for My yoke is easy and My burden is light. You can do nothing apart from Me anyway, so why waste time on fruitless works done by the arm of the flesh?

Come to My feet daily, and you will receive such a blessing you will not be able to contain it. See distraction as one of the ultimate enemies of your soul, and keep your eye single. For there are many good things in the world that will keep you from My best. Come back, Daughter, come back to our quiet place and you will know no end of satisfaction, peace, and joy in the Spirit.

I love you, My dear Child. Don't lean on what you think or what you feel, but on My Word alone. Your spirit hears Me in the night seasons, even when your emotions are in turmoil and all seems to be darkness without. But I AM within, and I will keep on speaking to you, My dear one; just open your ears and your heart that we might commune together.

My Child, know that I AM doing a new thing in your life. You have been told repeatedly to not lean on your own understanding for a reason – because you keep trying to under-

stand. But you won't, because My ways are higher than yours and past understanding. A child does not always understand his parents' reasoning when they say "no" to a certain request of his, but he must obey nevertheless. So it is with you, My Child. There are many things you will not understand until you reach heaven. I have given you a good, keen mind, but the temptation to use it when I just need you to trust Me is great. Go to My Word for understanding and wisdom, for in it lies buried treasure just waiting to be discovered.

You still don't trust Me, Child. You continue striving and straining as though you were the one required to "make things happen." Why not rest instead and let me work out all these things that concern you? I know your heart's desire, but I want it to conform to Mine. There is still much work to be done in the perfecting of your soul. But I have shown you repeatedly that I AM tender, gentle, and patient with you. Do you think I AM surprised by your reactions to these great pressures? No! I, who know the end from the beginning, see the panorama of your life and know that you will fulfill your destiny. I will see to that.

Spend much more time gazing into My face and you will learn who I AM and will love Me much more than you can imagine now. For I AM goodness and lovingkindness personified, and I AM working all these afflictions together for your good. But you must let go of the controls of your life and give them back to Me, or I AM bound in what I can accomplish through you. Observe little children, babies even, and you will see the utter peace, trust, and tranquility they experience with their earthly parents who are, after all, but dust. They allow themselves to be cared for and aren't laboring to make things work out in their lives. Observe their joy in simple pleasures and the delight they experience over some new discovery. That is how you will become like a little child and experience peace in My embrace and the freedom to walk the course I have destined for you.

My Daughter, though you forget Me at times, I can never forget you, for you are precious to Me and engraved on the palm of My hand. You have been traversing a rocky path – full of dangers and obstacles. You only need to look straight ahead and not focus on the scary obstacles in your path. Is anything too hard for Me, the great I AM, the King of the Universe? These obstacles and dangers have only been put in your path to test and try you – to see whether you will continually turn to Me with all your questions, confusion, heartaches and tears. You know I AM waiting for you, even at the end of the road as the father waited for the prodigal son. My three main gifts to you are righteousness, peace, and joy, which have so eluded you the last year and a half. Don't look at the circumstances you are in now, or the people, for they only distract you. Put all else aside except your passion to know Me and be My Child. Nothing else matters in this world.

My little one. Never give up… never give up… NEVER GIVE UP! I know you are being buffeted by the cruel blows of your enemy. I AM is bottling your tears and I AM writing them in My book. Behold, I have not forgotten you; I AM forging a new strength, a new purity in you through these fiery trials. Please stay put on the Potter's wheel as I form, mold and shape you into a vessel of beauty in My eyes. Not in the world's eyes, but in <u>My</u> eyes. What you are experiencing is the pain of the clay being slapped into a slab again and re-thrown on the wheel. I AM remaking you, My Daughter – removing the flaws, imperfections, yes, even the air bubbles that would interfere with the final firing. I AM doing a secret work, a hidden work that will <u>in due time</u> produce a vessel of such beauty and usefulness that the angelic hosts will marvel and exclaim.

Walk worthily as a tested and tried soldier, seasoned in battle and prepared to pull down strongholds in My Name. You must hold your head high, not with arrogance but with the dignity that befits one holding a high position. Did I not tell you that you would reign with Me? Don't let your enemy steal that and reduce you to a despairing, bowed down, and craven figure. No, STAND UPRIGHT and continue to fight the good fight. I AM will protect, guide, shelter, and undergird you. You have become completely distracted and entangled in the world's affairs, and today signals a break from all that – a fresh start. Know that I AM a God of new beginnings, and I delight in My children who get up and walk again once they've been knocked down.

My dear Child, I love you very much. I don't want you to be afraid about being out of a job, for My perfect love casts out all fear (this includes that low-grade anxiety that plagues you whenever you start thinking about the near future). I say in My Word that with fear comes torment, and Satan takes advantage of you at that point and steals your faith. I hold all of your tomorrows in My great and mighty hand. Keep trusting Me for

the step you're on, and I promise to lead and guide you into My perfect will. Your future is far more glorious than you can even comprehend at this time, so I say to you "just keep on doing the next thing." I will orchestrate the events, circumstances, and people around you to produce the next work I have for you to do. Just don't lean on your own understanding in this, but keep on acknowledging Me in all your ways and I will direct your paths.

Stand strong in these battles in the power of My might. Crucify your flesh, as in you dwells no good thing. Quit trying to be "the good person" and let Me (the only One who is good) transform you so completely that people see My light emanating from you... then I will get the glory and you will rest, since My yoke is easy and My burden is light.

Ask Me specific questions, listen, and wait for the answers. You are in too much of a hurry in our times of communion. Yes, I speak through many means, but I want to speak directly to your heart – from Me to you in an intimate way, rather than through books, articles, speakers, etc. Quiet yourself at My feet and let Us simply commune together. You will never regret the time that it takes for this to happen. I love you deeply and completely, My Beloved.

Stand firm, My Daughter, as it is always darkest before the dawn. Your circumstances will change – there will be a breakthrough as long as you relax and trust in Me to do it. Lean not upon your own understanding, as is so easy to do in these circumstances. I AM your Source, your Provision, and I know exactly where I want to place you and the timing of it. Fret not and fear not – these only lead to more distress on your part. Do your part and I will do mine. I AM showing you not to trust in man by surrounding you with so many believers who lack integrity and don't keep their word. Let it never be so said of you, My Daughter. For now, be encouraged, My lovely one and continue to redeem your time. I love you devotedly, Daughter.

My dearest one, I AM pleased that you want to return to our intimate times together. I have missed you and our sweet fellowship. Do I not always confirm My words to you in the most miraculous ways? My sheep know My voice and are not deceived by strange voices of false shepherds and prophets.

⸻

Give Me your work, dedicate it all to Me and let Me be in charge. For you will, in your flesh, jump ahead of Me as you have in the past. I raised you up for this venture, and I will keep honoring you as you honor Me.

⸻

Ah, My Child, you are finally getting it! This season has been for your good, even as you have chafed against it, railed at Me, and become faint, weary, and numb. It has been to show you that people will always disappoint, but I never will – the great I AM is your Source. Just as Jesus was led out into the wilderness by the Spirit, My Spirit has brought you to this place. Jesus quoted Scripture to Satan and so must you! Didn't He emerge from the wilderness <u>filled</u> with My power? So will you, if you keep your eyes on the goal – dying to self, becoming exactly like Me. Every son or Daughter I love I will chasten – FOR HIS OR HER GOOD. I love you more than you can even begin to take in right now.

⸻

Just keep pressing into Me, Daughter. Ignore everything else around you and press into Me. I want to comfort, strengthen and sustain you as <u>no</u> man ever could. You are on the brink of breaking through – you are learning humility and obedience by your very inability to die to yourself. But you want to know the answers, to walk them out... and that is what I see, My Child – your heart is "bent" in the right direction. You see your own helplessness, so keep on crying out to Me, and I will fill and flood you with My Spirit. I have had My hand on your life from before you were born, and I'm not about to let you fail now.

⸻

Keep climbing the mountain of holiness, but do not forget to stop and refresh yourself with My streams of living water. Hold onto My hand and know that I AM with you wherever you go and in all circumstances that you face. My beloved Child, I AM indeed teaching you much of eternal value during this your wilderness time. Only in retrospect will you be able to see the fruit of the trials and tests you are currently enduring. I know what I AM doing, although it makes no sense to your natural mind. That is why I give you the mind of Christ. See with spiritual eyes and hear with spiritual ears what the Spirit is doing in these last days. My righteousness will keep you during this hour of trial.

Learn to depend totally on Me. Reach not out to the arm of flesh, as you will continue to be devastated and overcome by the disappointments that come to you at the hands of men. But I will NEVER disappoint, betray, tempt or in any way harm you, My Beloved. I ask only that you trust even when you are bewildered and tired and have no sense of where I AM leading you, for you can't see the way ahead.

Keep on acknowledging Me in all your ways – your thoughts and actions – and I will lift you up at the appointed time. My timing is not slack, even as you are thinking right now. No work that I AM doing in your life is ever wasted time in My divine economy. It seems to be taking such a long time in your eyes, because you cannot see the beginning from the end as I do.

Rest, cease striving, and come to a point of just reveling in My presence, even when no "service" is resulting. I love you because You are mine and never for what you do. So please get off that performance orientation track and relax in being loved for just who you are – My beloved Daughter.

Yes, I AM leading and guiding each step of the way. You are never to doubt My hand in everything that is transpiring in your life. In patience, you must possess your soul and bring every thought captive to the obedience of Christ. Your soul must be sanctified, if you are to be My Bride. Bring to me those hurts and wounds that go so deep, and I <u>will</u> heal them. Yes, your reaction to the trials sent to you <u>is</u> your test. But through it all, I AM shaping you, molding you, perfecting you, and yes even conforming you to the image of My dear Son. Do not resist the work of My Spirit within you, even though it is only natural to want to pull back. For I AM with you in all these trials and afflictions, and I know all the feeling of your infirmities. I want you to get to that place of utter desperation, where surrender to Me in all things is the only answer.

My Child, continue to press on toward your goal of intimacy with Me. Let nothing hinder you; be single-minded in your pursuit of Me and My ways, and you shall <u>never</u> be disappointed again. It is only when you lean on the arm of the flesh or put people on pedestals that you become so wounded. People are never to be your source of trust – no, only the great and mighty I AM.

Render good for evil to those who slander and persecute you. At this point, you retaliate by murmuring against them in the privacy of your friendships. You do not bring these things to Me to deal with until that root of bitterness is already springing up. My Child, this ought not be so. If you bring the hurt immediately to Me, I will heal you and the wound will not fester and become infected, thus prolonging the period of healing. No, Child, your way of dealing with this is not right, but I will rectify it if you repent and return to the old paths. For I want you to be free – at liberty even as the children you observe with such delight. See how pure-hearted they are and free in their expression of worship to Me?

My beloved Daughter, you think I AM angry with you. I AM not! I have tenderhearted mercy and compassion on My children who simply want to know Me and do My will. Again, you must remember that your life with Me is not about performance or how many times you may falter, but getting up and continuing to follow Me. You need more knowledge of Me as a loving and kind Abba who is always waiting breathlessly to commune with you. Those thoughts of Me being angry with you have been implanted in your mind by the devil himself to keep you stuck in an oppressive circle, going round and round. My Word to you will always inspire, propel, and motivate you to walk forward and make progress. Whenever you are stuck, recognize the devices of your enemy. Do you feel him handcuffing you and making you feel as though you were slogging through the mud? I, instead, give you hinds' feet that traverse the rocky crags with ease and grace. The heaviness you do indeed feel surrounded by is only him, so shake the dust off your feet, get up, and begin walking again. Because of your temperament and sensitivity, this is the strategy that your enemy employs constantly against you, to vex and torment you. Keep on recognizing him for who he is and bringing Me the sacrifice of praise. When you do this, the dark and gloomy clouds will indeed be blown away and a beautiful azure sky and glorious Son-shine will envelop you instead.

Remember Daughter, I'm always looking at your heart. Remember also, that I AM gentle and meek with My lambs, and that I AM not just waiting to club you and beat you. My intent is to bless and not curse, encourage, and lift you up. Selah.

Keep climbing and do not look back. The past is removed, wiped clean. You just keep pressing on toward the goal of the high call. Nothing and no one can defeat you if you keep your focus on Me and disregard the distractions and hindering forces around you. Just keep pressing through, and you will overcome the many obstacles that will be put in your way. Daughter, I love you with an unfathomable love.

Daughter, I AM pleased with what you have resolved in your heart this day. Begin anew, and do not look back at the past months as wasted, rather as a lesson about not leaning on your own understanding. True wisdom comes from seeking My face and My will in all situations, whereby My plans shall be worked out on the earth. So look not behind, but look straight ahead. Great and glorious things await you, as you determine with all your heart to be obedient and surrendered to My perfect will for you. That restlessness you feel is the result of My making you so uncomfortable that you would return to acknowledging Me in all your ways.

Daughter, <u>now</u> begins the adventure. We shall do great exploits together for you are broken and don't know which way to turn. So you shall follow My lead and direction and <u>not</u> wander again. Stay with your Shepherd, and I will lead you to soft, plush, green pastures in which to feed. You have been eating dead grass, weeds, thistles and thorns. My Daughter, this ought not be so! I desire to bless you with rest, including My joy and peace, which has only continued to elude you. No more, My Child – this is it! Do not take one step without consulting Me and <u>waiting</u> on an answer. So many times, you are impatient and do not wait, but run out ahead of Me in the strength of the flesh. I cannot emphasize strongly enough that you mustn't do this again. Great grief, turmoil, and regret are the byproducts of this impetuosity. Come to be known as one who really does <u>wait</u> on Me for <u>all</u> her answers to the perplexities and quandaries of life.

———∞∞∞———

I ask and beseech you this day to inquire of Me, wait on answers, rest in My perfect peace, and finally proceed step by step, listening to My still, small voice that says, "This is the way... walk ye in it." Go in peace knowing that this day you have come to the crossroads and chosen correctly.

———∞∞∞———

These tests and trials are showing you how little you do trust Me. Have I not been faithful and trustworthy over the years? Have I ever abandoned or forsaken you? You leave Me regularly to isolate yourself when you are in pain instead of running into My arms for comfort. Child, you must learn that I AM the perfect Parent who will <u>always</u> be there for you. It is time that you learn this way down deep – internalizing it – forever.

———∞∞∞———

Let Me love you, Child, and give you the security you still lack. I will pour out My love and favor on you even as the latter rains will be greater than the former…. I will pour out in abundance, if you will only relax, stop struggling, and let Me give.

———∞∞∞———

Think not that I have left, forgotten, am being too hard on, or don't love you because of the onslaught of trials you have faced and are facing. These are the prerequisites for My crown of glory, which I long to set on your brow. I have told you several times now, Daughter, that you are a precious gem, a living jewel in My diadem. You are being cut and polished to enhance the brilliance with which you will shine. Continue to hang onto Me, nestle close, stay in My arms, and dwell in My covert until the storm passes. You will not suffer permanent harm if you are obedient in this.

———∞∞∞———

I long to promote and elevate you, My lovely one, but this process must come first. You need to quit counting the hours, days, months, and years. While you constantly calculate the time, you are actually growing in resentment for how long it is taking. <u>Instead,</u> I want you to rejoice that you are counted worthy to share in My Son's sufferings and fill them up. You are extremely blessed to even undergo this process, as no servant of mine who refuses it will truly prosper in My Kingdom. Remember that the first shall be last and *the last first. Humble yourself under My Mighty hand, and I will exalt you in due time. You must learn to flow in My timing and not your own or that of the world. I AM pulling impatience out of you by the roots so that you truly may have the quality and fruit of patience. I love you deeply, unreservedly, and unconditionally, My little one. Your Abba.*

Give Me your tongue, that I may eradicate the cursing that comes from it. No, not blasphemy or vulgarity, but careless, negative, judgmental words that fall from your lips and put curses on others. Remain silent when this rises up in you, and I will correct it. I will give you My eyes to see those whom you are tired of and with whom you are disgusted. I want to change the way you think about people. I want you to see them as lost sheep, which I dearly love and poured out My blood for on Calvary. When you can do that, mercy and compassion will re-enter your life. Your pain has been so great that those My gifts in you have been in hibernation. Awake, shake off the snow, for the winter is past and I AM bringing you into the full bloom of your calling – what I have intended for you all along.

Forgive your brothers and sisters in Christ who wound you. This is not their intention. You have wounded others when it was not your intention to do so. Make a concerted effort to live at peace with all men, so far as it depends on you. When you do this, I will make even your enemies to be at peace with you. Go with My love in your heart and My Name on your lips to minister to those <u>I</u> send to you.

Precious one, love others with the love I have for you. As I empty you of self, do <u>not</u> resist. That way, you can become an instrument that I can use in building My house. We must get you out of the way, that I would receive glory. Come to Me when you are weary, confused… and I will <u>fill</u> you up completely with My peace. Don't struggle to figure everything out, for there are many things that only I know. If you understood every detail of My great plan, there would be no need for faith, for trust. Surrender your mind, your intellect, all the knowledge you have gained to Me and be as a little child who is being taught things for the very first time. I AM always patient with My students, and I will not ridicule you or expect you to have all the answers.

Really, life can be very simple for you, My dear Child. Just become obedient to Me, and I will work out the distressing circumstances of your life before you even know what happened. Only be still and KNOW that I AM God – King of the entire Universe and more mighty than you can comprehend. Rest in My finished work on the cross for you, My Child. Remember that I came to seek and save that which was lost, and you are never so close to heaven as when you are humbled, broken, reaching out to Me for your very sustenance. I will never disappoint or let you down when you reach toward Me, My beloved one.

Though this valley has been a very dark one for you, precious Child, look and glimpse the glory, the brightness of My coming to you. The Sun of Righteousness rises upon you with healing in His wings. Come unto Me and rest. Rest your head on My bosom and give your weary heart to Me. I will refresh and reinvigorate you in such a powerful way that you will truly be a new creation. You will be capable of doing mighty works in My Name, and you will give Me all the glory since you have been broken and know your own wretchedness. Lean not on the arm of flesh, but lean on Me completely, for I AM lowly and gentle of heart, and you will feel the balm of Gilead healing your soul, My beloved Daughter. I love you with a fierce and everlasting love. Your Abba.

My beloved little Daughter, how could you think that I would withdraw My love from you? My lovingkindness and mercy is from generation to generation for those who fear Me. You may measure My love for you in terms of performance, but I <u>never</u> do. I love you because you are Mine and for no other reason than that - pure and simple!

You are filled with guilt, condemnation, and self-loathing – all kinds of foul things from your enemy. I AM not putting those things on you… for I only want to lift up, nurture, encourage, set on your feet again, and have you begin to walk closely with Me once again. You have been distracted, tormented, harassed and feel as though you are unable to even be in My presence for long periods of time. But I long for your presence, the sound of your voice, your heartbeat. Bring Me that huge load of cares and pain and dump it all out at the foot of the Cross. Leave it there, because those are all things My Son died to deliver you from.

———— ⚭ ————

My lovely one, My deepest desire is that you walk in freedom, lightness – as carefree as the most secure little girl in all the world, who does not doubt and knows the warmth of her daddy's embrace is always there for the taking. You are indeed battered, bruised, and bleeding, and I will heal you, for AM Jehovah Rapha. But you must stay still long enough for me to perform my healing of your heart. Be still, My Child, and know that I AM God, that I love you, that I will heal you, that I will set you free, that I will enable you to fulfill all that I have called you to be and do. I will finish that good work that I have begun in you. Quit looking to the fleshly, frail human beings around you for answers to this pain you're suffering. I'm not saying that they can't be helpful, but I AM the only One who can bring you through. So take My hand, trust Me, and we will walk out your healing together.

———— ⚭ ————

Continue to lay all things on the altar that are important to you and bring every concern and heartache to Me, as I will perfect that which concerns you. Only believe that I AM able to do this… that your life is not such a mess or you so sinful that I cannot redeem and use you for My highest purposes. For indeed, I AM grooming you for a front-line position, but I must break and humble you before that can take place. Do you think that for one second I have forgotten you or am not using all these trials to forge you into the soldier I would have you to be? No, I waste nothing of circumstances and tests – it is you that needs to repeat most things several times to be fully broken and molded into a vessel that I can use. You can speed that process up by submitting to, not resisting, the process.

———— ⚭ ————

The battle rages on two fronts. One, yes, most certainly is with the enemy of your soul, but the other is with your flesh, which dies so hard. The first calls for resistance, the second for lying down and dying. I will give you the power and strength to do both if you will only call on Me. I wait for My children to call on Me when they are utterly spent and broken, for it is only then that great victory will come and all glory will be given to Me.

You have only begun to taste of My goodness. The more you turn your eyes away from your circumstances and your ears from the voice of man, the more profound our fellowship will be. Continue to forgive your enemies and pray for them, and your liberation will be complete. You have no idea how free and whole I desire to make you, but you must do your part – otherwise I AM hindered in doing Mine. Keep coming back to the fountain of blood from Immanuel's veins for that cleansing, that deliverance from sin. Keep coming back to My Word for the washing by pure water.

My precious Daughter, you do not know how this kind of confession blesses My heart. For you are yielding your stony heart to Me to refashion, reshape and remold into a heart of flesh that I can write My law upon. See that you walk carefully, for the days are evil. Without becoming paranoid, do be aware that the enemy wants to <u>destroy</u> you. But I AM faithful and well able to deliver you from that destruction. Only rest in Me; lean on Me; give all your cares and burdens to Me; for I love you with an everlasting love. My little one, I see the anger deep in your heart for having to go through this pain. Remember how I said to you in My Word today that you must cease from your anger (Ps. 37:8)? I see it when no one else can. Repent of it and I will remove it so utterly, so completely, that you will marvel that you could ever be so angry with Me, because My goodness to you is from everlasting to everlasting. Yes, indeed, place your anger on the altar and forsake it, and your rewards will be too numerous to count.

Yes, Daughter, I AM <u>in the process</u> of restoring your joy and peace. I know where you have been and the heartaches and devastation you have endured. You think no one else can grasp the enormity of the pain you have suffered during the last three years… but My Son, who had His own Gethsemane, His own dark night of the soul, can comprehend <u>exactly</u> what you are going through. <u>EVERYTHING</u> has been stripped away from you; props have been removed, haven't they? You feel hopelessly stuck, even paralyzed; you can't go back, you can't go forward, and the present feels agonizing to you. Hold onto Me, Child – for I will see you through this time of complete desolation, this wilderness that seems to have lost both entrance and exit. It looms behind and ahead of you further than the eye can see. That is why I AM asking you to open your spiritual eyes and discern the reality that I want to reveal to you. Spend time with Me, My Beloved, and you will gain peace and joy to an extent that you have <u>never</u> experienced before. That *is the only way, and you must will to walk in it. I cannot force you. I know you are dry, withered up, and ready to blow away in the winds of adversity. But even as I put flesh and sinew on the dry bones in Ezekiel's vision, I long to restore health and vitality to you – spirit, soul, and body. Those bones did nothing to accomplish their transformation; the great I AM, the Ruach ha Kodesh [Holy Spirit in Hebrew], performed it. The zeal of the Lord of Hosts performed it indeed. So hold on just a little bit longer, and you will begin to see My promises made manifest to you. You will begin to move into the Promised Land. You will not die in the desert; you will thrive in paradise. But you must lay down you will every day, so that Mine can be accomplished. Remember, obedience is better than sacrifice. Obey Me in the small things, and I will reward you largely.*

⸺ ❧ ⸺

Once again, I tell you that you haven't lost My love – that that is impossible. You have walked away from Me, but I AM standing here with outstretched arms, waiting for you to come into My embrace and rest there. I love you with a fiery and unquenchable love, My dear little Daughter.

⸺ ❧ ⸺

O My beloved one, how I have longed and yearned for you to return to our tabernacle to seek My heart and Me. I have been as an abandoned lover, thrown aside to pursue any and everything else. My great heart has been broken over you, yet I have never stopped looking for you even as you were afar off, waiting for you to return to My arms of tender love and compassion. For truly, I AM the lover of your soul, the Light of your life, the One altogether lovely and to be desired. But you have settled for the husks, My Child, and for eating the garbage, the leftovers. No wonder you have become so sick at heart – so malnourished. You have not been feeding on My Word, and so you have starved yourself of real nourishing food and "pigged out" on junk food. But alas, you have come to your senses and returned even as the prodigal son did… and Daughter, even as the father in the parable did, I run toward, embrace, and fully reinstate you. It is as though no time has passed and I bury your sin in the sea of forgetfulness. Do not bring it up to Me again; let it stay under the Blood where it belongs.

⸺ ❧ ⸺

Little one: Keep on returning to Me, and you will truly find rest for your soul. A quiet and calm will settle over you that will never come to you in any other way. You need to keep on snuggling up to Me, for My way is perfect and filled with light. You will leave behind the cares, burdens, and anxieties of this present world and enter the supernatural realm for which you were created.

Do you notice that every time you look at circumstances, you become overwhelmed, despairing, or agitated? It is because you are not looking at Me – Jehovah Shalom – the One who brings you perfect peace – a peace the world cannot attain nor understand. So you must keep your eyes fixed and fastened on Me, or you will be sucked into the whirlwind consuming the world.

Daughter, even as you build memorials to your fallen soldiers, I want you to raise up a memorial to Me each time I move in a sovereign way in your life. For I would not have you forget My mighty works as they apply to you. I AM Alpha and Omega, the Author and Finisher of your faith. Therefore, I will finish the good work I have begun in you, even though that seems to you to be remote and unlikely right now. For I AM the God of tomorrows, of new beginnings, of fresh starts. Is anything too hard for Me? No, but you limit Me in your life with your doubts and fears. You need to remember who I AM and what I have wrought in you, lo these many years. It has been a silent work, not visible to the eye but very important to Me, as I form you into a living stone to be used in My house.

Arise and look up. For too long you have been decimated and prostrate with despair over your circumstances. The great and mighty I AM is bringing a reversal of all that seems hopeless, broken, and destroyed in you. If I can raise your mortal body from the dead, can I not resurrect the ashes of your walk with ME? Of course, I can, My little one. I desire to do that very thing when you yield up all that you have harbored and nursed in your heart of bitterness and resentment toward your fellow brothers and sisters in Christ. You must give it all up, else you'll remain stuck, as if in concrete, forever. Let Me do it through you, with My grace and mercy, which is sufficient for every situation. Is anything too hard for Me? I wait until you are utterly broken, have no human resources left, and are on the ash heap – then I AM released to move in mighty ways. But as long as there exists in you even a tiny portion of self-will or human strength, I cannot do anything. Even for you to surrender is an act empowered by My grace, for you can't do it in your own strength. One of the things you must remember is that I will do the restoration in My own way and own time. Do not try to help Me with this. It is a delicate surgery of the soul, as I will be cutting out the diseased, infected, and putrefying flesh that is poisoning your whole system. Return home, even as a wounded soldier would. That soldier would allow himself to be ministered to by the medical personnel. Lie quietly on the stretcher and let Me dress your wounds. Once surgery is complete, what does a patient do? He rests and heals. There may be some physical therapy necessary to prevent muscles from atrophying and to strengthen them. In a similar way, I will take you through some spiritual exercises that may seem very basic to you but are necessary to build you back up to where you need to be an effective soldier in My army.

I want you to be peaceful, Daughter. As the waves roar and crash around you, I want you to be free from distress and agitation. Learn to give Me those heavy burdens that are impossible to bear. Know that I will never reject you, no, I, your Heavenly Father, will embrace you and always be a very present help in time of trouble. I long to pull that root of rejection right out of you that your garden would be lush and fruitful, plentiful and abounding. King David said that his cup was running over. I desire to bless you with spiritual abundance so that your cup also runs over.

You now eat the deep meat of My Word. This privilege has come with the price tag of suffering, but Daughter, you have passed the test. You have not turned your back on Me and walked away. You have held on, endured, even through your agony and bewilderment. I know your heart, My Child, as no one else does, and I see your longing to really know Me. Well, now you have had but a taste of the fellowship of My Son's sufferings. Consider yourself honored that you have been counted worthy to suffer with Him. You are a jewel in My crown, and I AM continually buffing and polishing you that you may shine brightly and brilliantly with My glory and light.

You have turned a corner in your walk with Me. You have made the commitment to keep pressing in to Me. For you see, if even from afar, My goodness, beauty, and mercy. Come beloved Daughter, come close up and climb into My lap. I want to cuddle you even as a father cuddles his little girl. Don't hold me at arm's distance! My heart beats with passion for you, as I AM seeing you take those first tottering steps back to Me. Yes, you have been a prodigal in a faraway land, but you have set your mind and heart to return home.

———— ⟨⟨⟩⟩ ————

Come out of the darkness! I AM holding your hand and will not let you slip. Come into the light where I dwell. Let My healing rays of warmth envelop you and be as a healing balm to you. For I long to heal you in every area... spirit, soul, and body. I want you whole – not so you can go out and perform for Me, but simply for the sake of My loving to make My children whole. I grieve when I see you as marred and scarred as you've become. I long to make you so pure that My image is reflected in you, even as one beholds oneself in a mirror.

———— ⟨⟨⟩⟩ ————

My Child, how I have longed for you to run into My arms. I deeply desire to embrace you, but you run away even as a frightened animal does when threatened. Bring all your fears of intimacy to Me, and I <u>will</u> heal you – totally, completely, 100 percent healing. Nothing less than complete wholeness is My perfect will for you. When you hurt, so do I. My great Father heart breaks over the pain you have endured. Only don't clutch it to your breast – give it to Me. All your grief, sorrows, and burdens I will carry. But you must give them to Me first and not take them back.

———— ⟨⟨⟩⟩ ————

Desperate times call for desperate measures. This is not "business as usual." You must be about your Father's business. Do not be entangled in the beggarly elements. I want you to soar above them, even as you have watched the birds soar in the thermal winds. You see how effortlessly and freely they fly in those currents. You have seen their joy as they perform exactly as I have created them to. Even so, My Child, when you walk in My Spirit daily, you will not strive and struggle but will be quiet and confident – you will walk in ease and rest because it will be My wings undergirding and strengthening you in your flight. Yes, you must have dove's eyes that look straight ahead at Me. For to look to the side or down at the ground will only distract you and distort reality. Reality and truth walk together. There will be no bewilderment, confusion, turmoil or stress engendered when you eyes are fixed on Me as dove's eyes.

———— ⟨⟨⟩⟩ ————

You see what happens when you get quiet and listen to Me? I will lead you into My perfect will. You still have that tendency to jump out ahead of My timing, but I will turn these things to your good. You need to learn the lesson of waiting on Me in utter stillness.

This you have yet to learn. Nevertheless, I will move and minister through you wherever you are, as long as you consecrate and dedicate your work unto Me.

—————

O dear one, would that you would lay down every care and burden at My feet. You still spend precious emotional and physical energy trying to deal with them yourself. My Daughter, this ought not be so. I would have you so free in every realm that you would, indeed, soar as the eagle. Take NO thought for the morrow, My sweet one, but let each day take care of itself under My watchful eye. I will not let the spoiler and devourer strip you.

—————

Rise up, O Daughter of Zion! Rise up and take your stand against the evil that spreads across your land, your neighborhood, your family. Tear down the strongholds and contend for the souls around you… for who will if you do not? Be done with complacency and weariness – let My Spirit uplift and sustain you. I will strengthen you to do the work I require.

—————

Ask of Me largely and you will receive. You do not have, because you do not ask. Open your mouth wide and I, the Sovereign Lord, will fill it with words that will not miss the mark. You feel weak and inadequate for the tasks at hand. Good! Then you will know that it is with My mighty, upraised hand that the works are accomplished. I will receive all the glory and honor, do not take any for yourself, even inwardly in the most subtle fashion. Indeed, Daughter, I will give you a new heart, cleanse, and purify you. You have reached the point of utter helplessness as far as climbing out of the pit you find yourself in by your own strength. Remember, My precious one, it is not by might nor by power but by My Spirit – the Ruach ha Kodesh [Holy Spirit in Hebrew] – that you will be an overcomer and more than a conqueror.

—————

I will remove those things from you that have such a grip on your life. All you have to do is to be willing to be made willing and I, the Sovereign King of the Universe, will remove them from your life. After this is all over, you will truly realize what grace is all about and will quit all your striving and enter into My rest. There is no true rest apart from Me, and I know your heart is in turmoil and clamors for peace. I will bring it to you softly and tenderly, My dove, and you will discern the difference between My rest and worldly relaxation. There is no comparison between the two.

———— ⦿⦿⦿ ————

My lovely Daughter, the time has come for you to step out, to launch out into the deep. Your days of hiding in the cave of Adullam have ended, and I AM setting you free to go forth, conquer, and take the land I set before you. You must not look behind you, but press on. For the enemy of your soul would like to keep you mired in the past, but I AM a God of new beginnings, and I love to restore the fortunes of My children that Satan steals. <u>I</u> restore, not you. No self-effort is involved. You receive My supply, deliverance, and healing.

———— ⦿⦿⦿ ————

It is time for you to rise up and become proactive. You have rested and been refreshed, renewed, and restored. I AM calling you to go out into the highways and byways to bring in the lost… the treasures of darkness. Yes, in the natural, this is impossible, but with Me, <u>all things are possible.</u> You do not have to know the details, the particulars of how I will work out My plan for you. All you must have is a willing heart – one that eagerly says "Yes" to My direction and guidance. When you feel lethargy and fatigue overtake you, shake them off – even as you shake flies off when they land on you. There is no effort in that – it is a natural response. I long to move through you in mighty ways. You are at a crossroads of life, as you can take the easy way out and coast on through or you can fight and resist the enemy and all his evil ways. I will not force you to fight… you must take the steps, and I will empower you to do so.

———— ⦿⦿⦿ ————

My word for you, today, dear Child, is to persevere in the face of the tests and trials of life. You must endure hardness as a good soldier, counting not the cost. If your soldiers are not afraid to risk their lives for their country, why should you be afraid?

———— ⦿⦿⦿ ————

My Child, I long to do the sanctifying work in you that will produce a vessel of honor. You are getting there, Daughter, you are getting there. It seems that only as you exhaust yourself… wear yourself out by striving in your own strength… do you come to Me and let Me do the work. It is not until you are desperate and sickened by your own sinfulness that I can deliver, because then you step out of the way. As long as there is one ounce left of you that believes, even subconsciously, that you can change yourself, I cannot and will not work.

O My lovely one, you are precious to My heart. You please Me exceedingly when you seek Me – when you quiet your heart and turn your face to Me, even as a flower turns its petals to the sun. I will have you blossom and bloom, even as a flower, as you continually turn to Me and My Word for direction and sustenance. It is time to lift your countenance toward the Son and receive of My life-giving rays. As long as you gaze at the world around you, you will not receive the joy, gladness, and lightness of heart that is part of your godly inheritance. Earthly parents may leave monetary inheritances, but the one I give you so far surpasses them that an analogy would be even as an elephant is to an ant. You have not because you ask not. Ask Me, Child; ask of Me because I AM a liberal giver of wonderful gifts that are hidden – not seen or perceived by the natural eye. They are discerned spiritually and are like valuable ore that is buried beneath the surface of the earth. They must be mined and dug for. But they are worth far more than any gifts the world has to offer, which are fleeting, to say the least.

Continue to seek My face and shut all else out. Nothing on earth can compare to the glory and beauty that is to be found in My presence. Enter the Holy of Holies, My Beloved, and we will enjoy sweet, satisfying, intimate communion together. Come, Love, come now.

Ah, My dear one, run into My arms, and there you will find grace to stand and the healing balm of Gilead for your soul. It will be found in no other or any place on earth. For I AM your Comforter, Counselor, Guide and I will ease your load and light your path. Come to Me with all that troubles you. You have not because you ask not. You do not converse with Me on a constant basis. This you must do if we are to be intimate. Speak with Me, My lovely one, of all that hurts you, all that angers you, all that brings you into a place of turmoil, for I long to give you My blessed rest.

The world is in an uproar and upheaval at this time. I came to bring peace in the midst of the storm. If you come to Me ever and always first, I will give you a sweet, satisfying peace that no man can take from you. This is the secret of abiding in Me.

Allow Me to come in and clean your house. I will remove those things that seem to be impossible hindrances to you. I will clean out the cobwebs and order your belongings to free you from unnecessary clutter in your soul. You feel as though you have been hit by a hurricane, and everything is in chaos. I will repair that which is broken and right that which has toppled. I will clear away the debris and strengthen the foundation. I will shed My sweet fragrance abroad in your heart to replace the stench of sulfur that your enemy leaves behind. Do not hinder Me in this work. I promise that I will be gentle with you as I AM setting things right. You feel as though you have been run over by a truck — crushed, broken, wounded, and bruised. Daughter, I will heal you. I WILL HEAL YOU. But you must stand still and let Me do it, or you will continue to limp along and just make do with your "lot in life." May it never be so! For I came to set you free and make you more than a conqueror… not have you live out a mediocre existence in some dark corner. I want your house (temple) to be ablaze with My glory! You are so fearful of surrender, My Child. Have I not proven My goodness over and over again to you? Review My work in your life and take note of the blessings, the faithfulness, and the steadfastness of My love toward you. I AM your Rock that will never be moved. So let Me rebuild your house into a magnificent edifice worthy of My Name.

You have many questions. Would the answers really help you? Wouldn't it be better to simply rest in quietness and confidence in Me – that I have everything in hand and know all things? Yes, for I do know the end from the beginning, and time is of no consequence to Me. I want you also to learn to flee the bounds of time and come into the certain knowledge of eternal life that is yours. I have given it to you as a gift, simply because of My great love for you and for no other reason.

You and I need to become One. You continue to "do you own thing," risking your own spiritual health. You have your own ideas about what My perfect will should be for you,

and they are just that – your own ideas. Remember how My thoughts and ways are so much higher than yours? I reiterate this, not to humiliate you but to drive home the point that when you take things into your own hands, you bring upon yourself great heartache. How much better for you to turn the reins of your life over to Me, as I will never steer you in harmful ways. What you perceive to be harmful, I use instead for building character, courage, and endurance into your life. Then you will be a shining example to others who have worn themselves out striving to "live the life" only to fail repeatedly. This will be a significant part of your testimony concerning the faithfulness of your Heavenly Father, who never lets go of you.

Do not try to understand My plan for you anymore – it is much higher and more complex than you can fathom. Be content to be as child just weaned from her mother's breast – resting safely still in her arms but ready to walk and then run. For I will give you the feet to run and the inner fortitude to withstand the pressures upon you. Find the quiet inner sanctuary where we can commune no matter what is going on outwardly.

Lovely one, do as I ask of you – forgive those who hurt you. More times than not, they do not know what they are doing – they are acting out of the wounded places in themselves. You must learn to quickly dispense of these hurts or you will become bogged down in a quagmire of rejection and bitterness. Lift each incident to Me immediately, and let that action become habitual. Commit each interaction with others to Me, and I will transform these hurtful incidents into blessings, because of the character that is formed in you as a result of the buffeting. Know you not that when My Son was on earth, people constantly criticized, accused, and doubted Him? No, you must learn to bear it and use it as an opportunity to bless that person as you become aware of their spiritual poverty. I have not given you that heart of compassion for nothing – I would have it extended to your enemies, for they need it the most. For your enemies will be of your own household, as I told you in My Word, and you must learn to treat them with kindness and gentleness befitting your position in Me. They no longer have power over you, because you are a true Daughter of the Most High God. As such, these family ties pale in comparison with the true family of God. I will give you eyes to view them with compassion, rather than being fearful or vulnerable to their taunts and reproaches.

Do not wait until you think you "have it all together," for that time will not come. I glory in using imperfect vessels to display My love and splendor. I will continue to polish you until you reflect My image to the world. Then you will shine brightly and as the many-faceted jewel I created you to be. Selah.

Give Me the glory due Me. This I do not ask for Myself because I need it, but because it benefits you. The more you praise, the more of My greatness I shall reveal to you. I will not be obscured behind the veil but will usher you into the Holy of Holies to commune with you there.

Who can know My mind, My thoughts, My plans, My ways? You cannot discern them for yourself, but I choose to reveal them to My friends. My Son called you "Friend" when He was on earth, that you might begin to comprehend the intimacy I so long to have with you, My Beloved. The thoughts I share with you will bypass your mind, but only your carnal reasoning, not the mind of Christ. Look to My mind for answers to the puzzling and perplexing quandaries that confront you. You have barely scratched the surface of a vast, untapped reservoir. You cannot fathom with your natural intellect the depth of wisdom and knowledge awaiting you.

Put your hand in Mine and walk with Me through lovely fields of wildflowers. Inhale the crisp, clean air – fill your lungs with it. Feel the freedom and simplicity of simply walking with Me. It is not a complex thing – this is what I mean when I say, "Walk in the Spirit." Do not complicate what is a simple matter of communing with Me. We don't even have to talk. We can simply enjoy one another. You need this desperately, My Child, as you find yourself weighed down with burdens and cares of this life. Leave them behind, and come walk with Me in the field. For I long to restore that childlike simplicity and trust that still lies within you. They has simply been pushed down and pressed down until it has been relegated to a tiny corner of your soul. They need to be revived, so you can truly blossom and exist in the peace and simplicity that I so desire for you. Come, My Beloved, come walk with Me. I love you with an everlasting love.

O My little one, do not despair. For I AM doing a work in you that will stand the test of time and affliction. I will use you, but I will not abuse you. You do right whenever you slow down to seek Me in My Word and presence. This fills My heart with delight! Do you see how fruitless it is to run hither and yon trying to meet everyone's expectations of you? The demands of men are infinite and exhausting, and that is why I AM constantly beckoning you to come away, My Beloved. You need the solace only I can provide... because only I understand you completely. I know your thoughts, your feelings, what you ruminate about, yes, even obsess on, at times. This is a waste of time, for if you would give Me every burden and care you would feel so much lighter in every way.

Learn what I AM teaching you during this season of your life. It is but a short one, as I have already told you. I will release you when you are soft, supple, and compliant in My hand – when you are not resisting My purifying work in your heart. I AM still pulling things out, but you have come a long way, Daughter. Do not feel condemned and believe the lie that you have totally regressed. For progress in My Kingdom is like that – two steps forward and one back. Fits and starts. But you are progressing well, Daughter, and I AM pleased with the building I AM constructing.

My beloved Daughter, how I long to gather you in My embrace and have you rest there. This is the only route to healing. You look in vain everywhere else, especially when you believe man has the answer. No man has the answer to what your heart is craving, only My Spirit will call as deep calls unto deep. So wait no longer at empty wells, but come to Me, your Fount of Living Waters that never runs dry. Come and slake your thirst. Come and drink until you are satisfied. Come and feel the cool refreshing water: the pure water of My Word, which will cleanse your soul of every spot and stain. Come, My little one, come.

Do not wait until you feel worthy. Now is the time to come when all seems bleak and unpromising all around you. I see your heart and know exactly what is in it. You may "put on a good face" for others, but I AM never fooled. Let Me bind up your wounds, press them out, pour in the oil and the wine. For I will heal in such a way that the pain will leave you and not come back. No infection, the poison of bitterness, will set in if you will truly give Me your heart and leave it in My safekeeping. But if you keep taking it back, it will be broken over and over again by the carelessness and the cruelty of man. I don't want to take your sensitivity from you, rather your proneness to being deeply hurt, the wound festering, and you withdrawing to nurse the wound. Come into the light, and I will eradicate all the darkness attached to the pain. The natural things of the earth that flourish in the dark you dislike. Should it be any less so in the spiritual realm?

Endnotes

Chapter One: *The Many Faces of Abuse: Why Dredge Up the Past?*

1. http://helpguide.org/mental/child_abuse_physical_emotional_sexual_neglect. html.
2. John and Paul Sandford and Norm Bowen, *Choosing Forgiveness* (Arlington, TX: Clear Stream, Inc. Publishing), 1996.
3. http://www.gotquestions.org/who-is-Jesus.html.

Chapter Two: *Why Forgive, Anyway?*

1. Ed. Neil Wilson, *The Handbook of Bible Application: A Guide for Applying the Bible to Everyday Life* (Wheaton, IL: Tyndale House Publishing, 2000).
2. http://online.pesi.com/catalog/aspx.
3. http://mayoline.com/health/forgiveness, Mayo Foundation for Medical Education and Research, Nov. 21, 2009.
4. http://www.academeca.com/amedco/seminarinfor.aspx.
5. R. T. Kendall, *Total Forgiveness: When Everything in You Wants to Hold a Grudge, Point a Finger, and Remember the Pain – God Wants You to Lay it All Aside* (Florida: Charisma House, 2007).
6. http://findarticles.com/articles/mi_hb1416/is_1_32/ex.
7. http://zikkir.com/health/38510.

Chapter Three: *What Happens When We Won't Forgive*

1. http://www.merriamwebster.com/netdict/bitterness.
2. http://hubpages.com/hub/Wormwood_What_the_Bible_says_about_it_is_amazing.
3. http://www.faithfulreader.com/authors/au-rubin-jordan.aspx.
4. Charles F. Stanley, *The Gift of Forgiveness* (Nashville, TN: Oliver Nelson, 1987).
5. Archibald D. Hart, *Adrenaline and Stress* (Dallas, TX: Word Publishing, 1995).

6. Ibid.
7. Cyril J. Barber and John Carter, *Always a Winner* (Glendale, CA: G/l Publications, 1977).
8. Charles F. Stanley, *The Gift of Forgiveness* (Nashville, TN: Oliver Nelson, 1987).
9. http://www.iloveulove.com/forgiveness/pettittforgive.html.
10. Ibid.
11. John & Paul Sandford and Norm Bowman, *Choosing Forgiveness* (Arlington, TX: Clear Stream Publishing, 1996).
12. R. T. Kendall, *Total Forgiveness, When Everything in You Wants to Hold a Grudge, Point a Finger, and Remember the Pain – God Wants You to Lay it All Aside* (Florida: Charisma House, 2007).
13. Sandra Wilson, *Hurt People Hurt People* (Nashville, TN: Thomas Nelson, 1993).

Chapter Four, *How Does the Lord Feel about Child Abuse?*

1. http://randyalcorn.blogspot.com/2009/12/does-god-have-emotions.html.
2. http://www.sodahead.com/united-states/does-god-have-emotions/question-763587/.
3. Steven R. Tracy, *Mending the Soul: Understanding and Healing Abuse* (Grand Rapids, MI: Zondervan, 2005).

Chapter Five, *What Forgiveness Is/Isn't and the Process of Healing*

1. Steven R. Tracy, *Mending the Soul: Understanding and Healing Abuse* (Grand Rapids, MI: Zondervan, 2005).
2. Ibid.
3. Ibid.
4. Ibid.
5. Ibid.
6. Ibid.
7. Ibid.
8. Ibid.
9. Ibid.
10. http://www.azfamily.com/news/local/Phoenix-dad-accused-of-molesting-daughters-2-pastors-arrested-for-not-reporting-abuse-99483409.html.
11. http://www.happynews.com/news/682009/power-forgiveness.html.
12. Excerpted from *A Woman's Guide to Healing the Heartbreak of Divorce.* Copyright © 2001 Hendrickson Publishers, Inc. Used by permission. All rights reserved.
13. http://christsbondservants.org/Home_Files/wys-Ch-Forgiveness.pdf.
14. http://youareforgiven.tribe.net/thread/9dbb64ab-dcdd-4fdf-aeef-03252248ec2d.

Chapter Six, *How Can I Possibly Trust God? He Let This Happen to Me!*

1. Steven R. Tracy, *Mending the Soul: Understanding and Healing Abuse* (Grand Rapids, MI: Zondervan, 2005).
2. Ibid.
3. Christa Sands, *Learning to Trust Again: A Young Woman's Journey of Healing from Sexual Abuse* (Grand Rapids, MI: Discovery House Publishers, 1999).
4. http://www.familyfriendpoems.com/sad/poetry.asp?poem=19034.

Chapter Seven, *Distorted and Corrected Views of Father God*

1. Neil T. Anderson, *The Steps to Freedom in Christ: A Step-by-Step Guide to Help You Resolve Personal and Spiritual Conflicts; Break Free from Bondage and Renew Your Mind; and Experience Daily Victory as a Child of God* (Ventura, CA: Regal Books, 2001).
2. Ibid.
3. http://www.nacronline.com/spirituality/recovery-from-distorted-images-of-god-seeing-god-in-new-ways-recovery-from-distorted-images-of-god.

Chapter Eight, *Suffering, Sovereignty, and Hope*

1. James Dobson, *Holding on to Your Faith Even When God Doesn't Make Sense* (Wheaton, IL: Tyndale House Publishers, Inc., 1993).
2. Lynda Hunter, *God, Do You Care? Trusting God Through the Storms* (Colorado Springs, CO: W. Publishing Co., 2009).
3. Randy Alcorn. *If God Is Good: Faith in the Midst of Suffering and Evil* (Colorado Springs, CO: Multnomah Books, 2010).
4. Ibid.
5. http://www.flbaptist.org/MinistryPrograms/DL/LeadershipLifeDevelopment/BiblicalServantLeadership/SullivanCommentary/SullivansPreviousArticles/TheSovereigntyofGodAdefinition.aspx.
6. http://www.christinyou.net/pages/sovereignty.html. © 1999 James A. Fowler
7. http://bible.org/seriespage/sovereignty-god-history.
8. Jerry Bridges, *Trusting God Even When Life Hurts* (Colorado Springs, CO: NavPress, 1988).
9. Ibid.
10. http://bible.org/article/hope.

Chapter Nine, *Implementing the Steps of Forgiveness*

1. Neil T. Anderson, *The Steps to Freedom in Christ: A Step-by-Step Guide to Help You Resolve Personal and Spiritual Conflicts; Break Free from Bondage and Renew Your Mind; and Experience Daily Victory as a Child of God* (Ventura, CA: Regal Books, 2001).
2. Ibid.
3. Ibid.
4. Ibid.
5. Stormie Omartian, *Stormie: A Story of Forgiveness and Healing* (Eugene, OR: Harvest House Publishers, 1986).
6. Sandra D. Wilson, *Released from Shame* (Downers Grove, IL: InterVarsity Press, 1990).
7. Lewis B. Smedes, The *Art of Forgiving: When You Need to Forgive and Don't Know How* (New York, NY: Random House Publishing Group, 1996).

Chapter Ten, *How Forgiveness Unlocks the Door to Trust*

1. http://www.allaboutgod.com/definition-for-forgiveness-faq.html.
2. http://www.keepbelieving.com/sermon/1990-01-07-Can-We-Still-Believe-In-Romans-8-28/.
3. http://www.preceptaustin.org/romans_828-39.html.
4. Ibid.
5. Ibid.
6. Ibid.
7. Ibid.
8. Ibid.
9. Ibid.

Chapter Eleven, *What Does Trust in God Look Like?*

1. http://www.ancient-hebrew.org/emagazine/010.html#biblicalword.
2. Deborah J. Kern, *Learning to Trust God* (Enumclaw, WA: Pleasant Word: 2009).
3. http://www.chosentoremember.com/inspirational_quotes/inspirational_stories_trusting_god.html.
4. http://www.learningplaceonline.com/stages/organize/Erikson.html.

Chapter Twelve, *Learning to Trust God*

1. Ruth Graham, *Fear Not Tomorrow, God Is Already There: Trusting Him in Uncertain Times* (New York, NY: Howard Books, 2009).

2. http://www.christianity.net.au/questions/from_christianitynetau_moblog87.
3. http://www.whatsaiththescripture.com/Fellowship/How.To.Trust.God.html.
4. http://www.whatsaiththescripture.com/Fellowship/How.To.Trust.God.html.
5. Deborah J. Kern, *Learning to Trust God* (Enumclaw, WA: Pleasant Word, 2009).
6. Ibid.
7. Ibid.
8. Ibid.

Chapter Thirteen, *Blessings for Believers Who Forgive Others and Trust God*

1. http://www.faithclipart.com/guide/Christian-Music/hymns-the-songs-and-the stories/trust-and-obey-the-song-and-the-story.html.
2. Sandra Wilson, Ph.D., *Into Abba's Arms: Finding the Acceptance You've Always Wanted* (Wheaton, IL: Tyndale House Publishers, Inc., 1998).
3. Ed Delph, Alan Heller, and Pauly Heller, *Learning to Trust... Again* (Shippensburg, PA: Destiny Image Publishers, Inc., 2007).
4. http://www.studylight.org/dic/hbd/view.cgi?number=T3001.
5. http://www.ancienthebrew.org/27_peace.html.
6. http://bible.org/seriespage/ration-appendix-2-nature-divine-blessings-grace-and-peace.
7. Ibid.
8. http://www.biblebb.com/files/mac/sg50-1.html.
9. http://www.kevindedmon.com/2009/08/yada-yada-yada/.
10. Ibid.
11. http://www.commentarypress.net/cpn-essays/English/1CA4A315-A40C-4650-8153-1D1BFB29959B.html.
12. http://www.intimacywithgod.com/knowgod.html.
13. http://www.bibletools.org/index.cfm/fuseaction/Topical.show/RTD/cgg/ID/198/Intimacy.html.
14. http://www.intimacywithgod.com/goodrelationship.html.
15. Deborah J. Kern, *Learning to Trust God* (Enumclaw, WA: Pleasant Word, 2009).

Chapter Fourteen, *My Sheep Know My Voice*

1. Sandra Wilson, Ph.D., *Into Abba's Arms: Finding the Acceptance You've Always Wanted* (Wheaton, IL: Tyndale House Publishers, Inc., 1998).
2. Ibid.
3. Frances J. Roberts, *Make Haste My Beloved* (Ojai, CA: King Farspan, Inc., 1978).
4. Ibid.
5. Ibid.

6. Sandra Wilson, Ph.D., *Into Abba's Arms: Finding the Acceptance You've Always Wanted* (Wheaton, IL: Tyndale House Publishers, Inc., 1998).
7. http://en.wikipedia.org/wiki/Rhema.
8. Dave and Linda Olson, *Listening Prayer: My Sheep Hear My Voice* (Kansas City, MO: Desert Stream Press, 1996).
9. Mark and Patti Virkler, *4 Keys to Hearing God's Voice* (Shippensberg, PA: Destiny Image Publishers, Inc., 2010).
10. Ibid.
11. Ibid.
12. http://www.fangraphs.com/blogs/index.php/odds-of-catching-a-foul-ball/.
13. Os Hillman, *Experiencing the Father's Love* (Cumming, GA: Aslan Inc., 2010).
14. http://www.ehow.com/about_6330727_history-sparrows.html.
15. http://www.goodnewsmedia.com/bible.studies.htm/recentquestionsb.html.

Afterword

1. J. R. Sloan, *The Culture of Excess: How America Lost Self-Control and Why We Need to Redefine Success* (Santa Barbara, CA: ABC-CLIO, LLC, 2009).

Appendix A, *Are You Born Again? If Not, You Can Be!*

1. http://www.freepres.org/tract_details.asp?tract_bornagain.
2. Rick Renner, *Paid in Full: An In-depth Look at the Defining Moments of Christ's Passion* (Tulsa, OK: Teach All Nations, 2008).

Appendix B, *Accounts of Abuse Survivors Who Chose to Forgive*

1. Joel Covitz, *Emotional Child Abuse: The Family Curse* (Boston, MA: Sigo Press, 1981).
2. Ibid.
3. Ibid.
4. Ibid.
5. http://en.wikipedia.org/wiki/It_Is_Well_with_My_Soul.

Appendix C, *The Abuse Jesus Suffered and His Choice to Forgive*

1. David A. Ball, M.D., *Crucifixion and Death of a Man Called Jesus: From the Eyes of a Physician* (Bloomington, IN: CrossBooks, 2010).
2. http://www.learnthebible.org/nakedness.html.
3. http://www.learnthebible.org/nakedness.html.

4. http://www.answerbag.com/q_view/1018526#ixzz13R2DYoDq.

5. http://www.cbn.com/spirituallife/onlinediscipleship/Renner_Crucified.aspx.

6. http://www.yhwh.com/Cross/cross2.html.

7. David A. Ball, M.D., *Crucifixion and Death of a Man Called Jesus: From the Eyes of a Physician* (Bloomington, IN: CrossBooks, 2010).

8. Mark A. Marinella, M.D. *Died He for Me: A Physician's View of the Crucifixion of Jesus Christ* (Ventura, CA: Nordskog Publishing, 2008).

9. http://www.teatimeforyoursoul.com/articles/thedarknessofthecross.html.

10. Pierre, Barbet, M.D., *A Doctor at Calvary: The Passion of Our Lord Jesus Christ as Described by a Surgeon* (Fort Collins, CO: Roman Catholic Books, 1953).

11. Corrie Ten Boom with John and Elizabeth Sherrill, *The Hiding Place* (New York, NY: Bantam Books, 1971).

12. Mark A. Marinella, M.D., *Died He for Me: A Physician's View of the Crucifixion of Jesus Christ* (Ventura, CA: Nordskog Publishing, 2008).

13. Ibid.

14. Ibid.

15. Ibid.

16. Rick Renner, *Paid in Full: An In-depth Look at the Defining Moments of Christ's Passion* (Tulsa, OK: Teach All Nations, 2008).

17. Frederick T. Zugibe, M.D., *The Crucifixion of Jesus: A Forensic Inquiry* (New York, NY: M. Evans and Company, Inc., 2005).

18. Rick Renner, *Paid in Full: An In-depth Look at the Defining Moments of Christ's Passion* (Tulsa, OK: Teach All Nations, 2008).

19. Mark A. Marinella, M.D., *Died He for Me: A Physician's View of the Crucifixion of Jesus Christ* (Ventura, CA: Nordskog Publishing, 2008).

20. Rick Renner, *Paid in Full: An In-depth Look at the Defining Moments of Christ's Passion* (Tulsa, OK: Teach All Nations, 2008).

21. Frederick T. Zugibe, M.D., *The Crucifixion of Jesus: A Forensic Inquiry* (New York, NY: M. Evans and Company, Inc., 2005).

22. Rick Renner, *Paid in Full: An In-depth Look at the Defining Moments of Christ's Passion* (Tulsa, OK: Teach All Nations, 2008).

23. Ibid.

24. Mark A. Marinella, M.D., *Died He for Me: A Physician's View of the Crucifixion of Jesus Christ* (Ventura, CA: Nordskog Publishing, 2008).

25. Ibid.

26. Frederick T. Zugibe, M.D., *The Crucifixion of Jesus: A Forensic Inquiry* (New York, NY: M. Evans and Company, Inc., 2005).

27. Mark A. Marinella, M.D. *Died He for Me: A Physician's View of the Crucifixion of Jesus Christ* (Ventura, CA: Nordskog Publishing, 2008).

28. Ibid.
29. "On the Physical Death of Jesus Christ"; March 8, 2010; William D. Edwards, M.D; Wesley J. Gabel, M.Div.; Floyd E Hosmer, M.S, AMI. Reprinted from *JAMA - The Journal of the American Medical Association,* March 21, 1986, Volume 256, Copyright 1986, American Medical Association.

1. Matthew 26:17-27:61, Mark 14:12-15:47, Luke 22:7-23:56, John 13:1-19:42, the "The Holy Bible" (New International Version). Grand Rapids, Mich., Zondervan Bible Publishers, 1978.
2. Lumpkin R: The physical suffering of Christ. "J Med Assoc Ala" 1978;47:8-10,47.
3. Johnson CD: Medical and cardiological aspects of the passion and crucifixion of Jesus, the Christ. "Bol Assoc Med PR" 1978;70:97-102.
4. Barb AA: The wound in Christ's side. "J Warbury Courtauld Inst" 1971;34:320-321.
5. Bucklin R: The legal and medical aspects of the trial and death of Christ. "Sci Law" 1970; 10:14-26.
6. Mikulicz-Radecki FV: The chest wound in the crucified Christ. "Med News" 1966;14:30-40.
7. Davis CT: The crucifixion of Jesus: The passion of Christ from a medical point of view. "Ariz Med" 1965;22:183-187.
8. Tenney SM: On death by crucifixion. "Am Heart J" 1964;68:286-287.
9. Bloomquist ER: A doctor looks at crucifixion. "Christian Herald", March 1964, pp 35 46-48.
10. DePasquale NP, Burch GE: Death by crucifixion. "Am Heart J" 1963;6:434-435.
11. Barbet P: "A Doctor at Calvary: The Passion of Our Lord Jesus Christ as Described by a Surgeon", Earl of Wicklow (trans). Garden City, NY, Doubleday Image Books, 1953, pp 12-18, 37-147, 159-175, 187-208.
12. Primrose WB: A surgeon looks at the crucifixion. "Hibbert J" 1949, pp 382-388.
13. Bergsma S: did Jesus die of a broken heart? "Calvin Forum" 1948;14:163-167.
14. Whitaker JR: The physical cause of the death of our Lord. "Cath Manchester Guard" 1937;15:83-91.
15. Clark CCP: What was the physical cause of the death of Jesus Christ? "Med Rec" 1890; 38:543.
16. Cooper HC: The agony of death by crucifixion. "NY Med J" 1883:38:150-153.
17. Shroud W: "Treatise on the Physical Cause of the Death of Christ and Its Relation to the Principles and Practice of Christianity" ed 2. London, Hamilton & Adams, 1871, pp 28-156, 489-494.
18. Allen AC: "The Skin: A Clinicopathological Treatise", ed 2. New York, Grune & Stratton Inc, 1967, pp 745-747.
19. Sutton RL Jr: "Diseases of the Skin", ed 11. St Louis, CV Mosby Co, 1956, pp 1393-1394.
20. Scott CT: A case of haematidrosis. "Br Med J" 1918;1:532-533.
21. Klauder JV: Stigmatization. "Arch Dermatol Syphilol" 1938;37:650-659.
22. Weaver KF: The mystery of the shroud. "Natl Geogr" 1980;157:730-753.
23. Tzaferis V: Jewish tombs at and near Giv'at ha-Mivtar, Jerusalem. "Israel Explor J" 1970;20:38-59.
24. Haas N: Anthropological observations on the skeletal remains from Giv'at ha-Mivtar. "Israel Explor J" 1970;20:38-59.
25. McDowell J: "The Resurrection Factor" San Bernardino, Calif, Here's Life Publishers, 1981, pp 20-53, 75-103.
26. McDowell J: "Evidence That Demands a Verdict: Historical Evidence for the Christian Faith." San Bernardino, Calif, Here's Life Publishers, 1979, pp 39-87, 141-263.
27. McDowell J: "More Than a Carpenter" Wheaton, Ill, Tyndale House Publishers, 1977, pp 36-71, 89-100.
28. Hengel M: "Crucifixion in the Ancient World and the folly of the Message of the Cross" Bowden J (trans) Philadelphia, Fortress Press, 1977, pp 22-45, 86-90.

29. Ricciotti G: "The Life of Christ" Zizzamia AI (trans). Milwaukee, Bruce Publishing Co, 1947, pp 29-57, 78-153, 161-167, 586-647.
30. Pfeiffer CF, Vos HF, Rea J (eda): "Wycliffe Bible Encyclopedia." Chicago Moody Press, 1975, pp 149-152, 404-405, 713-723, 1173,1174, 150-1523.
31. Greenleaf S: "An Examination of the Testimony of the four Evangelists by the Rules of Evidence Administered in the Courts of Justice." Grand Rapids, Mich, Baker Book House, 1965, p. 29.
32. Hatch E, Redpath HA: "A Concordance to the Septuagint and the Other Greek Versions of the Old Testament (Including the Apocryphal Books) Graz, Austria, Akademische Druce U Verlagsanstalt, 1975, p 1142.
33. Wuest KS: "Wuest Word Studies From the Greek New Testament for the English Reader." Grand Rapids, Mich. WB Eerdmans Publisher, 1973, vol 1, p 280.
34. Friedrich G: "Theological Dictionary of the New Testament", Bremiley G (ed-trans). Grand Rapids, Mich. WB Eerdmans Publisher, 1971, vol 7, pp 572,573,632.
35. Aradt WF, Gingrich FW: "A Greek-English Lexicon of the New Testament and Other Early Christian Literature." University of Chicago Press, 1057, p 673.
36. Brown F, Driver SR, Briggs CA: "A Hebrew and English Lexicon of the Old Testament With an Appendix Containing the Biblical Aramaic." Oxford, England, Clarendon Press, 1953, pp 841, 854.
37. Robertson AT: "A Grammar of the Greek New Testament in Light of Historical Research." Nashville, Tenn, Broadman Press, 1931, pp 417-427.
38. Jackson SM (ed): "The New Schaff-Herzog Encyclopedia of Religious Knowledge." New York, Funk & Wagnalls, 1909, pp 312-314.
39. Kim H-S, Suzuki M, Lie JT, et al: Nonbacterial thrombotic endocarditis (NBTE) and disseminated intravascular coagulation (DIC): Autopsy study of 36 patients. "Arch Pathol Lab Med" 1977;101:65-68.
40. Becker AE, van Mantgem J-P: Cardiac tamponade: A study of 50 hearts. "Eur J Cardiol" 1975;3:349-358.

30. Frederick T. Zugibe, M.D., *The Crucifixion of Jesus: A Forensic Inquiry* (New York, NY: M. Evans and Company, Inc., 2005).
31. Rick Renner, *Paid in Full: An In-depth Look at the Defining Moments of Christ's Passion* (Tulsa, OK: Teach All Nations, 2008).
32. Ibid.
33. John MacArthur, *The Murder of Jesus: You've Seen The Passion of the Christ; Now Discover What It Means to You* (Nashville, TN: Thomas Nelson, Inc., 2000).
34. Ibid.
35. Ibid.
36. Ibid.
37. Ibid.

Appendix F, *Words to Me from the Father*

1. http://www.associatedcontent.com/article/41258/the_israelites_forty_year_trip_to_the.html?cat=34.

Bibliography

Adams, Jay. *From Forgiven to Forgiving*. Amityville, NY: Calvary Press, 1994.

Alcorn, Randy. *If God Is Good: Faith in the Midst of Suffering and Evil*. Colorado Springs, CO: Multnomah Books, 2009.

Allender, Dan B. *The Healing Path: How the Hurts in Your Past Can Lead You to a More Abundant Life*. Waterville, ME: WaterBrook Press Books, 2003.

Anderson, Neil T. *The Steps to Freedom in Christ: A Step-by-Step Guide to Help you Resolve Personal and Spiritual Conflicts; Break Free from Bondage and Renew Your Mind; Experience Daily Victory as a Child of God*. Ventura, CA: Gospel Light, 2002.

Arthur, Kay and David and B. J. Lawson. *How Do You Know God's Your Father?* Waterville, ME: WaterBrook Press Books, 2001.

Arthur, Kay and Pete De Lacy. *Trusting God in Times of Adversity*. Eugene, OR: Harvest House Publishers, 2003.

Backus, William. *The Healing Power of a Christian Mind: How Biblical Truth Can Keep You Healthy*. Minneapolis, MN: Bethany House Publishers, 1996.

Baker, John. *Life's Healing Choices: Freedom from Your Hurts, Hang-ups, and Habits*. New York, NY: Howard Books, 2008.

Ball, David A., M.D. *The Crucifixion and Death of a Man Called Jesus: From the Eyes of a Physician*. Bloomington, IN: Crossbooks™, 2010.

Bannister, Nonna with Denise George and Carolyn Tomlin. *The Secret Holocaust Diaries: The Untold Story of Nonna Bannister.* Carol Stream, IL: Tyndale House Publishers, Inc., 2009.

Barbet, Pierre (M.D.). *A Doctor at Calvary: The Passion of Our Lord Jesus Christ as Described by a Surgeon.* Fort Collins, CO: Roman Catholic Press, 1953.

Bateman, Lana L. *Bible Promises for the Healing Journey: Break Free from the Destructiveness of the Past through the Transforming Power of God's Word.* Westwood, NJ: Barbour Books, 1991.

Billheimer, Paul E. *Don't Waste Your Sorrows: New Insight into God's Eternal Purpose for Each Christian in the Midst of Life's Greatest Adversities.* Fort Washington, PA: CLC Publications, 1977.

Brauns, Chris. *Unpacking Forgiveness: Biblical Answers for Complex Questions and Deep Wounds.* Wheaton, IL: Crossway Books, 2008.

Bridges, Jerry. *Trusting God: Even When Life Hurts.* Colorado Springs, CO: Navpress, 1998.

Brown, Walt A. and Newman, Thomas A. *Emotional Abuse and Neglect of Children.* Tallahassee, FL: William Gladden Foundation, 2008.

Collins, R. Dandridge. *The Trauma Zone: Trusting God for Emotional Healing.* Chicago, IL: Moody Publishers, 2007.

Connolly, Peter. *Living in the Time of Jesus of Nazareth.* Benei Brak, Israel: Steimattzky Ltd, 1983.

Covitz, Joel. *Emotional Child Abuse: The Family Curse.* Boston, MA: Sigo Press, 1986.

Davis, Anne A. Johnson. *Hell Minus One: My Story of Deliverance from Satanic Ritual Abuse and My Journey to Freedom.* Tooele, UT: Transcript Bulletin Publishing, 2008.

Delph, Ed, Heller, Alan, and Heller, Pauly. *Learning How to Trust... Again.* Shippensburg, PA: Destiny Image Publishers, Inc., 2007.

DeMoss, Nancy Leigh. *Choosing Forgiveness: Your Journey to Freedom.* Chicago, IL: Moody Press, 2006.

Dittman, Anita with Jan Markell. *Trapped in Hitler's Hell: A Young Jewish Girl Discovers the Messiah's Faithfulness in the Midst of the Holocaust.* Eureka, MT: Lighthouse Trails Publishing, 2005.

Dobson, James. *Holding on to Your Faith Even When God Doesn't Make Sense.* Wheaton, IL: Tyndale House Publishers, Inc., 1993.

Edwards, Sue. *Daddy's Girls: Discover the Wonder of the Father.* Grand Rapids, MI: Kregel Publications, 2007.

Einhorn, Lois. *Forgiveness and Child Abuse: Would You Forgive?* Bandon, OR: Robert D. Reed Publishers, 2006.

Enright, Robert D. *Forgiveness is a Choice: A Step-by-Step Process for Resolving Anger and Restoring Hope.* Washington, D.C.: APA Life Tools, 2001.

Evans, Craig A. and N.T. Wright. *Jesus, the Final Days: What Really Happened.* Louisville, KY: Westminster John Knox Press, 2009.

Flanigan, Beverly. *Forgiving the Unforgivable: Overcoming the Bitter Legacy of Intimate Wounds.* New York, NY: Wiley Publishing, Inc., 1992.

Flanigan, Beverly. *Forgiving Yourself: A Step-by-Step Guide to Making Peace with Your Mistakes and Getting on with Your Life.* New York, NY: Wiley Publishing, Inc., 1996.

Frank, Jan. *A Graceful Waiting: When There's Nothing More that You Can Do, God's Deepest Work Has Just Begun.* Ann Arbor, MI: Servant Publications, 1996.

Freeman, Joel A. *When Life Isn't Fair: Making Sense Out of Suffering.* Green Forest, AR: New Leaf Press, 2002.

Goertz, Lisa. *I Stepped into Freedom.* London, England: Lutterworth Press, 1960.

Graham, Ruth. *Fear Not Tomorrow, God Is Already There: Trusting Him in Uncertain Times.* New York, NY: Howard Books, 2009.

Griffith, Naomi Haines and Zigler, Janet S. The *Unkindest Cut: The Emotional Maltreatment of Children.* Nashville, TN: Red Wine and Vinegar, LLP, 2002.

Halamandaris, Bill. *Love and Hate: The Story of Henri Landwirth.* Self-published, 2007.

Heald, Cynthia. *When the Father Holds You Close: A Journey to Deeper Intimacy with God.* Nashville, TN: Thomas Nelson Publishers, 1999.

Hengel, Martin. *Crucifixion.* Philadelphia, PA: Fort Press, 1977.

Hunter, Lynda. *God, Do You Care? Trusting God Through the Storm.* Nashville, TN: Word Publishing Group, 2001.

Huston, Paula. *Forgiveness: Following Jesus into Radical Loving.* Brewster, MA: Paraclete Press, 2008.

Hutchison, John C. *Thinking Right When Things Go Wrong: Biblical Wisdom for Surviving Tough Times.* Grand Rapids, MI: Kregel Publications, 2005.

Jacobsen, Wayne. *He Loves Me! Learning to Live in the Father's Affection.* Newbury Park, CA: Windblown Media, 2007.

Janiz, Gregory L. with Ann McMurray. *Healing the Scars of Emotional Abuse.* Grand Rapids, MI: Fleming H. Revell, 2003.

Johnson, Elliot. *Hope in Suffering.* Grand Rapids, MI: Full Court Press, 1993.

Kearney, R. Timothy. *Caring for Sexually Abused Children: A Handbook for Families and Churches.* Downers Grove, IL: InterVarsity Press, 2001.

Keller, W. Phillip. *Walking with God: Wholeness and Holiness for Common Christians.* Grand Rapids, MI: Kregel Publications, 1980.

Kendall, R. T. *How to Forgive Ourselves – Totally: Begin Again by Breaking Free from Past Mistakes.* Lake Mary, FL: Charisma House, 2007.

Kendall, R. T. *Total Forgiveness Experience: A Study Guide to Repairing Relationships.* Lake Mary, FL: Charisma House, 2004.

Kendall, R. T. *Total Forgiveness: When Everything in You Wants to Hold a Grudge, Point a Finger, and Remember the Pain – God Wants You to Lay It All Aside.* Lake Mary, FL: Charisma House, 2007.

Kern, Deborah J. *Learning to Trust God.* Enumclaw, WA: Winepress Publishing, 2009.

Ketterman, Grace. *Verbal Abuse: Healing the Hidden Wound.* Ann Arbor, MI: Servant Publications, 1992.

Kor, Eva Mozes as told to Mary Wright. *Echoes from Auschwitz: Dr. Mengele's Twins, the Story of Eva and Miriam Mozes.* Terre Haute, IN: Candles, Inc., 1995.

Kor, Eva Mozes and Lisa Rojany Buccieri. *Surviving the Angel of Death: The Story of a Mengele Twin in Auschwitz.* Terre Haute, IN: Tanglewood Publishing, Inc., 2009.

Kreeft, Peter. *Making Sense of Suffering.* Ann Arbor, MI: Servant Publications, 1986.

Klein, Charles. *How to Forgive When You Can't Forget: Healing Our Personal Relationships.* Bellmore, NY: Liebling Press, 1995.

Landwirth, Henri with J. P. Hendricks. *Gift of Life.* Self-published, 1996.

Linn, Dennis and Matthew. *Healing Life's Hurts: Healing Memories through the Five Stages of Forgiveness.* Mahwah, NJ: Paulist Press, 1978.

Long, Brad and Cindy Strickler. *Let Jesus Heal Your Hidden Wounds: Cooperating with the Holy Spirit in Healing Ministry.* Grand Rapids, MI: Chosen Books, 2001.

Loth, Peter as told to Sandra Kellogg Rath. *Peace by Piece: A Story of Survival and Forgiveness.* Longwood, FL: 2008.

Lotz, Anne Graham. *Why? Trusting God When You Don't Understand.* Nashville, TN: Thomas Nelson Books, 2004.

MacArthur, John F. *Forgiveness: The Freedom and Power of Forgiveness.* Wheaton, IL: Crossway Books, 1998.

MacArthur, John F. *The Murder of Jesus: You've Seen The Passion of the Christ; Now Discover What it Means to You.* Nashville, TN: Thomas Nelson, Inc., 2000.

MacKenzie, Carine. *Trusting God As: Provider, Leader, Shepherd, Healer, Peacegiver, Friend, Saviour.* Great Britain: Christian Focus Publications, 2007.

Maisel, Eric. *Toxic Criticism: Break the Cycle with Friends, Family, Co-workers, and Yourself.* New York, NY: McGraw-Hill.

Manning, Brennan. *Ruthless Trust: The Ragamuffin's Path to God.* New York, NY: Harper Collins Publishers, 2000.

Marinella, Mark. *Died He for Me: A Physician's View of the Crucifixion of Jesus Christ.* Ventura, CA: Nordskog Publishing, 2008.

Matzat, Don. *Christ Esteem: Where the Search for Self-Esteem Ends.* Eugene, OR: Harvest House Publishers, 1990.

McGinn, Linda R. *Dancing in the Storm: Hope in the Midst of Chaos.* Grand Rapids, MI: Fleming H. Revell, 1999.

Mead, Frank S. (Ed.). *12,000 Religious Quotations.* Grand Rapids, MI: Baker Book House, 1989.

Miller, Alice. *For Your Own Good: Hidden Cruelty in Child-rearing and the Roots of Violence.* New York, NY: The Noonday Press, 1990.

Missler, Chuck and Nancy. *Faith in the Night Seasons: Understanding God's Will.* Coeur d'Alene, ID: Koinonia House, 1999.

Montero, Danilo. *The Father's Embrace: Opening Yourself to Feeling His Loving Touch.* Lake Mary, FL: Charisma House, 2005.

Müller, George and H. Lincoln Wayland (Ed.). *Life of Trust: Being a Narrative of the Lord's Dealings with George Müller.* New York, NY: Sheldon and Company, 1861.

Niequiest, Shauna. *Bittersweet: Thoughts on Change, Grace, and Learning the Hard Way.* Grand Rapids, MI: Zondervan Books, 2010.

Olson, Dave and Linda. *Listening Prayer: My Sheep Hear My Voice.* Kansas City, MO: Desert Stream Press, 1996.

Omartian, Stormie. Stormie: *A Story of Forgiveness and Healing.* Eugene, OR: Harvest House Publishers, 1986.

Omartian, Stormie. *Lord, I Want to Be Whole: The Power of Prayer and Scripture in Emotional Healing*. Nashville, TN: Thomas Nelson Publishers, 2000.

Omartian, Stormie. *Praying God's Will for Your Life: A Prayerful Walk to Spiritual Well-Being*. Nashville, TN: Thomas Nelson Publishers, 2001.

Ortlund, Anne. *Fix Your Eyes on Jesus*. Dallas, TX: Word Publishing, 1991.

Ortlund, Anne and Ray. *You Don't Have to Quit: How to Persevere When You Want to Give Up*. Nashville, TN: Thomas Nelson Publishers, 1986.

Pelzer, Dave. *A Man Named Dave: A Story of Triumph and Forgiveness*. New York, NY: Penguin Group, 2009.

Price, Rose. *A Rose from the Ashes*. San Francisco, CA: Purple Pomegranate Productions, 2006.

Prince, Derek. *God's Remedy for Rejection*. New Kensington, PA: Whitaker House, 1993.

Rath, Sandra Kellogg as told by Peter Loth, *Peace by Piece: A Story of Survival & Forgiveness*. Longwood, FL: Xulon Press, 2008.

Renner, Rick. *Paid in Full: An In-depth Look at the Defining Moments of Christ's Passion*, Tulsa OK: Teach All Nations, 2008.

Richards, Larry. *Forgiveness: The Gift that Heals and Sets Free*. Nashville, TN: Thomas Nelson Publishers, 1996.

Richards, Nancy. *Heal and Forgive: Forgiveness in the Face of Abuse*. Nevada City, CA: Blue Dolphin Publishing, 2005.

Richards, Nancy. *Heal and Forgive II: The Journey from Abuse and Estrangement to Reconciliation*. Nevada City, Blue Dolphin Publishing, 2008.

Roberts, Frances J. *Come Away My Beloved*. Ojai, CA: Kings Farspan, Inc., 1970.

Roberts, Frances J. *Dialogues with God*. Ojai, CA: King's Farspan, Inc., 1968.

Roberts, Frances J. *Make Haste My Beloved*. Ojai, CA: Kings Farspan, Inc., 1978.

Roberts, Frances J. *On the Highroad of Surrender.* Palos Verdes Estates, CA: The King's Press, 1973.

Roberts, Frances J. *Progress of Another Pilgrim.* Ojai, CA: Kings Farspan, Inc., 1970.

Roberts, Frances J. *Total Love.* Uhrichsville, OH: Barbour Publishing, 2007.

Sande, Ken. *The Peace Maker: A Biblical Guide to Resolving Personal Conflict.* Grand Rapids, MI: Baker Books, 1991.

Sandford, John and Paula, and Norm Bowman. *Choosing Forgiveness.* Arlington, TX: Clear Stream, Inc., Publishing, 1996.

Sands, Christa and Joyce K. Ellis (Ed.). *Learning to Trust Again: A Young Woman's Journey of Healing from Sexual Abuse.* Grand Rapids, MI: Discovery House Publishers, 1999.

Sittser, Jerry. *A Grace Disguised: How the Soul Grows through Loss.* Grand Rapids, MI: Zondervan Books, 2004.

Simon, Sidney and Suzanne. *Forgiveness: How to Make Peace with Your Past and Get on With Your Life.* New York, NY: Warner Books, 1990.

Slosar, J. R. *The Culture of Excess: How America Lost Self-Control and Why We Need to Redefine Success.* Santa Barbara, CA: ABC,-CLIO, LLC, 2009.

Smedes, Lewis B. *The Art of Forgiving: When You Need to Forgive and Don't Know How.* New York, NY: Ballantine Books, 1996.

Somers, Suzanne. *Wednesday's Children: Adult Survivors of Abuse Speak Out.* New York, NY: Putnam/Healing Vision Publishing, 1992.

Spring, Pat. *Trusting – The Issue at the Heart of Every Relationship: Learning Who and How to Trust Again.* Ann Arbor, MI: Servant Publications, 1994.

Stafford, Wess with Dean Merrill. *Too Small to Ignore: Why the Least of These Matters Most.* Colorado Springs, CO: WaterBrook Press, 2007.

Stoop, David. *Forgiving the Unforgivable.* Ventura, CA: Gospel Light, 2001.

Tada, Joni Eareckson. *A Place of Healing: Wrestling with the Mysteries of Suffering, Pain, and God's Sovereignty.* Colorado Springs, CO: David C. Cook, 2010.

Tada, Joni Eareckson and Steven Estes. *When God Weeps: Why Our Sufferings Matter to the Almighty.* Grand Rapids, MI: Zondervan Publishing House, 1997.

Ten Boom, Corrie with John and Elizabeth Sherrill. *The Hiding Place.* New York, NY: Bantam Books, 1971.

TerKeurst, Lysa. *Becoming More than a Good Bible Study Girl.* Grand Rapids, MI: Zondervan Books, 2009.

TerKeurst, Lysa, *What Happens When Women Walk in Faith: Trusting God Takes You to Amazing Places.* Eugene, OR: Harvest House Publishing, 2005.

Townsend, John. *Where is God? Finding His Presence, Purpose, and Power in Difficult Times.* Nashville, TN: Thomas Nelson, Inc., 2009.

Tracy, Steven R. *Mending the Soul: Understanding and Healing Abuse.* Grand Rapids, MI: Zondervan Books, 2005.

Vamosh, Miriam Feinberg. *Daily Life at the Time of Jesus.* Herzlia, Israel: Palphot Ltd., 2000.

Virkler, Mark and Patti: *4 Keys to Hearing God's Voice.* Shippensburg, PA: Destiny Image Publishers, Inc., 2010.

Virkler, Mark and Patti: *Prayers that Heal the Heart: Prayer Counseling that Breaks Every Yoke.* Gainesville, FL: Bridge-Logos Publishers, 2001.

Walsh, Sheila. *Beautiful Things Happen When a Woman Trusts God.* Nashville, TN: Thomas Nelson Publishers, 2010.

Willis, Rosalie. *When God Speaks to My Heart: A Daybook of Personal Moments with God.* Lakeland, FL: White Stone Books, 2005.

Wilson, Neil S. (Ed.). *The Handbook of Bible Application.* Wheaton, IL: Tyndale House Publishers, Inc., 2000.

Wilson, Sandra D. *Into Abba's Arms: Finding the Acceptance You've Always Wanted.* Wheaton, IL: Tyndale House Publishers, Inc., 1998.

Wilson, Sandra D. *Released from Shame: Moving Beyond the Pain of the Past.* Downers Grove, IL: InterVarsity Press, 2002.

Wolter, Dwight Lee. *Forgiving Our Parents: For Adult Children from Dysfunctional Families.* Minneapolis, MN: CompCare Publishers, 1989.

Worthington, Everett. *Five Steps to Forgiveness: The Art and Science of Forgiving.* New York, NY: Crown Publishers, 2001.

Wright, H. *Healing for the Father Wound: A Trusted Christian Counselor Offers Time-Tested Advice.* Minneapolis, MN: Bethany House, 2005.

Yancey, Philip: *Disappointment with God: Three Questions No One Asks Aloud.* Grand Rapids, MI: Zondervan Books, 1988.

CPSIA information can be obtained at www.ICGtesting.com
Printed in the USA
BVOW06s1113080315

390772BV00003B/46/P